MW00618829

F. Scott Fitzgerald

F. SCOTT FITZGERALD

A COMPOSITE BIOGRAPHY

Niklas Salmose and David Rennie, Editors

University of Minnesota Press
Minneapolis
London

THE FRIENDS
MINNESOTA CENTER FOR THE BOOK

This publication is supported in part by The Friends of the Saint Paul Public Library in honor of Richard P. McDermott, who helped restore Fitzgerald's birthplace in the 1970s and remained an avid supporter of Fitzgerald activities until his death in 2012. The Friends, as the Minnesota Center for the Book, continues to steward Fitzgerald's legacy through programming that celebrates his life and literature.

Published by the University of Minnesota Press
111 Third Avenue South, Suite 290
Minneapolis, MN 55401-2520
http://www.upress.umn.edu

ISBN 978-1-5179-1585-8 (hc)
ISBN 978-1-5179-1609-1 (pb)

A Cataloging-in-Publication record for this book is available from the Library of Congress.

Printed in the United States of America on acid-free paper

The University of Minnesota is an equal-opportunity educator and employer.

32 31 30 29 28 27 26 25 24   10 9 8 7 6 5 4 3 2 1

This work is dedicated to
Ronald Berman (1930–2022) and
Scott Donaldson (1928–2020)

 Contents

Introduction

> There never was a good biography of a novelist. There
> couldn't be. He is too many people, if he's any good.
> —F. Scott Fitzgerald, "The Crack-Up"

It was a hot day in Paris on Tuesday, June 24, 2018. The editors of this book, along with many other members of the F. Scott Fitzgerald Society, were in town for the Eighteenth International Ernest Hemingway Conference. After witnessing several presentations in the stifling heat of the Sorbonne's Amphithéâtre Richelieu, we relocated to the enticing shade beneath the trees of the Place de la Sorbonne. Over the civilizing influence of rosé wine, talk turned to literary biography. What, for authors like F. Scott Fitzgerald, was the future? A five-volume treatment such as Michael Reynolds had provided for Hemingway? A new monolith somehow surpassing the empirical richness of Matthew J. Bruccoli's classic Fitzgerald biography from 1981, *Some Sort of Epic Grandeur*? Or would some new and ostensibly revelatory angle be put forth?

Recent work by Fitzgerald Society grandee and preeminent literary biographer Scott Donaldson (1928–2020) inspired exploration of the topic. Donaldson claimed the literary biography would endure "until humans lose their curiosity about each other, and about the way they lived and loved and did their work," but he nevertheless made that comment in a book about biography writing titled *The Impossible Craft* (2015).[1] Rather than a new solo-author account falling into the pitfalls of the pathography Donaldson deplored ("warts and all" accounts "attributing the worst possible motives" to the subject's "behavior") or the equally rebarbative "sash-weight heft" tome "of insignificant detail,"[2] perhaps what is needed is a multiauthor approach, which by its inherent plurality of perspectives would avoid a myopic, reductive biographical treatment—a task no less impossible, perhaps, but one replete with new possibilities.

Fitzgerald, after all, had left a clue in his *Notebooks*: the enigmatic statement on literary biography that is the epigraph to this Introduction. An author is "too many people, if he's any good." What does that mean?

That the good writer may be a complex, multifaceted individual? Few would bar Fitzgerald from such a characterization. But his statement also implies the necessary scope of the author's imaginative life: the requirement to project (out of inventive propensity, literary craftsmanship, and one's repository of lived experience) the creative mind into multiple characters and situations. A limitation of literary biographies, then, Fitzgerald suggests, is the presentation of the writer as "one" person, when—by definition of being identified as a literary author—he or she cannot be said to form a single entity.

Donaldson opened his own Fitzgerald biography, *Fool for Love* (1983), by invoking Henry James's comment: "The whole of anything is never told; you can only take what groups together."[3] The present biography parts from previous studies in that it does not advance a single interpretive theory or field of focus. Rather, by uniting the perspectives of twenty-three biographers, *F. Scott Fitzgerald: A Composite Biography* aims not to tell the "whole" of Fitzgerald's life but to present a new way of "grouping together" biographical material and perspectives. We offer a unique and self-reflective commentary on the subjectively constructed nature of biography, collectively emphasizing that a biographer's choice of emphasis, methodology, and theoretical approach results in an idiosyncratic presentation of Fitzgerald's life and work.

Given that Fitzgerald died at age forty-four, a two-year period seemed an appropriate time frame to assign each contributor. Such division gives each writer responsibility for a reasonably broad expanse of time—enough to track important developments—while allowing the biography to present a wide range of authorial perspectives. We gave contributors complete freedom to write about whichever subjects, texts, and contexts they felt were important to their two-year span. Some editing was required to weed out repetition and ensure continuity in formatting, but we tried, as much as possible, to preserve the idiosyncratic nature of the contributions.

F. Scott Fitzgerald: A Composite Biography is the latest in a long line of Fitzgerald biographical writing—one initiated by the author himself. Autobiographical pieces like "What I Think and Feel at 25" (1922), "How to Live on $36,000 a Year" (1924), "A Short Autobiography" (1929), and the "Crack-Up" series (1936) present a stream of autobiographical reflection at turns irreverent and analytical. Indeed, Fitzgerald twice, in 1934 and 1936, proposed a collection of autobiographical writings to Maxwell

Perkins at Scribner's. Unconvinced such a volume would be unified or would possess public appeal, Perkins demurred. He may have been wary of encouraging further exposure of Fitzgerald's starkly confessional mode in the "Crack-Up" essays. Donaldson observes that as a result of Fitzgerald's (deliberate or unintentional) self-mythologizing, "With Fitzgerald as with no one else in American Literature save Poe, the biography gets in the way." Despite the reputation of *The Great Gatsby* or the superlative heights of his best stories, Fitzgerald is still, to a degree, tainted by the indelible tags "Chronicler of the Jazz Age," "the Artist in Spite of Himself," or "the Writer as Burnt-Out Case," or draped in the "non-specific glamour" of his profligacy.[4]

Fitzgerald drew on his experiences for literary material. While the Basil Duke Lee stories or *Tender Is the Night* are not strictly autobiographical, Fitzgerald demonstrably transmuted elements of his personal life into creative fiction. He kept a ledger in which he carefully recorded biographical material he would write about.[5] Furthermore, when Zelda attempted to follow up her novel *Save Me the Waltz* (1932) with a play touching on their shared time on the Riviera (material that, as the professional writer in the marriage, Fitzgerald regarded as his), he was irate.[6] So the extent to which we can—or should—see Fitzgerald in Amory Blaine, Dick Diver, or Dexter Green (or Zelda in Nicole Diver and Ginevra King in Daisy Buchanan) is a central contention biographers must negotiate.

Of course, the objection may be raised that single-author biographies have already explored these issues and presented Fitzgerald as a many-sided author with a rich imaginative and creative life. Depending on how one tallies them, there are around twenty-five biographical works devoted exclusively to Fitzgerald; that figure does not include the cluster of biographical studies devoted to Zelda Fitzgerald. Career-wide biographies of Fitzgerald often present a certain emphasis or biographical "thesis." As Kirk Curnutt notes, the standard volume, Bruccoli's *Some Sort of Epic Grandeur,* "remains the most reliable resource for a simple reason: it keeps to the facts, avoiding the prurient speculation that has come to dominate biographical studies."[7] Part of Bruccoli's empirical approach centers on Fitzgerald as a professional author, in terms of textual editing, volumes sold, and money made. Donaldson's *Fool for Love,* meanwhile, focuses on Fitzgerald's "overweening desire to please," to win admiration, and to be loved.[8] Jeffrey Meyers's *Scott Fitzgerald* (1994), claiming to be "more analytical and interpretive" than previous biographies and to "illuminate recurrent patterns," dwells on self-destructive tendencies such as alcoholism, sexual insecurity, and cynically exploited marital volatility.[9] Additionally, historian David Brown treated Fitzgerald as a "cultural historian" in *Paradise Lost: A Life of F. Scott Fitzgerald* (2017) by tracing the "personal dynamics that formed Fitzgerald's thinking on the urban-industrial" transformation in American society.[10] More recently, Robert Garnett in *Taking Things Hard: The Trials of F. Scott Fitzgerald* (2023) argues Fitzgerald's unusual sensitivity to formative personal experiences (chiefly the intensity and disappointments of his relationships with Ginevra King and Zelda Fitzgerald) provided him with the material for his most powerful fiction. The heightened emotional output could not, however, be sustained, as Fitzgerald eventually exhausted his store of personal material that held the most potent personal significance. Fitzgerald's later years, while abounding in drama, were not experienced with the kind of youth-accentuated vigor that could be transmuted into the exhilarating brilliance of *The Great Gatsby* or "Winter Dreams." Such biographies present Fitzgerald within the bounds of a particular methodological or emotional emphasis, each implicitly delineating an apt conception of the "whole." While undoubtedly necessary in generating a cohesive text, such focus is, arguably, a form of distortion: a veneer of unity glossing over a vast and intractable biographical project.

In addition to career-spanning biographies are volumes focusing on particular sections of Fitzgerald's life, such as Aaron Latham's look at Fitzgerald's time in Hollywood, *Crazy Sundays* (1971), or James L. W. West III's study of the Fitzgerald–Ginevra King relationship, *The Perfect Hour* (2005). And Fitzgerald's intimates produced several examples of what Jace Gatzemeyer calls the "secondary memoir."[11] These works, such as Sheilah Graham's *Beloved Infidel* (1958), Anthony Buttitta's *After the Good Gay Times* (1974), and Frances Kroll Ring's *Against the Current* (1985), provide readers with a "'moderated' image" of Fitzgerald—moderated both in the sense of being the author's "subjective impressions" and in the sense of lying between "scholarly biography and aggrandized pop cultural myth."[12]

It is implausible that an author—as a complex, developing biopsychological being—could be best defined in the light of a single characteristic. Similarly, fiction is unlikely to be of enduring value if it can be explained as a reflection of one defining property. *F. Scott Fitzgerald: A Composite Biography,* therefore, offers a methodology appropriate to the heterogeneity of the biographical subject. While foregrounding and celebrating the diversity of possible approaches, our volume suggests that biography offers a partial, not a definitive, assessment of Fitzgerald's life. There have been forays into composite biographical studies before. Edward Nehls edited a three-volume series (1957–59) of reminiscences by D. H. Lawrence's contemporaries. Similarly, William L. Stull and Maureen P. Carroll's *Remembering Ray: A Composite Biography of Raymond Carver* (1993) collects essays from Carver's associates. In a sense, *The Crack-Up* (1945), Edmund Wilson's edited collection of Fitzgerald's nonfiction, also contains an element of composite biography in its closing section of reminiscences of Fitzgerald by Paul Rosenfeld, Glenway Wescott, and John Dos Passos. Our biography, however, is the first scholarly composite biography, as far as we are aware.

While the editors regret that Ronald Berman and Scott Donaldson did not live to see this volume in print, we hope dedicating the biography to them will stand as a fitting tribute to their redoubtable work as scholars and advocates of the Fitzgerald Society. This book is fortunate to include contributions from numerous eminent Fitzgerald scholars, including James L. W. West III, general editor of the Cambridge Edition of the Works of F. Scott Fitzgerald; Ronald Berman, former chair of the National Endowment for the Humanities; Jackson R. Bryer, current president of the Fitzgerald Society; Kirk Curnutt, managing editor of the *F. Scott Fitzgerald Review*; and international scholars William Blazek, Elisabeth Bouzonviller, Marie-Agnès Gay, and Philip McGowan.

While the volume as a whole eschews attempting a definitive biographical portrayal of Fitzgerald, individual chapters do employ targeted methodological lenses and present a variety of emotional and stylistic approaches. David Page and Sara Kosiba, for instance, make St. Paul and the Midwest the focus of their chapters. Ronald Berman discusses the years 1912–13 in relation to contemporary American educational philosophies. Ross K. Tangedal considers architecture and authorship; David Rennie looks at golf and the country club; Jade Adams, Kirk Curnutt, and William Blazek discuss less-well-known Fitzgerald short stories, including "The Dance," "The Adolescent Marriage," "Jacob's Ladder," "The Love Boat," "The Hotel Child," "Indecision," and "Flight and Pursuit." To turn to the "mood" of the chapters: There is a notable optimism in Martina Mastandrea's take on 1898–99, which explores the dawning American Century and feelings of national expectancy. William Blazek's treatment of 1934–35 bears the far darker imprint of the years when Fitzgerald's health, creativity, marriage, and finances were failing—circumstances Blazek broaches through the nostalgic tone of Fitzgerald's letters and the poignancy of his increasing inability to write salable magazine fiction. The chapters are shaped by the contributors' intellectual predilections and, to a degree, the distinctive emotional emphases they chose to place on their allotted time span within Fitzgerald's life.

This biography offers a panoramic view of Fitzgerald's enthralling career: from the heights of artistic mastery and Jazz Age decadence to the lows of the dissolution of his marriage, health, and career—all set against peripatetic wanderings through St. Paul, Paris, the Midwest, Italy, the Riviera, New York, and Hollywood. While the multiauthor nature of the volume deliberately precludes the possibility of a definitive biographical approach, we believe that this collaboration is a way of "grouping together" that more closely approximates the "too many people" Fitzgerald claimed to be.

NOTES

1. Scott Donaldson, *The Impossible Craft: Literary Biography* (University Park: Pennsylvania State University Press, 2015), 6.

2. Donaldson, *Impossible Craft*, 4–5.

3. Henry James, *The Notebooks of Henry James*, ed. F. O. Matthiessen and Kenneth B. Murdock (New York: George Braziller, 1955), 18.

4. Scott Donaldson, *Fool for Love: F. Scott Fitzgerald* (Minneapolis: University of Minnesota Press, 2012), ix.

5. James L. W. West III, "Interpreting Fitzgerald's Ledger," in *F. Scott Fitzgerald in Context*, ed. Bryant Mangum (Cambridge: Cambridge University Press, 2013), 21.

6. F. Scott Fitzgerald, *A Life in Letters*, ed. Matthew J. Bruccoli (New York: Charles Scribner's Sons, 1994), 220–21.

7. Kirk Curnutt, *The Cambridge Introduction to F. Scott Fitzgerald* (Cambridge: Cambridge University Press, 2007), 122.

8. Donaldson, *Fool for Love*, x.

9. Jeffrey Meyers, *Scott Fitzgerald: A Biography* (London: Macmillan, 1994), viii.

10. David Brown, *Paradise Lost: A Life of F. Scott Fitzgerald* (Cambridge, Mass.: Harvard University Press, 2017), 1, 9.

11. Jace Gatzemeyer, "'Scott Fitzgerald As I Knew Him': F. Scott Fitzgerald and the Secondary Memoir," *F. Scott Fitzgerald Review* 13 (2015): 236–59.

12. Gatzemeyer, "'Scott Fitzgerald As I Knew Him,'" 238–39.

in modeling a way of confronting disappointment and failure that did not sacrifice a sense of self at the altar of public opinion and recognition. Similarly, he noted that the frustrating relationship he had with his mother was a trigger for his artistic ambitions, in part because she did not approve of them. Perhaps she thought he could more easily restore the family's fortunes by following his grandfather into commerce. Her lack of enthusiasm, which was perhaps a driver for his, is revealed in a letter he wrote toward the end of his life, in which he noted that his mother had done him "the disservice of throwing away all but two of [his] very young [writing] efforts."[5] This, despite Mollie Fitzgerald's preservation of many childhood artifacts, including her son's baby book, which recorded his childhood in considerable detail and is now held at the Princeton University Library.

Edward Fitzgerald, Failure, and the South

Despite his ambivalence toward his father, F. Scott Fitzgerald always exhibited greater sympathy for his paternal line, tied to the history of the nation, than for his pioneering immigrant maternal forebears. His father, Edward Fitzgerald, was born near Rockville, Maryland, in 1853 to a family who had for generations been deeply embedded in southern society. His home state was crucial during the Civil War, acting as a buffer between the capital, Washington, D.C., and Confederate Virginia. Its position as a slave-holding state that did not secede from the Union generated an environment marked by shifting allegiances, fractured communities, and espionage. The childhood world that Edward Fitzgerald presented to his young son was one of action and historical significance. A Southern sympathizer, throughout his son's childhood he recounted his experiences of the conflict: how he had ferried spies across the Potomac River, cheered on Jubal Early's army at the Battle of Monocacy, and aided and abetted a member of Mosby's Raiders (disrupters of Union supply chains and communication channels) in avoiding arrest. It is easy to imagine the young Scott in the midst of an unforgiving Minnesota winter spellbound by stories of rebellion in the warm and fertile South. This contrast between the geography, climate, and character of the southern states with those of the North is most evident in Fitzgerald's short story "The Ice Palace" (1920). The heat and slowness of the South is contrasted with the cold, the speed, and the productivity of the North. Sally Carrol Happer, the southern girl who heads north for love, is shown to be constitutionally ill-suited to the place, and at the end of the story she is back where she began, talking lazily from her bedroom window to people passing by. Edward Fitzgerald had no such possibility of return and was trapped, by his son's own admission, in a world he was unable to successfully navigate.

Compounding the romantic narrative of the Lost Cause was Edward Fitzgerald's familial links to a number of historical figures, including Francis Scott Key (the composer of "The Star-Spangled Banner") and the notorious Mary Surratt, who was executed in 1865 for her role in the conspiracy to murder Abraham Lincoln. In the wake of Southern defeat, Edward's life of action shifted to a passivity that lasted until the end of his life. As the South and Southerners attempted to reconcile themselves to Northern victory and a recalibration of their way of life, Edward headed west, perhaps dreaming of the pioneering frontier, but ended up in the industrial city of St. Paul, after a brief stint in Chicago. In February 1890 he married Mollie McQuillan and was attempting life as a businessman amid the bustle of an energetic Victorian midwestern city.

If, as social historians such as Gail Bederman and Michael Kimmel suggest, there was a crisis of masculinity at the end of the nineteenth century, then by the 1890s Edward Fitzgerald was a perfect example of it.[6] Rapid industrialization, growing calls for female emancipation, high levels of immigration from Europe, and the movement of black people from the southern states to the North appeared to pose a threat to the authority of white, middle-class men. In the early 1890s Edward was running his own furniture business, but it would eventually fail; the company's demise was no doubt helped along by the financial panic of 1893. He took a position with Procter & Gamble, a situation of dependency rather than self-determination. In time, this too would come to an end, and he would remain financially dependent on his wife's family for the rest of his life. This final, personal defeat would have a profound effect on his son: it framed Scott's opinion of Edward until he was confronted with his own experience of financial and emotional collapse in the early 1930s, at the same time his father died.

As Fitzgerald was rising to fame in the 1920s, his father was an object of scorn in both his personal letters and his public essays. In his essay "Wait Till You Have Children of Your Own!" (1924), Fitzgerald denigrated his father and his entire generation as unproductive and unimaginative. They were symbols of failure sandwiched between the successful or sacrificed men of the Civil War and World War I. Fitzgerald's treatment of his father was no better in his personal correspondence. Edward was at best an object of pity. Scott wrote to his agent Harold Ober in 1926 that his father's "own life after a rather brilliant start back in the seventies has been a 'failure'—he's lived in mother's shadow and he takes an immense vicarious pleasure in any success of mine."[7] At worst, Edward was subjected to cruel and dismissive scorn. In the same year, Fitzgerald wrote the following to his editor, Maxwell Perkins: "Why shouldn't I go crazy? My father is a moron and my mother is a neurotic, half insane with pathological worry. Between them they haven't and never had the brains of Calvin Coolidge. If I knew anything I'd be the best writer in America."[8]

At that time, Fitzgerald's own personal success made it impossible for him to sympathize with the disappointments and frustrations of his father's life. That changed, however, when he left success and prosperity behind and was confronted by the horror that would be his life in the 1930s. His wife Zelda's first mental collapse occurred in April 1930, mere months after the Wall Street crash. The combination of these events ensured that Fitzgerald's life would be plagued by debt, anxiety about Zelda's health, and an unmanageable problem with alcohol. Failure had come knocking just as it had done for his father, who died in January 1931. His father's death and Fitzgerald's own experiences with despair led him to reevaluate Edward's influence on his life and vocation. This reassessment is best illustrated in the incomplete essay "The Death of My Father," first published posthumously in the *Princeton University Library Chronicle* in 1951; the "Crack-Up" essays published in *Esquire* in 1936; and the interview he gave to Michel Mok, also in 1936, which was published in the *New York Evening Post* on September 25, the day after Fitzgerald turned forty and mere weeks after his mother's demise. In these reflections on his father, his own life, and the definition of success and failure, Fitzgerald recognizes that success is perhaps a matter of chance but is certainly dependent on events that are often outside the control of the individual. In the interview with Mok, he identifies wholeheartedly and completely with Edward: "My father lost his grip and I lost my grip."[9]

This alignment with his father is indicative of Fitzgerald's own sense of failure at this time; he is identifying with a man whom a decade before he had dismissed as a "moron." It is also evidence of a growing awareness that failure teaches us about ourselves. The broken Fitzgerald of the

Edward Fitzgerald

1930s was far more capable of empathizing with the defeat experienced by others and by his father in particular. In "The Death of My Father," for example, he is able to write, "I loved my father—always deep in my subconscious I have referred judgment back to him, what he would have thought or done."[10] He acknowledged in this remark that the value of an individual is not tied exclusively to the external trappings of a materialistically driven definition of success. It can be seen in the resilience and sound judgment of a man who is confronted with failure but remains faithful to a personal code of conduct that values integrity over a shallow pursuit of social acceptance.

If You Can Meet with Triumph and Disaster and Treat Those Two Imposters Just the Same

A similar depiction of a man misunderstood by the society in which he operates appears in a play written by Fitzgerald while he was at Princeton. "Shadow Laurels" (1915) was published in the university's *Nassau Literary Magazine* and recounts Jacques Chandelle's pilgrimage to find out more about his deceased, drunken, and supposed failure of a father, Jean. Significantly, Jean Chandelle's importance to his friends is located not in his actions but in his words. His is a poetic voice that articulates experience on behalf of others. He "would tell us about men and women of history," states Jean's friend Lamarque, just as Edward would recount the stories of the South and the Civil War that changed it.[11] The son's response to his father's brilliance being (oral) storytelling rather than action jumps immediately to the question of transcending one's own time: "And he's forgotten. He left nothing. He'll never be thought of again."[12] This is dismissed by Destage, another of Jean Chandelle's friends: "Remembered! Bah! Posterity is as much a charlatan as the most prejudiced tragic critic that ever boot-licked an actor."[13]

This concern over what warrants success and whether society and posterity reward the right people looms in Fitzgerald's fiction. After all, established society is made up of "a rotten crowd" and the parvenu Jay Gatsby is "worth the whole damn bunch put together."[14] As the 1930s swamped Fitzgerald's confidence with self-doubt, the matter became increasingly pressing in the author's mind. This issue came into sharper focus when he positioned himself next to Ernest Hemingway—his sometime friend, sometime nemesis whose popularity was ascending as Fitzgerald's rapidly headed the other way. In his notebooks, Fitzgerald states, "I write with the authority of failure—Ernest with the authority of success. We could never sit across the table again."[15] What is often focused on in this assertion is the contrast between success and failure, but, importantly, Fitzgerald recognizes the authority that emerges from both experiences.

By the 1930s he was well versed in both, suggesting he had a more comprehensive artistic authority than his rival, yet it had become clear to him that success and failure on the public stage were transient. Despite his many frustrations during the period and the bouts of depression that plagued him in his final years, he never really lost sight of his great talent. In May 1940, seven months before his fatal heart attack, he wrote to Perkins, noting his public failure, "I wish I was in print." The letter offers a number of suggestions to restart his lagging career. He continues, perhaps echoing the son's lament for his father in "Shadow Laurels": "But to die, so completely and unjustly after having given so much!" He finally asserts, "Even now there is little published in American fiction that doesn't slightly bear my stamp—in a *small* way I was an original."[16]

In the closing lines of "Shadow Laurels," the son toasts his father: "I drink to one who might have been all, who was nothing—who might have sung; who only listened—who might have seen the sun; who but watched a dying ember—who drank of gall and wore a wreath of shadow laurels."[17] There is, of course, contradiction in the lament. After all, his father was praised by his friends for being a poet, and so he did sing rather than only listen. This contradiction highlights rather than obscures the suggestion that the father's success or failure is to a large extent a matter of perspective. Like Plato's captives in the cave, the son has been tricked, seeing only the shadow of his father's life rather than its reality. In Edward Fitzgerald, his son invoked the historical narrative of America, the battle between North and South, as a means of exploring personal failure. When his son shined this light on him, Edward Fitzgerald was a victim of circumstances beyond his control, a victim of historical forces that determined he would—to return to his son's play—wear not the laurels, but only their shadow.

For a Southerner, Words Speak Louder Than Actions

The association Fitzgerald made between his father and (oral rather than written) storytelling continued after Edward was deceased. In part this was the result of his father's passivity in the wake of his failed working life, which contrasted so powerfully with his activity during the Civil War. Fitzgerald's father replaced a childhood of action with an adult life of remembering, telling, and retelling stories from his own past but also from the past of a world that was lost in the defeat of the South. Fitzgerald wrote in "The Death of My Father" that he was repeatedly told his father's stories of the Civil War, often in the aftermath of damaging action or conflict. On one occasion, Fitzgerald disappeared on July 4 and was missing long enough to warrant the involvement of the police. On his return his father thrashed him:

> Afterwards, seeing in his face his regret that it had to happen I asked him to tell me a story. I knew what it would be—he had only a few—the story of the spy, the one about the man hung from his thumbs, the one about Early's march.
>
> Do you want to hear them I'm so tired of them all that I can't make them interesting. But maybe they are because I used to ask father to repeat + repeat + repeat.[18]

Accordingly, domestic acts of violence resulted in feelings of guilt, shame, and remorse. Action was a source of failure, and in the anecdote it was replaced by storytelling. Fitzgerald's request to "repeat + repeat + repeat" is significant, as it suggests there is comfort in the familiarity and certainty that the repetition of familiar stories offers. The words assigned to Edward are equally important: "Do you want to hear them I'm so tired of them all that I can't make them interesting." The retold story was not a straightforward recounting of events; it was a narrative that altered and changed and may have borne little resemblance to the events actually experienced. Fitzgerald learned from his father that action could be replaced with the retelling and reimagining of events. In the essay "Author's House" (1936), Fitzgerald provided an example of following in his father's footsteps and replacing failed action with storytelling that reframed and reimagined the event. While at school, he was taken off the field during a football match with the coach's words in his ears: "We can't depend on you." On reflection Fitzgerald reasoned, "I had been playing listlessly." He continued:

> I've been afraid plenty of times but that wasn't one of the times. The point is it inspired me to write a poem for the school paper which made me as big a hit with my father as if I had become a football hero. So when I went home that Christmas vacation it was in my

mind that if you weren't able to function in *action* you might at least be able to *tell* about it, because you felt the same intensity—it was a back-door way out of facing reality.[19] [emphasis added]

Here, Fitzgerald accepts the role of the observer. He replaces in this incident the all-American-hero football player with the introspective poet, an exchange that made him "a hit with my father," not with school friends, teachers, or wider society. If action resulted in failure, then it could be replaced with the act of telling, and events could be perfected and reimagined. This transformation of reality into an imagined, fictionalized world was a process Fitzgerald associated with his father. Despite his largely scornful dismissal of Edward early in his career, Fitzgerald did come to recognize the role his father played in his development as a writer. Edward demonstrated the cathartic nature of stories: the possibilities they presented to make right through words what was wrong in life.

Mollie Fitzgerald and a Family in Decline

Fitzgerald's complex relationship with his father was, in many respects, mirrored in his relationship with his mother. Contrasted to his father's rootedness in the American South, his mother's family were examples of the immigrant narrative. Fitzgerald's maternal grandfather, Philip Francis McQuillan, emigrated from Ireland's County Fermanagh in 1842 at the age of eight and settled with his large family in Galena, Illinois. By 1857, McQuillan was in St. Paul working as a bookkeeper for Beaupre and Temple, a large wholesale grocery business. He was married to Louisa Allen, and the couple would have a total of eight children, three of whom died in infancy. Fitzgerald's mother was born on August 8, 1859. At the age of thirty-eight, McQuillan had taken over the running of the grocery business and had generated considerable personal wealth, but he barely saw his forty-third birthday, succumbing in April 1877 to chronic nephritis complicated by tuberculosis.[20] In many respects McQuillan was the embodiment of the possibility of America: through hard work and ingenuity, abject poverty could be transformed into financial prosperity. At the time of his premature death, McQuillan had accumulated wealth in excess of a quarter of a million dollars, a significant sum of money that gave his surviving wife and children financial stability. Over the coming decades, the fortune would slowly but surely shrink, as none of McQuillan's offspring possessed his business acumen. Despite living in relative comfort, the Fitzgeralds were haunted by financial anxiety, a central component in Scott Fitzgerald's social insecurity.

Fitzgerald's familial background contrasts a pioneering spirit rooted in individual ambition and achievement with a traditional imported European principle of inherited status. Yet his family history does not entirely map over these two ideas of America. After all, the wealth generated by his pioneering maternal grandfather's ambition was on the wane, and the historical glory of his paternal line was faded, to say the least. His social anxiety was compounded by this disconnection with

Mollie McQuillan Fitzgerald

both American identities, leading to an ambivalence that can be traced through much of his work. The pioneering spirit evident in James Gatz and the vocational drive of Dr. Richard Diver are destroyed as their alter egos Jay Gatsby and Dick Diver are seduced by the allure of unearned wealth and social standing. Fitzgerald also exposes the folly of permitting such seduction as both men are destroyed by their pursuit of social status and acceptance, symbolized by union with a woman.[21] Of course, over time Fitzgerald recognized his own act of self-betrayal. In a letter written in 1938 to his daughter, Scottie, he articulated his inability to nurture his own talent and attempted to lay the blame squarely on his wife: "I was a man divided—she [Zelda] wanted me to work too much for her and not enough for my dream. She realized too late that work was dignity and the only dignity and tried to atone for it by working herself but it was too late and she is broke and is broken forever."[22] Fitzgerald is talking as much about himself as he is about his wife. He repeatedly, throughout his working life, allowed distractions to interfere with his creative life. This lack of focus would be compounded by the alcoholism that had taken hold of him by the mid-1920s at the very latest. Fitzgerald felt that his mother's indulgence of him in childhood and her overprotectiveness contributed to the weaknesses in his character that led to a lack of stamina and commitment. In addition to resenting her overindulgence, Fitzgerald was also embarrassed by Mollie's many eccentricities. In contrast to Edward's meticulous attention to dress, her appearance was rather haphazard: "The plumes of her antique bonnets drooped as if perpetually rained on," and her skirts were "apt to be trailing in the dust." She was referred to by some as "a witch" and mocked "for wearing high buttoned shoes with the top button undone to relieve her swollen ankles."[23]

Grieving Motherhood and the Depiction of the Feminine

Fitzgerald's embarrassment about his mother and his resentment of her eccentricities would reveal themselves in his fiction and his essays of the early 1920s. In his first novel, *This Side of Paradise,* Fitzgerald made the protagonist's mother the antithesis of Mollie. The figure of the mother is rarely evident in Fitzgerald's fiction with this exception, Beatrice Blaine, a maternal figure conjured up from the fantasy life of her creator. She is a woman of fashion, taste, and adventure. Elsewhere in Fitzgerald's novels, mothers are dead or absent or simply not mentioned, and not even the glamorous Beatrice will survive until the end of the novel. Two notable exceptions are Daisy Buchanan in *The Great Gatsby* and Nicole Diver in *Tender Is the Night.* Daisy is shown as remote from her daughter; the only reference she makes to her is an anecdote to illustrate her own frustrations. Nicole is presented as a more engaged mother, although this role is secondary to her identities as wife, daughter, patient, lover, and victim.

Mollie is also evident in her son's essay "Imagination—and a Few Mothers" (1923), where he depicts a neurotic and overly anxious mother figure, clearly drawing on Mollie and contrasting her with an alternative version of motherhood: Mrs. Paxton. Fitzgerald states that when Mrs. Paxton's son went to college he was on his own: "He never felt that there was someone standing behind him with all forgiving arms. . . . If he failed he would not be blamed, lectured, or wept over."[24] Significantly,

Mrs. Paxton is applauded for having been "wise enough never to pretend she owned her children. She had had enough imagination to see that they were primarily persons."[25] The benefits of Mrs. Paxton's manner of parenting and the dynamic of larger families, according to the essay, are that "each child is not ineradicably stamped with the particular beliefs, errors, convictions, aversions and bogeys that haunted the mother in the year 1889 or 1901 or 1922 as the case might be."[26] Fitzgerald asserts that the haunting of the mother is the haunting of the child. Overprotective mothers did not let their children be hurt or fail, but as a result they stopped those same children from succeeding through the process of learning that failure offers or from developing the self-reliance and resilience that life experience instills. Mrs. Paxton is the woman that Mrs. Fitzgerald should have been, according to her son, and Mollie's maternal legacy is carried on in what he identifies as his own personal weaknesses.

Mollie Fitzgerald's overprotectiveness was no doubt in part a response to the loss of two daughters in the months before the birth of her son. Fitzgerald cited those deaths in his essay "Author's House" as a trigger for his creativity: "Three months before I was born my mother lost her other two children and I believe that came first of all though I don't know how it worked exactly. I think I started then to be a writer."[27] He is linking his creativity to loss and to "the feminine." Greg Forter suggests that "had there been no loss, neither would Fitzgerald have felt any impulse or reason to create."[28] Forter also points out the peculiarity of this loss: it is a loss Fitzgerald inherited from his mother, not one that he personally experienced. André Le Vot contends that, as a result, "Fitzgerald would thus come to spend his life in a search to cure the insatiable longing produced by internalizing someone else's grief."[29] Fitzgerald was unable to mourn because he did not know what he grieved for. The loss of two children associated with his mother and not his parents, set up "associations that link up creativity, unmournable loss, and an internalized femininity."[30] It is important to note that these reflections were made at a particular time in Fitzgerald's life and that the essay "Author's House" was one of three pieces that made up a series published by *Esquire* magazine. "Author's House," "Afternoon of an Author," and "An Author's Mother" ran in consecutive issues between July and September 1936, in the final months of Mollie Fitzgerald's life. She died on September 2. In the first article, Fitzgerald uses the metaphor of the house as a means of reflecting on the motivations and influences that led to the decision to write. The essay draws on autobiographical details from Fitzgerald's life, but the author in the essay is not identified as Fitzgerald. The writing takes the form of a conversation between the "author" and an unnamed third party.

The focus of the first half of the essay is the past. It recounts the factors that led to a desire—indeed, a compulsion—to write. One of these events is the death of Fitzgerald's two sisters before he was born. One of a series of episodes mentioned, its privileged position highlights its traumatic significance but also reflects the chronological sequence that "the author" follows. This first memory, inherited rather than experienced, is identified as the beginning of his literary vocation. Writing in this context is a response to loss or, more particularly, absence. The second phase of childhood that contributes to his eventual vocation is also one based on loss. The "author" refers to killing "my first childish love of myself, my belief that I would never die like other people, and that I wasn't the son of my parents but a son of a king, a king who ruled the world."[31] What is lost is an imagined version of himself, but this loss can be overcome through writing, which allows the self to be reimagined, re-created, refashioned, and reparented. The third moment is the previously cited schoolboy performance on the football field where he was—in his mind—unjustly accused of cowardice. The accusation led to a retreat from performance to recollection. Writing "was a back-door way out of facing reality" and a way of escaping the loss of meaningful and successful action. All three events are associated with one or both of his parents: the first is his mother's grief, the second Fitzgerald's acute embarrassment regarding his parentage, and the third a recognition by Fitzgerald, through his father's response, that there was value in storytelling as well as in action.

There is something of a shift in the second half of the essay. It could be read as a mea culpa (albeit a humorous one) as "the author" demonstrates how the act of writing can disrupt and damage real-life relationships. Following an anecdote about the author toying with a woman who is under the misapprehension that one of the author's characters is actually her brother, Fitzgerald writes, "'But it's too late,' he [the author] continued as he and his visitor went upstairs. 'You can pay a little money but what can you do for meddling with a human heart? A writer's temperament is continually making him do things he can never repair.'"[32] Writing may be a retreat from action, but it is not without its own set of risks, especially for a writer who used his own life and emotional experiences as the source for much of his creative output. The remark

NOTES

1. F. Scott Fitzgerald, *The Apprentice Fiction of F. Scott Fitzgerald, 1909–1917,* ed. John Kuehl (New Brunswick, N.J.: Rutgers University Press, 1965), appendix (unnumbered pages).

2. F. Scott Fitzgerald, *Dreams of Youth: The Letters of F. Scott Fitzgerald,* ed. Andrew Turnbull (London: Little Books, 2011), 561.

3. Jerome Bruner, "Life as Narrative," *Social Research* 71, no. 3 (2004): 692.

4. Bruner, "Life as Narrative," 693.

5. Fitzgerald, *Dreams,* 613.

6. Gail Bederman, *Manliness and Civilization: A Cultural History of Gender and Race in the United States, 1880–1917* (Chicago: University of Chicago Press, 1995), 11; Michael Kimmel, *Manhood in America* (New York: Oxford University Press, 2006).

7. F. Scott Fitzgerald, *A Life in Letters,* ed. Matthew J. Bruccoli (New York: Charles Scribner's Sons, 1994), 141.

8. Fitzgerald, *Life in Letters,* 138.

9. F. Scott Fitzgerald, *Conversations with F. Scott Fitzgerald,* ed. Matthew J. Bruccoli and Judith S. Baughman (Jackson: University of Mississippi Press, 2004), 123.

10. Fitzgerald, *Apprentice Fiction,* 178.

11. Fitzgerald, *Apprentice Fiction,* 74.

12. Fitzgerald, *Apprentice Fiction,* 75.

13. Fitzgerald, *Apprentice Fiction,* 75.

14. F. Scott Fitzgerald, *The Great Gatsby: A Variorum Edition,* ed. James L. W. West III, Cambridge Edition of the Works of F. Scott Fitzgerald (Cambridge: Cambridge University Press, 2022), 185.

15. F. Scott Fitzgerald, *The Notebooks of F. Scott Fitzgerald,* ed. Matthew J. Bruccoli (New York: Harcourt Brace Jovanovich / Bruccoli Clark, 1978), 318.

16. Fitzgerald, *Life in Letters,* 308–9.

17. Fitzgerald, *Apprentice Fiction,* 77.

18. Fitzgerald, *Apprentice Fiction,* 182.

19. F. Scott Fitzgerald, "Author's House," in *My Lost City: Personal Essays, 1920–1940,* ed. James L. W. West III, Cambridge Edition of the Works of F. Scott Fitzgerald (Cambridge: Cambridge University Press, 2014), 170.

20. David S. Brown, *Paradise Lost: A Life of F. Scott Fitzgerald* (Cambridge, Mass.: Harvard University Press, 2017), 18.

21. The protagonists in Fitzgerald's two most accomplished novels are men who surrender the pursuit of individual self-realization in favor of social acceptance symbolized by union with a woman. Despite the lyricism of Fitzgerald's description of Gatsby uniting himself to Daisy, it is also quite clearly a mistake: "He knew that when he kissed this girl, and forever wed his unutterable vision to her perishable breath, his mind would never romp again like the mind of God." Fitzgerald, *Great Gatsby: Variorum,* 134. Similarly, in the relationship between Dick and Nicole in *Tender Is the Night,* a kiss is a moment when a permanent change in destiny occurs for the protagonist: "He [Dick] felt the young lips, her body sighing in relief against the arm growing stronger to hold her. There were now no more plans than if Dick had arbitrarily made some indissoluble mixture, with atoms joined and inseparable; you could throw it all out but never again could they fit back into atomic scale. . . . He

was thankful to have an existence at all, if only a reflection in her wet eyes." Fitzgerald, *Tender Is the Night,* ed. James L. W. West III, Cambridge Edition of the Works of F. Scott Fitzgerald (Cambridge: Cambridge University Press, 2022), 178. Both Jay Gatsby and Dick Diver come to be associated with leisure and society through their roles as hosts. Their work ethos (the driving force of pioneering America) is abandoned, which leads inevitably to both men's decline.

22. Fitzgerald, *Life in Letters,* 363.

23. Andrew Turnbull, *Scott Fitzgerald* (New York: Charles Scribner's Sons, 1962), 31–32.

24. Fitzgerald, "Imagination—and a Few Mothers," in *My Lost City,* 63.

25. Fitzgerald, "Imagination," 64.

26. Fitzgerald, "Imagination," 64.

27. Fitzgerald, "Author's House," 169.

28. Greg Forter, "F. Scott Fitzgerald, Modernist Studies, and the Fin-de-Siècle Crisis in Masculinity," *American Literature* 78, no. 2 (2006): 301.

29. André Le Vot, *F. Scott Fitzgerald: A Biography,* trans. William Byron (New York: Doubleday, 1983), 54; quoted in Forter, "F. Scott Fitzgerald," 301.

30. Forter, "F. Scott Fitzgerald," 302.

31. Fitzgerald, "Author's House," 169.

32. Fitzgerald, "Author's House," 172.

33. The exact date of Mollie's death has been established through the Find a Grave website, which lists the dates of Mollie's birth and death as well as the location of burial. Find a Grave, "Mary 'Mollie' McQuillan Fitzgerald," www.findagrave.com /memorial/24531573/mary-fitzgerald.

34. Fitzgerald, *Dreams,* 554.

35. Fitzgerald, *Life in Letters,* 306.

36. Fitzgerald, "Imagination," 65.

37. Fitzgerald, "An Author's Mother," in *My Lost City,* 181–82.

38. Fitzgerald, "Author's Mother," 184.

1898–1899

Martina Mastandrea

Winter 1898: Of Scott's First Specialist and Edward's First Business Failure

As 1897 gave way to 1898, the stroke of midnight marked the beginning of a fateful year that saw the United States emerge as an imperial power and New York as the second-biggest city on the globe.[1] The moment the hands of the clock pointed to twelve, a button pushed thousands of miles away in San Francisco electrically unfolded a new flag over Manhattan's city hall: New York City was starting to glow with "all the iridescence of the beginning of the world."[2] On January 1, 1898, the sun was rising, reported the *New York Daily Tribune*, "upon the greatest experiment in municipal government that the world has ever known—the enlarged city."[3] When Robert A. Van Wyck took office as the first mayor of the enlarged New York City, William McKinley and Queen Victoria were president of the United States and matriarch of the British Empire, both three years away from the ends of their lives.

The year 1898 started with a sense of excitement and confidence in the increasing prestige of the United States and the newly consolidated Metropolis of America. A contemporary observer reported that New Yorkers celebrated the beginning of the greater city by crowding saloons and cafés, where liquor flowed "in reality like water, a thing it is often said to do, but seldom really does."[4] About one thousand miles to the west, in St. Paul, Minnesota, far from taking part in the New Year's celebrations, two parents were struggling with their baby's illness. In a building known as the San Mateo Flats at 481 Laurel Avenue in the Summit Avenue neighborhood, Mollie McQuillan Fitzgerald and Edward Fitzgerald were considering summoning a doctor to examine their fifteen-month-old child, Francis Scott Key, who had been suffering from severe bronchitis since Christmas Day. Scott's baby book reveals Mollie's worry over her only son's condition, especially as her father and her sister Clara had been afflicted by the disease.[5]

The local press only increased her motherly concern. Throughout 1897,

St. Paul newspapers reported that one-third of the deaths occurring in the United States were caused by bronchitis and consumption, while advertisements scared people into buying lung balsams, specialists' health books such as *Winter Catarrh,* and even malt whiskeys, presenting them as "healthful stimulants" to cure an illness that was often marked by "serious endings."[6] According to pediatric manuals of the time, the inflammation of the air tubes was more to be feared than serious pneumonia and could prove rapidly fatal, and thus "called for the advice of a skillful doctor"[7]—which Mollie and Edward enlisted. On January 1, in the "Extraordinary Events" section of the baby book, Scott's mother recorded, "His first specialist."[8] An entry in the "Health Record" section reveals that Mollie "did not do what [the specialist] wanted after all which required a good deal of nerve" on her part.[9] Mrs. Fitzgerald did not specify what medical advice she ignored, but four days later her infant started to feel better again: F. Scott Fitzgerald was out of harm's way, for now.[10]

Having already lost two daughters to illness predisposed Mollie to fuss over her son's fragile health. Although Scott was born weighing ten pounds and six ounces,[11] at fifteen months he was not a robust child. In fact, "during his first fourteen months of life, his health was repeatedly threatened by colic and colds."[12] In Fitzgerald's most openly autobiographical novel, *This Side of Paradise* (1920), Amory Blaine's refined and glamorous mother Beatrice O'Hara has been described as a "complete makeover" of the eccentric and embarrassing Mollie.[13] Among the facts Fitzgerald took from real life and fictionally re-created in the book are two episodes in which his alter ego falls sick and the overly worried Beatrice summons specialist doctors and nurses to attend him:

> When Amory had the whooping-cough four disgusted specialists glared at each other hunched around his bed; when he took scarlet fever the number of attendants, including physicians and nurses, totalled fourteen. However, blood being thicker than broth, he was pulled through.[14]

Like Mollie, Beatrice believed her child to be "entirely sophisticated and quite charming—but delicate,"[15] and thus needing to be constantly under medical surveillance. Acute health episodes like the bronchitis Scott

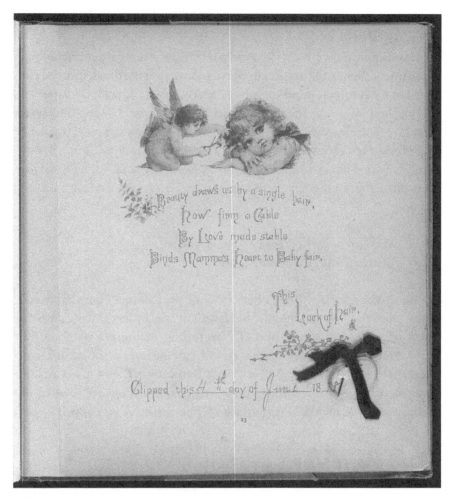

Baby Fitzgerald's lock of hair in F. Scott Fitzgerald's baby book

Summer 1898: Of Hawaiian Songs and "Eukalalis"

On July 7, 1898, President McKinley signed the Newlands Resolution, which officially annexed Hawaii to the United States. After a contentious and controversial year-long annexation process, in which divisions remained over the propriety of the U.S. role in the 1893 overthrow of the Hawaiian Kingdom, the appropriation of the islands was facilitated by the U.S. Navy's victory in Manila (May 1, 1898) during the Spanish–American War. Six months prior to the annexation, the last monarch of the Hawaiian Kingdom, Queen Liliʻuokalani, had published *Hawaii's Story by*

Hawaii's Queen (1898), which challenged the U.S. colonial construction of the Hawaiian nation.

Hawaiian culture soon became part of the average American's entertainment. Hawaiian music, in particular, was rapidly assimilated into mainland American popular songs. According to Elizabeth Tatar, the development of postcontact Hawaiian music can be divided into seven periods.[41] This historical and cultural context shows how Fitzgerald's contemporaries received his song "Take Those Hawaiian Songs Away" (1916). Included in act 2, scene 2, of *Safety First!,* the song complained that "they push Hawaii too far. . . . When will they switch to a new locality?"[42] The lines

> You can hear the strum on the eukalali
> Mingled with the sliding guitar

can be situated within Tater's Period III of postcontact Hawaiian music (circa 1895–circa 1915), which saw Hawaiian music integrating into the realm of American music and the beginning of the era of American urban music, when ragtime seeped into Honolulu and the ukulele was discovered. A month after the Newlands Resolution, the Battle of Manila (August 13, 1898) marked the end of the Spanish–American War in the Philippines. Meanwhile, Fitzgerald's second birthday was approaching.

Autumn 1898: Of Scott's Second Birthday and His Inheritance of a World of Hope

The family spent September 24, 1898, in Buffalo. Describing her son's special day, Mollie simply noted that she and Edward were "glad to think [Scott's] second year was safely passed."[43] One month later, three local newspapers announced that "Mr. and Mrs. Edward Fitzgerald of The Lenox" were entertaining family from St. Paul. The careless Buffalo journalists identified the Fitzgeralds' guests either as "Mr. Allan McQuillan and Miss McQuillan" or as "Mr. Allen Usquillan."[44] The articles were probably referring to Allen and Annabel, Mollie's unmarried brother and sister, who at the time were living with their mother in St. Paul at the McQuillan residence, 623 Summit Avenue.[45]

Shortly after her siblings returned to St. Paul, Mollie started worrying that Buffalo's harsh colder months could be dangerous for Scott's fragile health. She decided to spend the winter season in a city with a more temperate climate, Washington, D.C., while her husband remained in upstate New York.[46] On December 7, Mollie left for the capital city alone with her child; on the next day, she wrote down one of the first "cute sayings and sensible remarks" of baby Scott, who impatiently ordered her "take this quick so I would get it."[47] That same month, with the Treaty of Paris, Spain renounced all claim to Cuba, ceded Guam and Puerto Rico, and transferred sovereignty over the Philippines to the United States. In a single "fateful year," the United States annexed Hawaii and took possession of a highly strategic part of the Spanish Empire. Remarking that within the space of some months, the "land of the American Dream" had developed new desires and ambitions, H. H. Powers declared in his September 1898 address before the American Academy of Political and Social Science: "A year ago we wanted no colonies, no European neighbors, no army and not much navy."[48] After having molded public opinion for a decade, Theodore Roosevelt's and Henry Cabot Lodge's Large Policy of 1898 contributed to make their country the "indisputably dominant power in the western hemisphere."[49]

Fitzgerald and his peers who were born in the last years of the nineteenth century were raised in this atmosphere of optimism, inheritors of a world of hope. As the author wrote retrospectively in 1940, they were "told, individually and as a unit, that we were a race that could potentially lick ten others of any genus."[50] The new year was going to start with this unique feeling of infinite potential and invincibility. Or, in the words of Fitzgerald: "In 1899, when [Ernest Hemingway] was born, there was faith and hope such as a few modern nations have known."[51]

Winter 1899: Of Washington, D.C., and the White Man's Burden

Two-year old Scott celebrated the beginning of 1899 in Washington, D.C., where he received his first pair of bloomers.[52] Baptized one month after his birth,[53] he was being raised as a Catholic. On January 4, 1899, the deeply religious Mollie recorded that Scott had offered up his first prayer, which consisted of a generic and universal "God bless you."[54]

Mollie might have chosen to spend that winter in Washington not only for its weather but also because it was the city where her parents-in-law had been married and where both she and her husband had relatives.[55] Even though her mother owned a house at 1815 N Street,[56] Mollie did not stay there, choosing the fashionable Cairo Hotel at 1615 Q Street Northwest as her winter residence. In its early years, the Cairo was a

Advertisement for the Cairo Hotel, *Evening Star,* May 25, 1899.

prestigious address in an up-and-coming neighborhood. Among the prominent Washingtonians living at the hotel at the same time as Mollie and Scott were Supervising Architect of the Treasury James Knox Taylor and Congressman James S. Sherman, later vice president of the United States.[57]

Just like the Lenox, the Cairo was a brand new, glamorous building. Completed in December 1894, the 350-room apartment house was a fourteen-story skyscraper, whose "electric plant was considered one of the finest and most complete in the country."[58] As Sue A. Kohler and Jeffrey R. Carson note, the Cairo had been a Washington "landmark" since its opening: "It was considered a skyscraper when it was built. Many decried its excessive height; others, more attuned to progress than tradition, saw in it a triumph of American engineering and technology."[59] As a rental brochure from 1894 read, the building was "the largest and most luxurious apartment house in Washington."[60] Just like the Buffalo building in which the Fitzgeralds had lived a few months before, the Cairo offered a café on the top floor and elevators that ran all day and night. The hotel's guests could enjoy a "large and elegant ballroom with adjacent retiring and dressing rooms [and] a first-class drug store" on the

The Cairo Hotel, Washington, D.C. *Upper left*: first floor, columns; *upper right*: first floor, elevator and stairway; *lower left*: detail of main entrance; *lower right*: west side and south front.

first floor, "bowling alleys and billiard rooms" on the ground floor, and "a view from its tropical roof-garden" that could "hardly be surpassed."[61]

The Fitzgerald family in its entirety returned to Washington in December of the next year, as reported by the *Buffalo Times*: "Mr. and Mrs.

Edward Fitzgerald and son will leave town today for Washington where they will remain for the winter."[62] The article did not mention whether the Fitzgeralds stayed at the Cairo on that occasion; a letter that Scott sent to his cousin Cecilia Taylor Delihant many years later suggests he stayed at the same hotel as an adult. In 1917, he visited Washington several times to meet with Monsignor Sigourney Fay and Shane Leslie. On June 10, he asked Cecilia to accept "the most sincere apologies for the cold you got listening to my inane ramblings (of course I don't really think they were inane) on the porch of the Cairo." A few years later, the Cairo began a gradual decline, as it was no longer considered modern.[63] When Scott and Zelda returned to the city in 1920 and 1927, they preferred to stay at the New Willard and the Roosevelt Hotel.[64]

On February 4, 1899, one mile from the Cairo Hotel within the walls of the White House, President McKinley was receiving cable dispatches from overseas informing him of the outbreak of hostilities in Manila.[65] It was the beginning of what would come to be known as the Philippine–American War. In the aftermath of the Spanish–American War, the United States was accepting the imperialists' charge to shoulder what Rudyard Kipling called "The White Man's Burden." The publication of Kipling's so-titled poem in that month's issue of *McClure's Magazine* coincided with the beginning of the Philippine–American War and became, in Stephany Rose's words, "one of the most circulated refrains in the discussion of U.S. imperialism."[66] Twenty-two years later, while on an unsatisfactory trip to Europe, Fitzgerald would write, "I believe at last in the white man's burden. We are as far above the modern Frenchman as he is above the Negro. . . . We will be the Romans in the next generations."[67] In the same letter, Fitzgerald recognized that his comments were "philistine, anti-socialistic, provincial and racially snobbish," reflecting, in Suzanne del Gizzo's words, his "complex attitudes toward issues of race and ethnicities," attitudes she says are most clearly visible in *The Great Gatsby*.[68] As Rose notes, Fitzgerald, in imitation of Joseph Conrad, placed the novel

> within an anglophone literary tradition and the culture of
> European exploration and imperialism. . . . In Nick's rumination
> on the past, the pre-colonized land, he thinks about the space of
> wonder Gatsby must have occupied in parallel as Gatsby saw the
> light at the end of Daisy's dock and dreamt of materializing his

mission. But as "Gatsby believed in the green light, the orgastic future," Nick understands the ever present history of a society bearing on its future and as a nation, "we beat on, boats against the current, borne back ceaselessly into the past." What has become of America, the West, is a consequence of the acts enacted by those colonizing nations of Europe, the East, seeking to conquer the globe as superpowers.[69]

According to Rose, one of Conrad's most evident influences on *Gatsby* is the concept of the "compulsive pursuit of desires by man, specifically in the consideration of white civilization wanting to control and conquer others."[70] Fitzgerald locates this influence in the novel's unsympathetic antagonist Tom Buchanan, in particular in his belief that he is a member of "the dominant race" that has to "watch out or other races will have control of things."[71]

Lionel Trilling famously argued that "Gatsby, divided between power and dream, comes inevitably to stand for America itself," a nation that "prides itself upon a dream" and that has sprung from its "Platonic conception" of itself.[72] In addition to reading the Great American Novel as a response to the United States during the Roaring Twenties, it is important to view it as a product of the eventful 1898–99 period, a time in which baby Fitzgerald was living steps away from Capitol Hill, where decisions were being made to take up "the white man's burden" and turn the United States into the next century's superpower.

Spring 1899: Of Mollie's Pregnancy and Orchard Park

After a four-month stay in Washington, D.C., waiting for the cold to subside, in April Mollie and the sickly Scott returned to Buffalo and moved with Edward into a flat at Summer Street and Elmwood Avenue.[73] Around this time, Mollie became pregnant for the fourth time, just as she was worrying again for Scott, whose cough had persisted after their return from Washington.[74] Fearing the cough could develop into consumption, on June 9 Mollie decided to embark on a new journey, this time to Orchard Park, New York.[75]

In the early 1800s, Orchard Park, a southern suburb of Buffalo, had become a destination for migrating agrarian Quaker families attracted by the fact that the place was detached from "corrupting influences."

According to municipal historian Suzanne S. Kulp, the Fitzgerald family "boarded with the Potters during the summer to enjoy the fresh, healthful climate for which the community was known."[76] By "the Potters" she probably means the two daughters of Allen Potter, "an entrepreneur of unrivaled proportions," who was a commissioner of the city and county in 1850, when the house in which the Fitzgeralds boarded was built.[77] Located in the heart of Orchard Park, the building was turned into a funeral home in the 1930s and now houses the Allen Potter House Museum, which tells the story of the historical site. Its director, Timothy Gardner, interviewed descendants of the Potter family. They confirmed that Fitzgerald visited the property with his parents, who became good friends with the Clarks and the Potters.

Summer 1899: Of Auto Crazes and Death Cars

After a two-month stay in Orchard Park, Scott and Mollie returned to St. Paul and spent the month of August at Louisa McQuillan's house on Summit Avenue near Dale Street.[78] As Andrew Turnbull observes, Mollie's mother had moved to "upper, residential St. Paul, the railroad yards having appropriated the site of her former house in Lower Town."[79] Whereas many railroads lines failed in the years immediately after the Panic of 1893, automobiles were becoming the new technological luxury. The *Minneapolis Journal* reported in 1899 that "the auto craze had hit the fashionable people, like children with new toys."[80] But that year the excitement over the new, stylish means of transportation was shadowed by tragedy. On September 14, Henry H. Bliss became the first person ever killed by a motor vehicle in the United States. Bliss was run over and killed by an automobile that "came along at high speed, veered, and struck him squarely, knocking him in front of the wheels."[81] The accident happened in New York City at Central Park West and Seventy-Fourth Street, a dozen miles from the Valley of Ashes, the fictional location based on the Corona Dump in the New York borough of Queens, where Myrtle Wilson's life is "violently extinguished" by Gatsby's "death car."[82]

Autumn 1899: Of Scott's Third Birthday and Insatiable Appetite

On Scott's third birthday, September 24, 1899, he weighed thirty-five pounds. Halfway through her pregnancy, Mollie described the day as a "a very quiet rainy day in Buffalo, an exceedingly peaceful time."[83] The

Fitzgeralds were back to the Summer Street apartment where, the following month, Scott slid on the hall carpet and got a scar on the right side of
his forehead, a scar he possessed for the rest of his life.[84] The precocious
child was also starting to articulate more complex concepts. Four days
after his birthday, Mollie recorded "Scott's way of expressing hunger" as
"I want—too much."[85] The insatiable appetite for food would turn into
an insatiable appetite for glamour, fame, and addictions.

The year 1899, just like 1898, ended with a feeling of hope and promise. Mollie's baby was due in a month, and Scott's health seemed more
stable. No one could predict that the family was going to suffer yet another infant's death the following month. Born on January 21, 1900,
Scott's sister lived only an hour.[86] In the same year that Mollie Fitzgerald
lost her third baby, Minnie Sayre gave birth to her fifth surviving child,
Scott's future wife Zelda. In her essay "Looking Back Eight Years" (1928),
Zelda gave readers an insight into the generation born between the 1890s
and the early 1900s to "parents who didn't experience the struggles and
upheavals of the Sixties and Seventies and had no inkling of the cataclys-
mic changes the next decade would bring." In such a period of pregnant
placidity, according to Zelda, "it was a romantic time to be a child."[87]

The years 1898 and 1899 were eventful ones in F. Scott Fitzgerald's
life and in U.S. history. The last twenty-four months of the nineteenth
century saw New York City take its current political and geographical
form, and the United States became the dominant power in the Western
world. Still unaware of being one of "the Great Inheritors" of the Spanish Empire and of a world of hope,[88] in those months baby Fitzgerald
took his first steps and said his first words and prayers; he took his
first train ride and had his first haircut; he lived in his first glamorous
hotel and recognized, for the first time, that he wanted "—too much."
If this two-year window sheds light on Mollie's overprotectiveness and
Edward's inability to keep a job, it also illuminates what Scott Donaldson
described as "the way [Fitzgerald had] been brought up by migratory
parents who shifted frequently between apartments and rented houses."[89]
Destined to live a nomadic life and to never own a house, by the age of
three Fitzgerald had already lived in four cities and three states.

In the lively 1898–99 period, Fitzgerald also went East for the first
time, to the place where he would "[rise] up to his position" twenty years
later,[90] just like his most celebrated character. During those first months
living in the East, on November 1, 1899, the three-year-old Scott was
heard saying a very Gatsbyesque sentence: "Mother, when I get to be a big

boy can I have all the things I oughtn't to have?"[91] Perhaps it was around this time F. Scott Fitzgerald was starting to believe he "wasn't the son of my parents but a son of a king, a king who ruled the whole world,"[92] like all the other American "great believers . . . born to power and intense nationalism"[93] at the turn of the nineteenth century.

NOTES

1. By incorporating Manhattan, the Bronx, Queens, Staten Island, and Brooklyn, in 1898 New York City became the world's second-largest urban conglomeration, after London.

2. F. Scott Fitzgerald, "My Lost City," in *My Lost City: Personal Essays, 1920–1940,* ed. James L. W. West III, Cambridge Edition of the Works of F. Scott Fitzgerald (Cambridge: Cambridge University Press, 2014), 108.

3. "Birth of the Greater City," *New York Daily Tribune,* January 1, 1898.

4. "Birth of the Greater City."

5. Andrew Turnbull, *Scott Fitzgerald* (New York: Charles Scribner's Sons, 1962), 7–8.

6. "Causes of Death," *St. Paul Globe,* November 21, 1897; "Only a Cold!," *St. Paul Globe,* December 24, 1897; "Catarrhal Bronchitis," *St. Paul Globe,* March 27, 1898; "Bronchitis and Sore Throat," *St. Paul Globe,* May 23, 1897.

7. Charles West, *The Mother's Manual of Children's Diseases* (New York: Longmans, Green, 1885), 130–31, 178.

8. "Scrapbook VI: F. Scott Fitzgerald's 'Baby Book' (1896–1915)," 39; accessed October 22, 2019. https://findingaids.princeton.edu/catalog/C0187_c03404?onlineToggle =false.

9. "Fitzgerald's 'Baby Book,'" 42.

10. Many years later, when he went back to his baby book to rewrite parts of his ledger, F. Scott Fitzgerald sarcastically questioned the doctor's ability, noting that he had pulled through only because the specialist's "advice was not followed." F. Scott Fitzgerald, "F. Scott Fitzgerald's Ledger, 1919–1938," Matthew J. and Arlyn Bruccoli Collection of F. Scott Fitzgerald's Ledger, 1919–1938, Irvin Department of Special Collections, Digital Collections Department, University of South Carolina, 2013, 152; accessed October, 20, 2019. https://digital.library.sc.edu /collections/f-scott-fitzgeralds-ledger-1919-1938/.

11. "Fitzgerald's 'Baby Book,'" 35.

12. John J. Koblas, *A Guide to F. Scott Fitzgerald's St. Paul* (St. Paul: Minnesota Historical Society Press, 2004), 15.

13. John T. Irwin, *F. Scott Fitzgerald's Fiction: "An Almost Theatrical Innocence"* (Baltimore, Md.: The Johns Hopkins University Press, 2014), 197–200.

14. F. Scott Fitzgerald, *This Side of Paradise,* ed. James L. W. West III, Cambridge Edition of the Works of F. Scott Fitzgerald (Cambridge: Cambridge University Press, 2012), 13.

15. Fitzgerald, *This Side of Paradise,* 13.

16. F. Scott Fitzgerald, *The Letters of F. Scott Fitzgerald,* ed. Andrew Turnbull (New York: Charles Scribner's Sons, 1963), 199.

17. "The American Rattan and Willow Works," *St. Paul Daily Globe,* July 21, 1892.

18. Matthew J. Bruccoli, *Some Sort of Epic Grandeur: The Life of F. Scott Fitzgerald* (London: Hodder and Stoughton, 1981), 12.

19. "Agreeable Reports," *St. Paul Globe,* May 21, 1893.

20. Quoted in Bruccoli, *Epic Grandeur,* 12.

21. "Home Product Exhibit," *St. Paul Globe,* May 13, 1897.

22. Koblas, *Guide,* 15.

23. Alice Hall Petry, *Fitzgerald's Craft of Short Fiction: The Collected Stories, 1920–1935* (Tuscaloosa: University of Alabama Press, 1989), 169.

24. Scott Donaldson, *Fool for Love: F. Scott Fitzgerald* (Minneapolis: University of Minnesota Press, 2012), 5.

25. "Fitzgerald's 'Baby Book,'" 39. Two years later, in 1900, Buffalo would become the second-largest railroad terminus in the United States, after Chicago.

26. James M. Volo, *A History of War Resistance in America* (Santa Barbara, Calif.: Greenwood, 2010), 294–96.

27. David Traxel, *1898: The Birth of the American Century* (New York: Alfred A. Knopf, 1998).

28. Spain signed the Armistice on August 12, 1898, ending the war less than sixteen weeks after it began. The formal peace treaty was signed in Paris in December 1898.

29. Fitzgerald, "My Lost City," 108.

30. F. Scott Fitzgerald, "The Curious Case of Benjamin Button," in *Tales of the Jazz Age,* ed. James L. W. West III, Cambridge Edition of the Works of F. Scott Fitzgerald (Cambridge: Cambridge University Press, 2012), 186.

31. Donald H. Dyal, *Historical Dictionary of the Spanish American War* (Westport, Conn.: Greenwood Press, 1996), 108–9.

32. F. Scott Fitzgerald, "My Generation," in *My Lost City,* 192–94.

33. Fitzgerald, "My Generation," 192.

34. Fitzgerald, "My Generation," 192.

35. Fitzgerald, "Ledger," 152.

36. Social Register, *Buffalo Commercial,* May 3, 1898.

37. "Why Buffalo Grows," *Buffalo Courier,* May 3, 1896.

38. "A Model Building. The Lenox Apartment House for North Street," *Buffalo Courier,* May 10, 1896.

39. "Fitzgerald's 'Baby Book,'" 39.

40. "Fitzgerald's 'Baby Book,'" 16.

41. Elizabeth Tatar, "Introduction: What Is Hawaiian Music?" *Hawaiian Music and Musicians: An Illustrated History,* ed. George Kanahele (Honolulu: University of Hawaii Press, 1979), xxv–xxvi.

42. F. Scott Fitzgerald, "Take Those Hawaiian Songs Away," in *Spires and Gargoyles: Early Writings, 1909–1919,* ed. James L. W. West III, Cambridge Edition of the Works of F. Scott Fitzgerald (Cambridge: Cambridge University Press, 2022), 95–96.

43. "Fitzgerald's 'Baby Book,'" 31.

44. Social Register, *Buffalo Enquirer,* October 25, 1898; The Social Circle, *Buffalo Enquirer,* October 26, 1898; "Those Whom We Welcome to Our Homes," *Buffalo Courier,* October 30, 1898.

45. David Page, *F. Scott Fitzgerald in Minnesota: The Writer and His Friends at Home* (St. Paul: Fitzgerald in St. Paul / University of Minnesota Press, 2017), 85.

46. As the *Buffalo Commercial* reported, "Mrs. Edward Fitzgerald of The Lenox has gone to Washington." Social Register, *Buffalo Commercial,* December 7, 1898.

47. "Fitzgerald's 'Baby Book,'" 51.

48. Quoted in Julius W. Pratt, "The 'Large Policy' of 1898," *Mississippi Valley Historical Review* 19 (September 1932): 219–42.

49. Pratt, "Large Policy," 222.

50. Fitzgerald, "My Generation," 192.

51. Fitzgerald, "My Generation," 192.

52. "Fitzgerald's 'Baby Book,'" 39. In his ledger, Fitzgerald rewrote this entry specifying the name of the hotel where they stayed: "He put on bloomers and went to Washington to spend the winter at the Cairo Hotel." Fitzgerald, "Ledger," 153.

53. Fitzgerald, "Ledger," 151.

54. "Fitzgerald's 'Baby Book,'" 36.

55. The Fitzgeralds visited Mollie's relatives on a number of occasions. When they traveled to Washington to visit them, "she'd take the sleeper and Edward would follow on the day coach." Donaldson, *Fool for Love,* 6.

56. Bruccoli, *Epic Grandeur,* 12.

57. Sue A. Kohler and Jeffrey R. Carson, *Sixteenth Street Architecture,* vol. 2 (Washington, D.C.: Commission of Fine Arts, 1988), 369.

58. "Doings of the Week in Labor Circles," *Washington Times,* December 23, 1894. The Cairo's unprecedented height prompted the D.C. Board of Commissioners to pass a regulation that limited the height of future residential buildings. Dana Hull, "The Cairo: The Tower of Style and Elegance," *Washington Post,* May 18, 1996.

59. Kohler and Carson, *Sixteenth Street Architecture,* 365.

60. Quoted in Kohler and Carson, *Sixteenth Street Architecture,* 366–67.

61. Quoted in Kohler and Carson, *Sixteenth Street Architecture,* 366.

62. Personal Mention, *Buffalo Times,* December 10, 1900.

63. Kohler and Carson, *Sixteenth Street Architecture,* 369.

64. F. Scott Fitzgerald and Zelda Fitzgerald, "Show Mr. and Mrs. F. to Number —," in *My Lost City,* 116, 121.

65. U.S. Congress, *Congressional Record: Containing the Proceedings and Debates of the Fifty-Seventh Congress, First Session, Also Special Session of the Senate,* vol. 25 (Washington, D.C.: Government Printing Office, 1902), 7134.

66. Stephany Rose, *Abolishing White Masculinity from Mark Twain to Hiphop: Crises in Whiteness* (Lanham, Md.: Lexington Books, 2014), 79.

67. Fitzgerald, *Letters,* 326.

68. Suzanne del Gizzo, "Ethnic Stereotyping," in *F. Scott Fitzgerald in Context,* ed. Bryant Mangum (Cambridge: Cambridge University Press, 2013), 224–33.

69. Rose, *Abolishing White Masculinity,* 102.

70. Rose, *Abolishing White Masculinity,* 102.

71. F. Scott Fitzgerald, *The Great Gatsby: A Variorum Edition,* ed. James L. W. West III, Cambridge Edition of the Works of F. Scott Fitzgerald (Cambridge: Cambridge University Press, 2022), 16.

72. Lionel Trilling, "F. Scott Fitzgerald," in *The Liberal Imagination: Essays on Literature and Society,* with an introduction by Lois Menand (New York: New York Review of Books, 2008), 251.

73. Fitzgerald, "Ledger," 153.

74. Turnbull, *Fitzgerald*, 7–8.

75. Fitzgerald, "Ledger," 153.

76. Suzanne S. Kulp and Joseph F. Bieron, *Orchard Park* (Charleston, S.C.: Arcadia Publishing, 2003), 95.

77. Kulp and Bieron, *Orchard Park*, 118.

78. Fitzgerald, "Ledger," 153.

79. Turnbull, *Fitzgerald*, 8.

80. *Minneapolis Journal*, quoted in Reynold M. Wik, *Henry Ford and Grass-Roots America: A Fascinating Account of the Model T* (Ann Arbor: University of Michigan Press, 1973), 15.

81. "Killed by an Automobile: Henry H. Bliss Crushed under a Horseless Vehicle's Wheels," *Washington, D.C., Evening Times*, September 14, 1899.

82. Fitzgerald, *Great Gatsby: Variorum*, 165.

83. "Fitzgerald's 'Baby Book,'" 31.

84. Fitzgerald, "Ledger," 154.

85. "Fitzgerald's 'Baby Book,'" 27.

86. "Fitzgerald's 'Baby Book,'" 39; Fitzgerald, "Ledger," 153.

87. Zelda Fitzgerald, *Collected Writings*, ed. Matthew J. Bruccoli (Tuscaloosa: University of Alabama Press, 1991), 606–7.

88. Fitzgerald, "My Generation," 192, 194.

89. Donaldson, *Fool for Love*, 96.

90. Fitzgerald, *Great Gatsby: Variorum*, 202.

91. "Fitzgerald's 'Baby Book,'" 51.

92. F. Scott Fitzgerald, "Author's House," in *My Lost City*, 169.

93. Fitzgerald, "My Generation," 192, 194.

1900–1901

Philip McGowan

At the close of World War I, F. Scott Fitzgerald began to keep a ledger in which he recorded his life, writing plans, and income from his published works. There are nine ledger entries in total for the first two years of the twentieth century: five for 1900 and four for 1901. To account for Fitzgerald's young boyhood in this period focuses on supplying contextual and historical information, either facts that the ledger overlooks or material that Fitzgerald deemed superfluous to his own immediate biographical time line. That said, significant events in America's social, political, and cultural histories occur during these two years when the Fitzgerald family was living in upstate New York, first in Buffalo and then in Syracuse. The importance of these incidents arises from the fact that they would later be incorporated into Fitzgerald's fiction, either as direct references or as more subliminally layered traces: Fitzgerald's accumulation of knowledge, no matter how apparently arbitrary or trivial, and his absorption of historical detail began at a very young age. While the ledger provides surface information about his first years that he recorded retrospectively, it also includes nods toward noteworthy material and incidents at the time that would hold a longer-term fascination for Fitzgerald as he began the work of formulating his fictional worlds.

The five ledger entries for 1900 consist of one each for the months of January, February, March, August, and September, the month he turned four years of age. The Fitzgeralds were living in an apartment at Summer Street and Elmwood Avenue, north of the center of Buffalo. The notable events for this February of Fitzgerald's life are health-related, one self-inflicted, the other not: "He celebrated the new century by swallowing a penny and catching the measles. He got rid of both of them."[1] In the United States, measles was added to the list of infectious diseases that cities and districts were required to report and catalog in 1912; in the first decade that reports were collated, there were on average 297,216 measles cases per year, resulting in an average of 5,948 deaths annually between 1912 and 1921.[2] Although statistics do not exist for 1900, the incidence

HOTEL LENOX
NORTH STREET AT DELAWARE AVENUE
BUFFALO, N. Y.

Hotel Lenox, one block from the Fitzgeralds' apartment on Summer Street and Elmwood Avenue in Buffalo, New York.

rate would have been similarly high. Given the general concerns about Fitzgerald's health as a child (concerns that continued into adulthood; for example, he was treated for tuberculosis in 1932 and 1935), it is not surprising that he mentions his bout of measles in the ledger. The fact that it appears to have been a short-lived illness, certainly given the brevity of Fitzgerald's own note about it, suggests it formed a brief part of a wider family commentary about Fitzgerald's first years that was later passed on to him as he grew up. He was certainly well enough for his parents to send him to school for the first time the following month, though "he wept and wailed so they took him out again after one morning."[3] Though school proved initially daunting for the three-and-a-half-year-old, it is unclear whether his distress was a result of the usual separation anxieties of a toddler or of Fitzgerald's own individual personality traits. That this particular nugget of information is added to the tally in his ledger is notable: no doubt it emanated from a family lore of stories about his behavior from childhood that, when added together with his health issues, sketch an outline of the young Fitzgerald as a boy closely watched by parents concerned that they might lose a fourth child before his own fourth year was out.

In March 1900, while Fitzgerald was dealing with the early trials of childhood in upstate New York at the turn of the century, the *Smart Set* magazine was founded in New York City by Civil War veteran Colonel William d'Alton Mann, who had moved into the publishing industry after his distinguished service in the war, including at Gettysburg under the command of General George Armstrong Custer. Subtitled the *Magazine of Cleverness*, the *Smart Set* was aimed squarely at an upper-class clientele, most notably the so-called 400 of fashionable society individuals as identified in 1892 by Samuel Ward McAllister, a lawyer and right-hand man to Mrs. Caroline Astor.[4] The *Smart Set* continued to offer column inches to new literary talents until its last issue in June 1930 and had its high-water mark under the joint editorship of H. L. Mencken and George J. Nathan between 1914 and 1923. It would also be the first magazine to publish a Fitzgerald story, "Babes in the Woods," in September 1919, six months before his debut novel *This Side of Paradise* was released by Scribner's. Indeed, the *Smart Set* also published three more Fitzgerald stories before *This Side of Paradise* established his position as the literary voice of a new, postwar American generation: between January and

March 1920, "Porcelain and Pink," "Benediction," and "Dalyrimple Goes Wrong" appeared within the magazine's pages.

The United States at the Turn of the Century

While the ledger's interlude between March and August 1900 would suggest a period of little interest or activity in the Buffalo homelife of the Fitzgeralds, in the United States during these months a number of events occurred that would shape Fitzgerald's later life and writing. At this point in its history, Buffalo was the second-largest city in New York State and the eighth-largest urban area in the country. It was a key railroad terminus, just behind Chicago in terms of importance, and its economy was driven by grain, steel, and the railroad industry.[5] As the nation developed its transport networks on the back of the industrial success of cities such as Buffalo and as more services were offered on the rail network, there was a concomitant litany of fatal train crashes across the United States, and loss of life became a frequent fact of the national news cycle.

The 1870s and 1880s had been punctuated with multiple-fatality incidents, and the 1890s and the first years of the new century were no different. On July 30, 1896, fifty people were killed in a train collision just west of Atlantic City, New Jersey;[6] a further seventeen lost their lives when a train derailed in Garrison, New York, on October 24, 1897.[7] While the data on railroad crashes are historical record, one particular crash, which claimed a single life, became part of the contemporary cultural imaginary of the period. In the early morning of April 30, 1900, an accident in Vaughan, Mississippi, 175 miles south of Memphis, Tennessee, spurred its own mini industry of newspaper articles, books, a film, popular songs, and eventually a museum. The crash of the Illinois Central Railroad express train, the Cannonball, resulted in the death of the train's engineer, John Luther "Casey" Jones, almost instantly converting him into a cultural hero. Despite the fact that the crash was in large part caused by Jones's attempt to make up time en route to New Orleans after leaving Memphis ninety-five minutes late, his bravery in the accident soon became the stuff of legend: Jones remained at the controls of the train after instructing his fireman Sim Webb to jump to safety. As Norm Cohen relates, in 1909 a song by T. Lawrence Seibert and Edward Newton, based on an original blues ballad composition by Wallace Saunders, became "a national rage."[8] "Everyone was singing it," Cohen reports—so much so that in *This Side of Paradise,* true to the historical details of the times, "Casey Jones" is the song played on the Graphophone in the Minnehaha Club at the conclusion of Myra St. Claire's bobbing party. Amory Blaine at this stage of the proceedings is thirteen years old, and the year is 1909.

On Wednesday, November 27, 1901, two passenger trains collided head-on one mile north of the town of Seneca, Michigan. Although the official death toll was registered at twenty-three, estimates pushed that figure up to and beyond one hundred,[9] because the westbound No. 13 train headed for Kansas City, Missouri, was carrying many Italian immigrant families who were packed into wooden cars that became fireballs after the crash. Looking ahead to later in Fitzgerald's life and writing career, and in particular to those "thrilling, returning trains" of Nick Carraway's youth, to "the murky yellow cars of the Chicago, Milwaukee and St. Paul railroad looking cheerful as Christmas itself on the track beside the gate,"[10] we can see that these images represented more than just nostalgic resonances particular to Nick Carraway, and Fitzgerald would have been well aware of the spate of fatal railroad crashes that occurred regularly in the years before and after 1901 and up to his completing the text of *The Great Gatsby* in 1924. Indeed, the very railroad line that Carraway reminisces about was not without its own tragic history. In the early morning of October 28, 1886, the Chicago, Milwaukee, and St. Paul train derailed on an open switch east of Rio, Wisconsin: seventeen people burned to death in the day car, though the passengers traveling in the sleeper carriages survived.[11]

The twelfth federal census in the United States, held on June 1, 1900, recorded that the nation's population had passed seventy-six million, a rise of 21 percent on the 1890 census total.[12] As Joel Kabot notes, cities in the northeastern and eastern states at the turn of the century were more heavily populated than other major American cities at this time: Los Angeles, for example, ranked as the thirty-sixth and Atlanta the forty-third urban areas by population in 1900.[13] With America growing at an increasingly rapid rate, the first presidential election of the century was a potential watershed moment for the nation. The Republican incumbent, William McKinley of Ohio, secured his party's nomination for a second term in office at the Republican National Convention held in Philadelphia on June 19–21. Given that his first vice president, Garret Hobart, had died in office in November 1899, the convention also had to nominate a new running mate for the McKinley ticket. Although New York's Theodore Roosevelt declined the invitation to run, he secured 925 of the 926 delegate votes available, with one state abstaining: Roosevelt's own.[14] In the ensuing presidential election on November 6, McKinley defeated the Democratic contender from Nebraska, William Jennings Bryan, who later became a vocal advocate in the campaign for national prohibition.

Nine hundred miles, multiple states, and a veritable world away from the northeastern bustle of industrial Buffalo, on July 24, 1900, a fourth daughter, Zelda, was born to Judge Anthony D. Sayre and Minnie Machen Sayre of Montgomery, Alabama, becoming the youngest sibling of Marjorie, Rosalind, Clotilde, and Anthony B. Sayre. Zelda Sayre was born into a prominent, if not rich, Montgomery family, her father having served as a state senator between 1894 and 1897 before being appointed as a city court judge in Montgomery, a position he would be reelected to in 1903. It would be eighteen years before Zelda Sayre and Scott Fitzgerald would meet at a country club dance in Montgomery while he, an infantry second lieutenant, was stationed at the nearby Camp Sheridan awaiting deployment to the war in Europe.

During Zelda's first summer, Fitzgerald was in Buffalo before holidaying briefly in New Jersey and then returning home to prepare for his fourth birthday. In his ledger, he takes up the potted history of his three-year-old self again in August 1900, noting, "He visited Atlantic City for the first time, later going through the Philadelphia Navy-yard."[15] Summer trips to the New Jersey resort town were very much part of East Coast life in the last decades of the nineteenth century, a trend that increased in the first decades of the twentieth century. As one report about Atlantic City in the *Indianapolis News* from August 17, 1895, observed: "The past week has conclusively shown that, generously proportioned as this city and everything in it is, it is entirely too small in many ways for the mighty throngs that are now making an August pilgrimage to the sea."[16] Famous for its raised wooden boardwalk, originally constructed as a temporary seasonal structure in 1870, Atlantic City offered a holiday destination to lower-income as well as higher-income families and proved readily accessible for urban populations across Pennsylvania, New York, and New Jersey after the completion of the Philadelphia and Atlantic City Railway in 1877.[17]

On September 8, two weeks before Fitzgerald's birthday on September 24, a category-four hurricane devastated the city of Galveston, Texas.

Home to more than thirty-seven thousand residents, Galveston at the time was Texas's fourth-largest city; once the storm passed, at least six thousand people had been killed.[18] Later estimates suggest a higher total, between ten and twelve thousand,[19] the equivalent of one-third of the city's population. It remains the largest single natural disaster in U.S. history. Fitzgerald's ledger makes no mention of the storm, just as it had failed to catalog any of the fatal railroad accidents of the time. Insulated from the local and national newspaper coverage of the year's industrial tragedies and deadly weather events, the young Fitzgerald characterized in the ledger is an (at that time) only child who "had a party to celebrate his birthday" and who "wore a sailor suit about this time." Whether or not the sailor suit was the inspiration, he recalls that he "told enormous lies to older people about being really the owner of a real yatch."[20]

If this is an example of Fitzgerald's own creative accounting for his younger self, it is not a huge leap to connect such "enormous lies" concocted in childhood with the events of chapter 6 of *The Great Gatsby*, in which Nick Carraway relates a vital incident in the backstory of his eponymous hero: "the specific moment that witnessed the beginning of his career—when he saw Dan Cody's yacht drop anchor over the most insidious flat on Lake Superior."[21] Owning a yacht appealed as much to the sensibilities and imaginative worlds of the four-year-old Fitzgerald as it would to his later seventeen-year-old fictional creation James Gatz: "To young Gatz, resting on his oars and looking up at the railed deck, that yacht represented all the beauty and glamor in the world."[22] The distillation of the self-evident falsehoods of an imaginative four-year-old into the idealized fantasies "that a seventeen year old boy would be likely to invent" highlights the use Fitzgerald made of incidents from across his life,[23] whether they were of a more personal nature or were accumulated from a wider historical panorama of interests and specific occurrences.

Life was relatively eventful for F. Scott Fitzgerald in the first twelve months of the new century: losing a sister, contracting measles, taking a trip away from Buffalo—all added to the early evidence of his creative potential. Unknown to Fitzgerald at this time, 1900 was also a year that witnessed the deaths of notable writers or intellectuals who either would influence him during his writing career or were important figures in the literary environs in which he would soon circulate. The naturalist writer and journalist Stephen Crane died at the age of twenty-eight in Badenweiler, Germany, on June 5; on August 25, the German philosopher Friedrich

The young sailor begins his great voyage.

Nietzsche passed away in Weimar, aged fifty-five; and on November 30 in Paris, the Irish poet and dramatist Oscar Wilde, a significant influence on Fitzgerald's earliest writings, died at the age of forty-six. Naturalism was arguably the dominant domestic literary tradition at the turn of the century and the one against which Fitzgerald's first fictions were positioned as he sought to establish his reputation. Michael Nowlin summarizes what he, correctly, terms Fitzgerald's "flirtation with" naturalism evident to varying degrees in *This Side of Paradise* and *The Beautiful and Damned*.[24] Where Fitzgerald's debut novel name-checks American and European exponents of naturalism, specifically Frank Norris, Theodore Dreiser, Théophile Gautier, and Hermann Sudermann in his "romance and a reading list,"[25] *The Beautiful and Damned* more directly engages a naturalist mode, most evident in its dissection of the Patches' deterioration in the novel's third book. The flirtation that Nowlin identifies would be a short-lived if "crucial step" for Fitzgerald along the road to a more recognizably modernist style in his third novel, *The Great Gatsby*.[26]

To Syracuse and the 1901 Buffalo World's Fair

For the Fitzgeralds, 1901 brought both a new year and a new city: "He now went to Syracuse where he took Mrs. Peck's appartment on East Genesee Street," notes Fitzgerald for January 1901 in his ledger.[27] Syracuse, smaller than the previous city they had called home, was New York State's fourth-largest city at this time.[28] It is situated 150 miles due east of Buffalo, and Edward Fitzgerald's job with Procter & Gamble included short-notice moves between the two locations. The Fitzgeralds would live in Syracuse until 1903, when they returned to Buffalo. No matter which location they were in, they could not have missed the news that came on January 22, 1901: the death, after a reign of sixty-three years, seven months, and two days, of Queen Victoria. A change of era was occurring: while an ocean and a history of revolutionary insurgence separated America from Britain, Victorian values had held sway throughout the nineteenth century on both sides of the Atlantic. Arguably, with Victoria's passing, the new century was about to begin in earnest.

Newly returned to office, McKinley was inaugurated for his second term as president on March 4, 1901, with his new vice president, Theodore Roosevelt, a hero of the 1898 Spanish–American War, by his side. With that war concluded, the business of the new administration was to anticipate the promises of the new century, and McKinley began his second stint with a tour of the western states. It was scheduled to begin with a visit to Buffalo to attend the 1901 Pan-American Exposition, the first World's Fair of the twentieth century and the first exposition held on

American soil since the 1898 Trans-Mississippi Fair in Omaha, Nebraska. Because his wife, Ida, was ill, McKinley changed his schedule so that his visit would fall in September, instead sending his vice president to the opening of the exposition:[29] the Buffalo event began on May 1 and had a scheduled end date of November 2, 1901. Located on 350 acres of land bordered by Elmwood and Delaware Avenues, the site was three miles north of where the Fitzgeralds had been living the previous year; by the time it closed, eight million people had visited the Pan-American.[30] The Fitzgeralds made their way there at an unspecified date that August and did so as a family of four: Fitzgerald's sister Annabel, his only sibling to survive into adulthood, was born on July 21, 1901, Fitzgerald noting that "his first certain memory" was "the sight of her howling on a bed."[31] Unlike her older brother, Annabel lived a long life, dying the day after her eighty-sixth birthday in 1987; at the age of twenty-three, on April 12, 1925, she married Clifton "Ziggy" Sprague, who later became a vice admiral in the U.S. Navy during World War II. The Spragues had two daughters, Patricia and Courtney Sprague Vaughan.

Before returning to Buffalo to visit the World's Fair, the Fitzgeralds made a summer trip to Atlantic City with their baby and four-year-old son in August. Fitzgerald recalled, "Some Freudian complex refused to let him display his <u>feet</u>, so he refused to swim, concealing the real reason. They thought he feared the water. On reality he craved it."[32] This is an intriguing memory to be recalled in relatively extensive detail, certainly when read in relation to the other ledger entries for this period in his life. It speaks as much to the adult Fitzgerald's own interest in psychoanalysis and Freudian theory as it does to his wish to reassemble his childhood via key moments, however accurately or not that impulse to (re) write may have been. After this observation about his feet, he records blankly, "Also he attended the Buffalo exposition, the Pan American."[33] This emptying-out of detail about the visit to the World's Fair draws as much attention as the issue relating to his self-consciousness about his feet: the Pan-American was the biggest thing ever to happen in the history of Buffalo, and it placed the city that he had been living in for the previous four years firmly in an international spotlight for six months of 1901. Fitzgerald's deadpan, matter-of-fact note is so cursory as to be almost unnecessary, and it is puzzling that he found the fair so unimportant.

The Fitzgeralds were drawn to the Pan-American for the same reasons eight million other visitors made their way to Buffalo during six months of 1901: the opportunity to view and participate in the latest technological advances of the day and to partake in the entertainments offered by the carnival's midway and sideshows. At the heart of the fair was the Electric Tower, visible from fifty miles away when illuminated and the centerpiece of an exhibition designed as an extravagant wonderland of multicolored lights covering the temporary buildings and carnival structures arrayed in two colonnades around the tower.[34] The imprint such a spectacularly visual event had on the young Fitzgerald is readily evident in the 1924 short story "Absolution," in which Father Adolphus Schwartz recommends that the eleven-year-old Rudolph Miller "go and see an amusement park. . . . It's a thing like a fair, only much more glittering."[35] It does not require much imagination to connect what Fitzgerald encountered at the Buffalo fair and Father Schwartz's revery about this carnival wonderland where "everything will twinkle," even though, he warns, "it won't remind you of anything. . . . It will all just hang out there in the night like a colored balloon—like a big yellow lantern on a pole."[36]

Before the Buffalo exposition, arguably the most famous World's Fair in U.S. history had been the 1893 Columbian Exposition in Chicago, named the "White City" after the neoclassical architecture of its exhibition buildings. Buffalo's commitment to the age of electricity was reflected in the light displays throughout the fairgrounds: the peripheral buildings as visitors entered the site were palely lit, while the central ones gathered around the Electric Tower were highly colored; all this resulted in the Pan-American suitably being nicknamed the "Rainbow City." As Mark Goldman notes, "Above all else it was electricity and the Electric Tower that attracted the attention of the millions of people" who attended the fair: "At dusk, peak time at the exposition, when over two million light bulbs were turned on simultaneously, the effect was staggering."[37] According to Paul Greenhalgh, as the visual representation of American aspiration and achievement, the park welcomed its visitors "into a carefully crafted allegory of America's rise to the apex of civilization."[38] The allegory was lost on F. Scott Fitzgerald, who at the time of his visit was a month short of his fifth birthday, but it is unlikely that he would have forgotten the light displays of this particular World's Fair staged so near to where he had been living up to eight or nine months previously.

Presidents, Assassinations, and Executions

The Pan-American Exposition's place in history has less to do with the electrical extravaganzas on display during its six months in the Buffalo suburbs than with the events that unfolded once President McKinley did eventually make it to the fair. Arriving on the evening of September 4, 1901, McKinley's presence helped swell the next day's crowds to a record for the Buffalo fair of 116,000 for a single day;[39] in addition, a specially devised fireworks event was held to welcome the president to the exposition. On September 6, following a visit to Niagara Falls, McKinley returned to the fair. Shortly after 4:00 p.m., among the crowds in the Temple of Music, he was shot twice in the stomach by a lone assailant, Leon Czolgosz, a twenty-eight-year-old former mill worker from the Midwest. McKinley, also a midwesterner, lived for another eight days but died on September 14 from complications following his injuries. Theodore Roosevelt was sworn in as the twenty-sixth president of the United States in the Ansley Wilcox Mansion in Buffalo; at the age of forty-two years and 322 days, he remains the youngest person to become president of the United States.

Despite these momentous goings-on, Fitzgerald's ledger records considerably more mundane matters: "He played with one Dixon Green whom he has entirely forgotten. 'Oh Gee! I wish I had a different look on my face.' He remembered a horrible day in a backyard where his nurse pricked his ear with a straw."[40] Kabot identifies the Dixon Green referred to here as "Grant Dickson Green, Jr., whose father was secretary of one of Syracuse's many steel companies,"[41] so it is clear that Fitzgerald's family at the very least rubbed shoulders with some of the more affluent and influential members of Syracuse society during their time there. While the stuff of assassinations and executions may not have piqued the interest of a young F. Scott Fitzgerald, and they certainly did not feature in his later-life reconstruction of the months before and after his fifth birthday, it is difficult now to read a novel such as *The Great Gatsby* and not think of the correspondences between what happened at the Buffalo fair in 1901 and the events at Gatsby's "World's Fair" of a house where guests "conducted themselves according to the rules of behavior associated with an amusement park" and in which, in keeping with the technological and electrical innovations of Fitzgerald's first fair, "there was a machine in the kitchen which could extract the juice of two hundred

Buffalo boys

oranges in half an hour if a little button was pressed two hundred times by a butler's thumb."[42]

Like the Rainbow City fair, Gatsby's grounds are bedecked with "enough coloured lights to make a Christmas tree of Gatsby's enormous garden."[43] Just as at a World's Fair, "people were not invited—they went there";[44] one uninvited visitor in particular, the working-class George Wilson, assassinates Gatsby, another midwesterner adrift in a carnival world of his own creation on, as it so happens, another September day. Fitzgerald's fusing of historical fact with fictional contingencies in his 1925 classic, which opens with Nick Carraway refuting claims "of being a politician," reactivates subliminal "memories within the cultural subconscious of the American nation" connecting the gardens of Gatsby's mansion with the show grounds of the Buffalo fair and the fictional accounts of Nick Carraway with the elided worlds of Fitzgerald's own childhood.[45]

NOTES

1. F. Scott Fitzgerald, *F. Scott Fitzgerald's Ledger: A Facsimile,* introduction by Matthew J. Bruccoli (Washington, D.C.: NCR/Microcard Editions / Bruccoli Clark, 1973), 154.

2. Alan R. Hinman, Walter A. Orenstein, and Mark J. Papania, "Evolution of Measles Elimination Strategies in the United States," *Journal of Infectious Diseases* 189 (2004): 17–18.

3. Fitzgerald, *Ledger,* 154.

4. Carl Dolmetsch, *The Smart Set: A History and Anthology* (New York: Dial Press, 1966), 4.

5. Joel Kabot, "Buffalo and Syracuse, New York," in *F. Scott Fitzgerald in Context,* ed. Bryant Mangum (New York: Cambridge University Press, 2013), 90.

6. Alan A. Siegel, *A Disaster! Stories of Destruction and Death in Nineteenth-Century New Jersey* (New Brunswick, N.J.: Rutgers University Press, 2014), 79.

7. Mark Aldrich, *Death Rode the Rails: Railroad Accidents and Safety, 1828–1965* (Baltimore, Md.: The Johns Hopkins University Press, 2006), 77.

8. Norm Cohen, "'Casey Jones': At the Crossroads of Two Ballad Traditions," *Western Folklore* 32, no. 2 (April 1973): 78.

9. Roger H. Grant, *Railroads and the American People* (Bloomington: Indiana University Press, 2012), 239.

10. F. Scott Fitzgerald, *The Great Gatsby,* ed. Matthew J. Bruccoli, Cambridge Edition of the Works of F. Scott Fitzgerald (Cambridge: Cambridge University Press, 2022), 137, 136–37.

11. Aldrich, *Death Rode,* 79.

12. U.S. Census Bureau, *1900 Census,* vol. 1, *Population,* part 1, xix. https://www2.census.gov/library/publications/decennial/1900/volume-1/volume-1-p2.pdf.

13. Kabot, "Buffalo and Syracuse," 89.

14. Milton W. Blumenberg, *Official Proceedings of the Twelfth Republican National Convention* (Philadelphia: Press of Dunlap Printing Company, 1900), 138–39.

15. Fitzgerald, *Ledger,* 154.

16. "In Their Summer Retreats," *Indianapolis News,* August 17, 1895.

17. George W. Cook and William J. Coxey, *Atlantic City Railroad, the Royal Route to the Sea: A History of the Reading's Seashore Railroad, 1877–1933* (Palmyra, N.J.: West Jersey Chapter of the National Railway Historical Society, 1980), 172.

18. John Edward Weems, "The Galveston Storm of 1900," *Southwestern Historical Quarterly* 61, no. 4 (April 1958): 496.

19. James B. Elsner and Kara A. Birol, *Hurricanes of the North Atlantic: Climate and Society* (New York: Oxford University Press, 1999), 152, 380, 382.

20. Fitzgerald, *Ledger,* 155.

21. Fitzgerald, *Great Gatsby,* 76.

22. Fitzgerald, *Great Gatsby,* 78.

23. Fitzgerald, *Great Gatsby,* 77.

24. Michael Nowlin, "Naturalism and High Modernism," in Mangum, *Fitzgerald in Context,* 180.

25. F. Scott Fitzgerald, *The Notebooks of F. Scott Fitzgerald,* ed. Matthew J. Bruccoli (New York: Harcourt Brace Jovanovich / Bruccoli Clark, 1978), 158.

26. Nowlin, "Naturalism and High Modernism," 180.

27. Fitzgerald, *Ledger,* 155.

28. Kabot, "Buffalo and Syracuse," 89.

29. Mark Goldman, *High Hopes: The Rise and Decline of Buffalo, New York* (Albany: State University of New York Press, 1983), 3.

30. *Niagara Land . . . The First Two Hundred Years: Reprinted from the Series Featured in Sunday "The Courier-Express Magazine"* (Buffalo, N.Y.: Courier Express, 1976), 67.

31. Fitzgerald, *Ledger,* 155.

32. Fitzgerald, *Ledger,* 155.

33. Fitzgerald, *Ledger,* 155.

34. Goldman, *High Hopes,* 6.

35. F. Scott Fitzgerald, "Absolution," in *All the Sad Young Men,* ed. James L. W. West III, Cambridge Edition of the Works of F. Scott Fitzgerald (Cambridge: Cambridge University Press, 2014), 92.

36. Fitzgerald, "Absolution," 92.

37. Goldman, *High Hopes,* 7.

38. Paul Greenhalgh, *Ephemeral Vistas: The Expositions Universelles, Great Exhibitions, and World's Fairs, 1851–1939* (Manchester: Manchester University Press, 1988), 131.

39. Goldman, *High Hopes,* 8.

40. Fitzgerald, *Ledger,* 156.

41. Kabot, "Buffalo and Syracuse," 94.

42. Fitzgerald, *Great Gatsby,* 64, 34, 33.

43. Fitzgerald, *Great Gatsby,* 33.

44. Fitzgerald, *Great Gatsby,* 34.

45. Fitzgerald, *Great Gatsby,* 5; Philip McGowan, *American Carnival: Seeing and Reading American Culture* (Westport, Conn.: Greenwood Press, 2001), 78.

1902–1903

Joel Kabot

In January 1902, when Fitzgerald was five years and three months old, the Fitzgerald family moved within Syracuse, New York, to the Kasson Apartments on James Street. The move was not the start of his peripatetic lifestyle (that had begun with the family's move from St. Paul, Minnesota, to Buffalo, New York, in April 1898), but it was certainly an intensification of it and a sign of things to come for a writer who would traverse western Europe and the American coasts later in his life. The Fitzgeralds would move three times in Syracuse over the span of almost three years before returning to Buffalo. It was not until their retreat to St. Paul in 1908 that the young Fitzgerald would experience a more settled existence. In spite of such instability, Fitzgerald's Syracuse years were extremely important and influential in his development. Syracuse was the setting of his first memory, in 1901, and the place where he experienced his first recorded social disappointment—a birthday party with no guests. His years in Syracuse also strengthened his presence among society's elite and, ironically, sparked his long-standing interest in the American South.

In Syracuse, as in Buffalo previously, the Fitzgeralds found a booming industrial city on the old Erie Canal, an engine of economic prosperity for a new world power. It was the kind of place that, while not as populous as Buffalo, was still quite dynamic: a place where men or women could make something of themselves, where inventors, engineers, and businessmen, and everyone in between, could find success. It was a haven for immigrants from all over Europe, drawn to the factories promising steady employment and a chance at the American Dream.

That being said, Edward Fitzgerald's transfer from Buffalo to Syracuse must have been somewhat of a disappointment, as the family left behind the second-most-important city in the most important state, the forthcoming site of the 1901 Pan-American Exposition, for a more provincial burg 150 miles east. Relocating from St. Paul to Buffalo might have been considered an upgrade if viewed through rose-colored glasses, even though it meant leaving family members and a settled life in Minnesota (and the failure of his father's business, the American Rattan and Willow Works, which precipitated his father's employment with Procter & Gamble in Buffalo); Buffalo to Syracuse could be seen as a further retreat into the hinterlands of upstate New York and away from the familiar.

Still, for the Fitzgeralds, it was a life not too different from their old one on Summit Avenue. Their January 1902 move to the Kasson brought them to residences designed for the "affluent middle class,"[1] as one local historian termed them, in an almost brand-new building located on James Street—which was, like Summit Avenue in St. Paul, Syracuse's most desired address. Even now, the Kasson is a building that catches the eye on a walk down James, with its tan brick and green columns, or when driving along the New York State Thruway's spur highway, looking north: the building rises above the low-lying houses, with balconies ascending upward on both sides to dark green cornices supporting a terra-cotta roof. It is a turn-of-the-century Second Renaissance revival with Mediterranean details for a cold, not very Mediterranean climate.

The Kasson was home not for Syracuse's elite but for its near-elite, as evidenced by that phrase "affluent middle class": it was a place for those who were doing well but not *quite* well enough to live in a detached home further east on the same street. Time and time again, we see in Fitzgerald's life and writing his proximity to the elite, his fascination and frustration with them; how he is *with* them but not really *of* them. From the very beginning, blessed with remarkable skills of observation and memory, the young Fitzgerald was, because of his very residences, destined to be a chronicler of those in his vicinity but not necessarily in his inner circle.

Interestingly, Fitzgerald's second year in Syracuse begins with tales of places far away—that is, the battlefields of the American South—and not the booming industrial city or the leafy residential streets outside his window. That was partly due to childhood friend Jack Butler, "who had two or three facinating books about the civil war"[2] and who might be given credit for introducing Fitzgerald to the conflict if not for the presence of Fitzgerald's father, born in Maryland and decidedly Southern in his temperament and outlook. Many years later, when an adult Fitzgerald lived in his father's native state while his wife, Zelda, received psychiatric treatment at Sheppard and Enoch Pratt Hospital and Johns Hopkins University Hospital, he wrote the foreword to a book of etchings, *Colonial and Historic Homes of Maryland,* in which he remarked:

The Kasson Apartments in Syracuse, New York, one of Fitzgerald's homes as a young boy.

The undersigned can only consider himself a native of the Maryland Free State through ancestry and adoption. But the impression of the fames and domains, the vistas and the glories of Maryland followed many a young man West after the Civil War and my father was of that number. Much of my early childhood in Minnesota was spent in asking him such questions as:

"—and how long did it take Early's column to pass Glenmary that day?" (That was a farm in Montgomery County.)
and:

"—what would have happened if Jeb Stuart's cavalry had joined Lee instead of raiding all the way to Rockville?"
and:

["]—tell me again about how you used to ride through the woods with a spy up behind you on the horse."
or:

"Why wouldn't they let Francis Scott Key off the British frigate?"[3]

Fitzgerald refers to Minnesota, not upstate New York, but unless he was a precocious child asking such questions at the age of one and a half years (the age at which he left St. Paul), or unless "early childhood" is a broad enough phrase to include the age of eleven (when he returned to St. Paul), we can assume the real setting is upstate New York.

In his ledger, his next reference for 1902 is about Maryland specifically, for what appears to be his first sustained visit to the state. (In 1899, at the age of two years and four months, he lived in Washington, D.C., for the winter; no mention is made of visiting Maryland, although he would have had to pass through the Old Line State to reach the nation's capital.) In May, "he went to Randolph to his aunt Eliza Delihant's place in Montgomery County, Maryland, where he made friends with a colored boy, name forgotten—name Ambrose."[4] This visit is significant not only because it gave shape and color to the Civil War stories Fitzgerald knew from his father's tales and from Jack Butler's books, but also because an old Maryland home later found its way into Fitzgerald's writing. In a later *Saturday Evening Post* story, "More Than Just a House," we follow the young, up-and-coming Lew Lowrie as he mingles with the three Gunther girls at their Maryland manse. Over the course of six years, we see the (almost inevitable) crumbling both of the house and the family. At that first visit,

Lew's eyes lifted over [Bess Gunther] . . . up to the house with its decorative balconies outside the windows, its fickle gables, its gold-lettered, Swiss-chalet mottoes, the bulging projections of its many bays. Uncritically he regarded it; it seemed to him one of the finest houses he had ever known.[5]

Though too young to critically regard anything architecturally, Fitzgerald in Randolph probably had a similar experience: hundreds of miles away from his apartment building in a crowded city, Randolph was the embodiment of his father's romantic tales about the Old South countryside and must have made quite an impression on the imaginative Fitzgerald. Such an influence might have been tempered by the recognition that while his father came from such environs, he was no longer of them. Things had changed. Unlike the Gunthers, or even Lowrie, himself a Marylander, Edward and Scott Fitzgerald were now much removed from their ancestral lands. Edward Fitzgerald had gone to seek success in the West, and at the time of their May 1903 visit to Randolph he was a resident in Yankee territory, a region with no time to dwell on the past.

In "More Than Just a House," Lew Lowrie sees the Gunther fortunes decline precipitously: the family money is lost, one of the sisters and the Gunther parents die, and another sister leaves for China, seemingly never to return. Only the youngest sister, Bess, remains, all alone, and the house is now in extreme stages of neglect and disrepair:

> It was a desperately forlorn house he came to, and a jungled garden; one side of the veranda had slipped from the brick pillars and sloped to the ground; a shingle job, begun and abandoned, rotted paintless on the roof, a broken pane gasped from the library window.[6]

The story gets a happy ending when Lowrie, a gardener's son who is now a rich man, swoops in to marry Bess. But the family is gone, as is the house, almost—when leaving the grounds after proposing, Lowrie "looked at the house over his shoulder. 'Next week or so we'll decide what to do about that,'" he says ominously, after earlier suggesting, "Suppose we begin by setting fire to this house."[7] Lowrie is joking, but there is something significant there: maybe the older F. Scott Fitzgerald knew that the stories and family lore of Edward Fitzgerald—whose side lost the war, who had to retreat to the West, whose business failed in St. Paul— were decayed and no longer for this world. He seems to have recognized this as well in the unpublished essay "The Death of My Father": referring to his father's war stories, he asks the reader, "Do you want to hear them? I'm so tired of them all that I can't make them interesting."[8]

The young Fitzgerald would wait less than a year before returning to Maryland—to Randolph, specifically—this time for the wedding of his older cousin Cecilia Delihant, at which he was a ribbon holder. Echoing his earlier trip, his playmates were African American. During this April 1903 visit, however, "he turned on his two black friends Roscoe and Forrest,"[9] tying them up with the assistance of another boy. In addition to being indoctrinated with tales of the Lost Cause, Fitzgerald's Old South experience was not without another common occurrence: white and black childhood friends inevitably taking divergent paths, with the former betraying the latter. Fitzgerald's time in the South, in the company of a diminished father returned from the North to his ancestral land, possessing only memories of a decayed history, also saw Scott as a contemporaneous participant in the South's inherent moral decay. More than just sympathizing with and romanticizing an abhorrent cause, as he would even into middle age, Fitzgerald, in his actions, perpetuated the real Southern tradition: the oppression of those who looked different from him.

Perhaps, then, it is fitting that it takes the nouveau riche Lowrie to rescue the lone Maryland-bound Gunther daughter. It is his world, now, and in this world, it is right that the Gunther house and family wither to almost nothing, representing something not worth sustaining. But, of course, romance always beckons. Lowrie knows the house as it once was, and something draws him back to save its last inhabitant, to carry on the Gunther legacy even if not its name. In Fitzgerald's foreword to *Colonial and Historic Homes of Maryland* we also see that sentimentality. In "The Death of My Father," he attempts to rationalize his lack of interest in re-telling his father's stories: "Maybe they are [uninteresting] because I used to ask father to repeat and repeat and repeat."[10] Old sentiments die hard, it appears. Fitzgerald's fascination with the South would remain for the rest of his life. After all, he would marry the Alabaman Zelda Sayre and write a number of stories set in the region, notably the Tarleton trilogy,[11] that often romanticized the white, upper-class people who inhabited it.

In January 1903, Fitzgerald was further removed from a northern city's elite as the family relocated for the third and final time within Syracuse, away from the gilded Kasson to a "flat on East Willow Street."[12] East Willow is the street just north of and parallel to James, and even now grand homes remain there, a few in conditions not unlike those of the Gunther house at story's end. Fitzgerald was therefore in the same neighborhood as the most fashionable, but slightly removed. He had experienced James Street, even if only as a member of the "affluent middle class"; now he was in eyesight, especially of the Kasson. He wasn't quite the boy "always on the outside looking in,"[13] as his high school love Ginevra King called him once, but he was moving in that direction.

He did not have to leave James Street entirely, however. In September 1902, at the age of six, prior to the family move from the Kasson, "he entered Miss Goodyear's school."[14] The coeducational Goodyear–Burlingame School was at 509 James Street, offering kindergarten through "Senior Departments," as a 1900 advertisement noted, "[preparing students] for any college." The advertisement boasted that (so good must Goodyear–Burlingame's reputation have been) "a certificate from the school admits a pupil to Cornell University, Syracuse University, and Smith College without an examination."[15] At the school, Fitzgerald noted that "he and another little girl, name unknown, worked out the phonetic spelling of C-A-T. Thus becoming the stars of the primary class."[16] Regardless of whatever his family's fortunes might have been, or the prestige of their address, Fitzgerald had become a "star" with words. It is hard not to imagine the young Fitzgerald recognizing then and there that no matter what else, his literary prowess could make him something, could allow him to shine.

After writing of his move to East Willow in his ledger, the memories started to flow:

> He begins to remember many things, a filthy vacant lot, the haunt of dead cats, a hair-raising buck-board, the little girl whose father was in prison for telling lies, a Rabelaisean incident with Jack Butler, a blow with a baseball bat from the same boy—son of an army officer—which left a scar that will shine always in the middle of ~~my~~ his forehead, a history of the United States which father brought me; he became a child of the American Revolution. Also he boxed with Edgar Miller the grocery man's son, egged on by his father. His nurse pierced her ear for rings and he howled.[17]

At least one of these details made its way into Fitzgerald's fiction. Fitzgerald includes the vacant lot in *This Side of Paradise* when the protagonist, Amory Blaine, thinks of a Princeton classmate's death: "Amory was reminded of a cat that had lain horribly mangled in some alley of his childhood."[18] (Of note, Amory is from Minnesota, but this is a Syracuse memory of Fitzgerald.) We also get a possible explanation for why Jack Butler had those "two or three facinating books"—his father is a military officer. Echoing that theme of fathers influencing sons, we learn the young Fitzgerald received a "history of the United States" from Edward Fitzgerald and so became interested in another of America's wars.

In July 1903, Fitzgerald spent Sunday mornings "[walking] down town in his long trousers and with his little cane and had his shoes shined with his father,"[19] another detail that makes its way into his fiction. This time, it is an upstate memory shared by an upstate protagonist: Dick Diver in *Tender Is the Night,* where "in the summer father and son walked downtown together to have their shoes shined."[20] The memory also found its way into "The Death of My Father," where it retains its regional identity, if not its actual city:

> We walked downtown in Buffalo on Sunday mornings and my white ducks were stiff with starch and he was very proud walking with his handsome little boy. We had our shoes shined and he lit his cigar and we bought the Sunday papers. When I was a little older I did not understand at all why men that I knew were vulgar gentlemen made him stand up or give the better chair on our verandah. But I know now. There was new young peasant stock coming up every ten years and he was of the generation of the colonies and the revolution.[21]

Dick Diver's father is not dissimilar to Edward Fitzgerald: he is from the South, gone to live in the North, married to a wife with a "small fortune."[22] It wasn't so much losing his job or losing his St. Paul business due to the "financial panic in the nineties [that] struck him"[23] that F. Scott Fitzgerald blames for the demise of the American Rattan and Willow Works, however. His father was, simply, of "tired old stock." In contrast to those making up the "peasant stock" who refreshed cities like St. Paul, Buffalo, and Syracuse, eager to make new lives for themselves in a new world, Edward Fitzgerald was unable to overcome his familial destiny, no matter where he lived.

Just as the Reverend Diver and Edward Fitzgerald share many characteristics, Dick Diver is similar to his author. There is the alcoholism, the rapid rise in a profession for which his talent is evident, the mentally ill wife, the expatriate lifestyle—and a childhood in Buffalo. In the novel, Diver announces that he is "from Buffalo"[24]—not Tarmes in the French Riviera, or Paris, places that at the time have a more recent claim to him. At the end of the novel, after witnessing Diver's downward spiral, we learn he has returned to his native region. Like Scott's father, though, Diver is now of "tired stock," so he does not stay in Buffalo, still a booming city, but finds himself in much smaller locales as he goes: Batavia, Lockport, Geneva, and Hornell. We are told "he is almost certainly in that section of the country, in one town or another"[25]—*town*, and not *city*, it is noted. Diver's exile is a real one indeed.

Earlier in the ledger, in the July 1901 entry, Fitzgerald tells us: "His first certain memory is the sight of [his sister Annabel] howling on a bed."[26] That occurred six months after his arrival in Syracuse. Fitzgerald's last memory of Syracuse, at least as recorded in the ledger, is much more forlorn—at the risk of hyperbole, even tragic. In September 1903, "he had a birth day party to which no one came."[27] As Andrew Turnbull notes, "The children stayed home because it rained. 'Then,' says Fitzgerald in another account, 'I went sorrowfully in and thoughtfully consumed one complete birthday cake, including several candles (for I was a great tallow eater until I was well over fourteen).'"[28]

That it rained was probably of no consolation to a sensitive, detail-oriented boy like Fitzgerald. Before leaving Syracuse forever, his birthday party had an attendance of just one. Parties figure prominently in the Fitzgerald canon (and a child's celebration, specifically, is the subject of his 1925 story "The Baby Party"), but the most famous are those thrown by Jay Gatsby, who organizes such events for the sole purpose of meeting his long-lost love Daisy Buchanan. While "in his blue gardens men and girls came and went like moths among the whisperings and the champagne and the stars,"[29] until Gatsby meets Daisy again it is as if he is actually giving a "party to which no one [comes]."[30] Not the one, that is, for whom it is all intended.

Fitzgerald's unfortunate seventh birthday party brings to mind another scene in *The Great Gatsby*: the titular character's funeral. While not a party per se, Gatsby's funeral is another social gathering to which, save Gatsby's father, "no one came": "The minister glanced several times at his watch so I took him aside and asked him to wait for half an hour. But it wasn't any use. Nobody came."[31] It also, notably, takes place in the rain, just like the seven-year-old's birthday party: Nick met in vain with Meyer Wolfsheim in an attempt to get him to attend the funeral, then "the sky had turned dark and [Nick] got back to West Egg in a drizzle."[32] At the cemetery, "four or five servants . . . [are] all wet to the skin."[33] Owl Eyes, who appears graveside after not being able to "get to the house," has "rain [pouring] down his thick glasses" after "splashing" after the funeral party "over the soggy ground."[34] "Dimly," Nick "[hears] someone murmur 'Blessed are the dead that the rain falls on.'"[35]

Gatsby's funeral is the ultimate reminder that all was not as it had seemed on the surface. As Nick Carraway notes, most of the guests at Gatsby's parties "were not invited—they went there. . . . Sometimes they came and went without having met Gatsby at all."[36] Fitzgerald was one of "the stars of the primary class," but his stay in Syracuse would end on a down note. His party taught him that success, especially of the social variety, can be fleeting.

That same month ("possibly in consequence" of the birthday party, Fitzgerald sardonically noted in his ledger), the Fitzgeralds returned to Buffalo, where they took up residence at 29 Irving Place. Here, relatively speaking, was some stability in address for Fitzgerald, as the family did not move for another two years. According to Turnbull, "Irving Place . . . was a single tree-lined block—a lovely, sheltered spot for a poet to grow up in. Children played ball in the dappled shade or raced their buckboards down the sloping street, one of the first where asphalt had replaced the universal cobbles."[37]

It was an idyllic existence, one full of friends, whose names Fitzgerald rattles off in his ledger: "Ted Keating, Dodo Clifton, Jack Kimberly and Dexter Rumsey," a group making up a "facinating army."[38] This was an army of privilege; some of the children traced their lineage back to Buffalo's earliest settlers, especially Rumsey, whose family name was a familiar one in Buffalo society.[39] Once again, Fitzgerald found himself among an upstate city's elite, in whose circles he stayed until his return to St. Paul in 1908. As in his experience in Syracuse living at East Willow Street, though, with its proximity to James Street, Irving Place was in the same neighborhood as the most exclusive street, Delaware Avenue—but one block removed. So, Fitzgerald was once more near, but not within, the home of the geographical elite.

Like to the aforementioned "peasant stock," Fitzgerald attended a parochial school in Buffalo: Holy Angels Convent, "under the arrangement that he need only go half a day and was allowed to choose which half." This is the first reference to religion in the ledger since Fitzgerald's baptism, and it is followed soon afterward by the statement: "He fell under the spell of a Catholic preacher, Father Fallon, of the Church of the Holy Angels."[40] Michael Francis Fallon, a Canadian American who later became bishop of the Diocese of London, Ontario, had arrived in Buffalo from Ottawa two years before the Fitzgeralds made their second residence in the city. A professor of literature in Ottawa, and an outspoken proponent of English-speaking Catholics in Canada, he was "wildly popular[,] but that did not stop the Oblates [of Mary Immaculate] from banishing him to Holy Angels parish in Buffalo":[41]

> Bitter, Fallon blamed a French-Canadian conspiracy for both his removal as vice-rector [of the University of Ottawa] and his banishment from the country. [But] from his new base at Holy Angels, he continued to do what he did best: preach and lecture and engage with lively controversy. In no time, he had built up a new base of support and admiration and was as popular as ever with the people.[42]

While he probably "fell under the spell" from afar, it is easy to draw the parallel between the young Fitzgerald's fascination with the dynamic and engaging Fallon and his later close relationship with Monsignor Cyril Sigourney Webster Fay at the Newman School for Boys in Hackensack, New Jersey, which he attended from 1911 to 1913. Fitzgerald wrote that Fay, along with Catholic writer Shane Leslie, made the church "a dazzling, golden thing, dispelling its oppressive mugginess"[43]—perhaps Fallon was the first to open his eyes to the splendor of Catholicism. Fallon seemingly served as a proto-Fay, then, a mesmerizing figure to a young man finding his way in the world. As Fay was the model for Monsignor Thayer Darcy in *This Side of Paradise,* perhaps there is more of upstate New York in Fitzgerald's first novel than just a childhood memory of a Syracuse alley. Fallon may have set the stage for Fitzgerald's eventual mentoring by Fay.

In the years 1902 and 1903, we have seen a young Fitzgerald who, as an upstate New Yorker, becomes enthralled with the Southern stories of his father, moves among the elite of two cities, finds academic success, suffers social disappointment, and finds a protomentor in a future Catholic bishop. All of these experiences, in some way, make their way into his fiction, from the Reverend Diver references in *Tender Is the Night,* to the countless stories about the upper class and the discontent an outsider feels among them, and even to Jay Gatsby's rain-soaked funeral. There was much more to come for Fitzgerald, even in the short term (his father losing his job in 1908 chief among them), but in just two years, Fitzgerald already had a relatively large amount of material to draw on for his later works, especially given how young he was at the time.

NOTES

1. Evamaria Hardin, *Syracuse Landmarks: An AIA Guide to Downtown and Historic Neighborhoods* (Syracuse, N.Y.: Syracuse University Press, 1993), 217.

2. F. Scott Fitzgerald, *F. Scott Fitzgerald's Ledger: A Facsimile,* introduction by Matthew J. Bruccoli (Washington, D.C.: NCR/Microcard Editions / Bruccoli Clark, 1972), 156.

3. F. Scott Fitzgerald, foreword to *Colonial and Historic Homes of Maryland,* by Don Swann Jr., 3rd ed. (Baltimore, Md.: The Johns Hopkins University Press, 1983), vii.

4. Fitzgerald, *Ledger,* 156.

5. F. Scott Fitzgerald, "More Than Just a House," in *A Change of Class,* ed. James L. W. West III, Cambridge Edition of the Works of F. Scott Fitzgerald (Cambridge: Cambridge University Press, 2022), 174.

6. Fitzgerald, "More Than Just a House," 192.

7. Fitzgerald, "More Than Just a House," 194.

8. F. Scott Fitzgerald, "The Death of My Father," *Princeton University Library Chronicle* 12, no. 4 (Summer 1951): 189.

9. Fitzgerald, *Ledger,* 157.

10. Fitzgerald, "Death of My Father," 189.

11. Fitzgerald set three stories in fictional Tarleton, Georgia, a city loosely based on Zelda's Montgomery, Alabama: "The Ice Palace," in *Flappers and Philosophers,* ed. James L. W. West III, Cambridge Edition of the Works of F. Scott Fitzgerald (Cambridge: Cambridge University Press, 2012); "The Jelly-Bean," in *Tales of the Jazz Age,* ed. James L. W. West III, Cambridge Edition of the Works of F. Scott Fitzgerald (Cambridge: Cambridge University Press, 2012); and "The Last of the Belles," in *Taps at Reveille,* ed. James L. W. West III, Cambridge Edition of the Works of F. Scott Fitzgerald (Cambridge: Cambridge University Press, 2014).

12. Fitzgerald, *Ledger,* 157.

13. Dinitia Smith, "Love Notes Drenched in Moonlight: Hints of Future Novels in Letters to Fitzgerald," *New York Times,* September 8, 2003; accessed July 5, 2020. https://www.nytimes.com/2003/09/08/books/love-notes-drenched-in-moonlight -hints-of-future-novels-in-letters-to-fitzgerald.html.

14. Fitzgerald, *Ledger,* 157.

15. Goodyear–Burlingame School, advertisement, *Syracuse Post-Standard,* September 13, 1900.

16. Fitzgerald, *Ledger,* 157.

17. Fitzgerald, *Ledger,* 157.

18. F. Scott Fitzgerald, *This Side of Paradise,* ed. James L. W. West III, Cambridge Edition of the Works of F. Scott Fitzgerald (Cambridge: Cambridge University Press, 2012), 86.

19. Fitzgerald, *Ledger,* 157.

20. F. Scott Fitzgerald, *Tender Is the Night: A Romance,* ed. James L. W. West III, Cambridge Edition of the Works of F. Scott Fitzgerald (Cambridge: Cambridge University Press, 2022), 232.

21. Fitzgerald, "Death of My Father," 188.

22. Fitzgerald, *Tender Is the Night,* 232.

23. Michel Mok, "A Writer like Me Must Have an Utter Confidence, an Utter Faith in His Star," in *F. Scott Fitzgerald in His Own Time: A Miscellany,* ed. Matthew J. Bruccoli and Jackson R. Bryer (Kent, Ohio: Kent State University Press, 1971), 296.

24. Fitzgerald, *Tender Is the Night,* 106.

25. Fitzgerald, *Tender Is the Night,* 352.

26. Fitzgerald, *Ledger,* 155.

27. Fitzgerald, *Ledger,* 158.

28. Andrew Turnbull, *Scott Fitzgerald* (New York: Charles Scribner's Sons, 1962), 18.

29. F. Scott Fitzgerald, *The Great Gatsby,* ed. Matthew J. Bruccoli, Cambridge Edition of the Works of F. Scott Fitzgerald (Cambridge: Cambridge University Press, 2022), 33.

30. Fitzgerald, *Ledger,* 158.

31. Fitzgerald, *Great Gatsby,* 135.

32. Fitzgerald, *Great Gatsby,* 134.

33. Fitzgerald, *Great Gatsby,* 136.

34. Fitzgerald, *Great Gatsby,* 136.

35. Fitzgerald, *Great Gatsby,* 136.

36. Fitzgerald, *Great Gatsby,* 34.

37. Turnbull, *Fitzgerald,* 19.

38. Fitzgerald, *Ledger,* 158.

39. Edward T. Dunn, *Buffalo's Delaware Avenue: Mansions and Families* (Buffalo, N.Y.: Canisius College Press, 2003), 153–62.

40. Fitzgerald, *Ledger,* 158.

41. Michael Power, "The Mitred Warrior: A Critical Reassessment of Bishop Michael Francis Fallon, 1867–1931," *Catholic Insight,* April 2000, 21.

42. Power, "Mitred Warrior," 21.

43. F. Scott Fitzgerald, "Homage to the Victorians," in *F. Scott Fitzgerald on Authorship,* ed. Matthew J. Bruccoli and Judith S. Baughman (Columbia: University of South Carolina Press, 1996), 73–74.

1904–1905

Ross K. Tangedal

"Steel inexhaustible, to be made lovely and austere in his imaginative fire . . ."

—F. Scott Fitzgerald, "'The Sensible Thing'"

In the penultimate paragraph of *Tender Is the Night,* Dick Diver is said to have opened a medical practice in Buffalo, prior to moving about upstate New York. He makes stops in Batavia and Lockport before leaving as a result of an entanglement with a girl who worked in a grocery store and a medical lawsuit, but he is said to be somewhere near Hornell, New York, "almost certainly in that part of the country, in one town or another."[1] Joel Kabot argues that the Basil Duke Lee story "That Kind of Party," rather than being one with its companion stories—which together are widely considered "St. Paul stories"—includes significant references to Buffalo, making Basil (like a young Scott), a fellow one-time Buffalo resident.[2] Aside from these two works, Buffalo makes no substantial appearance in any of F. Scott Fitzgerald's fiction. There is St. Paul and New York, Long Island and Montgomery, Paris and the Riviera, but Buffalo, New York, remains almost invisible in the writer's fiction. In his short time there, however, he would live in a city filled with great buildings and modern structures, wealthy industrialists and their equally wealthy daughters, and the shine of an urban landscape that glittered, to use one of Fitzgerald's favorite words. But with the glittering high society of the up-and-coming, upstate New York "Queen City" came the onset of Scott's disappointment with his father, who would fail both Scott and his mother by 1908, when Scott felt the need to pray to stay clear of the poorhouse.

The Fitzgeralds lived at 29 Irving Place in Allentown, the neighborhood not far from Edward Fitzgerald's office at Procter & Gamble. Biographer Andrew Turnbull gives the most detailed account of the Fitzgeralds in Buffalo, calling their home "a lovely sheltered spot for a poet to grow up,"[3] though Scott continued to enjoy the company of friends, owing in part to the superiority of their living arrangements. He and his best friend would frequent the Teck Theatre, reenacting what they had seen for friends and others in the neighborhood. As early examples of artistic creativity and imagination, the restagings were opportunities for Fitzgerald to show off, if only for a few friends. Fitzgerald's Buffalo, to Turnbull, was a coming-of-age, boyhood romp, where Scott found his early desire to lead, rather than follow, other boys. He was eloquent, charming, and keenly self-aware, but it is well documented that there was always a tension in Scott regarding his father's shortcomings and the fact that his mother was able to provide for the family during his father's hard times. She was the ambitious one, while Edward did his best to support his young family.

In Buffalo, Scott made the girls swoon with his green eyes and blond hair, and he carried with him a sense of superiority, going so far as to believe that he was a foundling of royal birth rather than the son of Mollie and Edward. When the family moved to 71 Highland Avenue in Buffalo, a more upscale Victorian home featuring an imposing turret (typical of the Queen Anne style), Scott saved a dance card he had filled out at the city's Century Club, a place that would have shown him the glitz and glamour of a world he hoped to join. According to the card, he danced with Harriet Mack and Dorothy Knox, daughters of Buffalo wealth and prestige. Harriet's father owned the *Buffalo Times,* and Dorothy's father was Seymour H. Knox, cofounder of the consolidated F. W. Woolworth Company in 1912 and major art patron of the Albright–Knox Art Gallery (formerly the Albright Art Gallery). But Scott impressed them. He liked connecting with the well connected, and he liked the well connected to find him interesting. Many of these anecdotes are mirrored in his St. Paul years, where the developing Scott showed more interest in the wealthy and the well-to-do than in the less successful Edward, who was becoming more of a hindrance to his son's advancement. But in Buffalo he gained many things, particularly the growing recognition that he was not like his father, that he would be successful rather than a failure, and that he would be a creator and a maker, not a cog in the machinery of other men's endeavors.

Kabot argues that spending nearly a decade of one's life in any region is formative, especially when that decade is one's first. In Buffalo, Fitzgerald went to the theater, fell in love with girls, and recognized his talents of observation and social movement. He wrote fiction and plays while attending first Holy Angels Convent and then the Nardin Academy, where he remembered arguing with a teacher about something. The cornices and porticos of the city's structures must have spoken to this young boy, as they would in St. Paul (evidenced by entries in his *Thoughtbook,* the short diary he kept as a boy). Turnbull highlights an episode where Scott would swing from the attic ceiling of the Highland Avenue home: Scott swinging and thinking, presumably about greatness or girls. His proclivity for social observation began here, gleaned, no doubt, from his reading and, possibly, from the bustle of Buffalo's architectural diversity.

The influence of specific writers on his early career cannot be overstated, given that he referred to *This Side of Paradise* personally as "A Romance and a Reading List,"[4] but what he may have been reading in Buffalo certainly played a suggestive role in his understanding of a literary career. And what he saw around the city—the people, the churches, the museums, the office buildings—could only feed his interests, given what he became just fifteen years later. Fitzgerald's Buffalo was a place of youthful transition, where the intellectual curiosity of an eight-year-old boy was energized by the professional worlds of men. Whatever his thoughts, and whatever influence Buffalo may have had on him, Scott routinely took elements from the places of his past and carefully stitched them into his fiction. Buffalo had the images, the sensations, and the majesty, but it also had the heartbreak of his father's firing, perhaps the greatest influence on a young boy becoming a young man.

Buffalo Buildings

To understand Buffalo is to understand the Rust Belt at the turn of the century.[5] Cities like Pittsburgh, Pennsylvania ("the Steel City"), Akron, Ohio ("the Rubber City"), and Detroit, Michigan ("the Motor City") led the economic boom from the late nineteenth into the early twentieth centuries. Buffalo, "the city of good neighbors," was a beneficiary of a boom in several industries, including grain, automobiles, and steel, thanks in large part to its status as a port city and a main stop on the Erie Canal and the famed St. Lawrence Seaway. The city flourished, collecting immigrants and new money as the manufacturing and trade markets continued to grow. The influx of new residents brought a yearning for culture, which led to a boom not only in industry but also in art and architecture.

The Albright Art Gallery was completed in 1905, bringing Greco-Roman-inspired design to the city, and, with it, a dedication to displaying the great art of the world. The neoclassical, temple-style monument, with its 120 columns (more than any American building save for the Capitol in Washington, D.C.), is an inspired gem on the landscape of an industrial city. The museum is as much an artwork as its exhibits. Coupled with the diverse buildings, factories, and homes peppered throughout the city, the art gallery defines Buffalo as a unique, architectural laboratory, where the great architects of the day flocked to build the future.

One company would capitalize on the modern striving for newness amid the remnants of the nineteenth century. The Larkin Soap Company was founded in Buffalo in 1875 by John D. Larkin, originally a manu-facturer of "Plain and Fancy Soaps." In the company's early days Larkin and his associates would sell wares like their original Sweet Home Soap door to door. "Soap slinging," as it was known, eventually led to whole-saling and retail, with several shops carrying Larkin products. Though they were known for producing primarily fancy soaps and toiletry items, the company expanded into the mail-order business, becoming one of the leading mail-order retailers in the country (second only to Sears, Roebuck, and Company at the time). Historian Jerome Puma reports that money came into the Larkin company so quickly and in such vol-ume that it was taken from envelopes and deposited directly into bar-rels.[6] With literally barrels of money (approximately $4 million in 1905, which adjusts to well over $50 million in today's dollars), the company wanted to construct an administrative building to facilitate its expan-sion. The Administration Building of the Larkin Company of Buffalo sprang from the mind of early-career Oak Park, Illinois, architect Frank Lloyd Wright, a man of vision and ambition.

Designed in 1903–4 and completed by 1906, the Larkin Building brought a new modernism to manufacturing design. Wright was com-missioned to design a building of great utility but also of great beauty. He designed every piece of furniture, every desk, every lamp, every fixture, to create in employees a sense of duty and wonder. His building featured the first steel furniture and an early air-conditioning system. Employees were given a pipe organ to play in a common area, and all spaces were de-signed to make the working environment pleasant, collegial, and, above all, more efficient. The roof doubled as a recreation space, as Wright's

Larkin Administration Building, circa 1940

concept of openness took on new meaning in an office environment. Happy employees made for quicker envelope openers, more ambitious order fillers, and more effective communicators.

At eight years old, Scott would have been aware of his surroundings, perhaps more so than his peers. We know of his great love for the spires and gargoyles of Princeton, the stately manors and golden cathedral of St. Paul's Summit Avenue, the posh beaches of the French Riviera, and the solemn office buildings lining Manhattan's business hubs. His stories feature all of these marvels, the iron and steel, the plaster and porticos, the stone and the majesty. George O'Kelly, Fitzgerald's protagonist in "'The Sensible Thing,'" recalls moving to southern Tennessee after living in cities his entire life:

> All his life he had thought in terms of tunnels and skyscrapers and great squat dams and tall, three-towered bridges, that were like

dancers holding hands in a row, with heads as tall as cities and skirts of cable strand. It had seemed romantic to George O'Kelly to change the sweep of rivers and the shape of mountains so that life could flourish in the old bad lands of the world where it had never taken root before. He loved steel, and there was always steel near him in his dreams, liquid steel, steel in bars, and block and beams of formless plaster masses, waiting for him, as paint and canvas in his hand. Steel inexhaustible, to be made lovely and austere in his imaginative fire . . .[7]

The eloquence of his architectural descriptions signals a keen interest in the beauty of construction, the framing of powerful opportunities. Scott was exposed to more than his fair share of artful buildings in Buffalo, canvases all for makers of great structures. Old County Hall, then known as the City and County Hall, is a stunning, Romanesque Victorian landmark and a prominent counter to the newer Buffalo City Hall, a modernist art deco–inspired building completed by 1931. The Gothic revivalist Hotel Touraine, with its 250 rooms and 100 bathrooms, cuts a striking silhouette in the middle of the Buffalo business district; the neoclassical Graystone Hotel faces it across the street. Near Lake Erie, the Kellogg Company had, at one time, the largest linseed oil elevator in the United States, and General Mills had a vast milling elevator on South Michigan Avenue, which remained the central milling operation for the company well into the 1960s. Though flour was its primary export in the early part of the century, the mill produced Cherioats (today's Cheerios) in 1941, followed by products like Wheaties and Bisquick, which kick-started the breakfast-cereal boom. The imperious and striking St. Paul's Episcopal Church, located in the heart of the city, features a three-hundred-foot-tall spire, typical of the Gothic revival, a stunning structure thought by its architect, Richard Upjohn, to be his best work. The funeral cortege of slain President William McKinley marched by the church in September 1901 on its way to Canton, Ohio, where he would be laid to rest. McKinley had been in Buffalo attending the Pan-American Exposition, where he was assassinated in the temporary Temple of Music. That building was demolished after the exhibition's conclusion, and a plaque resides where McKinley was killed, a somber reminder of a key moment in local and national history.

Although the World's Fair brought art and culture to the city,

Hotel Touraine, 1905

St. Paul's Episcopal Church, 1905

American exceptionalism at the time was represented chiefly by industrialists, railroad tycoons, mineral barons, and oil magnates, particularly
at the turn of the century. There is something to be said for this mode
of aspirationalism, the taking of raw material and making it glow with
the power of progress. Fitzgerald was coming of age at a pivotal time in
American industrial history, when the Gilded Age of the century prior
was still flexing its muscles over the country created from its combination of ruthlessness and majesty. He saw men making their marks on this
place, which only fueled his desire to do the same. His chosen monu-
ments, like those of writers before and after him, would be creations
that were realized in dark letters typed on sheets of paper sewn between
boards, creations that have outlasted the Standard Oil Company, the
Anaconda Copper Mining Company, and the Larkin Administration
Building of his youth: books.

So how does Buffalo connect to Scott's biography? Nothing of note
happened to him while his family lived there, other than his father again
losing his job and forcing the family to relocate. It would be a stretch to
say that the young boy was influenced directly by, for instance, Wright's
at the time still-unfinished Larkin Administration Building. Buildings
always mattered to Fitzgerald, however. Amory Blaine experiences "the
Gothic halls and cloisters" of Princeton, which "were infinitely more

mysterious as they loomed suddenly out of the darkness, outlined each by myriad faint squares of yellow light."[8] Dexter Green, lost and forlorn at his inability to grieve for his Judy Jones, wanders New York City: "The gates were closed, the sun was gone down, and there was no beauty but the gray beauty of steel that withstands all time."[9] Green and George O'Kelly, the protagonist of "'The Sensible Thing,'" experience their conflicts through the metaphor of steel and power, and Fitzgerald's play on structure would come to pass with his masterpiece, *The Great Gatsby,* whose structure is as meticulously crafted and pored over as Wright's designs.

Even late in his career he wrote "Author's House" for *Esquire,* an essay that features "the author" (code for Fitzgerald) giving a visitor a tour of his house, from cellar to turret. The home is Victorian (no doubt a holdover image from his time in Buffalo and St. Paul), and the author recalls burying his youthful image of himself in the cellar (in contrast to Buffalo, where he thought himself the son of a king). But he leaves the most impactful moment of the conversation for the turret at the home's highest point, the same manner of turret that topped his homes in St. Paul and Buffalo:

> "Up to the cupola—the turret, the watch-tower, whatever you want to call it. I'll lead the way."
>
> It is small up there and full of baked silent heat until the author opens two of the glass sides that surround it and the twilight wind blows through. As far as your eye can see there is a river winding between green lawns and trees and purple buildings and red slums blended in by a merciful dusk. Even as they stand there the wind increases until it is a gale whistling around the tower and blowing birds past them.
>
> "I lived up here once," the author said after a moment.
>
> "Here? For a long time?"
>
> "No. For just a little while when I was young."[10]

Fitzgerald's most publicly successful period came the earliest, when *This Side of Paradise* flew off the shelves in 1920, and his stories in the *Saturday Evening Post* were the talk of the town. Many of his *Esquire* essays serve as laments for a past he could not repair in the present. While the protagonist of "Author's House" felt that his house (Fitzgerald's career) was unique when he built it, he comes to understand, like Fitzgerald, that "in the end, I suppose it's just like other houses after all."[11] The books have been written, the reviews have been placed, and history has begun the slow process of either accepting or denying the author's legacy as something more than the man who lived in the turret for a short time. It would take Fitzgerald's death to launch his literary life, so to speak, a life populated by influences great and small. Though we cannot determine just how much Scott cared about the bounty of buildings surrounding him in Buffalo, the city formed one of many metropolitan backgrounds in Fitzgerald's life, where grand—and increasingly modern—architecture reflected the scale and ambition of the emerging American Century. Architecture can create an influence on a literary life. If material of any artistic sort must be, according to Fitzgerald, "purified by an incorruptible style and the catharsis of a passionate emotion,"[12] then the blending of architectural function and aesthetics in cities like Buffalo parallels the merging of literary form and style that spurred him to represent and reformulate his own times in a body of written work both lasting and unmistakable.

Professionalism and American Publishing, 1904–5

The difficulty of writing a biography of a genius before he becomes one is that biographers tend to then connect everything to that genius, perhaps at the cost of doing a disservice to their subject. The buildings of Buffalo are my attempt at connecting strands of influence, though a greater and arguably deeper influence was growing steadily throughout the United States during Fitzgerald's childhood: the further development of the professional writer as a serious trade in American letters. Writers in the early twentieth century benefited from a century of disputes over copyright law, reprinting and piracy protections, and, above all, the cost of creating an "American" literature from nothing but a new republic populated by ex–British citizens. Did literature belong to the people? Meredith McGill, in her study of the rampant reprint culture in the nineteenth century, *American Literature and the Culture of Reprinting, 1834–1853*, ponders this question, among others, as it relates to the Jacksonian model of democracy, with its belief in the superiority of the common man over the aristocrat, pitting the reader against the author in the marketplace—and, for a time, readers won out over the rights of writers.

Authors were treated with an interesting mix of honor and removal;

publishers would use the names of authors to sell reprints, though the authors would receive little, if any, remuneration for their toil. McGill argues that "the culture of reprinting does not eliminate authors so much as suspend, reconfigure, and intensify their authority, placing a premium on texts that circulate with the names of authors attached."[13] An odd place for writers to be: respected for their work but removed from the financial rewards of that respect. International copyright became law immediately prior to the beginning of the twentieth century, and a new interest in periodicals and magazines catapulted writers to popularity seemingly overnight, with the *Atlantic Monthly, Harper's Weekly, McClure's,* and the *Saturday Evening Post* providing ample space for writers to make sizable incomes. "During the first half of the twentieth century the American author," according to James L. W. West III, "could publish stories and serialize novels in an unprecedented number and variety of such magazines."[14] Owing to the rapid urbanization and industrialization of the country (in contrast to the agricultural economy that had dominated much of the nineteenth century), writers like Jack London, Booth Tarkington, Theodore Dreiser, Edith Wharton, Willa Cather, and Ida Tarbell were featured in national magazines; they earned healthy sums from these sources, and many chose to serialize their work prior to trade publication, with some writers making considerably more from serialization than from book publication. Fitzgerald would enter into this market at its zenith, revolutionize the magazine story for an entire generation, and eventually decry his ability to write "*Post* stories" rather than more novels. Fitzgerald patterned much of his career on those he had seen succeed in the business, tapping multiple sources of literary income to sell the same work multiple times as literary property, a key concept in the twentieth century.[15]

Many writers in America up until the twentieth century made little from their writing, instead opting to work a day job to make ends meet. Herman Melville worked as a U.S. customs inspector for nearly two decades after the publication of *Moby-Dick* proved less than successful in America; early in his life Nathaniel Hawthorne held several government posts while attempting a career as a novelist; aside from being a newspaper editor and war nurse, Walt Whitman worked for the Department of the Interior and the Office of the Attorney General. Some writers were able to make their living exclusively by the pen: Washington Irving, James Fenimore Cooper, Susanna Rowson, and Catharine Maria Sedgwick, to name a few, are prime examples of America's "professional writers."[16] The nineteenth century offered writers a chance to advocate for a new "American" literature, as the country was only a quarter century old when the century began. "The problem of the professional writer," according to William Charvat, "is not identical with that of the literary artist; but when a literary artist is also a professional writer, he cannot solve the problems of the one function without reference to the other."[17] Fitzgerald learned, perhaps from seeing how his early idols navigated their careers, that money and art went hand in hand. The industry made him rich, got him the girl, broke him, used him up, and eventually threw him away. Fitzgerald was a man always looking for a second, third, or fourth act. He knew recuperating was possible because he had seen it done for decades by writers he admired, some of whom he would have been reading while living in Buffalo in the early 1900s.

With authorship now established as a trade, Fitzgerald's Buffalo years saw some of his later influences publish pivotal books in their considerable canons. According to Fitzgerald, he would "rather have written [Joseph Conrad's 1904 *Nostromo*] than any other novel";[18] he called it "the great novel of the past fifty years."[19] That year also saw the publication of *The Golden Bowl* by Henry James, a writer, William Blazek contends, who "for Fitzgerald . . . represented—along with Conrad, Edith Wharton, H. G. Wells, and W. M. Thackeray—the epitome of career achievement, a figure to be emulated, as James himself viewed Balzac and Flaubert."[20] Also in 1904, Thorstein Veblen released *Theory of Business Enterprise,* his critique of the corporate domination of American industry, which paired well with his earlier *Theory of the Leisure Class* (1899). Both books play an important role in our understanding of Fitzgerald's fiction prior to and during the Great Depression, with scholars citing Veblen as an influence on *The Great Gatsby* and *Tender Is the Night.*[21] The next year, 1905, Upton Sinclair released *The Jungle,* the great muckraking novel of the Chicago stockyards, which became the model for socially conscious fiction for the next forty years. As for Fitzgerald, he was reading a small smattering of adventure novels and books for boys in 1904 and 1905. He makes reference to reading *The Scottish Chiefs,* a historical novel by Jane Porter. He also was buying a "Henty book a day" while vacationing in the Catskills in July 1905, a reference to English novelist G. A. Henty, who wrote a series of historical adventure novels, five of which came out between 1904 and 1905.[22] Fifteen years later, certain influences made multiple appearances in letters and public pieces after the success of *This Side of Paradise*. A broad grouping of British and American writers would help make the young Scott into the writer he would become, and his Buffalo years would have put him much closer to the center of the American publishing universe in New York, making St. Paul feel like a foreign land in comparison.

We know the names of some of those influencers: native Indianan Booth Tarkington, whose book *The Magnificent Ambersons* played a significant (if underanalyzed) role in Fitzgerald's writing of *This Side of Paradise* and who won two Pulitzer Prizes during Fitzgerald's early career; Compton Mackenzie, whose *Sinister Street* (split into *Youth's Encounter* and *Sinister Street* in the United States) peppers several early letters between Fitzgerald and his friends in the lead up to *This Side of Paradise*; H. G. Wells, whose "quest" novels, rather than his prolific science fiction, gave Fitzgerald a form to imitate; George Bernard Shaw, whose books looked "cheerful and important";[23] and his newly discovered (by 1920) chestnuts Joseph Conrad and Frank Norris, who pushed him past the initial influence of the former writers. Like Amory Blaine in *This Side of Paradise*, young Fitzgerald was a walking, talking librarian of books both important and forgotten, and he used their names as points of pride in several letters for most of his life. This love of reading, at least according to Matthew J. Bruccoli and other biographers, really began during Fitzgerald's short time at Princeton, yet works of major writers from 1904–5 may very well have been on the young man's radar, especially if he were spending his time trying to impress the girls (and, perhaps more important, the girls' fathers).

H. G. Wells's *Kipps: The Story of a Simple Soul* was published in 1905 to critical success and had steady sales well into the 1920s. With *Kipps* and with his 1909 novel *Tono-Bungay*, Wells became noted for writing social, intellectual, bildungsroman novels, and Fitzgerald soaked them up with excitement. He mentions *Tono-Bungay* in several letters well into the 1920s, leading one to believe a novel like *Kipps* had, at one time or another, made its way onto Fitzgerald's reading list. In *This Side of Paradise*, writing about these kinds of "quest" novels, Fitzgerald said, "In the 'quest' book the hero sets off in life armed with the best weapons and avowedly intending to use them as such weapons are usually used, to push their possessors ahead as selfishly and blindly as possible, but the heroes of the 'quest' books discover that there might be a more magnificent use for them."[24] The use of "magnificent" may be coincidence, but another quest novel, Tarkington's *The Magnificent Ambersons* (1918), mirrors much of Fitzgerald's first novel. Tarkington's most famous novel for young readers was *Penrod* (1914), so Fitzgerald would not have encountered Tarkington as an eight-year-old, though he would find him with the novel *Seventeen* (1916) and most certainly with *Ambersons*.

But novels were not the only reading material for someone as curious as Fitzgerald. Magazines were regularly publishing novels in serial form, and many of those serials would become the best-selling novels of their time when they appeared in hardback. American writer Winston Churchill and British writer Mary Augusta Ward had their number-one bestsellers (Churchill's *The Crossing*, 1904; Ward's *The Marriage of William Ashe*, 1905) first published in *Collier's* and *Harper's* magazines, respectively. Though Fitzgerald was not influenced directly by either writer, he would have seen these magazines in Buffalo, perhaps even in his home. One writer who would influence Fitzgerald was Edith Wharton, whose novel *The House of Mirth* became a top-ten bestseller in 1905, soon after running as a successful serial in *Scribner's Magazine* earlier that year. She won the Pulitzer Prize for a Novel in 1921, becoming the first woman to do so, with *The Age of Innocence,* beating Sinclair Lewis's runaway bestseller *Main Street*. Some years later Fitzgerald would link himself with Wharton and other craftsmen, namely Joseph Hergesheimer and Booth Tarkington, in a June 1925 letter to his editor Maxwell Perkins denouncing Fitzgerald's one-time friend Thomas Boyd's writing about "the Great Beautiful life of the Manure Widder."[25] He respected Wharton's work, and her treatment of the social class structure of New York City can be seen running through some of Fitzgerald's best fiction. He was always a boy with less trying to be more. Much as the buildings of Buffalo may have played a part in a young man's artistic development, the magazines and best-selling novels of the era may have suggested to Fitzgerald a life of professional accomplishment and independence. After all, he had watched (and was watching) his father jump from employer to employer, only to be let go and cast back into the world jobless and unfulfilled. The serials and bestsellers glittered with possibility, even if he may not have read or understood them. The impact was there, for his friends and their families to see along with his mother and father.

Other books appeared over those two years, targeted particularly to young readers. The first in the Bobbsey Twins series was released in 1904, along with *Freckles* (Gene Stratton-Porter), *Rebecca of Sunnybrook Farm* (Kate Douglas Wiggin), and *The Marvelous Land of Oz* (L. Frank Baum); 1905 saw the release of *A Little Princess* (Frances Hodgson Burnett), two new titles by Baum, and *The Story of the Champions of the Roundtable,* the second volume in Howard Pyle's Knights of the Roundtable series. Children's literature was a lucrative market, given the increase in readership thanks to serial publication and primary school texts. More-adult fare was also published, including *The Golden Bowl* (Henry James), *The Deliverance* (Ellen Glasgow), and *The Sea-Wolf* (Jack London) in 1904, and *The Clansman* (Thomas Dixon Jr.)—a virulently racist novel that inspired D. W. Griffith's film *The Birth of a Nation* (1915)—was released in 1905 and quickly became one of the year's best-selling books. Of course, James was one of the most critically acclaimed writers in the United States and Britain, only a few years away from releasing his major works in an multivolume edition for Charles Scribner's Sons. Glasgow would win the Pulitzer Prize for her final novel, *In This Our Life* (1941), and Dixon's work remains a troubling reminder of the at times misguided nature of America's reading tastes.

An understudied connection exists between Jack London and Fitzgerald, who both wrote for the magazines, were adept at short-form writing for income, understood their literary value and markets, and wrote as a trade. London's career never intersected with Fitzgerald's, since he died in 1916 at the age of forty, but the former's great works were published during the latter's early years. If the young boy yearned for adventure, he needed look no further than the three novels London released in the early century: *The Call of the Wild* (1903), *The Sea-Wolf* (1904), and *White Fang* (1906). London's reputation (and sales power) rested on the success of these books. And he too became disillusioned with the publishing industry that had given him so much opportunity. *Martin Eden* (1909), London's great novel of the professional writer in America, reads as a novel-length treatment of themes similar to those Fitzgerald would mine in his infamous "Crack-Up" essays for *Esquire* three decades later. Martin learns to write by force of will, achieving success in the national magazine and trade publication markets, only to become disillusioned at the business of it all, what Ernest Hemingway would call "the lousy racket."[26] In a long response to his love interest Ruth, Martin reveals that he is uneasy that editors and readers who rejected him early and often are now clamoring for his services, given his newfound success. "I've got the

same flesh on my bones," he tells her, "the same ten fingers and toes. . . .
I am personally of the same value that I was when nobody wanted me.
And what is puzzling me is why they want me now. Surely they don't
want me for myself, for myself is the same old self they did not want."[27]
Martin is cracking up, as many writers do. Getting one's head around the
business of literature is generally fraught with anxiety, and no one is safe
from its vicissitudes.

When Fitzgerald cracked up, he wrote of the "first wild wind of success and the delicious mist it brings with it" in his essay "Early Success,"
charting his reaction to his debut novel doing well, albeit with "a certain
bonus and certain burden." "The compensation of a very early success,"
he wrote, "is a conviction that life is a romantic matter. In the best sense
one stays young."[28] Fitzgerald would begin to see his work fade in the
late 1930s, eventually becoming something editors and readers no longer
wanted. Why didn't they want what he wanted to write? There is a kinship, therefore, between London's fictional Martin Eden and Fitzgerald,
as if the latter were the real-life post-success version of the fictional former. Had Martin, "with his work all performed,"[29] continued to navigate
the rough waters of publishing as he had the South Seas, he may have
become Fitzgerald, who wrote, "Of course all life is a process of breaking down, but the blows that do the dramatic side of the work—the big
sudden blows that come, or seem to come, from outside—the ones you
remember and blame things on and, in moments of weakness, tell your
friends about, don't show their effect all at once."[30] Even if there is no
literal connection between these two writers, there is a spiritual one: the
professional writer and his anxieties about that profession have become a
central part of understanding Fitzgerald in his late career. At eight years
old, he could not know his trajectory, nor could he forecast his destiny.
But he knew he wanted more than his father could give him. Publishing
historian Charles Madison reminds us that "the peculiarity of publishing
is that while it is and must of necessity remain a business, it tends to attract a fair percentage of men who seek from it a satisfaction that money
alone cannot provide."[31] Seeing success on the front pages of magazines
and on the spines of new books would give anyone the impression that a
good life was one story, one salable narrative, one glittering thing away
from being realized. By 1904–5, writing was established firmly as a trade
in America, with major writers of fiction, nonfiction, and children's literature producing lasting works read by a newly established reading public,

and it was a trade whose ongoing forces would later influence Fitzgerald's career. The writer's trade became an art, an expression, and a means of satisfaction for F. Scott Fitzgerald, and the complications of that business mixed with his deep desire to capture moments of beauty built him and broke him. He would become more like his father than he could ever know.

NOTES

1. F. Scott Fitzgerald, *Tender Is the Night: A Romance,* ed. James L. W. West III, Cambridge Edition of the Works of F. Scott Fitzgerald (Cambridge: Cambridge University Press, 2022), 352.

2. Joel Kabot, "Buffalo and Syracuse, New York," in *F. Scott Fitzgerald in Context,* ed. Bryant Mangum (New York: Cambridge University Press, 2013), 100.

3. Andrew Turnbull, *Scott Fitzgerald* (New York: Charles Scribner's Sons, 1962), 11.

4. F. Scott Fitzgerald, *The Notebooks of F. Scott Fitzgerald,* ed. Matthew J. Bruccoli (New York: Harcourt Brace Jovanovich / Bruccoli Clark, 1978), 158.

5. In lieu of individual in-text citations, see Buffalo Architecture and History, https://buffaloah.com, for the particular buildings, companies, and industrialists discussed in this chapter. All photographs courtesy of Buffalo Architecture and History.

6. Jerome Puma, "The Larkin Building, Buffalo, NY: History of the Demolition," *Frank Lloyd Wright Association Newsletter* 1, no. 5 (1978); reprinted in *Buffalo Architecture and History,* https://buffaloah.com/h/larkin/admin/index.html.

7. F. Scott Fitzgerald, "'The Sensible Thing,'" in *All the Sad Young Men,* ed. James L. W. West III, Cambridge Edition of the Works of F. Scott Fitzgerald (Cambridge: Cambridge University Press, 2014), 152.

8. Fitzgerald, *This Side of Paradise,* ed. James L. W. West III, Cambridge Edition of the Works of F. Scott Fitzgerald (Cambridge: Cambridge University Press, 2012), 57.

9. Fitzgerald, "Winter Dreams," in *All the Sad Young Men,* 65.

10. F. Scott Fitzgerald, "Author's House," in *My Lost City: Personal Essays, 1920–1940,* ed. James L. W. West III, Cambridge Edition of the Works of F. Scott Fitzgerald (Cambridge: Cambridge University Press, 2014), 173.

11. Fitzgerald, "Author's House," 174.

12. F. Scott Fitzgerald, "How to Waste Material: A Note on My Generation," in *My Lost City,* 79.

13. Meredith L. McGill, *American Literature and the Culture of Reprinting, 1834–1853* (Philadelphia: University of Pennsylvania Press, 2003), 17.

14. James L. W. West III, *American Authors and the Literary Marketplace since 1900* (Philadelphia: University of Pennsylvania Press, 1988), 103.

15. For a more detailed account, see West's chapter "The Magazine Market" in *American Authors.*

16. See William Charvat, *The Profession of Authorship in America, 1800–1870,* ed.

Matthew J. Bruccoli (New York: Columbia University Press, 1992), for case studies on Cooper, Irving, and other early American writers.

17. Charvat, *Profession of Authorship*, 3.

18. F. Scott Fitzgerald to Fanny Butcher, May 10, 1923, quoted in Donald W. Rude, "F. Scott Fitzgerald on Joseph Conrad," in *Conradiana* 31, no. 3 (1999): 217.

19. F. Scott Fitzgerald, "10 Books That I Have Read," *Jersey City Evening Journal,* April 24, 1923, 9, quoted in Matthew J. Bruccoli, *Some Sort of Epic Grandeur: The Life of F. Scott Fitzgerald,* 2nd rev. ed. (Columbia: University of South Carolina Press, 2002), 173.

20. William Blazek, "Literary Influences," in Magnum, *Fitzgerald in Context,* 50.

21. See E. Ray Canterbery, "Thorstein Veblen and *The Great Gatsby,*" *Journal of Economic Issues* 33, no. 2 (1999): 297–304.

22. F. Scott Fitzgerald, *F. Scott Fitzgerald's Ledger: A Facsimile,* introduction by Matthew J. Bruccoli (Washington, D.C.: NCR/Microcard Editions / Bruccoli Clark, 1972), 159.

23. John Kuehl and Jackson R. Bryer, eds., *Dear Scott / Dear Max: The Fitzgerald–Perkins Correspondence* (New York: Charles Scribner's Sons, 1971), 22.

24. Fitzgerald, *This Side of Paradise,* 115.

25. Kuehl and Bryer, *Dear Scott / Dear Max,* 111.

26. Ernest Hemingway, *The Letters of Ernest Hemingway,* vol. 5, *1932–1934,* ed. Sandra Spanier and Miriam B. Mandel (New York: Cambridge University Press, 2020), 146.

27. Jack London, *Martin Eden* (New York: Penguin, 1984), 460.

28. F. Scott Fitzgerald, "Early Success," in *My Lost City,* 186, 190, 190.

29. London, *Martin Eden,* 461.

30. F. Scott Fitzgerald, "The Crack-Up," in *My Lost City,* 1139.

31. Charles Madison, *Book Publishing in America* (New York: McGraw-Hill, 1966), 163.

1906–1907

Kayla Forrest

In the years 1906 and 1907, Theodore Roosevelt was in the second term of his presidency at the height of the Progressive Era and Upton Sinclair exposed the abysmal state of the meat-packing industry in *The Jungle,* leading to the establishment of the Food and Drug Administration. The Panama Canal was in progress, and a major stock-market crash was avoided after the brief Panic of 1907. These were also the years when F. Scott Fitzgerald was transitioning into adolescence: on September 24, 1906, he turned ten years old in Buffalo, New York. Less focused on national and global issues than on his immediate world, he was preoccupied with which college football teams were having winning seasons, his rank in the order of affection of the girls in his dance class, and whether nearby theaters were showing any Wild West films. Though by no means entirely innocent, the shift into double digits from 1906–7 marked a significant period in his life, as he was beginning to conceptualize his individuality, ask questions, and observe his immediate environment more closely.[1]

While childhood pictures of Fitzgerald mark his physical growth, his ledger, correspondence, and early writing offer a glimpse into his emotional and intellectual development through details about his familial relationships; experiences at summer camp, church, and school; friendships with boys his age and pursuit of girls; growing passion for football and other sports; and the stories that fascinated him, including American history, books, and films. Fitzgerald's boyhood observations and recollections of this period do more than simply paint a picture of this important stage of life: they elucidate the formation of his individuality, pride, self-reliance, desire for love and social mobility, and passion for narratives, all in conjunction with a burgeoning sense of himself as a writer.

Boyhood in Buffalo

The Fitzgerald family lived in Buffalo in 1906 and 1907, and in the early 1900s the city was still thriving as a result of strong industry and the harnessing of Niagara Falls as an energy source. Scott's father had a job as a salesman with Procter & Gamble, and the Fitzgerald family resided at 71 Highland Avenue, a cozy house with a turret in the front, located not far from downtown Buffalo. Highland Avenue was, and remains, a residential street with houses pressed close to one another. Scott would play with children from the neighborhood, and as Andrew Turnbull notes, he would frequent the neighboring Powells at number 80.[2] Fitzgerald describes playing football "on the Highland corner" and taking part in "pom-pom-pullaway," a street game the neighborhood kids played in the evening.[3] Though the Fitzgeralds had lived on Highland Avenue since 1905, the family was never listed in *Dau's Society Blue Book,* suggesting they were not recognized as a prominent Buffalo family, despite their investment in raising their social status.

Of his relationships with family during this time, there is not much to be said regarding his younger sister, Annabel. His January 1906 ledger entry recalls that "he used to scare Annabel by a game called 'Bad Brownie come to eat you up' and 'Good Brownie come to see what you want for Christmas,'"[4] indicating both affection for her and an older brother's amusement at tormenting a younger sibling. His parents, however, contributed considerably to his self-formation and perception of his social standing.

The lessons Fitzgerald's father, Edward, imparted to his son were often tied to the manifestation and practice of decorum, with the implied message that individuals' outward appearances reflected their interior morality and respectability. Scott records that "he had to wear black suits because father thought blue was common in dancing school."[5] He also writes, in his August 1906 ledger entry, that his father had a habit of getting drunk and playing baseball in their yard.[6] Despite Edward's flaws, he recognized that his son was a bright child, even encouraging him in his writing, as Scott would later acknowledge: "The first help I ever had in writing in my life was from my father who read an utterly imitative Sherlock Holmes story of mine and pretended to like it."[7] Though that story may have been "The Mystery of the Raymond Mortgage," which Scott completed in 1909, we know from his ledger that he had begun writing "a detective story about a necklace that was hidden in a trapdoor under the carpet" in 1907,[8] so it is possible this lost story was the one his father read. Regardless of which story Fitzgerald shared with his father, it is clear that he trusted his father with his early writing and appreciated Edward's encouragement of his early literary efforts.

Fitzgerald's mother, Mollie McQuillan Fitzgerald, also saw him as a bright and talented boy, and she doted on her son. As Turnbull writes, she "seldom intruded on her son's occupations, but she was ambitious for him."[9] The only mention of his mother in his 1906–7 ledger entries points to this ambition as he recalls Mollie's belief in his talent: "His mother got the idea that he could sing so he performed 'Way down in colon town' and 'Don't get married any more' for all visitors."[10] Mollie's influence on his life also included his education in Catholicism. As Matthew J. Bruccoli notes, though his father and mother were both Catholic, Mollie was more dedicated to her faith, and she made sure her son was properly instructed in Catholic doctrine.[11]

Faith and Challenging Authority

Religion played a significant role in Fitzgerald's young life, as not only did he go to church with his mother but he also attended two Catholic schools while the family lived in Buffalo. Though there are no known records of the family's attendance, it is probable that they attended Holy Angels Catholic Church, given its connection and proximity to the Holy Angels school, which Scott attended, and given the mention of a church rector, "Father Fallon, of the Church of the Holy Angels," whose orations captivated a seven-year-old Fitzgerald.[12] In 1906 and 1907, Fitzgerald was not only beginning to partake in the sacraments but he also felt guilty about his perceived sins. His September 1907 ledger entry recounts a time in confession when "he hid by saying in [a] shocked voice to the priest 'Oh no, I never tell a lie.'"[13]

Bruccoli makes the connection between this moment from the ledger and the story "Absolution" (1924), where Rudolph Miller lies in confession.[14] Rudolph bears several similarities to young Fitzgerald, including being eleven years old, exactly the same age as Fitzgerald when the confession incident occurred. Rudolph also believes he is a changeling, swapped at birth with another child, and he feels embarrassed about not having money to offer for collection, both sentiments Fitzgerald also felt as a child.[15] Finally, Rudolph repeats Scott's own lie in confession. In the story, Rudolph suffers from his guilt, fearing he will be struck down by God if he tries to take Communion without confessing this sin.

Eventually, he decides God must surely understand that he "had done it to make things finer in the confessional, brightening up the dinginess of his admissions by saying a thing radiant and proud."[16] Given the similarities between young Fitzgerald and Rudolph, the story could be said to explore the conflict between the inner angst of recognizing one's sinful nature and the rebellion of becoming one's own person, able to think for oneself. As Rudolph confronts his fear and respect for his father while deciding how to navigate his religious transgression, Fitzgerald seems to draw on the tension between individual belief and autonomy and the Catholic doctrine of sin and its consequences that he grappled with as a boy.

This tendency to challenge and even rebel against authority points to Fitzgerald's growing sense of pride and independence. In September 1906, for example, he records an incident in school when he had corrected a teacher, telling her, "Mexico City was not the capitol of Central America."[17] Though this is all that is recorded of this specific incident, his admonishment probably had the same result as it did in Fitzgerald's story "That Kind of Party" for Terrence Tipton, who was sent to the principal's office when he corrected his teacher for the same mistake. Fitzgerald's indignation at being punished for being right is evident in Terrence's reaction to the "forces of injustice [that] were confusingly arrayed against him,"[18] but so too is his pride in calling out what he knew was wrong.

Becoming Independent

While the classroom incident reflects Fitzgerald's desire to think for himself, his travel to attend Camp Chatham in Orillia, Ontario, in July 1907 reflects a more formative experience of self-reliance, as he was away from home for the first time and was several hours away from his parents. His ledger describes his participation in camp activities: "He swam and fished and cleaned and ate fish and canoed and rowed and caught behind the bat and was desperately unpopular and went in paper chases and running contests."[19] Though he acknowledges his lack of popularity among his peers, revealing the negative impact it had on him, this sentiment is outweighed by the triumph tied to his successes with fishing, running, and other camp activities. His descriptions of camp underscore Fitzgerald's growing independence, having, for the first time, managed on his own. Rather than expressing homesickness, his letters home and his ledger relate his experience as one rooted in feelings of accomplishment and pride, even despite the adversity of being unpopular.

His camp letters also included requests for money, and Fitzgerald used other boys' financial situations to justify his own need, hinting that, even at this young age, he recognized the economic stratification of society and the fact that having money could bring insider status. The letters also convey his desire for agency in his own life and his confidence he could manage on his own. These feelings are apparent in one letter to his mother, dated July 18, 1907, where he discourages her from visiting, stating reasons such as "You know no one hear except Mrs. Upton and she is busy most of the time" and "It is only a small town and no good hotels."[20] His efforts to dissuade his mother could have been in earnest, but it is more likely Fitzgerald's increasing self-reliance made a visit from his mother not only unnecessary but also undesirable. Instead, he asks her to send him money, attempting to enlist guilt to ensure its delivery, telling her "all the other boys have pocket money besides their regullar allowance." His request for a dollar is coupled with a justification: "becaus there are a lot of little odds and ends i need. I will spend it causiusly."[21] Scott's request acknowledges his financial reliance on his parents, while also reassuring them he is capable of exercising discernment in his spending. Here he expresses confidence in his abilities to take care of and rely on himself.

His self-reliance would later play a significant role in his life, especially when it came to his career and finances. From his determination to finish *This Side of Paradise* and prove his financial worth to Zelda to his decision to go back to work in Hollywood in the lean years of the late 1930s, Fitzgerald used his talent to provide for himself and his family, recognizing that wealth allowed him to control where and how he lived. Though his conscientious approach to spending would not last long, Fitzgerald's childhood resolve to take care of himself persisted into adulthood.[22] Even in his financial distress from the responsibility of paying for Zelda's institutionalization and his daughter Scottie's schooling, Fitzgerald relied on himself and his prowess as a writer to pay the bills.

Fitzgerald was also confronted with the restrictions of economic status and social stratifications during his time at school. He attended the school at Holy Angels Convent from September 1903 to September 1905, but when the school closed he moved to Miss Nardin's Academy.[23] Named for one of its original founders, Ernestine Nardin, a Daughter of

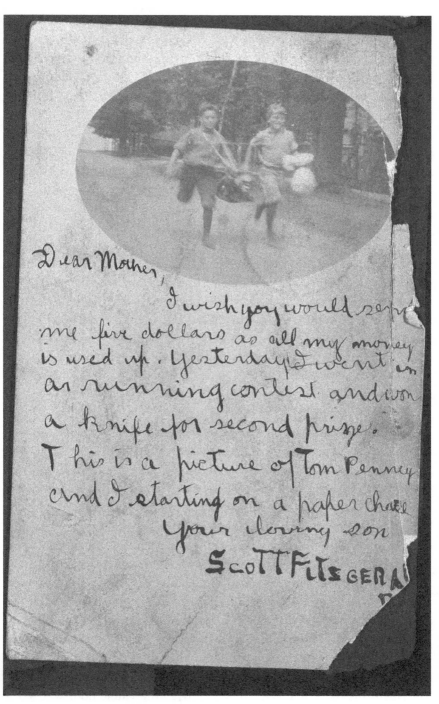

Dear Mother,

I wish you would send me five dollars as all my money is used up. Yesterday I went in a running contest and won a knife for second prize. This is a picture of Tom Penney and I starting on a paper chase

Your loving son

SCOTT FITSGERA
D

Letter from Scott to his mother, requesting money

the Heart of Mary, the school was founded in 1857 as a Catholic school for girls, but in 1874 it opened its doors to boys as well.[24] Attending school at Miss Nardin's was a continuation of his Catholic education, but the school's location across from the mansion built by John J. Albright also continued his education regarding the way the wealthy lived in comparison to his own family. Betsy Taylor, in her history of the Albright estate, notes that the mansion, built in 1901, had grounds of more than twelve acres. Albright was a successful businessman in several industries, including coal, asphalt, and steel. He was well known in Buffalo for having helped bring industry to the city through the Lackawanna Steel Company.[25] Although Fitzgerald never discusses Albright specifically in his work or ledger, the observant boy would have been aware of him and his success, especially as Scott had to walk around the Albright estate every day to get to Miss Nardin's on Cleveland Avenue. As he walked around the high brick wall enclosing the estate, part of which still exists across from the present-day Nardin Academy, he may have recognized the symbolic representation of this wall—a physical barrier isolating the wealthy Albright and keeping himself out, much like the material and social barriers that kept his family on the fringe of high society.

Girls and "That Kind of Party"

Fitzgerald's emerging adolescence also included an increased interest in girls. Much of his interaction with them came from Charles H. Van Arnum Jr.'s classes at dancing school, but he also attended several city dances and carnivals, such as an Easter carnival on April 20, 1906, where he and his dance classmates performed in groups. Fitzgerald danced the "Humpty Dumpty" with other boys in his class, and Nancy Gardner, one of Scott's early love interests, did a solo dance.[26] One of the events where Scott was listed as an attendee by the Buffalo newspapers was the inaugural Children's Charity Ball on January 2, 1906. He was favored with inclusion in Mrs. Norman E. Mack's box, along with her daughters and several of their peers. As Mrs. Mack was a known society woman and the organizer of the ball, this was a marker of social acceptance that Fitzgerald would have recognized as important, as he was beginning to share his parents' desire for social mobility. The *Buffalo Evening News* described this particular ball romantically: "The whole floor was like a flower garden, with its whirling, tiptoeing, lovely children in white and pink and blue, be-ribboned, with saches [sic] and hair bows only slightly smaller than themselves."[27] These public performances and events were opportunities to dance and socialize with his various crushes and to begin to discover the complexities of love.

His first mention of love in his ledger comes in November 1905, when he declares his love for Nancy Gardner, but in 1907 Kitty Williams has caught his attention. Of October 1907 Fitzgerald writes, "He asked Kitty to lead the grand march in dancing school the first day."[28] This incident, and the events occurring after it, are described in greater detail in an August 1910 entry in his *Thoughtbook* (a boyhood diary) titled "My Girls":

Kitty Williams is much plainer [than Nancy Gardner] in my memory. I met her first at dancing school and as Mr. Van Arnumn (our dancing teacher) chose me to lead the march I asked her to be my pardner. The next day she told Marie Lautz and Marie repeated it to Dorothy Knox who in turn passed it on to Earl, that I was third in her affections. I don't remember who was first but I know that Earl was second and as I was already quite overcome by her charms I then and there resolved that I would gain first place.[29]

Fitzgerald writes in both his ledger and the *Thoughtbook* about delivering a box of candy to Kitty's house at Christmas. He was "scared silly,"[30] and he "nearly fell down with embarrassment" but "finally stammered 'Give this to Kitty,' and ran home" when Kitty herself opened the door.[31] In early 1908, Fitzgerald would gain first place in Kitty's esteem at a so-called kissing party, but this experience of vying for her affection and the anxiety of making his feelings known to her reveal his awareness of a physical attraction to girls and his growing understanding of the vulnerability accompanying pursuit of the opposite sex. These uncomfortable romantic efforts are also mirrored in his fiction, such as Amory Blaine's bumbling attempt to impress and kiss Myra St. Claire, a girl he met at dancing school. While Amory succeeds in kissing Myra after telling her he likes her "first and second and third,"[32] he is overcome by a sort of revolted panic and his refusal to kiss Myra again angers her—a painful representation of the conflicting feelings and agonizing difficulty of adolescent courtship.

The mystique of kissing parties, as well as the awkwardness of young romance, is well represented in Fitzgerald's short story "That Kind of

Party." The story was meant to be a part of the Basil Duke Lee stories, but it was rejected by editors even after Fitzgerald tried to publish it on its own, replacing Basil with Terrence R. Tipton.[33] Jackson R. Bryer and John Kuehl have made connections between the story and Fitzgerald's ledger entries for his tenth year, including Fitzgerald's noting of his cigar-band collection, the charity ball he attended where he "was chased by a cripple named Sears McGraw," and the incident where he corrected his teacher's error.[34] Given the additional similarities between the names of Terrence's school (Mrs. Cary's Academy) and Fitzgerald's real school (Miss Nardin's Academy) and the names of Terrence's friend Joe Schoonover and Fitzgerald's playmate from across the street, Joe Powell, the story seems to primarily reflect the details and experiences of Fitzgerald at ten years old, though he also includes details from earlier in his life. For instance, Terrence gets into a fight outside school with Albert Moore, a bespectacled boy whose nose he bloodies before fleeing, resembling an incident when Fitzgerald was eight: he "gave a boy a bloody nose and ran home in consequence with a made up story."[35] In the story version, this is another setback for Terrence, who, fearing punishment for fighting, frets about not being able to go to the party and kiss Dolly Bartlett.

Additionally, Terrence and Joe cook up a plan to get Joe's mother out of the house for the party by sending a fake telegram from her sister. In order to get money for the telegram, Terrence goes to his aunt's house, where he eats a raw egg in exchange for a quarter, telling his friends, "I had to eat it raw. She's a health fiend."[36] The consumption of the raw egg, done in the name of love, resembles another ledger entry from Fitzgerald's eighth year: he "ate an egg every day on the bidding of his Aunt Clara. She gave him 25¢ a raw egg."[37] Though these incorporations from his eighth year are represented in the story, Fitzgerald's primary personal inspiration does seem to be his tenth year, as the characters in the story are ten and eleven. Indeed, as a fictional representation of adolescent love and the kissing parties he attended, this story draws on all the excitement, jubilation, fear, and embarrassment of Fitzgerald's youthful attempts at romance.

Love of Sports

While navigating relationships with girls had a significant impact on his emerging identity, Fitzgerald also prized athleticism, and his fixation on sports at this age is well represented in his ledger. In his January 1907

Ted Coy, captain of Yale's 1909 varsity football team

entry, he recalls attending a basketball game with Joe Powell where he "fell madly into admiration for a dark haired boy who played with a melancholy defiance."[38] Fitzgerald deeply respected the physical prowess and raw emotion involved in sports; however, while he enjoyed playing them, his athletic talent was not particularly stunning. His ledger records from 1906 and 1907 indicate that he played golf, baseball, and football, which appears to have been his favorite sport. By late 1905, his investment in football was such that he had the uniform and all the equipment, and in September 1906 he was playing regularly as the "guard or tackle and usually scared silly."[39] In September 1907, he played "on a team of which Norbert Sullivan was the star. He [Fitzgerald] weighted sixty-eight llbs."[40] The note about his weight at eleven years old, the fear he remembers from playing the sport at ten, and the implied comparison between himself and Norbert Sullivan point to his feelings of athletic inadequacy, despite his enthusiasm for the game.

Young Fitzgerald also kept track of college football scores and admired players like Ted Coy, the handsome captain of Yale's varsity team who played fullback and later went on to coach at Yale. Coy's National College Football Hall of Fame entry conveys his heroism on the field: "It was a familiar sight when Ted would burst through an enemy defense, his long blonde hair held back by a white sweatband. Coy was a pressure player who always seemed to come up with the big play. He ran through the line with hammering, high knee action then unleashed a fast, fluid running motion through the secondary."[41] This description illustrates why Fitzgerald looked up to Coy as a paragon of athleticism and leadership, as he led his team to win nine games with only one tie and no losses in 1907, his first year on the Yale varsity team. Fitzgerald followed Yale's season through the local newspapers in Buffalo. Despite being less than a decade older, Coy was a role model for Fitzgerald and one of his heroes even into adulthood.[42] James L. W. West III notes that the character Ted Fay in "The Freshest Boy" (1928) is inspired by Coy.[43] Basil describes Fay's "sculptured profile," depicts him as "a well-built blond young man of about twenty with a strong chin and direct grey eyes," and refers to him as a "hero" and "legend."[44] The description matches Coy's physical features, but, more important, it reflects Fitzgerald's admiration for Coy as a representation of greatness. Fitzgerald would never be a football icon like Ted Coy, as his lightweight frame, blunders with the ball, and injuries precluded a sustained career in football, but he envisioned a different version of himself in some of his stories, notably "Reade, Substitute Right Half" (1910). Reade resembles his creator in being an underweight, "light haired stripling,"[45] but when he intercepts the ball for a touchdown, Fitzgerald writes himself into the moment of glory he sought but never attained on the field.

Despite his unrealized desire to become a star player, his enthusiasm for the game came from an appreciation of the grittiness and physicality of the sport, the tactical battle between teams, and the talent he witnessed as a player and fan of the game. His descriptions of on-field action, in stories like "Basil and Cleopatra," mirror the play-by-play coverage of a live game: "Basil called for a short pass over the line, throwing it himself for a gain of seven yards. He sent Cullum off tackle for three more and a first down. At the forty, with more latitude, his mind began to function smoothly and surely."[46] The precision with which he describes plays like this one and his use of football terminology reveal Fitzgerald's deep understanding of the game he fell in love with as a child, playing in the streets of Buffalo.

History, Media, and Fitzgerald's Emerging Creative Consciousness

In addition to stories of heroes on the field, young Fitzgerald sustained an affinity for narratives of all sorts, including cinematic, historical, and fictional ones. Both his parents encouraged him to read and provided him with books and magazines that fueled his imagination. In 1906 and 1907, he read children's magazines like *St. Nicholas* magazine and *The Youth's Companion*; Edward Stratemeyer books, which were probably *The Rover Boys* and the *Dave Porter* series; and Byron Archibald Dunn's *The Young Kentuckians Series*.[47] The stories he read were mostly written for children, and many included stories of adventure or intrigue that would have engaged a clever boy like Scott.

Of the stories he read during this period, Walter Scott's *Ivanhoe* left a lasting imprint on his memory. He read the novel in January 1906 while recovering from a nose operation,[48] and it seems to have fueled an interest in the Middle Ages that persisted throughout his life. His appreciation for *Ivanhoe* and fascination with medieval stories endured throughout adulthood, as Scottie recalls "his annoyance when I kept falling asleep during his background briefings on *Ivanhoe*."[49] His attempts to turn this interest into historical fiction were poorly executed, however. The Philippe or "Count of Darkness" stories chronicled the adventures of a medieval count in France, and though they were published in *Redbook*, a reputable outlet, Bruccoli describes them as "among the worst fiction Fitzgerald ever published."[50] These stories were unsuccessful, but they reveal how his fascination with the Middle Ages still inspired him long after his first reading of *Ivanhoe*.[51]

In addition to his interests in sports, reading, and history, Fitzgerald also notes an appreciation for film and live performances in his ledger. Specifically, he remembers going to see "Wild West movies and the Tech Stock Company."[52] "The Tech Stock Company" was a reference to one of the stock company shows performed regularly at the Teck Theatre in downtown Buffalo.[53] Turnbull also notes that Fitzgerald's friend Hamilton Wende "got two complimentary tickets to the matinee at the Teck Theatre and always gave one to Scott. Chin cupped in hands, elbows on knees, Scott seldom spoke or took his eyes off the stage during the performance."[54] Many theaters also showed moving pictures, such as the Wild West films Fitzgerald mentions in the ledger. Though he doesn't cite the specific films or shows he saw, his interest in westerns is consistent with his interest in history and the stories inspired by it. His fascination with shows and films influenced his own ideas about narratives and what makes them captivating, and many of his stories include cinematic plotlines. To give two examples: in "The Offshore Pirate," a young woman, Ardita, falls in love with a man she thinks is a pirate, and "The

Augustus Post in a White Steamer automobile in front of the Teck Theatre in Buffalo, New York, 1906.

Night before Chancellorsville" is a first-person account of another young woman, Nora, whose train runs into the middle of a Civil War battle. Such texts illustrate Fitzgerald's prowess in writing theatrical plotlines, a skill that was developing even at a young age.

Many influences were shaping Fitzgerald into the person and writer he was becoming during this impressionable period of preadolescence. He was, even then, an astute observer of the world around him, and his experiences, relationships, and memories would feed his imagination and inspire his work. At this age, he was writing prize-winning essays for school, trying his hand at short fiction, and soaking up the stories around him—from the books he was reading to the history he was learning. As an adult, he would recognize these years as the beginning of his writing career. In a letter from 1920 he stated, "Started writing when I was 10 yrs old + have been hard at it ever since."[55]

NOTES

1. At age seven Fitzgerald "began to hear 'dirty' words," and he had a "curious dream of perversion." F. Scott Fitzgerald, *F. Scott Fitzgerald's Ledger: A Facsimile,*

introduction by Matthew J. Bruccoli (Washington, D.C.: NCR/Microcard Editions / Bruccoli Clark, 1972), 158.

2. Andrew Turnbull, *Scott Fitzgerald* (New York: Charles Scribner's Sons, 1962), 13.

3. Fitzgerald, *Ledger*, 161.

4. Fitzgerald, *Ledger*, 160.

5. Fitzgerald, *Ledger*, 160.

6. Fitzgerald, *Ledger*, 160.

7. F. Scott Fitzgerald, *Correspondence of F. Scott Fitzgerald*, ed. Matthew J. Bruccoli and Margaret M. Duggan (New York: Random House, 1980), 322.

8. Fitzgerald, *Ledger*, 161.

9. Turnbull, *Fitzgerald*, 12.

10. Fitzgerald, *Ledger*, 161.

11. Matthew J. Bruccoli, *Some Sort of Epic Grandeur: The Life of F. Scott Fitzgerald*, 2nd ed. (Columbia: University of South Carolina Press, 2002), 16.

12. Fitzgerald, *Ledger*, 158. Mary Goldman and her colleagues note that the school was at the corner of Porter and West Avenues, which means it diagonally faced the church. Mary Kunz Goldman, Elizabeth Barr, and Lauri Githens, "F. Scott Fitzgerald: The Buffalo Years," *Buffalo News*, February 19, 1994, accessed January 1, 2020. https://buffalonews.com/1994/02/19/f-scott-fitzgerald-the-buffalo-years/.

13. Fitzgerald, *Ledger*, 162.

14. Bruccoli, *Epic Grandeur*, 20.

15. In his January 1906 ledger entry Fitzgerald records, "Suspicion that he is a changeling," and in his October 1907 entry he writes, "In church one little girl made him frightfully embarrassed when he didn't have a penny to put in the collection box." Fitzgerald, *Ledger*, 160, 162.

16. F. Scott Fitzgerald, "Absolution," in *All the Sad Young Men*, ed. James L. W. West III, Cambridge Edition of the Works of F. Scott Fitzgerald (Cambridge: Cambridge University Press, 2014), 93.

17. Fitzgerald, *Ledger*, 161.

18. F. Scott Fitzgerald, "That Kind of Party," in *The Basil, Josephine, and Gwen Stories*, ed. James L. W. West III, Cambridge Edition of the Works of F. Scott Fitzgerald (Cambridge: Cambridge University Press, 2022), 6.

19. Fitzgerald, *Ledger*, 161.

20. F. Scott Fitzgerald, *A Life in Letters*, ed. Matthew J. Bruccoli (New York: Charles Scribner's Sons, 1994), 5.

21. Fitzgerald, *Life in Letters*, 5.

22. Fitzgerald, *Life in Letters*, 5. Another letter from camp with an unspecified date includes a proud comment about winning second place in a race and a request for five dollars "as my money is used up" (5).

23. Holy Angels Catholic Church was established in 1852 and closed permanently in July 2020.

24. History & Tradition, *Nardin Academy*, accessed January 1, 2020. https://www.nardin.org/about-nardin/history-tradition.

25. Betsy Taylor, *The Ivy Grows Again: A History of the Albright Estate from 1890 to the Present* (Buffalo, N.Y.: Nardin Academy, 1998), as excerpted in "John J. Albright Illustrated Biography: 1848–1931," History of Buffalo, https://www.buffaloah.com/h/alb/index.html.

26. "The Easter Carnival," *Buffalo Evening News*, April 18, 1906.

27. "The Children's Charity Ball," *Buffalo Evening News*, January 3, 1906.

28. Fitzgerald, *Ledger*, 162.

29. F. Scott Fitzgerald, *The Thoughtbook of F. Scott Fitzgerald: A Secret Boyhood Diary*, ed. Dave Page (Minneapolis: University of Minnesota Press, 2013), 4.

30. Fitzgerald, *Ledger*, 162.

31. Fitzgerald, *Thoughtbook*, 5.

32. F. Scott Fitzgerald, *This Side of Paradise*, ed. James L. W. West III, Cambridge Edition of the Works of F. Scott Fitzgerald (Cambridge: Cambridge University Press, 2012), 21.

33. F. Scott Fitzgerald, *The Basil and Josephine Stories*, ed. Jackson R. Bryer and John Kuehl (New York: Charles Scribner's Sons, 1973), vii–viii.

34. Fitzgerald, *Basil and Josephine Stories*, ed. Bryer and Kuehl, xxiii. The incident of correcting the teacher's error is also mentioned in "Absolution," another Buffalo-based story.

35. Fitzgerald, *Ledger*, 159.

36. Fitzgerald, "That Kind of Party," 7.

37. Fitzgerald, *Ledger*, 159.

38. Fitzgerald, *Ledger*, 161.

39. Fitzgerald, *Ledger*, 161.

40. Fitzgerald, *Ledger*, 162.

41. Ted Coy, National Football Foundation and College Hall of Fame, accessed January 1, 2020. https://footballfoundation.org/hof_search.aspx?hof=1256.

42. Fitzgerald includes Ted Coy in his list of heroes in "Wait Till You Have Children of Your Own!" (1924).

43. F. Scott Fitzgerald, *My Lost City: Personal Essays, 1920–1940*, ed. James L. W. West III, Cambridge Edition of the Works of F. Scott Fitzgerald (Cambridge: Cambridge University Press, 2014), 240.

44. Fitzgerald, "The Freshest Boy," in *Basil, Josephine, and Gwen Stories*, 70.

45. F. Scott Fitzgerald, *The Apprentice Fiction of F. Scott Fitzgerald, 1909–1917*, ed. John Kuehl (New Brunswick, N.J.: Rutgers University Press, 1965), 31.

46. Fitzgerald, "Basil and Cleopatra," in *Basil, Josephine, and Gwen Stories*, 178.

47. In a letter to Corey Ford at Oak Hall, Tryon, North Carolina, in April 1937, Fitzgerald added a note next to the address: "That always reminds me of you + your Rover Boys—didn't you read Dave Porter too?" Oak Hall is also the name of the boarding school in *Dave Porter at Oak Hall: At Oak Hall, the Schooldays of an American Boy*, by Edward Stratemeyer. Fitzgerald, *Life in Letters*, 320.

48. Fitzgerald, *Ledger*, 160.

49. Bruccoli, *Epic Grandeur*, 496.

50. Bruccoli, *Epic Grandeur*, 387–88.

51. Bruccoli, *Epic Grandeur*, 496. Scottie notes that they were "so inferior to his other work that *Redbook* asked him to discontinue them."

52. Fitzgerald, *Ledger*, 161.

53. Fitzgerald spells the theater's name "Tech." A stock company is a permanent group of actors who perform from a repertoire of "stock" plays in a specific theater.

54. Turnbull, *Fitzgerald*, 12.

55. Fitzgerald, *Correspondence*, 60.

1908–1909

David Page

Last Days in Buffalo

In a frequently quoted March 1908 ledger entry, F. Scott Fitzgerald explained the family's retreat from Buffalo, New York, to St. Paul, Minnesota, by writing in the third person: "His father's services were no longer required by Proctor and Gamble."[1] Fitzgerald elaborated on the circumstances during an interview with journalist Michel Mok in 1936:

> One afternoon—I was 10 or 11—the phone rang and my mother answered it. I didn't understand what she said but I felt that disaster had come to us. My mother, a little while before, had given me a quarter to go swimming. I gave the money back to her. I knew something terrible had happened and I thought she could not spare the money now.
>
> Then I began to pray. "Dear God," I prayed, "please don't let us go to the poorhouse; please don't let us go to the poorhouse." A little while later my father came home. I had been right. He had lost his job.
>
> That morning he had gone out a comparatively young man, a man full of strength, full of confidence. He came home that evening, an old man, a completely broken man. He had lost his essential drive, his immaculateness of purpose. He was a failure the rest of his days.[2]

The anecdote demands sympathy, as it should, but the Fitzgeralds' financial situation was far from bleak in the spring of 1908. During the next couple of months, Scott noted in his ledger that he received some history books wrapped in "crisp tissue" and "played golf with Inky on the public links"[3]—hardly the kinds of episodes one would expect from a family destined for destitution. Nonetheless, Scott Fitzgerald relived the humiliation of being forced to patronize the *public* links in "A Freeze-Out," his 1931 short story set in St. Paul. In that tale, members of the Kennemore

Golf Club are deciding whether the Rikker family can join their private club. Alida Rikker suspects the vote may not go well: "Maybe I won't be a member," she tells her hostess at the Kennemore; "you'll have to come and play with me on the public links. . . . I played on the public links in Buffalo all last spring"[4]—exactly as Scott had done after his father lost his job. Although there were a few humiliating moments, clearly the time Scott spent in Buffalo socializing with the children of the city's well-to-do, including Inky, prepared him to hobnob with the elite families of St. Paul. In addition, several of the incidents that occurred in 1908–9 found their way into Fitzgerald's most noteworthy fiction.

Born the month before Fitzgerald, Inky was James Ingham, whose father, Clark Leonard Ingham, was vice president of Buffalo Realty Company and one of the principals behind the construction of the Lenox,[5] the fashionable apartment building that was the Fitzgeralds' first address when they moved to Buffalo in 1898.[6] In 1908, the Inghams were living at 1088 Delaware Avenue, nicknamed Buffalo's "Millionaires' Row." The Fitzgeralds never rented on Delaware Avenue, but they always lived near the city's elite street during the time they called Buffalo home, and Fitzgerald easily parlayed his academic and dance-class connections to situate himself in the highest circles of young Buffalo society.

The year 1908, for example, began quite auspiciously for eleven-year-old Scott Fitzgerald. On the evening of New Year's Day, he took part in the Children's Charity Ball at Buffalo's Convention Hall.[7] Fitzgerald's dance instructor, Charles H. Van Arnam Jr., directed the ball, which was chaired by Mrs. Norman E. Mack. At the event, he was invited by Seymour H. Knox II (called Earl in Fitzgerald's ledger) to sit in a private viewing box leased by the Knoxes.[8] Earl lived with his family in a twenty-seven-room Italian Renaissance mansion at 1035 Delaware Avenue. Located just a couple of blocks southeast of the Fitzgeralds' residence on Highland Avenue, the Knox mansion stood near the Inghams' home. In 1911, the senior Knox would merge his one hundred five-and-dime stores with those of two cousins, Frank W. and Charles Woolworth, to form F. W. Woolworth Company. The same month as the Charity Ball, Scott got an opportunity to wear his "little tuxedo" at a party given by the Ramsdells.[9] Like the Inghams, the Knoxes, and the Macks, the Ramsdells lived on Delaware Avenue in a large barnlike brick mansion located at 1132. The head of the family, William Mayhew Ramsdell, published the *Buffalo Express*.

Although the denizens of Delaware Avenue figured prominently in Fitzgerald's social circle, he was most smitten by Kitty Williams, whose family lived a block south of the Fitzgeralds. He had met her in Van Arnam's dance class. Through the Knox children, Fitzgerald learned he was third in Kitty's affections. "I then and there resolved that I would gain first place," Scott wrote in his *Thoughtbook* (a boyhood diary).[10] Scott first wooed Kitty in Honey Chittenden's yard. Since "Honey" is sometimes a nickname for "Hortense," it is probable that Honey's father was John L. Chittenden, a broker who lived with his wife, three daughters, and two servants at 81 Highland Avenue, only a few doors away from the Fitzgeralds. In February 1908, Fitzgerald attended a party where the children played "postoffice, pillow, clap in and clap out," and Fitzgerald was able to kiss Kitty countless times.[11] He would later include the episode in his short story "That Kind of Party." By the end of the fete, Fitzgerald had secured the "coveted 1st place" in Kitty's affections.[12] Fitzgerald soon lost his top rank with Kitty to Johnny Gowans.[13] John's father, Grosvenor Gowans, was in the soap manufacturing business, making him a direct competitor to Procter & Gamble.

Before Fitzgerald's father was laid off, Scott regularly attended artistic events. Scott's ledger for February 1908 mentions that he "almost died laughing" at Edward Hugh Sothern's portrayal of Lord Dundreary in *Our American Cousin,* the play at which Abraham Lincoln had been assassinated in 1865.[14] Sothern was reprising his father's famous role at the Lyric Theater in New York City at the time, so Scott would have had to travel there to see the show.[15]

The first mention of Princeton University in Fitzgerald's ledger occurs in a February 1908 entry. Although Scott indicated he had attended a performance by the Princeton Glee Club with his mother and Inky that month, this may have been one of the few times Fitzgerald's memory was incorrect, since there is no newspaper evidence that the Princeton Glee Club performed in Buffalo that year. It is more likely the trio was in the audience at an April 18, 1908, performance in Buffalo's Star Theater of Princeton Triangle Club's *When Congress Went to Princeton.* The show made stops in Cleveland, Indianapolis, and Chicago as well as Buffalo during Easter Break in 1908.[16] The events depicted occurred in Princeton at the close of the Revolutionary War when Congress was holding its sessions at Nassau Hall. And, just as he would do after he relocated to St. Paul, Fitzgerald created costume dramas in his friends' attics. In

Buffalo, he and Inky based their production on the American Revolution.[17] Fitzgerald's scrapbooks from about this time include a fuzzy picture of Fitzgerald wearing a tricorne hat—all clear clues that he and Inky took in *When Congress Went to Princeton* rather than a Glee Club performance, since he and Inky would have been delighted to see the Triangle Club's take on the end of the American Revolution. What role his introduction to the Princeton Triangle Club played in his decision to attend Princeton is uncertain, but it probably appeared on his list of reasons.

Back to St. Paul

Midway through 1908, the Fitzgeralds gave up on Buffalo and returned to St. Paul. Mollie Fitzgerald (and presumably Edward Fitzgerald) stayed with their friends the Fultons on Summit Avenue, St. Paul's equivalent of Buffalo's Millionaires' Row.[18] The Fultons' daughter, Laura, would befriend Scott's sister, Annabel, who lived with Scott and Grandmother Louisa McQuillan a couple blocks away at 294 Laurel Avenue.

That first summer back in St. Paul, Fitzgerald met several children who resided on or near Summit Avenue. Many became close friends, some for the rest of his life. Samuel D. Sturgis lived at 123 Nina Avenue, in the same line of row houses but around the corner from Fitzgerald's grandmother. Sturgis's father, also Samuel D. Sturgis, was a major in the U.S. Army and was stationed at Fort Snelling.[19] Sam's grandfather, also Samuel D. Sturgis, achieved the rank of brevet major general in the regular army during the American Civil War, one of Fitzgerald's favorite subjects.[20]

Across the street from the Fultons lived Arthur Foley. Born a year before Fitzgerald, he grew up in a four-story Victorian mansion next to James J. "Empire Builder" Hill's house on Summit Avenue. Despite later being spoofed by Fitzgerald in a comic newspaper, Foley's older brother, Frederick Foley, would go on to invent the balloon catheter, which is often called a Foley.

In the row house next to Grandmother McQuillan lived Roscoe Hersey, whose niece Marie Hersey would become one of Fitzgerald's greatest friends. Roscoe's daughter Eva married Dan Mudge, and the Mudges were living at Roscoe's Laurel Avenue property when Scott moved next door. Scott mentions "walking the fence" with the Mudges' daughter, Betty, who later would be a member of Scott's dance class and an actress in one of the juvenile plays Scott wrote for the Elizabethan

Dramatic Club between 1911 and 1914.[21] Fitzgerald once spanked one of the Mudges' sons, Archie, for telling a lie.[22]

A Lock of Red Hair: Violet Stockton

Other Summit Avenue friends included John L. "Jack" Mitchell and his sister, Eleanor. They lived with their brother, Raymond, and father, bank president John R. Mitchell, at 251 Summit Avenue. Jack performed in a couple of the plays Fitzgerald wrote, and Eleanor was in Scott's 1910 dancing class.

Although esteemed Fitzgerald biographer Matthew J. Bruccoli described Violet as a "Southern girl visiting the Finches on Summit Avenue in the summer of 1910,"[23] and Fitzgerald's friend and biographer Andrew Turnbull called her "a summer visitor from Atlanta,"[24] she actually hailed from New Jersey, and the events recorded in Fitzgerald's *Thoughtbook* about Violet occurred in the summer of 1908. Fitzgerald indicated that Violet "spoke with a soft southern accent leaving out the r's,"[25] but that would have been more of the East Coast "pahk the cahr" variety of leaving out the r's than an accent from the South. Violet's father, Richard Stockton, the U.S. consul to Rotterdam, married Clemence Finch in St. Paul on January 19, 1887. Because Clemence's father, George Finch, was president of the first St. Paul Winter Carnival, Clemence laid the cornerstone of St. Paul's first Ice Palace, which opened to the public in February 1886 and was among the inspirations for Fitzgerald's short story "The Ice Palace."[26]

No doubt young Scott Fitzgerald was as pleased with Violet's appearance as he was with her pedigree. She was described as "petite and dainty and, in coloring, an attractive brunette" in the *Trenton Evening Times* when she came out to society on December 6, 1912.[27] With good looks and unimpeachable family connections, Violet made a deep impression on Scott. Because some of his Basil and Josephine stories are set at the same time as episodes involving Violet covered by the *Thoughtbook*, it's possible Scott drew part of the portrait of Ermine Gilberte Labouisee Bibble (Minnie)—a popular New Orleans girl who is in St. Paul visiting a cousin—from his encounter with Violet. The reference to New Orleans may have originated with the fact that Sara Marks, Violet's paternal grandmother, hailed from the Crescent City. In 1845, at the age of sixteen, Marks married nineteen-year-old John Potter Stockton in New Orleans.[28]

In "He Thinks He's Wonderful," Basil puts Minnie's age at fifteen,

A photograph of Violet Stockton published in the St. Paul papers after her marriage to Charles Ashley Voorhees. *St. Paul Pioneer Press,* October 3, 1915.

although Violet would have actually been fourteen when she first met Scott. The writer's biggest clue about Minnie's identity occurs in the line "Her head had reminded otherwise not illiterate young men of damp blue violets."[29] Due in part to a stubborn, self-centered streak, Scott lost

Violet to a rival, just as Basil loses Minnie because (as the story title confirms) "He Thinks He's Wonderful." At the end of the *Thoughtbook* section on Violet, Scott is downtrodden, writing, "Not much has happened since Violet went away."[30]

Basil is also disconsolate in "He Thinks He's Wonderful" after Minnie leaves for Glacier National Park. In both the *Thoughtbook* and the short story, however, new girls come into the picture. Unfortunately for Basil's heart, he runs into Minnie again in the story "Forging Ahead" after he first sees her younger sister, an episode Scott refers to in his ledger in July 1908 with a comment about "Little Ellen Stockton," Violet's younger sister.[31] How much time, if any, Scott spent with Violet after 1908 is open to debate. An invitation to a party at Ivy Tower is pasted in Scott's scrapbooks at Princeton. It reads: "Mr. and Mrs. Richard Stockton / Miss Stockton / will be home / on Friday the sixth of December / from four until six o'clock." Next to it is a lock of reddish hair, and underneath, written in Scott's hand, is "Violet—and 7 years after."[32] Since the only year close to 1908 for which December 6 falls on a Friday is 1912, that is probably the date of the invitation. Scott was boarding at Newman School in New Jersey at the time, so it's possible he made the trip to Trenton for the open house.

Soon after returning to Trenton following a trip to St. Paul during the fall of 1915, Violet married Charles Ashley Voorhees.[33] Immediately after the wedding, Violet and Charles moved to Florida, where he eventually became a contractor.[34] On October 29, 1917, the *Trenton Evening Times* reported, "Mrs. Charles Ashley Voorhees, formerly Miss Violet Stockton, daughter of Mr. and Mrs. Richard Stockton, of Ivy Tower Greenwood Avenue" had arrived at her parents' home from Orlando, Florida, two days earlier for a weeks-long visit but would be returning south before Christmas.[35]

The next month, on November 14, Scott wrote a letter to his mother from Princeton's Cottage Club, where he was staying while waiting to receive his military orders. In it he stated, "Went down to see Ellen Stockton in Trenton the other night. She is a perfect beauty."[36] Had Violet still been visiting, it would seem natural that Scott would have mentioned her, but he didn't. Nonetheless, throughout the remainder of his life, Violet continued to pop into Fitzgerald's consciousness. On a couple of occasions in the mid-1930s, he checked into the Oak Hall Hotel in Tryon, North Carolina, out of concern for his tubercular lungs. On a pamphlet advertising Tryon's resorts, Fitzgerald wrote a dozen or so names in a shaky hand; among those recognizable are Mudge, Donahoe, Shepley, and Violet.[37] In the last year of his life, Scott created a list labeled "Fixations," mostly girls and women who had turned his head. At the end of the list, he included "Nancy, Kitty, Violet?"[38]

Frontenac and "The Diamond"

In April 1909, Grandmother McQuillan went abroad, so Scott's parents moved into her house.[39] They had been living a few blocks away at the Aberdeen Hotel since the previous September. That June, Scott remained active, playing baseball and riding his bike to Hastings, Minnesota, with his Summit Avenue friend Wharton Smith. The twenty-mile ride was probably undertaken to cruise around the spiral of Hastings's Mississippi River bridge, which was already a tourist attraction at the time.[40]

Later in the summer, Scott and Annabel vacationed in the resort town of Old Frontenac, Minnesota. Made popular by James J. Hill and the Reverend Henry Ward Beecher, the town was located on a wide spot in the Mississippi River sixty miles south of St. Paul. Scott signed the ledger of the Frontenac Inn on July 27, 1909. A postcard view of the inn is affixed in his Scrapbook 7 at Princeton.

Soon after he arrived in Frontenac, Scott met Evelyn Stuart Garrard and once more fell hard. Like Violet, she was older than he and had noteworthy credentials. Her grandfather, Brigadier General (Bvt.) Israel Garrard, had helped found Frontenac and had eventually come to own several thousand acres along the river. Her great-grandfather, James Garrard, was a governor of Kentucky, and her grandmother was a descendant of Israel Ludlow, one of the original owners of the site of Cincinnati, Ohio.[41]

Evelyn and her family lived in one of the large Victorian houses that overlooked the inn. Given Fitzgerald's amazing memory and his predilection to ask questions, he may have learned enough about the Garrard family from Evelyn to fill in the biographies of the Washington family in "The Diamond as Big as the Ritz." Like Garrard, Colonel Fitz-Norman Culpepper Washington comes from a southern state (Kentucky and Virginia, respectively) to a western state (Minnesota and Montana, respectively). They both establish mining operations (limestone and diamonds, respectively).

Garrard's son, George Wood Garrard, took over the family estate after the death of the general in 1901. Washington's son, Braddock, in-

Evelyn Stuart Garrard in the St. Paul society pages. *St. Paul Pioneer Press,*
April 18, 1915.

herits the diamond mine after the death of his father in 1900. To keep
his property secluded, Colonel Washington has a river diverted. To keep
his property pristine, General Garrard had a railroad redirected. Both
sons had three children. The only thing Braddock feared was airplanes.
Interestingly, General Garrard's brother Jeptha experimented with the
making of heavier-than-air craft on the general's property. The general
preferred sailboats, and he named his favorite *Daisy.* In the short story,
the sister of the heroine wants to come out in London. In real life, Evelyn's
sister married a British army major and moved to London.[42]

Since the Garrards traveled to St. Paul regularly, it's difficult to know how often Evelyn and Scott saw one another, but when he visited the Garrards again in June 1913, he noted in his ledger: "I love her—oh—oh—oh."[43] Her son, Stuart Beck, remembered his mother talking about F. Scott Fitzgerald. "They obviously had something going on," he said.[44]

Another youngster Fitzgerald socialized with in Frontenac during the summer of 1909 was Billy Webster Jr. By the spring of 1922, Billy had taken over the family laundry business and was appearing as "Frisco Billy" in the St. Paul Junior League Show that Fitzgerald had helped write and direct.[45] Fitzgerald may have been thinking about Billy later that summer when he based the wealth of Dexter in "Winter Dreams" on a laundry business.

Another of the Frontenac gang was Billy Butler, whose father, Pierce Butler, represented James J. Hill's Great Northern Railroad in litigation and was named to the U.S. Supreme Court in 1922. Published posthumously in *Esquire,* the Fitzgerald story "Three Hours between Planes" revolves around name confusion among children at Frontenac. Perhaps Fitzgerald was musing about the two Billys when he wrote it. "Oh, yes. It was at Frontenac," the main female character says to a man whom she is confusing with another with the same first name, "the summer we—we used to go to the cave."[46] In-Yan-Teopa, the old "Indian cave" at Frontenac, was the subject of nighttime ghost stories and one of the favorite hangouts of the children who populated Frontenac.[47]

Duluth and a Nascent Gatsby

From Frontenac, Fitzgerald traveled with his mother and sister north to Duluth in order to catch a Great Lakes passenger steamer for a return visit to Buffalo.[48] The Fitzgeralds arrived just in time for Venetian Night, a large gathering sponsored by the Duluth Boat Club on the evening of August 9.[49] The festivities included a line of "140 canoes, rowboats, and sailboats ablaze with Japanese lanterns" that paraded around the *Alvina,* Thomas F. Cole's pleasure yacht.[50] One of Fitzgerald's acquaintances, Bob Kerr, told him about rowing out to help a yacht owner from Long Island Sound; Fitzgerald transferred the story to Lake Superior in *The Great Gatsby* and also provided Dan Cody with many of Cole's attributes in the novel: "Cody was fifty years old then, a product of the Nevada silver fields. . . . Transactions in Montana copper . . . made him many times a millionaire."[51] Cole was forty-seven when Fitzgerald visited Duluth that summer; he owned mining interests in Nevada; and he was president of a copper company in North Butte, Montana, which became famous for its bonanza ore.

Thomas Cole's daughter Elcey occasionally socialized in the same circles as Scott at the White Bear Yacht Club just north of St. Paul.[52] No proof exists that Fitzgerald gleaned information about her father from Elcey, but Fitzgerald did give Cody's yacht a name, *Tuolumee,* similar to the name of one of Cole's Montana copper holdings: Tuolumne.[53]

New Home

September 1909 proved to be an important month. For the first time in more than a year, Scott's nuclear family rented their own home at 514 Holly Avenue. As Scott started his second year at St. Paul Academy, his first published story, which he had written the previous June, was published in the academy's magazine, *Now and Then.* "The Mystery of the

Thomas F. Cole was a media darling during the early 1900s. *Los Angeles Times,* February 7, 1906.

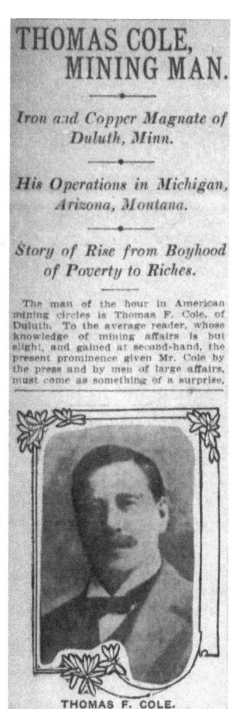

THOMAS COLE, MINING MAN.

Iron and Copper Magnate of Duluth, Minn.

His Operations in Michigan, Arizona, Montana.

Story of Rise from Boyhood of Poverty to Riches.

The man of the hour in American mining circles is Thomas F. Cole, of Duluth. To the average reader, whose knowledge of mining affairs is but slight, and gained at second-hand, the present prominence given Mr. Cole by the press and by men of large affairs, must come as something of a surprise,

THOMAS F. COLE.

Scott's bedroom at 514 Holly Avenue, St. Paul.

Raymond Mortgage" never resolves the mystery of the missing mortgage, but its publication thrilled the nascent author:

> Never will I forget the Monday morning the numbers came out. The previous Saturday I had loitered desperately around the print-

ers down-town and driven the man to indignation by persisting
in trying to get a copy when the covers had not been bound on—
finally, I had gone away and almost in tears. Nothing interested
me until Monday, and when at recess, a big pile of the copies were
brought in and delivered to the business manager I was so excited
that I bounced in my seat and mumbled to myself, "They're here!
They're here!" until the whole school looked at me in amazement.
I read my story through at least six times, and all that day I loitered
in the corridors and counted the number of men who were reading
it, and tried to ask people, casually, "if they had read it?"[54]

Continuing his interest in football, Fitzgerald played for Art Foley's team
in pick-up games and followed the career of University of Minnesota
quarterback John McGovern, who was named an All-American by *Look*
magazine in 1909.[55]

In December Scott had dancing lessons with Professor William H.
Baker. Janey Ingersoll, the mother of one of Scott's friends, organized
the classes and invited Scott to join because she "liked him."[56] Mollie responded positively, and Scott began spending his Saturday afternoons
at Ramaley School of Dance on Grand Avenue. Baker was a pear-shaped
little man with a bald dome and a gray-white mustache. Moonlighting as
a bartender at the White Bear Yacht Club, he frequently smelled slightly of
spirits, but he was "light on his feet," the students acknowledged. While
some enjoyed the lessons, others were not so happy. Philip Stringer, one
of Scott's classmates, recalled, "The dancing lessons lasted all of Saturday
afternoons and completely ruined our Saturdays. After going to school
all week, the only day we had to ourselves was Saturday, and it had to
be wasted learning the Grand March."[57] Not surprisingly for someone
who so easily gave his heart away, Scott ended the year on an enigmatic
romantic note, sneaking off a half dozen blocks to Gerber's Dry Goods
and Notions at 368 Selby Avenue to purchase "a return present for the
unexpected one."[58]

NOTES

1. F. Scott Fitzgerald, *F. Scott Fitzgerald's Ledger: A Facsimile,* introduction by
Matthew J. Bruccoli (Washington, D.C.: NCR/Microcard Editions / Bruccoli Clark,
1972), 162.

2. Michel Mok, "The Other Side of Paradise: Scott Fitzgerald, 40, Engulfed in

Despair," in *Conversations with F. Scott Fitzgerald*, ed. Matthew J. Bruccoli and Judith S. Baughman (Jackson: University Press of Mississippi, 2004), 122.

3. Fitzgerald, *Ledger*, 162.

4. F. Scott Fitzgerald, "A Freeze-Out," in *A Change of Class*, ed. James L. W. West III, Cambridge Edition of the Works of F. Scott Fitzgerald (Cambridge: Cambridge University Press, 2022), 41.

5. *Memorial and Family History of Erie County, New York*, vol. 2, *Biographical and Genealogical* (Buffalo, N.Y.: Genealogical Publishing Company, 1906–8), 88.

6. When Mary Hill (railroad tycoon James J. Hill's wife and a good friend of Mollie Fitzgerald's sister Annabel McQuillan) traveled to Buffalo in 1908, she noted in her diary for September 6: "Mollie McQuillan is in Buffalo at the Lenox." "Mary T. Hill Diary: 1898," accessed October 8, 2014. http://www2.mnhs.org/library /findaids/00718/pdf/00718_MTH1898.pdf.

7. Fitzgerald, *Ledger*, 162. "Early Days of the New Year Filled to the Brim with Gaiety," *Buffalo Courier*, January 2, 1908.

8. Seymour Knox II is listed in the census as Earl. Earl's son, Seymour H. Knox III, helped organize the Buffalo Sabres hockey team.

9. Fitzgerald, *Ledger*, 162.

10. F. Scott Fitzgerald, *Thoughtbook*, in *Last Kiss*, ed. James L. W. West III, Cambridge Edition of the Works of F. Scott Fitzgerald (Cambridge: Cambridge University Press, 2022), 4.

11. Fitzgerald, *Ledger*, 162.

12. Fitzgerald, *Thoughtbook*, 5.

13. A local amateur athletic star, Gowans earned mention in a book covering the first forty years of U.S. tennis history. Roger W. Ohnsorg, *Robert Lindley Murray: The Reluctant U.S. Tennis Champion* (Bloomington, Ind.: Trafford, 2011), 212.

14. Fitzgerald, *Ledger*, 162.

15. "Theatrical Attractions in the Metropolis," *Buffalo Sunday Morning News*, January 19, 1908.

16. "Princeton Triangle Club," *Buffalo Enquirer*, March 23, 1908.

17. Fitzgerald, *Ledger*, 161.

18. Fitzgerald, *Ledger*, 162.

19. *War Department Annual Reports, 1911*, vol. 3 (Washington, D.C.: Government Printing Office, 1912), 84.

20. The South Dakota town that hosts the famous motorcycle rally is named for the eldest Sturgis.

21. Fitzgerald, *Ledger*, 162.

22. Fitzgerald, *Thoughtbook*, 8.

23. Matthew J. Bruccoli, *Some Sort of Epic Grandeur: The Life of F. Scott Fitzgerald* (New York: Harcourt, Brace, and Jovanovich, 1981), 29.

24. Andrew Turnbull, *Scott Fitzgerald* (New York: Charles Scribner's Sons, 1962), 19.

25. Fitzgerald, *Thoughtbook*, 6.

26. Christina H. Jacobsen, "The Burbank–Livingston–Griggs House: Historic Treasure on Summit Avenue," *Minnesota History* 42, no. 1 (Spring 1970): 27.

27. "Miss Stockton Introduced at Violet Reception," *Trenton Evening Times*, December 6, 1912.

28. "Sara Marks," Henigan Family Tree, Ancestry.com, accessed July 21, 2019. https://www.ancestry.com/family-tree/person/tree/10365067/person/24103350994 /facts.

29. F. Scott Fitzgerald, *The Basil, Josephine, and Gwen Stories*, ed. James L. W. West III, Cambridge Edition of the Works of F. Scott Fitzgerald (Cambridge: Cambridge University Press, 2009), 92.

30. Fitzgerald, *Thoughtbook*, 12.

31. Fitzgerald, *Ledger*, 162.

32. F. Scott Fitzgerald, "F. Scott Fitzgerald Scrapbooks," *Princeton University Digital Library*, 19, accessed July 21, 2019. https://findingaids.princeton.edu/catalog /C0187_c03405.

33. George Norbury MacKenzie, ed., *Colonial Families of the United States of America*, vol. 6 (Baltimore, Md.: Seaforth Press, 1917), 435.

34. "1920 Census Place: Pine Castle, Orange, Florida," roll T625_228; page 8A; enumeration district: 123; image 999. www.ancestry.com.

35. "Personal Mention," *Trenton Evening Times*, October 29, 1917.

36. F. Scott Fitzgerald, *The Letters of F. Scott Fitzgerald*, ed. Andrew Turnbull (New York: Charles Scribner's Sons, 1963), 451.

37. "Series 3: Documents; 1926–1931," F. Scott Fitzgerald Papers, box 55, folder 24, Manuscripts Division, Department of Rare Books and Special Collections, Princeton University Library.

38. "Subseries 1N: Notes; 1930 April–June," F. Scott Fitzgerald Papers, box 37, folder 14, Manuscripts Division, Department of Rare Books and Special Collections, Princeton University Library.

39. Fitzgerald, *Ledger*, 163.

40. Dave Page, *F. Scott Fitzgerald in Minnesota: The Writer and His Friends at Home* (St. Paul, Minn.: Fitzgerald in St. Paul / University of Minnesota Press, 2017), 45.

41. Frances Densmore, "The Garrard Family in Frontenac," *Minnesota History*, March 1933, 32. collections.mnhs.org/MNHistoryMagazine/articles/14/v14i01p031 -043.pdf.

42. Densmore, "Garrard Family," 43.

43. Fitzgerald, *Ledger*, 167.

44. Stuart Beck, telephone interview with author, August 28, 1996.

45. Page, *Fitzgerald in Minnesota*, 254.

46. F. Scott Fitzgerald, "Three Hours between Planes," in *The Lost Decade: Short Stories from* Esquire, *1936–1941*, ed. James L. W. West III, Cambridge Edition of the Works of F. Scott Fitzgerald (Cambridge: Cambridge University Press, 2014), 81.

47. Page, *Fitzgerald in Minnesota*, 244.

48. Fitzgerald, *Ledger*, 163.

49. Fitzgerald placed his trip to Buffalo during the month of July, but we know from several sources he did not make it to Duluth until August.

50. "Thousands Enjoy Water Spectacle," *Duluth News Tribune*, August 10, 1909.

51. Dave Page and John Koblas, *F. Scott Fitzgerald in Minnesota: Toward the Summit* (St. Cloud, Minn.: North Star Press, 1996), 41.

52. "Miss Cole Honored Guest," *St. Paul Daily News*, August 27, 1913.

53. Since the Tuolumne River (San Francisco's main water source), after which the mine is probably named, is pronounced Twal-oo-mee, Fitzgerald may have spelled

it in *The Great Gatsby* the way he heard it, either from Cole's daughter Elcey or from his neighbor Stuart Shotwell, an owner of Tuolumne Mining shares. The Fitzgeralds moved into Shotwell's house after his death in the summer of 1910. Edward Fitzgerald was one of the pallbearers at Shotwell's funeral. "Miss Cole Honored Guest"; "Girl Autoist Kills Broker," *St. Paul Pioneer Press,* May 23, 1910; "Won't Sue Miss Stark," *St. Paul Dispatch,* May 24, 1910.

54. Quoted in Turnbull, *Fitzgerald,* 28–29.

55. Fitzgerald, *Ledger,* 164.

56. Page and Koblas, *Fitzgerald,* 51.

57. Quoted in Page and Koblas, *Fitzgerald,* 52.

58. Fitzgerald, *Ledger,* 164.

1910–1911

Sara Kosiba

F. Scott Fitzgerald sums up January 1910 in his ledger with the words "Bert Egbertson boxing. Bob-rides. Sliding. Skeeing. Praying. Saving up Now I Lay Mes."[1] For July 1910 he recalled, "Went to Grandma's. Fussed about dog. . . . ate vegetables for Aunt Annabel."[2] Fitzgerald was a thirteen-year-old student at St. Paul Academy, actively socializing with neighborhood kids, and a participant in a dancing school he entered in September 1908. Among this litany of teenage activity, Fitzgerald was learning his early craft as a published story writer and playwright.

In September 1910, Fitzgerald entered his third, and last, year at St. Paul Academy. That month the Fitzgerald family moved from 514 Holly Avenue to an address on the opposite side of the street: an 1887 brownstone Romanesque revival townhouse at 509 Holly Avenue. A remark in his ledger indicates this move betokened the failure of Fitzgerald's father, Edward, to support his own family during this time. "Grandfather McQuillan: 'Well, if it wasn't for him where would we be now."[3] While Edward's stagnating career was ameliorated by Grandfather McQuillan's fiscal prosperity, Edward's son was forging a path of his own. Scott's first published work, "The Mystery of the Raymond Mortgage," a murder mystery involving a curious newspaper reporter and a rather inept chief of police, was published in St. Paul Academy's student magazine *Now and Then* in October 1909. On the strength of this initial coup, Fitzgerald "became an inveterate author and a successful, not to say brilliant debater and writer."[4]

He followed that early success with two other publications in the same periodical: "Reade, Substitute Right Half" in February 1910 and "A Debt of Honor" in March 1910.[5] "Reade, Substitute Right Half" shows Fitzgerald's early interest in football and presents a romanticized glory that comes with victory, as Reade, a "light haired stripling" and rather unlikely athletic star, makes an impressive touchdown by the end of the story.[6] "A Debt of Honor" similarly romanticizes glory and sacrifice through the tale of a Confederate soldier who atones for an earlier error

The title of "The Mystery of the Raymond Mortgage," Fitzgerald's first published story.

by rushing into battle to capture an enemy location, forfeiting his life in the process. While neither story is particularly noteworthy for its narrative or characterization, they both contain the basic theme of desiring recognition for accomplishments, a theme that Fitzgerald often embodied in his own life and future writing.

In August 1911 Fitzgerald's first play, *The Girl from Lazy J,* was performed at the St. Paul home of Elizabeth Magoffin. This farce was the first of four Fitzgerald dramas performed by the St. Paul Elizabethan Dramatic Club between 1911 and 1914 and acted as a harbinger of the success Fitzgerald would later achieve as an author of lyrics for the Princeton Triangle Club performances. In September 1911, the family moved yet again to another house, 499 Holly Avenue, after which Fitzgerald left to begin his two-year period at the Catholic preparatory Newman School in New Jersey.

Fitzgerald's juvenilia shows glimpses of the talent that expanded and deepened with age. These early literary productions are clearly juvenile in their composition. However, in addition to his early published works, Fitzgerald was sketching down material in his childhood diary, the *Thoughtbook,* a series of vignettes he added to from August 1910 to February 1911. Virtually all of this short document is devoted to cataloging his and his friends' social and romantic status. For example: "Alida Bigelow is the most popular girl I know of. I know five boys who like her best. These are the girls and boys I like best in order."[7] Such keen at-

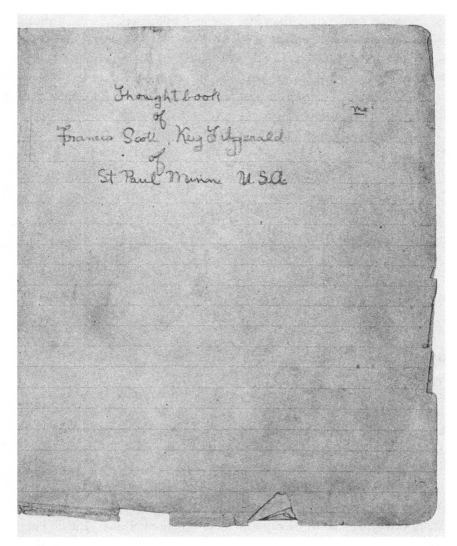

First page of Fitzgerald's *Thoughtbook*.

tention to hierarchy and communal standing colors "Reade, Substitute Right Half" and "A Debt of Honor" and would carry through to the acute social one-upmanship of Princeton in *This Side of Paradise*.

Fitzgerald had published three stories by the time he began the *Thoughtbook* in August 1910, yet the "inveterate author" is focused solely on the social scene among his St. Paul cohort. As Dave Page notes, "Fitzgerald clearly showed at a young age that his best fiction would develop from the 'personal note' rather than any 'literary' influences. . . . Fitzgerald's talents lay in the interweaving of his own experiences into the warp and woof of his fiction."[8] A sense of close emotional connection to his material would be central to the passion and vitality of Fitzgerald's work. In the *Thoughtbook* Fitzgerald was already narrativizing important personal material. Chronicling his youthful romance with Violet Stockton, Fitzgerald corrects himself for making an aside concerning "a game called Indians which I made up" by noting "However, I am getting from my story."[9] He chose to record the following dialogue with Violet:

> "Violet," I began, "Did you call me a brat."
> "No."
> "Did you say that you wanted your ring and your picture and your hair back."
> "No."
> "Did you say that you hated me"
> "Of course not."[10]

For all its callow triviality, the exchange thrills with charged emotion because of the (genuine, if immature) intensity with which it was experienced at the time. Fitzgerald concluded this section with a single line: "And that is the story of Violet Stockton."[11] A clumsily conventional finale, to be sure, but enough to indicate Fitzgerald was consciously converting emotional experience into literary narrative.

Page notes of the Stockton passage that it contains "the kind of dialogue that fills the pages of Fitzgerald's novels,"[12] suggesting that Fitzgerald was using real-life experiences to work out what would translate to print and that those experiments were foundational. The St. Paul world imprinted upon him and formed the foundations of Fitzgerald's literary career, and he drew on aspects of the *Thoughtbook,* in particular, in later stories such as "The Scandal Detectives" and "Some Kind of Wonderful," both set in a fictionalized St. Paul and starring the character of Basil Duke Lee. Basil, often a stand-in for a youthful Fitzgerald, agonizes over adolescent interactions and is keenly aware of neighborhood dynamics.

Many Fitzgerald biographers note his father's propensity for storytelling, and Fitzgerald wrote about his mother's love of Ohio poets Alice and Phoebe Cary in "An Author's Mother."[13] Other literary influences were also not far away during Fitzgerald's childhood. The local novelist Grace Hodgson Flandrau—who in 1909 married William (who went by the name Blair) Flandrau, the son of a local dignitary, Judge Charles E. Flandrau Sr.—mentored Fitzgerald in late 1919, after Scribner's accepted *This Side of Paradise* (published 1920). She recommended him to the Paul Revere Reynolds Agency and advised him about the value of selling movie rights to his fiction.[14] Grace Flandrau's early works, including *Miss Julia* (1917) and *Being Respectable* (1923), focused on characters in St. Paul. Fitzgerald reviewed *Being Respectable,* and while he noted some shortcomings in structure, he declared the book "a thoroughly interesting and capable novel" and better than Sinclair Lewis's *Babbitt* (1922). He also jokingly observed that with works like those by Lewis and Flandrau, "Sauk Center, Minneapolis, and St. Paul have been flayed in turn by the State's own sons and daughters. I feel that I ought to take up the matter of Duluth and make the thing complete."[15] The nearby influences of successful writers who used their surroundings as literary inspiration and material probably encouraged young Fitzgerald's own literary ambitions.

As much as Fitzgerald was writing in and about St. Paul at a young age (at least through the *Thoughtbook*), he avoided using much of that local material in his early fiction. There are limited references to the Midwest or to St. Paul in his juvenilia and in his writing at Princeton. Other than two pieces in the 1917 *Nassau Literary Magazine* (a review of Booth Tarkington's *Penrod and Sam* in January and a short story, "Babes in the Woods," in May) that had connections to the Midwest (with no real focus on the region in the literature itself), his writing more often focused on East Coast locales or more exotic, dramatized settings. Matthew J. Bruccoli notes that "Babes in the Woods" has some midwestern influence as it is based on "Fitzgerald's meeting with Ginevra King in St. Paul," but other than some scenes taking place during winter, no other details necessarily make it a definitively midwestern narrative.[16] "The Camel's Back" (1920) is also a St. Paul tale with no distinctive references to that locale. The story has midwestern location, with its Toledo, Ohio, setting, but Page describes the way the tale was influenced by a costume party at Louis Hill's home on Summit Avenue in St. Paul.[17] Some of this failure to use familiar material from his St. Paul days in more concentrated ways in the early years could be due to Fitzgerald's desire to construct an image for himself that transcended his adolescent struggle with feeling "within and without an exclusive social enclave," as so many critics have

Fifteen-year-old Fitzgerald at the Newman School

ascribed to Fitzgerald's literary motivations.[18] Bruccoli, for instance, argues, "Once he was away at school, Fitzgerald gradually stopped thinking of himself as a Midwesterner," and yet he felt the "emotional pull" of the region.[19]

Revisiting the Past? The Midwest in Fitzgerald's Mature Fiction

Even with limited focus on the Midwest in his early career, looking at the breadth of Fitzgerald's work it is clear that he felt drawn to midwestern material and regional influence throughout his life, despite spending more time living outside the region than in it. Barry Gross notes, "Fitzgerald spent about seven of his first twenty-six years in the Midwest—two of them years of infancy and only two of them adult years."[20] However, he returned to the region again and again in his later writing and reflections, showing how foundational those midwestern experiences were. Edmund Wilson wrote in 1922 in the *Bookman* that Fitzgerald

> comes from the middle west—from St. Paul, Minnesota. Fitzgerald is as much of the middle west of large cities and country clubs as [Sinclair] Lewis is of the middle west of the prairies and little towns. What we find in him is much what we find in the prosperous strata of these cities: sensitivity and eagerness for life without a sound base of culture and taste. . . . And it seems to me a great pity that he has not written more of the west: it is perhaps the only milieu that he thoroughly understands.[21]

Wilson's comments were not necessarily complimentary, but he astutely acknowledges the impact the region had on Fitzgerald. While the author's early published stories deal with midwestern spaces only more tangentially, the region's continual recurrence in Fitzgerald's work demonstrates its considerable influence on him and his career.

The Midwest takes on a more prominent and overt role in Fitzgerald's fiction starting with "The Ice Palace" (1920). Amid the youthful interactions in this story, Fitzgerald makes distinctions between the South and the North, distinctions he admitted were drawn from his knowledge of St. Paul and Montgomery, Alabama.[22] In the story, Harry Bellamy tries to contextualize life in the North for Sally Carrol Happer after she arrives, and he explains that she needs to remember "this is a three-generation town. Everybody has a father, and about half of us have grandfathers. Back of that we don't go."[23] Fitzgerald reaffirmed the importance of local generational depth three years later in his review of Flandrau's *Being Respectable,* explaining that "St. Paul, although a bloodbrother of Indianapolis, Minneapolis, Kansas City, Milwaukee and Co., feels itself a little superior to the others. It is a 'three generation' town, while the others boast but two."[24] Fitzgerald felt that imprint of place from all his time on Summit Avenue in St. Paul, surrounded by houses built by "lumber barons, transportation tycoons, and wholesalers," and he watched the ebb and flow of that generational wealth and success.[25]

The material that connects most directly to Fitzgerald's 1910–11 experiences in St. Paul are the Basil Duke Lee stories, which were not written until the late 1920s. Basil's escapades are based on Fitzgerald's own life, albeit adjusted and dramatized for greater effect. The first of the tales, "The Scandal Detectives," appeared in the *Saturday Evening Post* in April 1928, and the details are drawn from the adolescent clubs Fitzgerald wrote about in the *Thoughtbook.* Basil's adolescent escapades are simultaneously juvenile and profound, revealing a thoughtfulness in Fitzgerald's writing that can come only with the passage of time and the reflection that allows. The introductory ruminations to "The Scandal Detectives" show Fitzgerald was still reflecting on the significance of St. Paul as a "three generation town" and what that meant:

> Some generations are close to that which succeed them; between others the gap is infinite and unbridgeable. Mrs. Buckner—a woman of character, a member of Society in a large Middle-Western city—carrying a pitcher of fruit lemonade through her own spacious backyard, was progressing across a hundred years. Her own thoughts would have been comprehensible to her great-grandmother; what was happening in a room above the stable would have been entirely unintelligible to them both.[26]

Fitzgerald describes a generational transformation taking place, one that elicited widespread nostalgia for midwestern ways. However, his handling of it was more complex than a mere reflection of the movement from farm to city, for example. As much as something is gained, something is also lost or irrevocably changed, and Basil's final reflection in the story, "His face was turned without regret toward the boundless possibilities of summer," highlights a choice between regret for the past and turning toward the future.[27]

The Midwest in *The Great Gatsby*

While the character of Amory Blaine in *This Side of Paradise* emerges from the Midwest, the book is not the most distinctive of midwestern novels, and therefore it is unfortunate that critic Carl Van Doren later included it in a Contemporary American Novelists column in *The Nation* that became so confining to discussions of midwestern literature. The column, "Revolt from the Village, 1920," highlighted *This Side of Paradise* alongside other midwestern works such as Sinclair Lewis's *Main Street,* Sherwood Anderson's *Winesburg, Ohio,* E. W. Howe's *Anthology of Another Town,* and Floyd Dell's *Moon Calf,* all of which Van Doren saw as lampooning small-town life. In his eyes, the appearance of all those novels focusing on small-town critique in such a short span of time constituted a literary trend of revolt, as books like *Main Street* demonstrate that "the villages of the Middle West . . . have been conquered and converted by the legions of mediocrity."[28]

The dichotomy identified by Van Doren is very much in evidence in *The Great Gatsby* (1925), Fitzgerald's most significant midwestern novel— particularly as protagonist Nick Carraway declares the tale is "a story of the West, after all."[29] The novel begins with Nick describing his family's credentials as "prominent, well-to-do people in this middlewestern city for three generations" (reminiscent of the 1923 comments Fitzgerald made about St. Paul being a "three generation town").[30] *The Great Gatsby* is very much a story grounded in youth, as most of the characters (Daisy, Nick, Gatsby) start out with youthful optimism about their lives and then later reflect on the ways that life has not turned out as they had hoped. We are told midway through the novel, for example, that James Gatz of North Dakota, in reinventing himself, "invented just the sort of Jay Gatsby that a seventeen-year-old boy would be likely to invent, and to this conception he was faithful to the end."[31] Despite the dissatisfaction that drove Nick from the Midwest to the East, by the end of the novel he notes that he is nonetheless tethered to his home region. Reminiscing about trains home from prep school and college, Nick lists prominent names that are reminiscent of the names Fitzgerald knew as he grew up in St. Paul (Ordway, Hersey, Schultz), and he claims that region as his own:

That's my middle-west—not the wheat or the prairies or the lost
Swede towns but the thrilling, returning trains of my youth and
the street lamps and sleigh bells in the frosty dark and the shadows
of holly wreaths thrown by lighted windows on the snow. I am part
of that, a little solemn with the feel of those long winters, a little
complacent from growing up in the Carraway house in a city where
dwellings are still called through decades by a family's name.[32]

While Fitzgerald always felt a bit of a misfit in a city like St. Paul, where a
name could convey such status, especially as the Fitzgerald family name
never achieved any level of prominence, he clearly felt the imprint of the
place, which he channels so well through Nick's reflections. That imprint
continued throughout Fitzgerald's life, to the point that he later wrote to
his friend Oscar Kalman in St. Paul that he wanted his daughter, Scottie,
to "have some sense of life in the middle-west" and "to know St. Paul."[33]
The region had been transformative to Fitzgerald's life and work, and he
wanted Scottie to have that same experience as well.

Careers Shaped by Midwestern Roots: Hemingway, Van Vechten, and Fitzgerald

Fitzgerald's impulses to use adolescent material not only to frame or
populate his fiction but also to reflect on and make sense of life was
shared by many of his contemporaries, and his fellow writers from the
Midwest similarly crafted stories that expand our understanding of the
region. For example, born in Oak Park, Illinois, Ernest Hemingway and
his family regularly traveled in the summer to their cottage on Walloon
Lake in northern Michigan, and the locale and events there shaped much
of Hemingway's fiction. Likewise, Carl Van Vechten, another friend and
contemporary of Fitzgerald, drew on his Iowa upbringing in his literary career. Van Vechten was born in Cedar Rapids, Iowa, and much like
Fitzgerald was shaped by the area as a child and adolescent but later left
the region behind for literary success and critical and cultural fame.

Fitzgerald, Hemingway, Van Vechten, and many others were influenced by the Midwest and would, in turn, shape the region's identity and
culture through their writing. Louis Bromfield captured the complexity
of that generation's relationship with place in an epigraph to his novel
The Green Bay Tree (1924):

Life is hard for our children. It isn't as simple as it was for us. Their grandfathers were pioneers and the same blood runs in their veins, only they haven't a frontier any longer. They stand . . . these children of ours . . . with their backs toward this rough-hewn middle west and their faces set toward Europe and the East and they belong to neither. They are lost somewhere between.[34]

These authors may not have spent their full career in the region or used the Midwest in their entire body of work, but it is obvious that their midwestern foundations were formative and inspired their careers as writers and artists. That inherent tension, navigating a midwestern past while also existing in the present and attempting to craft a successful literary future, exists in their writing and is essential in understanding what they wrote and who they were as people.

As a result, tracing the actual Midwest in Fitzgerald's fiction is almost beside the point, as the details of which place is evoked on which page or who formed the real-world influence for which character is actually secondary to the larger significance of what the Midwest is for Fitzgerald. Ronald Weber discusses Nick Carraway's difficulty finding a place that would function as a "warm center" or a safe and secure home—a problem paralleled and evidenced in Fitzgerald's own life by his almost constant movement from house to house or town to town—and states that the feeling stems from an ambivalent feeling toward the Midwest, part of "complex displays of within and without feelings" from which "the region's most enduring literary expressions have emerged."[35] Fitzgerald was wise to that often emotional, sometimes contradictory—and ultimately unresolved—puzzle.

In 1910–11, all of that creativity and reflection was yet in Fitzgerald's future. While penning the pages of the *Thoughtbook* and writing his early stories in St. Paul, he was beginning to shape a nascent literary career, and that career was gaining its foundations from the midwestern landscape around him. He was absorbing the legacies of the past and assessing the weight those histories placed on the future, mulling over the influence of generational evolution and its impression on modern identity. What is it to be carrying the weight of a "three generation" town? How does that balance a sense of the past with an evolving future? As Fitzgerald entered the Newman School in the fall of 1911 and began the path that led to Princeton and later literary success, he carried that midwestern complexity with him and returned to the region again and again, at times in person but always in memory, revisiting those early people and places and contemplating the accuracy of those definitions and expectations in his writing.

NOTES

1. F. Scott Fitzgerald, "Ledger, 1919–1938," Matthew J. and Arlyn Bruccoli Collection of F. Scott Fitzgerald, Digital Collections, University of South Carolina University Libraries. https://digital.tcl.sc.edu/digital/collection/fitz/id/0.

2. Fitzgerald, "Ledger," 164.

3. Fitzgerald, "Ledger," 165.

4. Fitzgerald, "Ledger," 165.

5. F. Scott Fitzgerald, *The Apprentice Fiction of F. Scott Fitzgerald,* ed. John Kuehl (New Brunswick, N.J.: Rutgers University Press, 1965), 17, 28, 35.

6. F. Scott Fitzgerald, *Spires and Gargoyles: Early Writings, 1909–1919,* ed. James L. W. West III, Cambridge Edition of the Works of F. Scott Fitzgerald (Cambridge: Cambridge University Press, 2022), 10.

7. F. Scott Fitzgerald, *The Thoughtbook of F. Scott Fitzgerald: A Secret Boyhood Diary,* ed. Dave Page (Minneapolis: University of Minnesota Press, 2013), 12–13.

8. Dave Page, "Afterword," in Fitzgerald, *Thoughtbook,* 55.

9. Fitzgerald, *Thoughtbook,* 6.

10. Fitzgerald, *Thoughtbook,* 7–8; punctuation Fitzgerald's.

11. Fitzgerald, *Thoughtbook,* 11.

12. Page, "Afterword," 55.

13. F. Scott Fitzgerald, "An Author's Mother," in *My Lost City: Personal Essays, 1920–1940,* ed. James L. W. West III, Cambridge Edition of the Works of F. Scott Fitzgerald (Cambridge: Cambridge University Press, 2014), 181.

14. Matthew J. Bruccoli, ed., *As Ever, Scott Fitz—: Letters between F. Scott Fitzgerald and His Literary Agent Harold Ober, 1910–1940,* with the assistance of Jennifer McCabe Atkinson (Philadelphia: J. B. Lippincott, 1972), 3, 6.

15. Matthew J. Bruccoli and Jackson R. Bryer, eds., *F. Scott Fitzgerald in His Own Time: A Miscellany* (Kent, Ohio: Kent State University Press, 1971), 141–42.

16. Matthew J. Bruccoli, *Some Sort of Epic Grandeur: The Life of F. Scott Fitzgerald,* 2nd ed. (Columbia: University of South Carolina Press, 2002), 68.

17. Dave Page, *F. Scott Fitzgerald in Minnesota: The Writer and His Friends at Home* (St. Paul: Fitzgerald in St. Paul / University of Minnesota Press, 2017), 30–31.

18. Davis D. Schlacks, "St. Paul, Minnesota, St. Paul Academy, and the *St. Paul Academy Now and Then,*" in *F. Scott Fitzgerald in Context,* ed. Bryant Mangum (New York: Cambridge University Press, 2013), 111.

19. Bruccoli, *Epic Grandeur,* 44–45.

20. Barry Gross, "Fitzgerald's Midwest: 'Something Gorgeous Somewhere'— Somewhere Else," *MidAmerica: The Yearbook of the Society for the Study of Midwestern Literature* 6 (1979): 113.

21. Edmund Wilson, "The Literary Spotlight: F. Scott Fitzgerald," *Bookman,* March 1922: 22.

22. F. Scott Fitzgerald, *Correspondence of F. Scott Fitzgerald,* ed. Matthew J. Bruccoli and Margaret M. Duggan (New York: Random House, 1980), 61–62.

23. F. Scott Fitzgerald, *Short Stories of F. Scott Fitzgerald,* ed. Matthew J. Bruccoli (New York: Charles Scribner's Sons, 1989), 56.

24. Bruccoli and Bryer, *Fitzgerald in His Own Time,* 141.

25. Page, *Fitzgerald in Minnesota,* 3.

26. F. Scott Fitzgerald, "The Scandal Detectives," in *The Basil, Josephine, and Gwen Stories,* ed. James L. W. West III, Cambridge Edition of the Works of F. Scott Fitzgerald (Cambridge: Cambridge University Press, 2022), 16.

27. Fitzgerald, "The Scandal Detectives," 36.

28. Carl Van Doren, "Contemporary American Novelists: Revolt from the Village, 1920," *The Nation* 113 (1921): 410.

29. F. Scott Fitzgerald, *The Great Gatsby,* ed. Matthew J. Bruccoli (Cambridge: Cambridge University Press, 1991), 137.

30. Fitzgerald, *Great Gatsby,* 6; Bruccoli, *As Ever,* 141.

31. Fitzgerald, *Great Gatsby,* 77.

32. Fitzgerald, *Great Gatsby,* 137.

33. F. Scott Fitzgerald, *The Letters of F. Scott Fitzgerald,* ed. Andrew Turnbull (New York: Charles Scribner's Sons, 1963), 432.

34. Louis Bromfield, *The Green Bay Tree* (New York: Grosset and Dunlap, 1924), epigraph.

35. Ronald Weber, *The Midwestern Ascendancy in American Writing* (Bloomington: Indiana University Press, 1992), 24.

1912–1913

Ronald Berman

In the most evidentiary terms, the years 1912–13 were a series of transitions for F. Scott Fitzgerald: his movement from the security of family and neighborhood in St. Paul to the Newman School on the East Coast; his academic and social failures at Newman; his adjustment to school regulations and student dogmas; his recognition as a personage by Monsignor Cyril Sigourney Webster Fay; and his acceptance at Princeton University.

André Le Vot's early biography states that the Newman School was Fitzgerald's entry into "the fabulous East of his reading."[1] David S. Brown's biography specifies that some of the books Fitzgerald read were a form of social romance. For Fitzgerald (and many others), a "steady diet of literary juvenilia, including the college-life narratives of C. M. Flandrau *(Harvard Episodes)* and W. J. Lynch *(Princeton Stories)*" offered examples of athletic glory and social success.[2] Horatio Alger stories, although their subject is rising through work, still mattered a great deal. The new literature promised considerably more: membership in an exclusive society. Fitzgerald read about success at Harvard and Princeton and also about the good life on Broadway. The college books generally have a plot about keeping faith with friends and ideals. They earnestly teach that respect is won through one's conduct. Many are about making a varsity team and gaining honor through sacrifice and teamwork. Broadway books describe a different but still idealized life. In Fitzgerald's Basil Duke Lee stories, the protagonist believes they show "fashion," or the upper class of New York. They also show human complexity.

The promise of the East in boys' stories was aristocracy—which had both powers and duties. In *The Great Gatsby* and "May Day," however, the East turns out to be a plutocracy. When we first meet Philip Dean in "May Day," he is polishing his body after a shower: "everything about him radiated . . . bodily comfort."[3] The new men are drunk, bored, and without empathy. They inherit wealth and understand power but not duty. The changing social world gave novelists urban characters such as the veteran returned from the war, the free woman, and the rich who

The Newman School for Boys in Hackensack, New Jersey

don't much care about that orbit around the self of community and nation. Possibly the most interesting thing about Dean and those others is their lack of social curiosity. Really, for them, truth is an inconvenience. This mindset recalls William James's statement to the contrary that, at the turn of the century, Americans "want to believe," by which he implies that there actually is a truth to find. And he says the most important thing is that the search for truth is one "in which our social system backs us up."[4] Fitzgerald seems to have adopted James's idea: we "*want* to believe." Amory Blaine says in *This Side of Paradise* that truth can be found in America's system of politics, prejudices, philosophy, and education.[5]

The Culture of American Prep Schools

In a time of economic expansion, institutions attract new money. Catholic prep schools, like their Protestant counterparts, wanted to be *haut bourgeois,* producing a certain *style* of graduate. Woodrow Wilson famously called his ideal undergrad a "Gentleman," while Protestant prep schools of that fabulous East wanted—no bones about it—to make a "Christian Gentleman" (so described by Fitzgerald in his review of educational flyers and catalogs in *This Side of Paradise*).[6] "A Catholic Boyhood" by Pearl James describes the internal conflict in Catholic education: a new bloc of consumers had appeared, the moneyed sons of immigrants who wanted entry and assimilation into the upper class. That could only be achieved by secular means, and she points out that teachers at Newman were not all clerics. Some were married. Students went to Mass once a week, and social life at Newman was much like that at a Protestant prep school. The school was also expensive and allowed wealthy families "to avoid the socioeconomic diversity of the parish school." In a dry aside, James states that wealthy Catholics wanted to pay more for exclusivity—and Newman School obliged.[7]

Even if Newman did succeed in its imitation of the Protestant American prep school, that did not mean that Fitzgerald was launched into the social world. He brought his problems with him. Matthew J. Bruccoli's *Some Sort of Epic Grandeur* cites Scott's ledger on the academic year 1911–12 that ended his first year at Newman: "A year of real unhappiness excepting the feverish joys of Xmas."[8] In the 1912 term he did badly in his exams, with the exception of ancient history. Life outside class was a constant struggle for redemption because the previous year he had managed to become the most unpopular boy at Newman. Scott, a spoiled brat at home, bullied and boasted his way to social exile when he tried to be popular at school. He wanted above all to be a football hero, but he was not big enough to take the game's pounding. Fitzgerald blamed himself for avoiding a tackle in one game and thought it a sign of bad moral character. It *was* bad social character, according to the new academic ideology of the 1910s, which insisted, in the words of James Axtell's history of Princeton, that applicants show "manhood," defined as honor, fearlessness, forcefulness, and successful "participation in athletics."[9] Axtell believes this language was "encoded," meant to encourage Protestant applicants, warn Catholics how to behave, and discourage bookish Jews who competed intellectually.

In 1912 at least some of Fitzgerald's hopes came true in this new environment. For the last time, he had some success in track and football; after that, he would never have sufficient size or weight to compete in college. He made friends. And he began to write interesting fiction and drama for the *Newman News*. "A Luckless Santa Claus," "Pain and the Scientist," and "The Trail of the Duke" all show a sharp interest in language, and they contain lines that show the condensed style of modern sensibility. Newman School allowed limited access to New York, with its theater and views of street life. Bruccoli cites certain of Scott's passages:

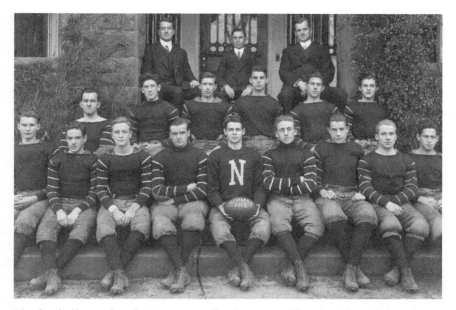

The football squad at the Newman School. Fitzgerald is third from left in the front row.

"From out [of] the night into the houses came the sweltering late summer heat. . . . In the flats that line upper New York, pianos (sweating ebony perspiration) ground out rag-time tunes of last winter and here and there a wan woman sang the air in a hot soprano."[10] Scenes with distant and unknown subjects, like that of New York, became part of his first three novels.

Bruccoli notes that Scott was uncertain about himself, willing and eager to be a hero-worshipper. At this stage, he wanted to imitate athletes; then he turned his admiration on men of letters like H. L. Mencken, Edmund Wilson, and Gerald Murphy. The appearance of Father Fay at Newman in late 1912 mattered greatly because "he was the first important person who responded to Scott" and who knew enough to be interesting.[11] Fay was more than a teacher: he had been part of the American Oxford Movement, before converting to Catholicism; he later worked at Newman and became headmaster. He liked the good life, could pay for it, and was a hard man to shock. Appearing as Monsignor Darcy in *This Side of Paradise,* he was exempt from Fitzgerald's usual deconstruction of his mentors. Darcy in the novel reflects the genuine virtues of his real-life model: looking like a Winston Churchill gone to seed, Fay was a great conversationalist, socially balanced, and fully aware that part of intellectual life was personal style. He had achieved something that eluded Fitzgerald. According to Pearl James, "Fay must have impressed Fitzgerald on many levels. He had wealth and the social assurance that came with it. He was Irish on his mother's side, like Fitzgerald, but made that heritage seem like a romantic badge of honor rather than a social demerit."[12]

Fay introduced Scott to the writer Shane Leslie, who was, Scott wrote, "a young Englishman of the governing classes" whose own life brought to mind the novels of Compton Mackenzie. Brown notes that Leslie "brought to the table all of the surnames, schools, and connections certain to impress Fitzgerald."[13] Leslie's connection to the upper classes meant a good deal to Scott because the idea of aristocracy retained exceptional power in the 1910s and 1920s. It became the great theme of H. L. Mencken, who often wrote that unalloyed democracy allowed the rule of boobs and yokels. Like Fitzgerald, he located aristocracy in the South, among "the Virginians and the older Marylanders" who retained the cultural values of the Old World.[14] Mencken theorized that America could never fulfill its promise if it were left to the middle class of the North: "Obviously, there is no aristocracy here. . . . But where is intelligence? Where are ease and surety of manner? Where are enterprise and curiosity? Where, above all, is courage, and in particular, moral courage— the capacity for independent thinking?"[15] Part of the disappointment evinced by Fitzgerald's novels and stories comes from the brutal fact that these desirable ends seem not to have American means. In an industrial democracy, wealth and productivity matter and style is a commodity.

Both Fay and Leslie (and the founders of the Newman School) wanted to make Catholicism stylish, intellectually respectable. But that was not what Scott had in mind. He wrote instead about individuals who worked against the most novelistic of the great forces identified by Sigmund Freud in "Creative Writers and Day-Dreaming": the power of the "common run of humanity" over the aspiring ego.[16] Instead of writing about Catholic nobility, he depicted careers and working society between the wars. Catholic romanticism had a limited audience, and Leslie has declined into a footnote to literature.

Capital in the Twentieth Century

Thomas Piketty's *Capital in the Twenty-First Century* has renewed interest in the American economy of the time, stating, "It is a well-established fact that wealth in the United States became increasingly concentrated over the course of the nineteenth century. In 1910, capital inequality there was very high, although still markedly lower than in Europe: the top decile owned about 80 percent of total wealth and the top centile around 45 percent. . . . Interestingly, the fact that inequality in the New World seemed to be catching up with inequality in old Europe greatly worried U.S. economists at the time." Piketty states that the period 1910–20 confirmed the democratic belief that enormous wealth was "deemed to be incompatible with U.S. values."[17] When Fitzgerald recalled this period in his fiction, he had much to say about the connection among values, ambitions, and education. He saw how a society based on money actually worked, how it enforced relationships.

What was in fact going on in American cities when Fitzgerald first began to consider the nature of class, money, and those values that the economists mentioned by Piketty worried about? The life of wealth was full of separate institutions—organizations such as social and country clubs and events such as dances and parties—that included few and excluded many. Membership required funds, whether from inheritance, salaries, or sometimes indebtedness. But life at the top of the social scale had its critics. In 1909, Herbert Croly had published *The Promise of American Life,* which criticized the narrow range of prosperity. In 1910, Theodore Roosevelt supported the book, writing articles in *The Outlook* seeing wealth as the current enemy of historical values: his American villain was "the dishonest man of swollen riches whose wealth has been made in ways which he desires to conceal from the law."[18] Fitzgerald follows a far more complex strain of thought, beginning with life in a world of increasing wealth and opportunity, then showing how dangerous the promise of American life could be. He was interested in the mechanisms of social mobility, first among them education.

Le Vot underestimated the spirit of place. He thought that because St. Paul was far from the large eastern cities, it was provincial. I couldn't agree less with his conclusion that "the narrowness of family life" alienated Scott, because the creation of a domestic world became so large a subject of his life and work.[19] James R. Mellow later said, "The two major themes of Fitzgerald's fiction were courtship and the conjugal life."[20] Fitzgerald's daughter, Scottie, in an interview with Bruccoli, affirmed that her father was as much interested in American social life as he was in the Jazz Age. Otherwise, she said, the body of his short stories, about middle-class careers, would make no sense at all. She was emphatic about that last point, reiterating that although Scott may have used the term "Jazz Age," he kept alive his memories of the music, sentiments, ideas, and social arrangements of the 1910s.[21] His audience understood that his life and their own had begun in an unforgotten social world.

Piketty wrote that life in the 1910s caused American economists anxiety about stability and the distribution of wealth. One of the first great sociological surveys, *Recent Social Trends* (1933), concluded that the American economy had become both great and unequal well before the 1920s. This was evident not only in corporate change but in the life of any observant individual. "At the turn of the century . . . the first book of American history was closed."[22] The new book opened with Fitzgerald as a witness to its social changes. Many of these involved rapid gains or declines in wealth and status.

Summit Avenue, St. Paul

Dave Page, in his *F. Scott Fitzgerald in Minnesota*, shows that the Summit Avenue neighborhood was part of a national economy, caught up in a stream of transactions and sales; marriages, births, and deaths; fortunes made, lost, squandered, and (like Mollie Fitzgerald's) dribbled away. The first-rate photographs by Jeff Krueger show the great houses of the town, saved by local preservationists, looking as if the past has been crystallized. Yet those houses, built to resist time, were sold and inherited, built and rebuilt as the economy rose and fell. One of the most beautiful belonged to Norris and Betty Jackson: just before the publication of "The Scandal Detectives" in the April 28, 1928, issue of the *Saturday Evening Post,* Jackson received a note from Fitzgerald saying that he had "finally included your house in a story." The point was not simply that the house was a great good place in their shared memories; rather, he added, "sooner or later time will wipe out that pleasant spot."[23]

Certain houses on Summit Avenue declined into apartments or boarding houses, and of course the Fitzgerald family moved from one rental to another. For Fitzgerald, Minnesota was more than a location for stories of his adolescence; it was where changes in his family's wealth became evident. A letter to Scott from his Aunt Lorena McQuillan, "whose financial situation had become precarious," predicts that she will end

Fitzgerald's home at 599 Summit Avenue. Photograph by Jeff Krueger.

up in an "Old Ladies Home."[24] He witnessed the impersonal grinding of the American economy while he was growing up.

Walter Lippmann chose Minnesota to illustrate the tectonic relationship of the American past and present. His 1927 essay on Sinclair Lewis and his world began: "By 1920 the American people were thoroughly weary of their old faith that happiness could be found by public work, and very dubious about the wisdom of the people. They had found out that the problem of living is deeper and more complex than they had been accustomed to think it was. They had, moreover, become rich. They were ready for an examination of themselves."[25] If we are to go by the Basil and Josephine stories, Fitzgerald agreed. At the end of the 1920s there was a surge of recollections of the generation before. *Middletown* and other work by the sociologists Robert and Helen Lynd began by observing that the 1920s could never be understood without measuring them against the years before the war. Edith Wharton's *A Backward Glance* (1933) showed how Darwinian was America's social history, how short the life span of a governing class. Edmund Wilson wrote in *I Thought of Daisy* (1929) that his own certainties about the recent past—to his embarrassment—had

"A CAPTURED SHADOW"

Original play by

SCOTT FITZGERALD

- CAST -

Dorothy Greene	Scott Fitzgerald
Ann Winchester	Lawrence Boardman
Margaret Winchester	John Mitchell, Jr.
Eleanor Alair	Paul Ballion
Julia Dorr	Theodore Parkhouse
	William Bannon
	James Porterfield

A Captured Shadow was presented by the Elizabethan Dramatic Club in August 1912. It was, according to Fitzgerald's handwritten note in his scrapbook, an early success.

become yesterday's news. And Fitzgerald's Basil stories of 1929, about a state at the edge of the map, sketched out the beginning of the big change.

Changes in the American Education System

St. Paul was in fact a center of urban growth and renewal. Fitzgerald lived through a time of "exponential U.S. population growth," reflected in the growth of high schools. "In Minneapolis, Minnesota, 23 new schools were built between 1900 and 1915." The concept of instruction changed completely:

In 1913 Central High School in Minneapolis opened with an enrollment of 1,600 students. It was one of the most modern high schools in the country. It included a greenhouse, a physics laboratory, an 1,800-seat auditorium, a running track, two gymnasiums, and a large library. A typical student's experience at Central has numerous similarities to those of current public high school students. . . . Manual training courses such as woodworking, shop, drawing, housekeeping, and sewing were available, as were liberal-arts courses including Greek, orchestra, chorus, creative writing and drama.[26]

This sounds impressive, although writers, including Mencken and Lionel Trilling, criticized educational ideology, arguing that the new high schools were in fact microcosms of American society rather than sources of instruction. To a surprising extent, education historians agreed.

Recent Social Trends admitted that schools had become miniature communities: they "have assumed responsibility for many phases of child care. . . . They are adopting special devices to equip everyone whom they can reach for success in vocations and participation in community activities." The attraction to education and also the disappointment it entails was a structural interest of Fitzgerald's. His characters are shown enrolled at schools, thinking about advancement in schools, mentioning their educational past. Money and education (as at St. Midas's School in "The Diamond as Big as the Ritz") are connected.

James L. W. West III describes higher education at the University of Minnesota:

> Basil's estimate of the state university betrays his snobbishness but is not altogether inaccurate for 1913, the year in which "Forging Ahead" is set. The University of Minnesota was then a relatively new institution, devoted primarily to applied knowledge and practical training. . . . Its enrollment in 1913 was approximately 4,200 students, most of them from Minnesota. Princeton, by contrast, enrolled some 1,350 young men in that year. The atmosphere at Minnesota was conservative, with an active Prohibition Club.[27]

Minnesota was part of a national civic order and Prohibition was a slick and successful movement uniting all regions. By this time it had become highly respectable, joining together both rubes and reformers. It certainly was the venue for literate, moneyed, middle-class organizations that worried about far more than booze. The coalition identified its enemies as immigrants from the wrong parts of Europe, the criminal classes otherwise known as the poor, and those Americans who rejected traditional values. Lisa McGirr begins her history of Prohibition arguing that it was a coalition of people who despaired about "Civilization."[28] They worried about economic fluctuations, about the loss of authority by family, church, and community. They understood that cities, unlike towns, were indifferent to moral suasion. They were coming to understand the role of political coercion and of public symbolism.

In "He Thinks He's Wonderful" Basil Duke Lee returns to his home in 1912 "after the college-board examinations." He has been thinking about himself (not unusual) but he has also been thinking about ideas transmitted to him: "He believed that everything was a matter of effort—the current principle of American education—and his fantastic ambition was continually leading him to expect too much."[29] That is a piercing observation, containing in it much more than the idea that egotism defines character. He understands his own life is part of institutional life. The new social sciences of anthropology and sociology had begun to define America in terms of family, work, education, and leisure. Those categories shape *Middletown,* which takes "Training the Young" as one of its main subjects. The section begins with the statement that learning has become part of a new and "institutional" world.[30] Schools developed their own bureaucracies, and teachers formed national associations. "The number of high school graduates per year tripled between 1900 and 1920," while in 1910, roughly when Basil starts thinking about schools as ladders up the social scale, the college student population "grew by more than half, to 355,000."[31] Fitzgerald's figures exist in a world of values defined by the public majority.

In *Middletown,* the Lynds state that the leveling powers of civic boosterism and the suffocating embrace of community values can be seen in the schools:

> Almost never is the essential of education defined in terms of the subjects taught. . . . In Middletown's traditional philosophy it is not primarily learning, or even intelligence, as much as character and good will which are exalted. . . . "You know the smarter the man the more dissatisfied he is," says Will Rogers in a Middletown paper, "so cheer up, let us be happy in our ignorance." "I wanted my son to go to a different school in the East," said a business class mother, "because it's more cultured. But then I think you can have too much culture. It's all right if you're living in the East—or even in California—but it unfits you for living in the Middle West."[32]

We think of boosterism and back-slapping in Sinclair Lewis's *Babbitt,* although *Middletown* states that religion was by far the most important influence on the schools. Such influence was exerted through campus visitations, school clubs, and, as Fitzgerald wrote in detail in 1920 and

PRINCETON UNIVERSITY

Place and Date _Princeton, N.J., June 1,_ 191_2_.

Received of _Francis Scott Fitzgerald_

Five Dollars in Payment of Fee for Entrance Examinations,

June and September, 191_2_.

_____

For the Registrar.

Fitzgerald's receipt of payment for the entrance exam to Princeton University

then again in the Basil stories of 1929, through the ideology of social "service." That meant the connection of schools with social betterment of a particular kind, combining Reform, Prohibition, and Protestant ideologies. Those ideas were on Fitzgerald's mind when he wrote about 1912–13.

Princeton

Fitzgerald took the entrance exams for Princeton in 1912 and failed them; he then began a campaign of reexamination and appeal. He was accepted with conditions—and then compiled a record of missing classes, failing grades, and challenging the codes that in 1913 governed the campus. By the end of 1913 Scott recognized that he was much more likely to impress by writing, but he needed to succeed at an art to justify his claim to being an artist:

> Near the end of my last year at school I came across a new musical-comedy score lying on top of the piano. It was a show called "His Honor the Sultan," and the title furnished the information that it had been presented by the Triangle Club of Princeton University. That was enough for me. From then on the university question was settled. I was bound for Princeton.

> I spent my entire freshman year writing an operetta for the
> Triangle Club. To do this I failed in algebra, trigonometry, coor-
> dinate geometry and hygiene. But the Triangle Club accepted my
> show.[33]

Academic requirements were difficult enough, but there were in addition
the social codes of form, manner, and style. Brown calls those rules "security in conformity."[34] Fitzgerald may have believed that an easy southern style could be acquired, but that came at a certain cost. The social
graces did not include self-advertising, talking about accomplishments,
or stating vast ambitions. Princeton valued studied grace and was somewhat alarmed by sincerity. Students were not impressed by budding intellectuals. Character and background turned out to mean as much on
this campus as at other Ivy League colleges. But Princeton was divided
over that ideal of "character." James Axtell states, "In his 1912 analysis
of Princeton's emerging social system, Owen Johnson characterized the
clubmen as 'a rather elastic autocracy, self-convinced that the same laws
that divide society in the outer world inevitably must form social divisions in college.' Opposed to their thinking was an 'aggressive democracy' led by [Princeton] President Wilson, who 'insisted that the university should exist independently of worldly cleavages.'"[35] Both Wilson and
his successor, John Grier Hibben, tried to raise standards and improve
teaching, but Edwin Slosson's 1910 history of Princeton concluded that
the school "offer[ed] one particular kind of college training to one rather
limited social class of the United States."[36] Even hard economic realities
(which we sometimes think are definitive in settling all issues) have to
be balanced against Fitzgerald's conviction that other aspects of life were
just as important. Christopher A. Snyder argues in *Gatsby's Oxford* that
Fitzgerald knew and admired much of the large body of literature about
Oxford and used it to transfer many years of reverent memory about
Oxford to Princeton. From John Henry Newman and Matthew Arnold
onward, the idea of a university transcending time (and the economy of
the moment) became part of cultural imagination.[37]

Before they can get to the dances and clubs and big games, Fitzgerald's
characters have to qualify for entrance. After entrance, they faced
the kind of problem that Fitzgerald exemplified at both Newman and
Princeton, for he was a writer impervious to assignments. Fitzgerald's
education in the classroom should not be downgraded—after all, he was

taught by Christian Gauss. But he mentioned later in life that he learned about texts from his friends John Peale Bishop and Edmund Wilson. He learned about scenes, particularly of New York, by observation. He learned (rather like Mr. Utsonomia, the Japanese exchange student who appears in Fitzgerald's "Forging Ahead" [1929]) about people by overhearing them.

Intellectual romance could descend into the conduct of life as a sonorous patrician pastime. How did Scott respond to the superficial undergraduate life and to inert courses that meant little to him? He was too combustive to live the role of the gallant southerner. His teachers, with the exception of Gauss, seemed unable to sever their ties to Victorianism. However, his "most durable and important friendships" with Wilson and Bishop led him to read more and become more critical of himself.[38] Of course, they were skeptical about Scott's ambitions and talents. Both thought that wealth and status dominated his imagination, and he often agreed with them on that point. But there was to be a crucial turn when he understood that there was more than one tale to tell about those who inherited and those who aspired to wealth. In the stories about life in 1912–13, education, money, and the constant pressure of community life are connected subjects.

NOTES

1. André Le Vot, *F. Scott Fitzgerald: A Biography*, trans. William Byron (New York: Doubleday, 1983), 22.

2. David S. Brown, *Paradise Lost: A Life of F. Scott Fitzgerald* (Cambridge, Mass.: Harvard University Press, 2017), 32. "W. J. Lynch" was actually Jesse Lynch Williams.

3. F. Scott Fitzgerald, "May Day," in *Tales of the Jazz Age*, ed. James L. W. West III, Cambridge Edition of the Works of F. Scott Fitzgerald (Cambridge: Cambridge University Press, 2012), 62.

4. William James, "The Will to Believe," *The Writings of William James*, ed. John J. McDermott (Chicago: University of Chicago Press, 1977), 722.

5. F. Scott Fitzgerald, *This Side of Paradise*, ed. James L. W. West III, Cambridge Edition of the Works of F. Scott Fitzgerald (Cambridge: Cambridge University Press, 2012), 200. Amory says that while thinking of the meaning of greatness. There is an obituary for men like Gatsby in this passage: there won't "be any more permanent world heroes" (199).

6. Fitzgerald, *This Side of Paradise*, 29.

7. Pearl James, "A Catholic Boyhood: The Newman School, the Newman News, and Monsignor Cyril Sigourney Webster Fay," in *F. Scott Fitzgerald in Context*, ed. Bryant Mangum (Cambridge: Cambridge University Press, 2013), 118–19.

8. Matthew J. Bruccoli, *Some Sort of Epic Grandeur: The Life of F. Scott Fitzgerald* (Columbia: University of South Carolina Press, 2002), 31. See Fitzgerald's self-assessment at Newman in Andrew Turnbull, *Scott Fitzgerald* (New York: Charles Scribner's Sons, 1962), 34–35.

9. James Axtell, *The Making of Princeton University: From Woodrow Wilson to the Present* (Princeton: Princeton University Press, 2006), 131–32.

10. Bruccoli, *Epic Grandeur,* 35.

11. Bruccoli, *Epic Grandeur,* 35.

12. P. James, "A Catholic Boyhood," 122.

13. Brown, *Paradise Lost,* 39.

14. Fred Hobson, *Mencken: A Life* (New York: Random House, 1994), 47.

15. H. L. Mencken, *Prejudices: Second Series* (London: Cape, 1921), 77–78.

16. Sigmund Freud, *The Freud Reader,* ed. Peter Gay (New York: W. W. Norton, 1989), 437.

17. Thomas Piketty, *Capital in the Twenty-First Century,* trans. Arthur Goldhammer (Cambridge, Mass.: Harvard University Press, 2014), 347–49.

18. Quoted in H. W. Brands, *T. R.: The Last Romantic* (New York: Basic Books, 1997), 684–85.

19. Le Vot, *Fitzgerald,* 39.

20. James R. Mellow, *Invented Lives: F. Scott and Zelda Fitzgerald* (Boston: Houghton Mifflin, 1984), 23.

21. Matthew J. Bruccoli, *Scottie Fitzgerald: The Stewardship of Literary Memory* (Columbia: Thomas Cooper Library, University of South Carolina, 2015), 8–9.

22. Edwin F. Gay and Leo Wolman, "Trends in Economic Organization," *Recent Social Trends in the United States: Report of the President's Research Committee on Social Trends* (New York: McGraw-Hill, 1933), vol. 1, 219–20.

23. Dave Page, *F. Scott Fitzgerald in Minnesota: The Writer and His Friends at Home* (St. Paul: Fitzgerald in St. Paul / University of Minnesota Press, 2017), 124. See Lloyd C. Hackl, "Still Home to Me," *F. Scott Fitzgerald and St. Paul, Minnesota* (Cambridge, Minn.: Adventure Publications, 1996), 13–37.

24. Page, *Fitzgerald in Minnesota,* 153.

25. Walter Lippmann, *Public Persons,* ed. Gilbert A. Harrison (New York: Liveright, 1976), 85.

26. Heather A. Beasley, "Education," in *The Age of Reform: 1890 to 1920,* ed. Rodney P. Carlisle (New York: Infobase, 2009), 115–18.

27. F. Scott Fitzgerald, *The Basil, Josephine, and Gwen Stories,* ed. James L. W. West III, Cambridge Edition of the Works of F. Scott Fitzgerald (Cambridge: Cambridge University Press, 2022), 347.

28. Lisa McGirr, *The War on Alcohol: Prohibition and the Rise of the American State* (New York: W. W. Norton, 2015).

29. Fitzgerald, "He Thinks He's Wonderful," in *Basil, Josephine, and Gwen Stories,* 78.

30. Robert S. Lynd and Helen Merrell Lynd, *Middletown: A Study in Modern American Culture* (San Diego, Calif.: Harcourt Brace, 1957), 181.

31. John Milton Cooper, *Pivotal Decades: The United States 1900–1920* (New York: W. W. Norton, 1990), 136–37.

32. Lynd and Lynd, *Middletown,* 229.

33. F. Scott Fitzgerald, *A Short Autobiography,* ed. James L. W. West III (New York: Charles Scribner's Sons, 2011), 1–2.

34. Brown, *Paradise Lost,* 47.

35. Axtell, *Making of Princeton,* 305–6.

36. Quoted in Axtell, *Making of Princeton,* 117.

37. Christopher A. Snyder, *Gatsby's Oxford* (New York: Pegasus, 2019), 30.

38. Mellow, *Invented Lives,* 331. See Edward Gillin, "Princeton, New Jersey, Princeton University, and the *Nassau Literary Magazine*" in Magnum, *Fitzgerald in Context,* 126–35.

1914–1915

David Rennie

> Here is a country in which it is an axiom that a business-
> man shall be a member of the Chamber of Commerce, an
> admirer of Charles M. Schwab, a reader of *The Saturday
> Evening Post*, a golfer—in brief, a vegetable.
> —Henry L. Mencken, *Prejudices: Third Series*

F. Scott Fitzgerald took the title for his 1923 play, *The Vegetable*, from H. L. Mencken's essay "On Being an American."[1] Here Mencken pejoratively locates golf—alongside championing industry and consuming mass-market media—within his axiomatic summation of the American businessman. Mencken's disdain for the sport, conveyed within a socially astute appreciation of its place within the national socioeconomic fabric, may be fairly compared to Fitzgerald's attitude toward golf. Unlike the football field, the golf course was never a site of heroic possibility for Fitzgerald. And this is perhaps why golf—and, more important, the country-club environment—has been an overlooked aspect of his fiction. In the year of Fitzgerald's birth, golf in America was limited to a handful of early (and exclusive) courses established toward the end of the nineteenth century. By 1915, country clubs and their attendant golf courses had spread throughout middle-class America. The evolution of the country club is an important index of the emerging United States: a reflection of increasingly available discretionary time, an expression of the values and identity of burgeoning suburban locales, and a means of regulating who was included and excluded.

As his writing demonstrates, Fitzgerald was cognizant that the country club had become a pervasive fact of national life by the time he returned to Princeton as a freshman in January 1914. And the country club was an important setting, personally, for Fitzgerald during 1914–15. His play *Assorted Spirits* was performed in September 1914 at the White Bear Yacht Club, located in Dellwood, approximately fifteen miles north of

St. Paul, and the following January he met Ginevra King at the St. Paul Town and Country Club. Having grown up near—and in—these clubs additionally shaped Fitzgerald's evaluation of Princeton, where he matriculated as a freshman in September 1913, as "the pleasantest country club in America."[2] Golf and the country club also offered a natural vehicle for depicting personal and national development in his writing. "Winter Dreams" and "The Diamond as Big as the Ritz," in particular, reflect on events of these years, such as Fitzgerald's visit to the family ranch of his friend Charles "Sap" Donahoe in Montana in 1915 and his failed pursuit of Ginevra.

By 1914–15, golf had, after a relatively short period of growth, become an established feature of American socioeconomic life. Richard J. Moss observes, "In the most general way, the people who founded the golf community were responding to modernization," most particularly to post–Civil War "suburbanization and urbanization." Moss continues:

> The rise of the new city eroded the sense of community that most had felt prior to 1870. . . . Golf was just one of the many ways that people sought to reconstitute community, to revive a sense of belonging. It was also one of the ways Americans sought to reconnect with nature.[3]

Early clubs included St. Andrews in Yonkers, New York (founded 1888); Shinnecock Hills in Suffolk County, New York (1891); Chicago Golf Club (1892); and the Onwentsia Club in Lake Forest, Illinois (1895). In 1913 amateur Francis Ouimet won the U.S. Open in a surprise victory over British golf greats Harry Vardon and Ted Ray. The victory of a relatable, working-class American over two of golf's elite players helped popularize the game in America, generating widespread demand for public golf courses that would be accessible to ordinary Americans, not just to the financial upper crust. The result was a surge in participation numbers: "In 1913 there were 350,000 golfers in the United States. A decade later the number had grown to two million."[4] While Ouimet's victory is credited with democratizing golf in America, social elitism did not disappear from the game. In fact, as Moss notes, "Until World War II the majority . . . of courses were created and maintained as private courses."[5]

An improving economy around the turn of the twentieth century did mean that "golf clubs began to slide down the social class structure becoming more attractive to the middle class."[6] The idea of establishing or joining a country-club environment for sport or social activity increasingly held an appeal in an America where "a pervasive culture of mass consumerism based on rising disposable income, increasing leisure time, and changing attitudes toward work and recreation . . . made sports more acceptable and even desirable for Americans."[7] This is a particularly significant context for Fitzgerald, who was not only an acute observer of national progress but one who did so from a somewhat ambiguous social position on the fringes of the upper middle class. The country club was a central institution for the middle classes, one where the tensions of social aspiration and stratification played out. And as Fitzgerald approached the end of his teenage years, golf and the country club had become firmly rooted in the fabric of national life: "By 1915 the country club–golf club idea had spread everywhere a middle class proud of its city existed."[8]

Golf, then, was more than just a pastime for the elite. It is intimately tied to the currents in American life in the late nineteenth and early twentieth centuries. Though more extensive than is usually supposed, Fitzgerald's participatory relationship with golf was sporadic and ambivalent. The country club, however, was a hugely important social milieu both for him as an individual and as a persistent—even ubiquitous—setting in his early fiction. A sensitive commentator on contemporary society and conscious of the place of the moment on the continuum of the nation's time line, Fitzgerald was highly attuned to the importance of the country club in American life. The game of golf, as A. Fletcher Cole remarks, is "exceptionally well-suited to exploring" Fitzgerald's "favorite themes: class conflict, social mobility, [and] pursuit of the 'American dream.'"[9] And 1914–15 were also years in which the country club played an important backdrop to milestone events in Fitzgerald's life. Accordingly, this two-year window represents an opportunity to explore the connections between the country club and Fitzgerald's life and fiction.

St. Paul Country Clubs

It would be hard to argue with Cole's assertion that "Fitzgerald never was a golf aficionado."[10] Yet Fitzgerald did have a long-standing relationship with the game, one he repeatedly drew on in his fiction. In his ledger entry for July 1906, Fitzgerald records that he "bought three golf-clubs and essayed the scotch [sic] game." Then, in June 1908, he recalled, "Played golf with Inky on the public links."[11] Though not a keen golfer, Fitzgerald grew up near two country clubs that would play important roles in his life and work: the St. Paul Town and Country Club and the White Bear Yacht Club.

The St. Paul Town and Country Club, "formally launched . . . on December 8, 1887," began as a year-round offshoot of the St. Paul Carnival Club (known as the Nuskhas), which had originated the year prior.[12] A clubhouse designed by Cass Gilbert was built near the Marshall Avenue bridge over the Mississippi River, and the club's early members included Charles E. Flandrau (father of Charles M. Flandrau—the essayist and owner of St. Paul's Kilmarnock Books), businessman Lucius Pond Ordway, and James J. Hill, who "used the club to entertain foreign investors when he was building the Great Northern Railway."[13] In 1893 the club added a five-hole golf course, which was extended to eighteen holes in 1907. The Town and Country Club formed the terminus of Fitzgerald's childhood bobsled rides, and he recalled going to the club for "the charity ball and Mack's party" in January 1907.[14]

The White Bear Yacht Club was founded as a sailing club in 1889, and a nine-hole golf course was added in 1912. Fitzgerald hints at this development in "A Freeze-Out" (1931), in which Chauncey Rikker—tarred by the stigma of bankruptcy and a reputation for nefariousness—returns to Minnesota and hopes to join the Kennemore Club. Forrest Winslow's father initially seeks to oppose Chauncey's application—much to the approval of his son, who takes pride in his family's long-standing social rectitude and the fact that "his grandfather had been a founder of this club in the 90s when it was for sailboat racing instead of golf."[15] Symptomatic of golf's rise across the nation, in 1915 the White Bear Yacht Club expanded its course into a full-sized, eighteen-hole facility.[16] Fitzgerald's father was a member at White Bear, but, Scott Donaldson notes, as the family could not afford a summer house there, Fitzgerald and his sister Annabel rode out on the trolley line to visit their friends' lakeside homes.[17] Fitzgerald's ledger records that he went to the White Bear Yacht Club in the summer of 1911,[18] and two years later his Civil War play *Coward* was performed at White Bear by the Elizabethan Dramatic Club.

Princeton: "The Pleasantest Country Club in America"

Fitzgerald's firsthand experience of these environments may have colored his attitude to Princeton. In *This Side of Paradise*, Amory Blaine describes Princeton as "the pleasantest country club in America."[19] This is presented as Amory's viewpoint, but Fitzgerald espoused a similar outlook in his 1927 essay "Princeton," which indicates that Amory's description strongly chimes with Fitzgerald's feelings toward his alma mater. If a young man desired a college that felt itself to be "passionately America's norm in ideals of conduct and success," he would be attracted to Yale, Fitzgerald opined. If, on the other hand, he found "at seventeen the furies that whip on America's youth have become too coercive for his taste," Princeton beckoned. "A green Phoenix," insulated from the railroads and urban slums of New York by "deer parks, pleasant farms and wood-lands," Princeton would allow a young man "the taste of pleasant pasture and a moment to breathe deep and ruminate before he goes into the clamorous struggle of American life."[20] These sentiments are reminiscent of the ideals behind the creation of the country club: to establish an enclave of green space separated from the ugliness and monotony of America's sprawling industrial and suburban spaces.

Though attractive to Amory and Scott Fitzgerald, Princeton's country-club associations were a source of concern for Woodrow Wilson, who, during his tenure as the thirteenth president of Princeton (1902–10), sought to bring in higher academic standards and to abolish the eating-club system. The Princeton clubs reflected, and offered a point of initiation to, the nationwide club structure. "Often clubmen as adults, [students] joined Princeton's eating clubs then moved on to a larger pattern of club membership that included country clubs, summer resorts and—the cap-stone of the system—the metropolitan men's clubs."[21] Wilson attempted to replace clubs with residential colleges (known as quadrangles), each with its own dining room and common room, but faced opposition from alumni and trustees. In *This Side of Paradise,* the club system is intact when Amory, having achieved a degree of prominence from his role on the board of the *Daily Princetonian,* is courted by upperclassmen from Ivy, Cottage, and Tiger Inn clubs. Amory, like Fitzgerald, plumps for Cottage, "architecturally the most sumptuous of the clubs" with "a large Southern following."[22]

After reading *This Side of Paradise,* John Grier Hibben, Wilson's successor as president at Princeton (1912–32),[23] wrote to Fitzgerald expressing the hope he would use his literary powers to promote the "instinctive nobility of man." Hibben lamented that, in his debut novel, Fitzgerald had instead given the impression that Princeton's "young men are merely living for four years in a country club and spending their lives wholly in a spirit of calculation and snobbery."[24] In his reply, Fitzgerald acknowl-

The Cottage Club, Princeton University

edged that the novel did "overaccentuate the gayety and country club atmosphere. . . . It is the Princeton of Saturday night in May. Too many intelligent classmates of mine have failed to agree with it for me to consider it really photographic any more."[25] As Donaldson observes, many of Fitzgerald's classmates—who attended more prestigious schools and came from wealthier families—"were less caught up in the struggle for social dominance than he was."[26]

During his freshman year, it became apparent that Fitzgerald would not earn the distinction he craved on Princeton's football field.[27] Instead, he applied himself to writing for the Triangle Club's 1914 show. Founded in 1891, the Triangle Club was, and still is, a theatrical troupe that premieres and then tours a student-produced musical every year. Fitzgerald's absorption with extracurricular activities quickly affected his grades. His ledger entry for February 1915 reads, "Began ▲ Play . . . Failed many exams."[28] In April, he met John Peale Bishop, an editor of Princeton's *Nassau Literary Magazine,* who helped Fitzgerald's literary aspirations by introducing him to the serious appreciation of poetry. Bishop would also serve as the basis for Thomas Parke D'Invilliers in *This Side of Paradise.*

Golf and World War I

Summer 1914 saw the outbreak of the 1914–18 Great War in Europe. America did not join the conflict until April 1917, and Fitzgerald, though conscripted, never saw active service in France. In August 1914 the war was an offstage phenomenon. In *This Side of Paradise* Fitzgerald writes, "Beyond a sporting interest in the German dash for Paris the whole affair failed either to thrill or interest" Amory.[29] In retrospect, however, Fitzgerald would identify the conflict as a defining moment for his age group. In "My Generation" (1939), he ascribed the "uniqueness" of his generation to the fact that they were "at once pre-war and post-war." Fitzgerald's cohort, he felt, "inherited two worlds—the one of hope to which we had been bred; the one of disillusion which we had discovered early for ourselves."[30] At the same time, Fitzgerald claimed his was "a husky generation."[31] As exemplars, alongside Tommy Hitchcock (a war veteran, a polo ace, and the model for Tom Buchanan) and Bill Tilden (the first American to win Wimbledon), Fitzgerald included golfers Dudley Mudge and Harrison Johnston.

Dudley Mudge, while also playing for the Yale baseball team, came to national attention when he was a medalist in the 1915 U.S. Amateur in Detroit. The same year, Mudge won the Minnesota State Amateur title. He repeated the feat in 1916, winning at the White Bear Yacht Club, where he was a member.[32] During the war, Mudge served with the aviation section of the Signal Corps. Stationed in England at the School of Military Aeronautics at Oxford University, he suffered a broken arm when his plane was "written off" in a crash landing. Mudge never served in combat but was made a first lieutenant in the aviation reserve.[33]

Harrison Johnston, the son of St. Paul architect Clarence Johnston, was born, like Fitzgerald, in 1896, grew up in St. Paul's prestigious Summit Hill area, and attended St. Paul Academy. In 1915 he reached the semifinals of the Minnesota State Amateur. During the war, Johnston served in the 337th Machine Gun Battalion and suffered shell shock. After the war, representing the White Bear Yacht Club, he went on to win eight straight Minnesota State Amateur events, from 1921 to 1928, and the U.S. Amateur in 1929.

Though far from a keen golfer himself, Fitzgerald grew up among players like Johnston and Mudge who achieved success in the years 1914–15 and, for Fitzgerald, symbolized the best of a generation that was shaped by its pre- and postwar duality.[34]

Ginevra King

On September 8, 1914, Fitzgerald's play *Assorted Spirits* was performed—with Fitzgerald serving as lead actor and stage manager—at St. Paul's Elizabethan Dramatic Club. The next day, a performance was given at the White Bear Yacht Club. This was the last of four plays Fitzgerald wrote for the Elizabethan Club. And he expanded his roster of theatrical works when the Triangle Club's musical comedy *Fie! Fie! Fi-Fi!* premiered in December 1914. His script was chosen by Triangle Club president Walker Ellis over a rival submission from Lawton Campbell. Ellis revised the script and took credit for the dialogue and characters, with only the plot and lyrics recognized as Fitzgerald's on the published program. Fitzgerald's poor academic performance meant he was excluded from appearing in the play and from participating in its subsequent tour.

Fitzgerald's contribution to the play's success may have encouraged him to feel that his creative star was rising as he returned to St. Paul for Christmas. There, at the St. Paul Town and Country Club, he met Ginevra King on January 4, 1915. Fitzgerald described his encounter with Ginevra in his 1917 story "Babes in the Woods." Originally published in the *Nassau Literary Magazine,* the story was later incorporated into *This Side of Paradise* as the scene where Amory Blaine meets Isabelle Borgé. Emerging from the dressing room of the Minnehaha Club, Isabelle encounters Amory "in the club's great room" and is intrigued by his daring verbal come-ons, including the tantalizing claim he has "an adjective that just fits" her. After dinner and a frenetic dance in which Isabelle is repeatedly cut in on, she and Amory retire to "the little den of the reading room."[35] Having declared he has fallen for her, Amory comes close to kissing Isabelle—until an interruption from fellow guests thwart the anticipated kiss.

Ginevra was one of the quartet of desirable Chicagoan society girls who styled themselves the "Big Four." Also of the four was Edith Cummings, who would go on to become a successful amateur golfer, winning the U.S. Women's Amateur (1923) and Western Amateur (1924) titles. She was the first woman—and first golfer—featured on the cover of *Time* magazine. Edith was a classmate of Ginevra's at Westover School, and it is

St. Paul Town and Country Club

probable that Fitzgerald met Edith when he visited Ginevra at the school in February 1915.[36] Fitzgerald later revealed to Maxwell Perkins that the basis of Jordan Baker in *The Great Gatsby* "was Edith Cummings."[37] Ginevra was also a proficient golfer, and her diary entries contain repeated mentions of playing golf with Cummings at the elite Onwentsia Club in Lake Forest.[38]

At Princeton, Fitzgerald carried on an intense epistolary romance with Ginevra, writing letters on an almost daily basis. In February 1915 he was elected Triangle Club secretary. Then, in March, he was admitted to the prestigious Cottage Club. Each year, Fitzgerald remarked, Princeton's clubs "take in an average of twenty-five sophomores, seventy-five percent of the class." Cottage—along with Tiger, Cap and Gown, and Ivy—was one of the "big four" clubs, and Fitzgerald had received bids from Cap and Gown, Quadrangle, Cannon, and Cottage.[39] Membership in Cottage—which contained a "wood-paneled reproduction of Merton College Library"—conferred an unmistakable mark of prestige on Fitzgerald and helped build his emerging reputation as a campus figure.[40]

"A Diamond as Big as the Ritz"

Fitzgerald's accrual of—again, extracurricular—accolades continued. In April and June, Princeton's *Nassau Literary Magazine* ("the *Lit*") published two of his pieces, "Shadow Laurels" (a one-act play) and "The Ordeal" (later rewritten as "Benediction"). These publications brought Fitzgerald closer to Edmund Wilson, who was on the editorial board of the *Lit*. Wilson would go on to have an important career as a literary critic and served, as Fitzgerald later remarked, as his "intellectual conscience."[41] Together they collaborated on the Triangle Club's 1915 production *The Evil Eye*, with Fitzgerald writing the lyrics and Wilson supplying the plot. Also in June, Ginevra attended the Princeton prom. Together, Fitzgerald and Ginevra went to New York, where they had dinner at the Ritz-Carlton and visited the Midnight Frolic Cabaret. On his return to St. Paul, Scott visited her at Lake Forest. They then went their separate ways for the summer—Ginevra to Maine and Scott to the family ranch of his friend Sap Donahoe in Montana, an experience that would provide the setting for Fitzgerald's story "The Diamond as Big as the Ritz" (1922).

A close friend of Fitzgerald from the Newman School, Donahoe also matriculated at Princeton in 1913 and joined the Cottage Club alongside Fitzgerald. Charles's father, Michael Donahoe, owned the Castle Mountain Livestock Company near White Sulphur Springs and was vice president of the Anaconda Copper Mining Company. In 1905 he bought "The Castle," an opulent stone mansion built in 1890–92 by Byron Roger Sherman (a cousin of Civil War general William Tecumseh Sherman). At the time of Fitzgerald's visit, "the ranch had grown to more than thirty thousand acres and ran 2,762 head of cattle and 4,436 sheep."[42] There is little evidence of how Fitzgerald spent the summer beyond cryptic hints in his ledger: "Aubrey & Olga Black. Attempts to cut out smoking . . . Drunk: The Cowboy song . . . $50 at cards . . . No news from Ginevra . . . The weakly bath."[43] As Landon Y. Jones notes, the conspicuous opulence of the Castle may have been an inspiration for Gatsby's mansion.[44]

A more definite connection exists between Fitzgerald's Montana summer and "The Diamond as Big as the Ritz," in which John T. Unger is invited by Percy Washington, a classmate from St. Midas's preparatory school, to spend the summer at his father's estate in the Montana Rockies. The Washingtons' fabulous wealth comes from a mountain-sized diamond whose existence is fiercely hidden—even to the extent that visitors, like Percy, are killed rather than being allowed to return to the outside world. The story can be read as an allegory of the moral corruption accompanying the unprincipled acquisition of extreme wealth. And golf plays a role in emphasizing the Washingtons' sheer opulence. In the story's second sentence, the reader is told John's father—from Hades on the Mississippi River—"held the amateur golf championship through many a heated contest."[45] This is a marker of John's affluent upbringing: only the wealthy had the leisure time to hone their game to the standard necessary to win tournament golf. The implied affluence of Unger Senior, however, is dwarfed by that of Percy's father, Braddock Washington, who has built a private golf course on his estate.

This course, as Percy explains, is "all a green, you see—no fairway, no rough, no hazards."[46] In golf, each hole concludes—after players have navigated hazards such as trees, sand traps, and standing water—with a green: an area of closely cut and rolled grass across which golfers putt their ball into a hole. The Washingtons' course being "all a green" exemplifies the vast wealth necessary to maintain such a facility; metaphorically, of course, this description suggests the "green" of the innumerable dollars in the Washington coffers. A private and hazardless course also implies the kind of life the Washingtons have attempted to buy: one where money secures total seclusion and control. Fitzgerald continues this imagery when Braddock concludes a conversation with a group of airmen he keeps imprisoned on his property. Ignoring their pleas, Washington strolls "toward the ninth hole of the golf course, as though the pit and its contents were no more than a hazard over which his facile iron had triumphed with ease."[47] The course is just one facet of the Washingtons' opulent, yet ultimately brittle, facade. After a prisoner escapes, the estate comes under attack by airplanes. His secret exposed, Braddock Washington detonates prelaid explosives and obliterates the mountain.

College Would Never Be the Same

Although he was garnering material for future work, in 1914–15 Fitzgerald's literary endeavors—and the strain of his largely written relationship with Ginevra—proved a distraction from his studies, and having failed a makeup exam in the fall, he was barred from extracurricular activities. In October he attended the Princeton–Yale game at New Haven and saw Ginevra in Connecticut. Then, in November 1915, he was hospitalized with fever, and the following month he dropped out of his junior year. While the Triangle Club toured that year's performance, *The Evil Eye* (of which Fitzgerald had written much of the material), he was in St. Paul. On

January 3, 1916, nearly a year to the day after meeting Ginevra, Fitzgerald obtained a note from the dean of Princeton allowing him to claim that his suspension of studies emanated from poor health rather than scholastic deficiency. Looking back in his ledger, Fitzgerald described 1915 as "a year of tremendous rewards that toward the end overreached itself and ruined me."[48]

It was perhaps cruel that Fitzgerald's concentration on creative activities ultimately prevented him from fully enjoying the rewards and recognition that he could, with reason, have felt his due. He had, for a second time, contributed to a successful Triangle Club production and was—again—barred from the production's tour. Ineligible for campus offices, he could not stand for the Triangle Club presidency. When Fitzgerald returned to Princeton in 1916, he discovered he would have to repeat his junior (third) year. Recalling this time, Fitzgerald came to view his failure as a turning point in the formation of his vocation as a writer:

> To me college would never be the same. There were to be no badges of pride, no medals, after all. . . .
>
> Years later I realized that my failure as a big shot was all right—instead of serving on committees, I took a beating in English poetry; when I got the idea of what it was all about, I set about learning how to write.[49]

Just as Fitzgerald had compensated for athletic shortcomings by throwing himself into work for the Triangle Club, writing once again formed a new way to fashion a viable response to failure. The distinction here, though, is different. In his freshman and sophomore years, Fitzgerald aspired to social success *within* orthodox boundaries: to attend an elite university, enter one of the "big" clubs, distinguish himself as a writer, and emerge as a leading figure on campus. "It was a harsh and bitter blow," he recalled, "to know that my career as a leader of men was over."[50] His refashioned self-conception, it is implied here, is of an individual now operating *outside* the conventional current of social advancement he had, hitherto, followed with some success.

Fitzgerald's vision of Princeton as "the pleasantest country club" may have been more reflective of personal ambition than of historical verisimilitude. As Edward Gillin observes, however, Fitzgerald's "sense of essential difference from his classmates afforded him a stance from which to observe and criticize."[51] Fitzgerald may have at some level craved social success—athletic prowess, scholastic ability, the attainment of campus offices—but his almost complete failure to achieve these is in some way a necessary condition of his later success as an astute literary observer of the vivifying effects of aspiration and the poignancy of disappointment.

Ginevra in Retrospect: Winter Dreams

Fitzgerald would rebound from this setback and from the further disappointment of the breakdown of his relationship with Ginevra. Again, he later transmuted personal disappointment into literary achievement by drawing on Ginevra for a number of female characters.[52] Alongside Isabelle Borgé in *This Side of Paradise* and Daisy Fay in *The Great Gatsby,* Fitzgerald recast Ginevra in "Winter Dreams," a story he wrote after living near and at the White Bear Yacht Club following his return to St. Paul in 1921. In August of that year, Scott and Zelda moved into a house at 14 Highway 96 in Dellwood, on White Bear Lake, just a few streets away from the White Bear Yacht Club. They were asked to leave in October and relocated to 626 Goodrich Avenue in St. Paul. The following year, from June to August, the Fitzgeralds returned to the White Bear Lake area, this time staying at the White Bear Yacht Club. Having been asked to leave there as well, the couple then relocated to the Commodore Hotel in St. Paul. Here Fitzgerald finished "Winter Dreams" prior to moving to Great Neck, New York. The experience of residing at White Bear Yacht Club offered the country club as an apt setting for Fitzgerald's retrospective reflection on his romance with Ginevra.

The chronology of "Winter Dreams" is difficult to map out. We can infer that the reacquaintance between Judy Jones and the now successful Dexter Green occurs in 1914 and that his ultimately failed pursuit of her takes place throughout 1914 and 1915. The only definite date in the story is February 1917, when Dexter heads east prior to America's entry into World War I. Tracing backward, we are told that Dexter and Irene Scheerer become engaged in January 1916 and plan to announce it in June of that year. This engagement, the narrator comments, happens "eighteen months after he first met Judy Jones."[53] This is not strictly true: they had met years previously when Dexter, aged fourteen, was a caddy at Sherry Island Golf Club and Judy, aged eleven, had been taken by her nurse to play golf. Fitzgerald provides another chronological marker that

White Bear Yacht Club

aligns with the remark that Dexter pursues Judy for approximately eighteen months after their reacquaintance: "Summer, fall, winter, spring, another summer, another fall—so much [Dexter] had given of his active life to the incorrigible Judy Jones."[54] It is in the summer of 1914, therefore, that Dexter, twenty-three years old and owner of a chain of prosperous laundries, is given a weekend guest pass to Sherry Island Golf Club by Mr. Hart, a man for whom Dexter had caddied as a boy.

Back then, Dexter, the son of the man with "the second-best grocery store" in Black Bear, was caddying for pocket money.[55] Now Dexter is a self-made man, a financial equal to the middle-aged golfers he once caddied for. Playing with three such individuals, he encounters Judy after she insouciantly hits one of Dexter's playing partners in the stomach with her drive. Later that day, he meets Judy on the lake and is invited to her house for dinner the following night. He is just one of many suitors, and "when autumn had come and gone again it occurred to him that he could not have Judy."[56]

While care has to be taken not to mistake fiction for biographical fact, it seems likely that, looking back in 1922, Fitzgerald was drawing on golf and the country club to reflect on both his relationship with Ginevra and his subsequent success. In 1915, he was, like the young Dexter, a middle-class boy infatuated with an upper-class girl. Dexter channels his feelings of inadequacy into practical action: he quits his job as a caddy, struggles financially through his education at a prestigious eastern university, and quickly builds a business empire. Early in the story, Dexter pictures himself "stroll[ing] frigidly into the lounge of the Sherry Island Golf Club," which, as a caddy, he would have been barred from doing.[57] Dexter's subsequent achievement secures exactly this. Fitzgerald never accomplished Dexter's disciplined commercial prosperity, but he did return to White Bear Lake with the aura of success—as someone established in a difficult profession who could afford not just to visit but to live at a country club. In "Winter Dreams" (as in *Gatsby*, which it anticipates), Dexter's exertions emphasize the reality that the object of his desire (an unproductive member of the leisure class) is ultimately unworthy of his pursuit. In "Winter Dreams," we can see Fitzgerald—via the vehicle of golf and the country club—retrospectively applying these feelings to his thwarted infatuation with Ginevra.

Coda: The Country Club in Fitzgerald's Fiction

The country-club phenomenon had become established as a nationwide suburban fixture by 1914–15. This accounts for the country club's pervasive presence in Fitzgerald's early fiction: it functioned as a socially acceptable place to meet members of the opposite sex. The opening passage of "Bernice Bobs Her Hair" neatly summarizes the social hierarchy of the country club. At a Saturday night dance, outside looking in, are "the heads of many curious caddies" not permitted access to the clubhouse. Inside, a different set of forces is juxtaposed as, on the balcony, "a great babel of middle-aged" female chaperones look down on an assortment of youths dancing. The youth culture unfolding below—despite being partly defined against its parents' mores—paradoxically gains a necessary degree of moral legitimacy from the supervision offered by the older generation's "stony eyes."[58] In "The Popular Girl," Fitzgerald refers to such spaces (a sort of improvised ballroom, "filled by day with wicker furniture") as "that nameless chamber wherein occurs the principal transactions of all the country clubs in America."[59]

For Fitzgerald, these "transactions" chiefly center around young love. The opening pages of "The Last of the Belles" are strewn with references to the "country club dances" where Lieutenant Canby and Bill Knowles pursue Ailie Calhoun.[60] In "The Jelly-Bean," Jim Powell—accompanying

Clark Darrow to a country-club dance in Tarleton, Georgia—encounters the beguiling Nancy Lamar. Excited by his suggestion of using gasoline to remove a stubborn piece of gum stuck to her shoe, Nancy drags him "toward a group of cars parked in the moonlight by the first hole of the golf course."[61] This image highlights not only the importance of the country club as a meeting place for romantic relationships but the centrality of the recently available motorcar in the logistics of such encounters. Fitzgerald observed that the "flapper movement" that "dispersed . . . to the country club" was not necessarily an innovation responding to nothing but itself; instead, it swelled to fill "new limits marked out for new youth to explore," limits partly expanded by the advent of the motorcar. "Remove the automobile," Fitzgerald determined, "and the bottom falls out of the whole hilarious spectacle."[62]

Outside of a few isolated stories, the country club becomes a less prominent social background as Fitzgerald's characters age. In one such exception, "What a Handsome Pair" (1932), Helen Van Beck and her husband, Stuart Oldhorne, are coenthusiasts of tennis and polo and "were golf crazy when it was still considered a comic game."[63] By 1915, Stuart's Wall Street career has collapsed, and he is reduced to giving lessons as a golf professional. As such he is humiliatingly barred from entering a clubhouse to congratulate his wife for winning an amateur tournament. Here the social divide between wealthy amateur and working professional signify the growing financial and personal distance between the two.

The country club does function as an occasional marker for maturation and aging. In "The Rich Boy," Anson Hunter, in his youth a habitué of exclusive venues such as Palm Beach and the Everglades Club, later finds that his friends have built "an intricate family life centering around some suburban country club," from which, as an aging single man, he feels estranged.[64] In "The Popular Girl," Yanci Bowman's father possesses a "complexion hearty from twenty years in the service of good whisky and bad golf." He does some "vague real-estate business," but "his chief concern in life [is] the exhibition of a handsome profile and an easy wellbred manner in the country club."[65] The orthodoxies of the initiates of American country-club life offered limited scope for Fitzgerald, however. Certainly, the staid, lecherous middle-aged businessmen in "Winter Dreams" hardly seem the material of Fitzgerald protagonists. Mr. T. A. Hedrick ("a bore and not even a good golfer anymore") comments that Judy Jones "always looks like she wanted to be kissed," and Mr. Sandwood observes, "My god, she's good looking."[66] Middle-class participation in golf and country-club life betokens success and stability and is, therefore, not obviously germane to Fitzgerald's preoccupation with themes of ambition, failure, and loss. Instead, he tended to revisit youth (in the Basil and Josephine stories), find other character types (Dick Diver and Monroe Stahr), or move on to fresh backdrops (Europe and Hollywood).

The country club is, nevertheless, a central location in Fitzgerald's life and works: in its historical rise as a nationwide institution by 1914–15, as it affected his life in those years, and as it would go on to be a backdrop to several key encounters in his writing. Fitzgerald met Ginevra King at a country club, used golf as a vehicle to convey Dexter Green's upward social mobility, drew on the sport to build the Montana-inspired "Diamond as Big as the Ritz," and depicted Princeton as a microcosm of the nation's adult country-club environments. At the close of 1915, he still had some youthful "transactions" of his own to make at the country club in Montgomery, Alabama, where he would meet Zelda Sayre. The country club would offer him a crucial setting in the novels and stories through which he would establish his literary reputation in the coming years.

NOTES

1. Henry L. Mencken, "On Being an American," in *Prejudices: Third Series* (New York: Alfred A. Knopf, 1922), 19.

2. F. Scott Fitzgerald, *This Side of Paradise*, ed. James L. W. West III, Cambridge Edition of the Works of F. Scott Fitzgerald (Cambridge: Cambridge University Press, 2012), 41.

3. Richard J. Moss, *The Kingdom of Golf in America* (Lincoln: University of Nebraska Press, 2013), x–xi.

4. John Williamson, *Born on the Links: A Concise History of Golf* (Lanham, Md.: Rowman and Littlefield, 2018), 59.

5. Moss, *Kingdom of Golf*, 34.

6. Moss, *Kingdom of Golf*, 55.

7. George B. Kirsh, *Golf in America* (Urbana: University of Illinois Press, 2009), 69.

8. Moss, *Kingdom of Golf*, 35.

9. A. Fletcher Cole, "Fairways of His Imagination: Golf and Social Status in F. Scott Fitzgerald's Fiction," in *Upon Further Review: Sports in American Fiction*, ed. Michael Cocchiarale and Scott D. Emmert (Westport, Conn.: Praeger, 2004), 75–85, 84.

10. Cole, "Fairways," 84.

11. F. Scott Fitzgerald, *F. Scott Fitzgerald's Ledger: A Facsimile*, introduction by Matthew J. Bruccoli (Washington, D.C.: NCR/Microcard Editions / Bruccoli Clark, 1972), 56, 58.

12. Rick Shefchik, *From Fields to Fairways: Classic Golf Clubs of Minnesota* (Minneapolis: University of Minnesota Press, 2012), 2.

13. Shefchik, *From Fields to Fairways*, 6.

14. Fitzgerald, *Ledger*, 57.

15. F. Scott Fitzgerald, "A Freeze-Out," in *Babylon Revisited, and Other Stories* (London: Alma Classics, 1914), 50.

16. Shefchik, *From Fields to Fairways*, 90, 92.

17. Scott Donaldson, *Fool for Love: F. Scott Fitzgerald* (Minneapolis: University of Minnesota Press, 2012), 11.

18. Fitzgerald, *Ledger*, 61.

19. Fitzgerald, *This Side of Paradise*, 41.

20. F. Scott Fitzgerald, "Princeton," in *My Lost City: Personal Essays, 1920–1940*, ed. James L. W. West III, Cambridge Edition of the Works of F. Scott Fitzgerald (Cambridge: Cambridge University Press, 2014), 6–7.

21. Jerome Karabel, *The Chosen: The Hidden History of Admission and Exclusion at Harvard, Yale, and Princeton* (New York: Houghton Mifflin Harcourt, 2005), 67.

22. Fitzgerald, "Princeton," 12.

23. From 1910 to 1912 John Aikman Stewart served as acting president.

24. F. Scott Fitzgerald, *Correspondence of F. Scott Fitzgerald*, ed. Matthew J. Bruccoli and Margaret M. Duggan (New York: Random House, 1980), 58.

25. F. Scott Fitzgerald, *The Letters of F. Scott Fitzgerald*, ed. Andrew Turnbull (London: Bodley Head, 1964), 462–63.

26. Donaldson, *Fool for Love*, 26.

27. David S. Brown, *Paradise Lost: A Life of F. Scott Fitzgerald* (Cambridge, Mass.: Harvard University Press, 2017), 48.

28. Fitzgerald, *Ledger*, 64.

29. Fitzgerald, *This Side of Paradise*, 58.

30. F. Scott Fitzgerald, "My Generation," in *My Lost City*, 194.

31. Fitzgerald, "My Generation," 196.

32. Shefchik, *From Fields to Fairways*, 14–15.

33. Marian Sperberg-McQueen, "Dudley Hersey Mudge," The Men of the Second Oxford Detachment, October 9, 2020, accessed February 20, 2021. https://parr-hooper.cmsmcq.com/2OD/the-biographies/mudge-dudley-hersey/.

34. Shefchik, *From Fields to Fairways*, 106–9.

35. Fitzgerald, *This Side of Paradise*, 67, 68.

36. James L. W. West III, *The Perfect Hour: The Romance of F. Scott Fitzgerald and Ginevra King, His First Love* (New York: Random House, 2005), 59.

37. F. Scott Fitzgerald, *F. Scott Fitzgerald: A Life in Letters*, ed. Matthew J. Bruccoli (New York: Charles Scribner's Sons, 1994), 91.

38. West, *Perfect Hour*, 111–23.

39. Fitzgerald, "Princeton," 12.

40. Edward Gillin, "Princeton, New Jersey, Princeton University, and the *Nassau Literary Magazine*," in *F. Scott Fitzgerald in Context*, ed. Bryant Mangum (New York: Cambridge University Press, 2013), 129–30.

41. Fitzgerald, "Pasting It Together," in *My Lost City*, 148.

42. Landon Y. Jones, "Babe in the Woods: F. Scott Fitzgerald's Unlikely Summer

in Montana," *Montana: The Magazine of Western History* 57, no. 3 (2007): 38–39, accessed February 20, 2021. www.jstor.org/stable/25485635.

43. Fitzgerald, *Ledger,* 65.

44. Jones, "Babe in the Woods," 38.

45. F. Scott Fitzgerald, "The Diamond as Big as the Ritz," in *Tales of the Jazz Age,* ed. James L. W. West III, Cambridge Edition of the Works of F. Scott Fitzgerald (Cambridge: Cambridge University Press, 2012), 127.

46. Fitzgerald, "Diamond," 146.

47. Fitzgerald, "Diamond," 150.

48. Fitzgerald, *Ledger,* 65.

49. Quoted in Mary Jo Tate, *Critical Companion to F. Scott Fitzgerald: A Literary Reference to His Life and Work* (New York: Infobase, 2007), 362.

50. Fitzgerald, *My Lost City,* 146.

51. Gillin, "Princeton, New Jersey," 129.

52. West, *Perfect Hour,* 91–107.

53. F. Scott Fitzgerald, "Winter Dreams," in *All the Sad Young Men,* ed. James L. W. West III, Cambridge Edition of the Works of F. Scott Fitzgerald (Cambridge: Cambridge University Press, 2014), 56.

54. Fitzgerald, "Winter Dreams," 57.

55. Fitzgerald, "Winter Dreams," 43.

56. Fitzgerald, "Winter Dreams," 57.

57. Fitzgerald, "Winter Dreams," 44.

58. F. Scott Fitzgerald, "Bernice Bobs Her Hair," in *Flappers and Philosophers,* ed. James L. W. West III, Cambridge Edition of the Works of F. Scott Fitzgerald (Cambridge: Cambridge University Press, 2012), 108.

59. Fitzgerald, "The Popular Girl," in *Flappers and Philosophers,* 263.

60. F. Scott Fitzgerald, "The Last of the Belles," in *Taps at Reveille,* ed. James L. W. West III, Cambridge Edition of the Works of F. Scott Fitzgerald (Cambridge: Cambridge University Press, 2014), 52–53.

61. F. Scott Fitzgerald, "The Jelly-Bean," in *Tales of the Jazz Age,* 21.

62. F. Scott Fitzgerald, "Girls Believe in Girls," in *My Lost City,* 101.

63. F. Scott Fitzgerald and Zelda Fitzgerald, *Bits of Paradise* (London: Bodley Head, 1973), 345.

64. F. Scott Fitzgerald, "The Rich Boy," in *All the Sad Young Men,* 33.

65. Fitzgerald, "The Popular Girl," 264.

66. Fitzgerald, "Winter Dreams," 49.

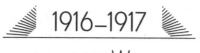

1916–1917

James L. W. West III

In January 1916 F. Scott Fitzgerald was living with his parents in St. Paul and contemplating his immediate future. The previous year had been full of promise. In January 1915 he had been introduced to Ginevra King, a child of wealth from Lake Forest, Illinois, who was visiting St. Paul over the holidays. She was beautiful and socially polished, as adept as he at the game of romance. Ginevra was smitten by Fitzgerald's looks and charm; he was captured by her beauty and poise. He and she carried on an intense romance, largely epistolary, through the spring of 1915. He took her on a whirlwind visit to New York, with her mother as chaperone, in early June.[1] That same spring he was elected secretary of the Princeton Triangle Club and accepted a bid to Cottage, one of the most prestigious of the college's eating clubs. He neglected his coursework that semester, cutting more than fifty classes; he assumed that with tutoring and cramming he could erase his academic failures before the beginning of the new year. Makeup exams were administered just before the start of each fall term at the university. Fitzgerald crossed his fingers and hoped he would squeak by.

In September 1915, however, he failed his makeup exam in qualitative analysis. This made him ineligible to hold office in Triangle and burdened him with an extra course—in ancient art, a subject in which he had little interest. He was bored with most of his classes and spent his time during the fall term working on lyrics for the Triangle show, a musical concoction called *The Evil Eye*. He soon fell behind academically and had no chance of recovery. His health deteriorated (either from a mild case of malaria, endemic around Princeton in those years, or from incipient tuberculosis) and he sought escape by withdrawing from the university. A reluctant dean allowed Fitzgerald to blame his exit on "ill health," but his academic transcript, the document of record, attributed the withdrawal to "scholastic deficiencies."[2]

Fitzgerald was marking time in St. Paul. He planned to resume his studies at Princeton in the fall of 1916, hoping somehow to become eligible for the campus honors he desired, but he must have known that his future would not lie in the world of learning. He was curious intellectually but temperamentally unsuited for academic work. Even courses in literature failed to capture his imagination. He found his preceptor for a class in the English Renaissance to be "a disagreeable silly ass" with a "small mind."[3] Literary scholarship held no attractions. Fitzgerald later set down the essence of the matter in a poem that Amory Blaine addresses to one of his teachers in *This Side of Paradise*:

> You are a student, so they say;
> You hammered out the other day
> A syllabus, from what we know
> Of some forgotten folio;
> You'd sniffled through an era's must,
> Filling your nostrils up with dust,
> And then, arising from your knees,
> Published, in one gigantic sneeze.[4]

Fitzgerald had a fertile imagination and a gift for words. Was there a place for him in American society? He possessed good looks and charm, was clever and inventive, and could spin out dramatic dialogue and song lyrics on command. These, however, were not trump cards for a young man of his middling social status. Fitzgerald did not come from a background of wealth and privilege; there was no job in a family business waiting for him after college, nor was there promise of a year in which to travel and find himself. He was beginning to have inclinations toward full-time authorship, but even this early he must have understood that writing was a precarious business. Certainly it was not a profession in the sense of medicine or law or finance. Like Amory in *This Side of Paradise*, Fitzgerald must have felt adrift. "How'll I fit in?" laments Amory. "What am I for?"[5]

St. Paul

Not much was happening around St. Paul in the winter of 1916, so Fitzgerald decided to manufacture some fun. The previous year at Princeton he had dressed up in a showgirl's costume, donned a woman's wig, and applied heavy cosmetics. A photograph of him in this getup, quite convincing, had appeared in publicity notices for the Triangle production of *The Evil Eye*. Now, in February, he attempted something similar, dressing in drag and persuading his friend Bobby Schurmier to escort him to a Psi Upsilon fraternity dance at the University of Minnesota. Fitzgerald carried off the deception for an hour or so, but when he attempted to use the men's restroom the game was up.

He continued to correspond with Ginevra, then in her junior year at the Westover School, a female academy in Middlebury, Connecticut. Ginevra had never cared much for Westover; activities there were tame, and her behavior was closely supervised. She was an indifferent student and, like her Princeton admirer, studied with only enough diligence to get by. Ginevra had a disobedient streak and seems to have enjoyed getting under the skin of the headmistress, Mary Robbins Hillard. In May things came to a head: Ginevra and two other girls broke the rules by leaning out of a dormitory window and talking to several boys who were at Westover for the senior dance. For this infraction she and her two friends were summoned to the office by Miss Hillard, who called them "bold, bad hussies" and "adventuresses." Their excuses were "honeycombed with deceit," and their "honour was stained."[6] The punishment was severe: Ginevra and the other girls would be allowed to take their end-of-year exams but must leave Westover immediately thereafter. Ginevra's father, Charles King, was informed of the crisis. He came to the school, had an acrimonious meeting with Miss Hillard, and withdrew Ginevra on the spot. She did not take her final exams or finish the school year.

News of this contretemps made its way to Fitzgerald, in gossip from friends and in letters from Ginevra, who was unrepentant. Her father enrolled her for the coming fall at Miss McFee's School, a finishing academy on West 72nd Street in New York City. She would be closer to Princeton there, and Fitzgerald must have hoped that she would come to the university to see him. In truth, though, their romantic disengagement had already begun. Ginevra's letters to him had become chatty and impersonal, and he had begun to think of her as a potential character in his fiction—an emotionally cool rich girl who liked to play at romance but who understood the ultimate importance of status and money. In the early months of 1916 Fitzgerald had written two stories about himself and Ginevra and had sent the manuscripts to her. One of these stories, "The Perfect Hour," was about their romance as it might have developed away from the distractions of family and schooling. In the other story, which

Fitzgerald called "The Ideal Day," Ginevra entertained him by flirting while they played golf. Neither story survives: once the romance was finally over, about a year later, Fitzgerald asked Ginevra to destroy his letters to her. She complied and, alas, must have destroyed these two stories as well.

In February Fitzgerald made a trip to Princeton to see his friends and check on the status of his enrollment for the fall term. When he returned to St. Paul he composed a poem for the *Nassau Literary Magazine* and sent it to the editor; "To My Unused Greek Book" was published in the June issue. The thirty-line composition is a parody of John Keats's "Ode on a Grecian Urn" and an expression of its author's attitude toward academic work. The poem, an amusing bit of japery, reads in part:

> Thou still unravished bride of quietness,
> Thou joyless harbinger of future fear,
> Garrulous alien, what thou mightst express
> Will never fall, please God, upon my ear. . . .
> Tasks all complete are sweet, but those untried
> Are sweeter, therefore little book, with page
> Uncut, stay pure, and live thy life inside,
> And wait for some appreciative age.[7]

During his first two years at the university, Fitzgerald had written primarily for the campus newspaper (the *Daily Princetonian*) and the humor magazine (the *Princeton Tiger*). During the remainder of his time in college, he would direct most of his writing to the *Nassau Lit,* where the serious student authors published their prose and verse.

That summer, in August 1916, Fitzgerald paid a visit to Ginevra in Chicago. He stayed with one of his aunts and attempted to socialize with Ginevra and her friends, but he found the experience frustrating. He had hoped for special treatment from her but found he was only one among many young men who were competing for her attentions. He could not penetrate the crowd of admirers that followed Ginevra everywhere. He was not on the firmest of ground with this social group; he was a Roman Catholic of Irish descent, two strikes against him at Princeton and in the world of the Chicago *haute bourgeoisie.* His father was a wholesale grocery salesman, not a stockbroker, an attorney, a railroad baron, or a department store magnate. This had not mattered when he was writing

Ginevra King, 1916

amusing letters to Ginevra the previous spring, but now it did. She was becoming more conscious of status and family and could see that Fitzgerald, though charming, did not really belong in her world.

Back to Princeton

The following month Fitzgerald returned to Princeton and resumed his studies. He celebrated his twentieth birthday on September 24. He seems to have made an initial effort to attend classes and to improve his marks, but he soon fell into his old habits of inattention and class-cutting. He spent most of his time on undirected reading and, as in the previous fall, composed lyrics for the Triangle show, a production called *Safety First!* These lyrics are among the best of Fitzgerald's collegiate writings. One song, "One-Lump Percy," concerns a young man of patrician manner, at ease at afternoon tea parties, where he always desires only a single lump of sugar in his cup. Herewith the chorus:

> One-lump Percy, Percy, the parlor snake,
> Please have mercy, Percy, for mercy's sake,
> Tender hearts you're breaking,
> Someone forsaking;
> When upon your knee your tea you balance,
> We lose sight of other gallants,
> King of parlor talents,
> Percy the parlor snake.[8]

Ginevra was now a student at Miss McFee's in New York. Fitzgerald made a final try for her affections, inviting her to come to campus for the Yale football game in November. In her letters to him she was evasive. "Please ask someone else if you can't wait," she urged him in one letter. "Be frank and earnest," she added.[9] Ginevra did end up coming to Princeton for the Yale game, but she and her companion, another girl from Miss McFee's, had made second engagements (known as "late dates") with two boys from Yale. Many years later, Ginevra remembered the deception. After the game Scott and another Princeton boy rode the train with Ginevra and her classmate back to Penn Station in the city. "My girlfriend and I had made plans to meet some other, uh, friends," Ginevra recalled. "So we said good-bye, we were going back to school, thanks so much. Behind the huge pillars in the station there were two guys waiting for us—Yale boys. We couldn't just walk out and leave them standing behind the pillars. Then we were scared to death we'd run into Scott and his friend. But we didn't. I think they'd just headed for the bar."[10]

Fitzgerald's poor academic record had again made him ineligible to perform in the Triangle show or to go on tour with the traveling production. He tried to manufacture his own version of an opening night by inviting two St. Paul girls, Elizabeth "Litz" Clarkson and Marie "Bug" Hersey, to come to Princeton for a performance of the show on Saturday, December 16. Both girls were attending the French School, a young women's academy on East 94th Street in New York. Fitzgerald was inviting them to a "*pre*formance," given for the faculty and, in particular, for Jenny Hibben, the wife of John Grier Hibben, the university president. Jenny Hibben was the unofficial censor for the production, alert to anything off-color or risqué in the plot or lyrics. With blue pencil in hand and a copy of the script on her lap, she would strike through offending elements that might put the university in a bad light during the traveling production.

Fitzgerald's letter to Elizabeth Clarkson, postmarked December 7, is light in tone. He had lined up another boy, Jimmie Ackerman, to make a foursome. They would dine at the Princeton Inn, he said, and then proceed to the Casino, the barnlike theater building on campus in which the show was to be presented. "On Sunday we will amuse you to the best of our ability," continued Fitzgerald, "though I havn't the slightest idea how as Sunday here is desolate." Fitzgerald continues the letter in a chatty mode: "Hear you met Dave Mcdougal. Do you aimez him? Non! I met your friend Harold Bulkley the other day. Seems very charming. Oh dear!"[11] The girls did come to Princeton to see the show, but for Fitzgerald this must have been a poor substitute for true participation in *Safety First!*—a production for which he, after all, had written the lyrics.

What is remarkable about Fitzgerald's letter to Clarkson, and about his other letters and writings from 1916, is their innocence. He seems to have been largely unaware of the war that was raging in France and Belgium, destroying much of European civilization and taking a bloody toll in the trenches. In February 1916 the lengthy Battle of Verdun had begun; by November it had produced more than seven hundred thousand casualties. From July to November 1916, at the first Battle of the Somme, one million men died or were wounded. There seemed to be no

Fitzgerald at Princeton in tennis togs

end in sight for this war. For the time being, the United States was remaining neutral. What Fitzgerald knew of the Great War came to him from newspapers and magazines or over the radio. Soon enough he and the other members of his generation in America would learn firsthand about the war, but for the time being he seemed largely unaware of it.

Years later Fitzgerald set down a summary of his twentieth year in his ledger: "A year of terrible disappointments + the end of all college dreams," he wrote. "Everything bad in it was my own fault."[12] And yet much of what happened to Fitzgerald during 1916 set the stage for his decision to become a writer. Princeton was cloistered and protected. The prizes and social recognition that the young men competed for could become all-consuming; the winners in these campus contests, many of whom considered their college years to be the best of their lives, often accomplished little thereafter. Fitzgerald was lucky to escape this trap. He was able to stay at Princeton and to use his time to read and ponder and make a start as an author. Perhaps he was already beginning to think of himself as the chronicler of his generation, as a social observer and critic and storyteller. Just how he would manage to support himself in the literary marketplace remained a mystery, but he must have known that, potentially at least, he could compete on a larger playing field than the one Princeton had provided.

He was now beginning to write about Ginevra and girls like her for publication. In January 1917 he published a one-act play, "The Debutante," in the *Nassau Lit*. The play, a closet drama, is set in the boudoir of a young society beauty named Helen. The room is filled with boxes, ribbons, strings, dresses, skirts, petticoats, and dance slippers, all lying about in disarray. Helen is gazing into a large pier mirror and practicing facial expressions for the debutante ball that she will shortly attend downstairs. She is "terrifically pleased with herself," the narrator tells us.[13] Helen can play the ingenue or the vamp with equal facility, and she is supremely confident in social situations. Her mother now enters the boudoir and instructs her about which of the men at the dance are most eligible for matrimony. Helen will have none of it. She means to pay attention only to those boys who catch her interest. The mother reluctantly leaves, and Helen continues her primping.

Now a disappointed suitor named John makes an appearance at her window and, with permission, climbs into Helen's *sanctum interiorem*. "You've been rotten to me this week," he complains. "You're tired of me." This prompts Helen to explain her approach to courtship. "I like the feeling of going after them," she tells him. "I like the way they begin to follow you with their eyes." Matters progress, she explains, until the young man is infatuated. "He's first lovesick, then discouraged, and finally lost," she says. Poor John, once favored, is now among the vanquished. "Please go now," Helen tells him. Crestfallen, he departs through the window. Helen, having finished her preparations for the evening, "dances toward the mirror, kisses the vague reflection of her face, and runs out the door."[14] This short play is filled with clever dialogue and witty asides. It is the first appearance in Fitzgerald's writings of his heroine, beautiful and headstrong, defiant of convention, and aware of her power over men. This young woman knows instinctively how to draw attention in social situations and is interested chiefly in herself.

Fitzgerald gave his heroine a second outing in a short story published in the May issue of the *Nassau Lit*. This story, "Babes in the Woods," is Fitzgerald's rendering of his first meeting with Ginevra, in January 1915, at a house party for teenagers in St. Paul. The Ginevra character, whose name is Isabelle, is a sixteen-year-old beauty from out of town, visiting with a school friend. The St. Paul girls have prepared Isabelle to meet and fall for the local champion—a handsome college sophomore named Kenneth Powers. All goes according to plan; the two young people meet, smile at one another, and begin their flirtation. Both are experienced at this sort of thing, though Kenneth likes occasionally to depart from the script. He has a clever "line" and a polished manner, while Isabelle proceeds intuitively, relying on her beauty and natural poise. Fitzgerald portrays Isabelle with considerable skill:

> All impressions and in fact all ideas were terribly kaleidoscopic to Isabelle. She had that curious mixture of the social and artistic temperaments, found often in two classes—society women and actors. Her education, or rather her sophistication, had been absorbed from the boys who had dangled upon her favor; her tact was instinctive, and her capacity for love affairs was limited only by the number of boys she met. Flirt smiled from her large, black-brown eyes and figured in her intense physical magnetism.[15]

Toward the end of the evening Kenneth maneuvers Isabelle into a little den near the music room. They are alone, having temporarily escaped Isabelle's other admirers. Kenneth is hoping for a kiss. He moves forward, but with hesitation: "I've fallen for a lot of people—girls—and I guess you have too—boys, I mean, but honestly you—," he tells her. Isabelle is "quite stirred" and feels Kenneth's hand close over hers. They lean forward for their first kiss but then, maddeningly, three younger boys from the party rush into the den. The moment is ruined, the kiss not achieved. After this disappointment the story comes to a quick conclusion. Kenneth must catch the late train east for his first day of classes. He and Isabelle exchange a glance—"on his side, despair, on hers, regret." Later, in bed, Isabelle is miffed. "Damn!" she mutters as she punches her pillow. "Damn!"[16]

"The Debutante" and "Babes in the Woods" introduce us to a character Fitzgerald would re-create again and again, with refinements, throughout his literary career. She is beautiful and alluring, aware of her good looks and charm, secure in her social status, and infinitely attractive to men. She is also willful, vain, and a bit coldhearted, not much interested in protestations of love and devotion. This young woman understands how society operates and how status is achieved and maintained. Eventually, she believes, she will marry successfully and follow a comfortable path through life, but for the time being she intends to enjoy her beauty and youth. Fitzgerald was a keen observer, alive to details of courtship and marks of status. He could sense that the social habits of American youths were beginning to change. His instinct was to set it all down before it vanished.

Fitzgerald's writings in the *Nassau Lit* demonstrate a growing skill with the mechanics of fiction and drama. He was learning to create believable characters, to construct a scene, to write lively dialogue, and to keep the plot moving. His models were not the avant-garde authors of the period; instead he was imitating such writers as H. G. Wells, Arnold Bennett, Compton Mackenzie, George Bernard Shaw, and Oscar Wilde. From these authors, all of them successful in the literary marketplace, he took a sense of writing for one's natural public rather than for a coterie of admirers. After he became a professional, Fitzgerald managed to balance on the line between popular appeal and artistic respectability as well as any writer of his generation. These lessons, which he learned early, are already apparent in his *Nassau Lit* publications.

Fitzgerald began to spend time with some of the more literary students on campus. He developed a friendship with Edmund Wilson, who later became the leading book critic of his generation, and with John Peale Bishop, who made a mark during the 1920s as a poet and essayist. Another friend was John Biggs Jr., who became a lawyer and later a judge but who maintained an interest in literature and published two novels in the 1920s. These new friends urged Fitzgerald to read "better stuff"—by which they meant fewer popular novels and fewer magazine stories with trick plots. Wilson, Bishop, and Biggs admired Fitzgerald for his obvious talent; they also envied him for his felicity with words and for the ease with which he could turn out poems and stories.

It now appeared that the United States was headed into the Great War and that Fitzgerald might be a part of that conflict. Germany had resumed unrestricted submarine warfare early in 1917; six American merchant ships carrying supplies to the Allies had been sunk by U-boats, without warning and with great loss of life. Big American banks had made large loans to England and France; it was manifestly in their interest for the Allies to win the war. Pro-British propaganda was everywhere in the newspapers, intermixed with reports of German atrocities in Belgium and other occupied countries. The British intercepted and published the Zimmermann Telegram, an encoded message from the German government to the Mexican government. The telegram made an offer: if the Mexicans would support the Central powers, Germany would help them regain the territory they had lost to the United States in the Mexican–American War of 1846–48. These various factors caused President Woodrow Wilson, on April 6, 1917, to ask Congress for a declaration of war. The legislators complied, and the United States entered the conflict.

Fitzgerald signed up for intensive military training in May. Under this plan he went through three weeks of drill at Princeton and was given a pass for the courses he had not completed. Fitzgerald wanted to be an officer and therefore applied for a commission. Most of the officers were drawn from the ranks of college men; Fitzgerald felt relatively confident that, as a Princeton man, his application would be approved. He spent most of the summer of 1917 in St. Paul, reading and loafing and wondering what it would be like to go to war. Many of his hometown friends were already in military training camps, and the summer social season was slow. Late that summer he visited Bishop in Charles Town, West Virginia, where he carried on a flirtation with a local girl named Elizabeth "Fluff" Beckwith. He returned to St. Paul and traveled to Fort Snelling, seven miles to the south, to take the examination for a commission in the infantry.

Fitzgerald was back at Princeton in September, but he did not formally enroll in classes. He attended a few lectures and waited for his commission to be approved. He roomed with John Biggs in Campbell Hall and helped Biggs, who was editing the *Princeton Tiger,* fill the issues. It was not unusual for the two young men to sit up all night and turn out an entire issue between sundown of one day and sunrise of the next. On September 24, Fitzgerald turned twenty-one. A little over a month later his commission as a second lieutenant came through. He signed the Oath of Allegiance, purchased his uniforms at Brooks Brothers in New York City, and reported for duty at Fort Leavenworth, Kansas, in late November.

Most of Fitzgerald's time in November and December 1917 was occupied by military training. He was not a natural officer; the posture of command did not come readily to him. He had a romantic attitude toward army service and saw possibilities for gallantry and heroism in combat, but he found the training exercises tedious. He had more important things on his mind. He had begun writing a novel that fall while still at Princeton, an autobiographical narrative that he was calling "The Romantic Egotist." A handful of chapters were finished. His first-person narrator, whose name is Stephen Palms, is a thinly veiled version of Fitzgerald. Like many young infantry officers, Fitzgerald suspected that he might not live through the war, and he wanted to leave behind a record of his experiences. He had brought his completed chapters with him to Fort Leavenworth. He attempted to produce more pages during mandatory study periods in the evenings but was found out by the instructors. He therefore resolved to do his writing on weekends. Each Saturday afternoon at one o'clock he settled in at the Officers' Club and went to work on his novel. "There, in a corner of a roomful of smoke, conversation and rattling newspapers," he later recalled, "I wrote a one-hundred-and-twenty-thousand-word novel on the consecutive week-ends of three months. There was no revising; there was no time for it."[17] This was Fitzgerald's first attempt at a long work of fiction, and he found himself struggling. The surviving pages of "The Romantic Egotist" reveal some of his difficulties:

> Here I am with not one chapter finished—scrawled pages with no
> form or style—just full of detail and petty history. I intended so
> much when I started, and I'm realizing how impossible it all is. . . .
> I don't seem to be able to trace the skeins of development as I ought.
> I'm trying to set down the story part of my generation in America
> and put myself in the middle as a sort of observer and conscious
> factor. . . . I'll never be able to do it again, well done or poorly. So
> I'm writing almost desperately—and so futily.[18]

By January 10 he could report to Edmund Wilson that he had completed eighteen chapters and had five to go. He had high hopes for the book: "I can most nearly describe it by calling it a prose, modernistic Childe Harolde," he boasted. If the novel was actually published, he told Wilson, "I'll wake some morning and find that the debutantes have made me famous over night."[19]

In the months between January 1916 and December 1917, Fitzgerald ended his romance with Ginevra King and learned many things about how social status operated. He accepted the fact that he was a poor student and ceased to compete for campus honors at Princeton. He joined the army but made no early mark as an officer. These failures, and others that were to come, became part of his conception of himself. They impelled him later in life to aim high and drive himself hard. He retained his faith in his talent and his belief in his destiny; eventually, he hoped, he would succeed in literature and in love. A few years later his star would indeed begin to shine, but for now he waited and pondered, wondering what the future might hold for him.

NOTES

1. James L. W. West III, *The Perfect Hour: The Romance of F. Scott Fitzgerald and Ginevra King, His First Love* (New York: Random House, 2005), 39–40.

2. Matthew J. Bruccoli, *Some Sort of Epic Grandeur: The Life of F. Scott Fitzgerald*, 2nd ed. (Columbia: University of South Carolina Press, 2002), 60.

3. Bruccoli, *Epic Grandeur*, 65.

4. F. Scott Fitzgerald, *This Side of Paradise*, ed. James L. W. West III, Cambridge Edition of the Works of F. Scott Fitzgerald (Cambridge: Cambridge University Press, 2012), 104.

5. Fitzgerald, *This Side of Paradise*, 200.

6. West, *Perfect Hour*, 48.

7. F. Scott Fitzgerald, "To My Unused Greek Book," in *Spires and Gargoyles: Early Writings, 1909–1919*, ed. James L. W. West III, Cambridge Edition of the Works of F. Scott Fitzgerald (Cambridge: Cambridge University Press, 2010), 123.

8. F. Scott Fitzgerald, "One-Lump Percy," in *Spires and Gargoyles*, 85.

9. West, *Perfect Hour*, 61.

10. West, *Perfect Hour*, 62, 63–64.

11. James L. W. West III, "F. Scott Fitzgerald's Last Triangle 'Preformance,'" *Princeton University Library Chronicle* 69, no. 3 (Spring 2008): 516.

12. F. Scott Fitzgerald, *F. Scott Fitzgerald's Ledger: A Facsimile*, introduction by Matthew J. Bruccoli (Washington, D.C.: NCR/Microcard editions / Bruccoli Clark, 1972), 170.

13. F. Scott Fitzgerald, "The Debutante," in *Spires and Gargoyles*, 144.

14. Fitzgerald, "The Debutante," 144–53.

15. F. Scott Fitzgerald, "Babes in the Woods," in *Spires and Gargoyles*, 189.

16. Fitzgerald, "Babes in the Woods," 193–95.

17. F. Scott Fitzgerald, "Who's Who—and Why," in *My Lost City: Personal Essays, 1920–1940*, ed. James L. W. West III, Cambridge Edition of the Works of F. Scott Fitzgerald (Cambridge: Cambridge University Press, 2005), 4.

18. F. Scott Fitzgerald, "The Romantic Egotist," facsimiled in *F. Scott Fitzgerald Manuscripts*, vol. 1, part 2, ed. Matthew J. Bruccoli (New York: Garland, 1990), 18–19.

19. F. Scott Fitzgerald, *A Life in Letters*, ed. Matthew J. Bruccoli (New York: Charles Scribner's Sons, 1994), 17.

1918–1919

Niklas Salmose

The Long Summer of Despair, 1919

God Damn, I have my darling. She is mine. Scott Fitzgerald will turn twenty-three in a handful of days. (In his ledger, he succinctly calls his twenty-third year the happiest since he was eighteen.) Ten minutes earlier, the postman rang the bell and Fitzgerald dived wildly down the stairs from his third-floor room in his parents' home at 599 Summit Avenue, St. Paul. Now he clutches in his hands a letter dated September 16 that will change his life. "Dear Mr. Fitzgerald," it opens.[1] The room smells of leftover milk and stale sandwiches, but he has not had an appetite for quite some time, subsisting only on Coke and the cigarettes he smokes on a small deck outside the window overlooking Summit Avenue.[2]

He glances at the cover of a book on his bedside table—Hugh Walpole's 1913 novel Fortitude: Being a True and Faithful Account of the Education of an Explorer, *which he read on the 4th of July that year on the "dry" train to St. Paul from New York.[3] One of Walpole's London novels, Fortitude* became an enormous success on both sides of the Atlantic. Fitzgerald noticed, and perhaps took inspiration from, the way the novel portrayed a novice writer struggling to find both an identity and an occupation in life, but he knew bad writing when he saw it. According to André Le Vot, Walpole's novel gave Fitzgerald renewed hope during a time when he had almost given up on a literary career. *"If Walpole can get away with it so can I."[4]*

Discharged from the army in mid-February 1919, Fitzgerald settled in New York at 200 Claremont Avenue, in "one room in a high, horrible apartment-house in the middle of nowhere."[5] In the daytime Fitzgerald worked at Barron Collier Agency, composing advertisements at a salary of ninety dollars a month for the Street Railway Advertisement Company. He was poor as a church mouse, but his literary talent earned him a raise when he composed a slogan for the Muscatine Steam Laundry in Iowa: "We keep you clean in Muscatine." His boss joked with him: "Pretty soon this office will not be big enough to hold you."[6] How right he was! At

Colliers, some of his slogans were illustrated by John Held Jr., who became one of the seminal art deco illustrators of the Jazz Age. Held also made the famous cover for Fitzgerald's second collection of short stories, *Tales of the Jazz Age* (1922), which would include stories inspired by the events of this time in Fitzgerald's life, most notably "May Day" (set in New York) and "The Jelly-Bean" (set in Alabama), both published in 1920. While in New York, Fitzgerald could not resist the temptation to look up Maxwell Perkins at Charles Scribner's Sons. The publishing house had already rejected Fitzgerald's first novel twice, but during the meeting Perkins pushed Fitzgerald to revise his manuscript again, stressing the need to create more distance by changing from first-person narration to third.[7]

Fitzgerald wrote stories in the evenings (nineteen that spring) and received 122 rejections. The walls of his tiny Claremont Avenue room were covered in rejection slips. His only sale was the 1917 story "Babes in the Woods," first published in Princeton's *Nassau Literary Magazine*, which the *Smart Set* bought for thirty dollars. That first acceptance letter was not even a great event: "Dutch Mount and I sat across from each other in a car-card slogan advertising office, and the same mail brought each of us an acceptance from the same magazine—the old 'Smart Set.'"[8] The story had been written in college two years before, and Fitzgerald was disappointed that his new stories were not good enough. "I was on the down-grade at twenty-two."[9]

The money from the *Smart Set* was used to buy a pair of white flannels for his fiancée, Zelda Sayre, but Fitzgerald's poverty was genuine. As Le Vot argues, "He began to lose some of the self-assurance that had borne him through college and the army."[10] As Fitzgerald testifies in "Early Success," the vernal Princeton beau, wearing shoes with cardboard in the soles, glanced longingly into the shop windows on Fifth Avenue: "It was like the fox and goose and the bag of beans," he claimed, referring to the famous river-crossing riddle.[11] "Lost and forgotten," he wrote, "I walked quickly from certain places—from the pawn-shop where one left the field glasses, from prosperous friends whom one met when wearing the suit from before the war—from restaurants after tipping with the last nickel, from busy cheerful offices that were saving the jobs for their own boys from the war."[12]

After three quarrelling and (at least for Scott) depressing visits in the first half of 1919 to Montgomery, Alabama, to visit Zelda, she broke off

In March 1919, a youthful Zelda Sayre had photographs taken of herself in costume that she then sent to Fitzgerald in New York City. She wrote to him in a personal letter dated March 1919: "I'm glad you liked those [photographs]—I wanted them to serve as maps of your property."

their engagement in May. She also returned the engagement ring (his mother's engagement ring) that Scott had sent her on March 24 with an accompanying note: "Darling: I am sending this just the way it came—I hope it fits and I wish I were there to put it on. I love you so much, much, much that it just hurts every minute I'm without you—Do write every day because I love your letters so—Good bye, my own wife."[13] Fitzgerald, sensing his own failures, tried to hasten their marriage plans through letters to Zelda's mother and father and extensive visits to Montgomery, but to no avail.

The strain in the relationship is evident in their intense correspondence. Zelda's letters started out as jovial, chatty, intense, and warm after their initial meeting at the Montgomery Country Club on the evening of July 13, 1918, but they became more and more reserved, informative rather than personal, and distanced—in short, anxious—from March to June 1919.[14] In May 1919 Zelda wrote to Scott, "I am so damned tired of being told that you 'used to wonder why they kept princesses in towers'— you've written that verbatim, in your last *six* letters! . . . And so many of your letters sound forced."[15] Toward the summer the letters from Scott became scarcer, to Zelda's distress: "No wonder I never hear from you . . . looks like wild nights and headachy mornings—I was scared you had forgotten me."[16] Zelda's final letter to Scott that summer is emblematic of how their relationship had stalled:

June 1919
Montgomery, Alabama

You asked me not to write—but I do want to explain—That note belonged with Perry Adair's fraternity pin which I was returning. Hence, the sentimental tone. He has very thoughtfully contributed a letter to you to the general mix-up. It went to him, with his pin.

I'm so sorry, Scott, and if you want the pictures, I'll mail them to you.

Zelda[17]

The note Zelda refers to was meant for someone else. At the Georgia Institute of Technology, Zelda had been infatuated with golfer Perry Adair and received his fraternity pin. Remorseful upon her return to Alabama, she had mailed the pin back but accidently mixed up her note to Adair with a letter to Fitzgerald, so Scott received Adair's note by accident.[18] After receiving this letter, Fitzgerald hurried to Montgomery one last time to try to settle the whole affair through an immediate marriage, an idea that Zelda rejected. Rebuffed and lost, Fitzgerald spent his last pennies on a three-week bender and returned home to St. Paul on July 4. The optimism he had aired to Zelda on first arriving in New York— "DARLING HEART AMBITION ENTHUSIASM AND CONFIDENCE I DECLARE EVERYTHING GLORIOUS THIS WORLD"—seemed far gone.[19]

September 17, 1919. "Dear Mr. Fitzgerald." He reads the letter he has just received. Pauses. The dazzling sound of the electric car on the Groveland Park Line outside his open window. This is the moment, the decisive moment for a career and a life that were to be so much the representation of the mythical structures forming the American nation for decades. "I am very glad, personally, to be able to write to you that we are all for publishing your book, 'This Side of Paradise.'"[20]

Scott "ran along the streets stopping automobiles to tell friends and

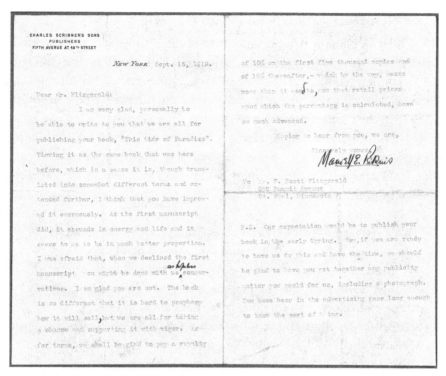

Letter from Maxwell Perkins and Scribner's, dated September 16, 1919, finally accepting *This Side of Paradise* for publication.

acquaintances" that his novel had been "accepted for publication."[21] That was, indeed, not only the end of his job repairing car roofs for the Northern Pacific Railway (which he had begun two weeks earlier, in early September, and where he was ridiculed for wearing a polo shirt and dirty white flannels instead of denim) but also the end of an education of a personage—Fitzgerald was now properly a persona of his own. On the way to Zelda, with a bottle of gin and a copy of the manuscript of *This Side of Paradise,* he sipped endless cups of tea to cure his Minnesota winter cold while the Tennessee purple maypops swayed in the wind of the train, unaware perhaps that he had found an editor, Max Perkins, who would back him for the rest of his life.[22] Little did he know that a drama had taken place at Scribner's before Perkins sent out the letter of acceptance. And in that train car he had not the faintest idea that within four months he would be both married and the hippest generational writer of the nation.

"I Am Now Lieutenant F. Scott Fitzgerald," 1918

"I am now Lieutenant F. Scott Fitzgerald of the 45th Infantry," Fitzgerald wrote to Edmund Wilson on January 10, 1918. This was the same day that a Russian delegation headed by Leon Trotsky recognized the Ukrainian People's Republic as a sovereign nation during opening peace negotiations with the Central powers, and one day after German flying ace Max Ritter von Müller was killed during a dogfight with three British planes over Moorslede, Belgium. In the final stages of the Great War, however, Fitzgerald's project was more internal than national, and in the letter to Wilson he announced:

> There are twenty-three Chapters, all but five are written and it
> is in poetry, prose, verse libre and every mood of a tempermen-
> tal temperature. It purports to be the picaresque ramble of one
> Stephen Palms from the San Francisco fire, thru School, Princeton
> to the end where at twenty one he writes his autobiography at
> the Princeton aviation school. It shows traces of Tarkington,
> Chesterton, Chambers Wells, Benson (Robert Hugh), Rupert
> Brooke and includes Compton-Mckenzie like love-affairs and
> three psychic adventures including an encounter with the devil
> in a harlot's apartment.[23]

As his ledger for his twenty-second year acknowledged, this was "a year of enormous importance. Work, and Zelda. Last year as a Catholic."[24] The twenty-three chapters would haunt him, just as the "devil in a harlot's apartment" haunts Amory in the novel, for more than two years. Everything he did was somehow intertwined with the literary task of writing the great generational novel—and, simultaneously, writing himself into the heart and family of Zelda, a free spirit and dancer who was soon to be voted the prettiest girl in Lanier High School's class of 1918.

One must trace the stylistic development of his first novel back to student life at Princeton University. Patriotic spirit spread over the college after the United States declared war against Germany on April 6, 1917, and the football fields were turned into drill grounds. During that year Fitzgerald sent off twenty-six poems, and they were all rejected. Although he gave up his poetic endeavors, his novel was highly influenced not only by these very poems but also by a poetic prose style that would mark his literary voice in decades to come. Similarly, as Henry Dan Piper argues, his fascination for the stage and play writing also encouraged his literary style, especially his ability to catch nuances in dialogue.[25] As he told his daughter, Scottie, much later, work on verse and poetry developed his impressionistic and concentrated prose style.[26]

On November 20, 1917, he started writing his novel. "Every evening, concealing my pad behind *Small Problems for Infantry*," he remembered, "I wrote paragraph after paragraph on a somewhat edited history of me and my imagination. The outline of twenty-two chapters, four of them in verse, was made, two chapters were completed; and then I was detected and the game was up. I could write no more during study period."[27] He either slept or wrote through lectures on "Trench Behaviour," "Sniping and Being Sniped," and "The Lewis Gun."[28]

The war brought about a strong sense of the limitations of time. "I had only three months to live," he wrote later; "in those days all infantry officers thought they had only three months to live—and I had left no mark on the world."[29] But for Fitzgerald, the urgency to write also seemed to have a different, although related, ambience:

> I am trying to set down the story part of my generation in America and put myself in the middle as a sort of observer and conscious factor.
>
> But I've got to write now, for when the war's over I won't be able to see these things as important—even now they are fading out against the back-ground of the map of Europe. I'll never be able to do it again; well done or poorly. So I'm writing almost desperately—and so futily.[30]

So, now working in the Officers Club, he toiled and sweated, all work and no play, and finished off 120,000 words in three months.[31]

One can read the development through multiple revisions of *This Side of Paradise* in many ways, but among Cyril Sigourney Fay, John Peale Bishop, Edmund Wilson, and Charles "Sap" Donahoe, Shane Leslie is perhaps the most unrecognized influence. Leslie was an Irish journalist, poet, and lecturer who toured the United States twice between 1911 and 1918. He was a very handsome man and had connections in high places. Although James Mellow argues that there was something suspect about

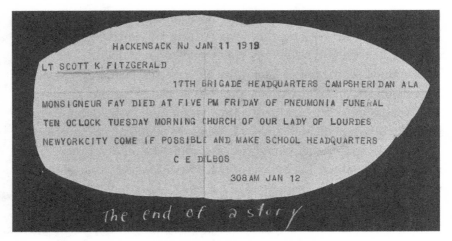

HACKENSACK NJ JAN 11 1919

LT SCOTT K FITZGERALD

17TH BRIGADE HEADQUARTERS CAMPSHERIDAN ALA

MONSIGNEUR FAY DIED AT FIVE PM FRIDAY OF PNEUMONIA FUNERAL

TEN OCLOCK TUESDAY MORNING CHURCH OF OUR LADY OF LOURDES

NEWYORKCITY COME IF POSSIBLE AND MAKE SCHOOL HEADQUARTERS

C E DILBOS

308AM JAN 12

The end of a story

The wire on January 12, 1918, announcing the death of Fitzgerald's mentor Monsignor Sigourney Fay.

Leslie's character,[32] Fitzgerald had great respect for him, as a mentor and also as an author, which shined through in his positive reviews of Leslie's poetry. Fitzgerald compared Leslie's *The Celt and the World* (1917) to the pessimistic but precise prose of Swedish author August Strindberg and related Leslie's *Verses in Peace and War* (1916) to that great "undercurrent of sadness" also permeating Leslie's prose.[33] Fitzgerald described Leslie as "the most romantic figure" he had ever known. "He had sat at the feet of Tolstoy, he had gone swimming with Rupert Brooke, he had been a young Englishman of the governing classes."[34] Most significantly, Leslie was a Scribner's author.

In early February 1918, Fitzgerald takes a week's leave and visits Leslie in Washington to discuss his novel. Scott later finishes his first version of the novel in the Cotton Club, Princeton, and sends the typescript to Leslie, who had offered to recommend him to Charles Scribner II. Leslie corrects the typescript and sends it on to Scribner's on May 6 with a cover letter describing the author as an American prose Rupert Brooke: "Though Scott Fitzgerald is still alive it has a literary value. Of course when he is killed, it will also have a commercial value. . . . In spite of its disguises, it has given me a vivid picture of the American generation that is hastening to war. I marvel at its crudity and its cleverness."[35]

This Side of Paradise was dedicated to the late Father Fay, who had also been the model for Monsignor Darcy, the most optimistic, spirited, and positively crafted character in the novel. Fay had written to Fitzgerald in December 1917 that although Fitzgerald "went to war as a gentleman should," it was "better to leave the blustering and tremulo-heroism to the middle classes; they do it so much better."[36] True enough, Fitzgerald never saw combat, but he did see beauty, for *de gustibus non est disputandum*. And it happened on July 13, 1918, at the Montgomery Country Club.

The Military Man

The Forty-Fifth Infantry moved from Kansas to Camp Zachary Taylor in Louisville, Kentucky, on March 15, 1918. Trained as an officer, Fitzgerald was scheduled to command a platoon but was deemed unfit for such responsibilities.[37] He also reconnected with John Peale Bishop, who had already been at the camp for several months. Bishop and Fitzgerald had become friends at Princeton, and this was an opportunity to develop their friendship. They intensively discussed literature; Bishop's poetry collection *Green Fruit* (1917) had just been published. The pair also took a whack at the social life of the streets of Louisville; the city had a reputation for beautiful architecture that was paralleled by equally appealing girls, and they were charmed by both. Louisville would later become an important setting for *The Great Gatsby,* where Daisy Fay first meets the soldier Jay Gatsby.

In April the Forty-Fifth moved to Camp Gordon, Georgia, before finally settling at Camp Sheridan, Montgomery, in June. Montgomery's capitol dome was where the first Confederate banner had floated, and the town was dominated by a coterie of proud, rural, and conservative Confederate sons and daughters. Andrew Turnbull sketches the town of some forty thousand inhabitants in a Fitzgeraldesque way:

> Each morning Negro drovers herded cattle down the main residential street, and in September when the cotton had been baled, a procession of mule-drawn drays took it through the town to the warehouse. Negro women in calico dresses and bright bandanas sat on the bales plucking banjos or laughing with the children, while the men in straw hats and overalls roused their dust-caked beasts with a crack of the whip or a loud "Geet-opp!"[38]

Officers of the Sixty-Seventh Infantry Regiment at Camp Sheridan in
Montgomery, Alabama. Scott Fitzgerald is in the center.

As had been the case with his platoon in Camp Zachary Taylor, several reports indicate Fitzgerald was not a successful officer. Although he
was promoted to first lieutenant at Camp Sheridan, his officers did not
show him much respect, and he was subjected to a series of pranks.[39] At

Sheridan he fell off his horse and was commanded to take riding lessons, and Le Vot relates an unfortunate incident with a boat, which was later used for the short story "I Didn't Get Over" (1936).[40] Whatever the reasons behind these military failures, it is interesting to note that several of Fitzgerald's cosoldiers experienced him as an odd person, deviating from the ordinary norms and personalities in the military and displaying an almost nervous desire to be liked. "I didn't particularly like him," said Colonel Benjamin W. Venable of Forty-Fifth. "He was more or less self-centered. He ran around chiefly by himself. He didn't date very often with anyone else."[41] Fellow soldier Deveraux Josephs, by contrast, claims that Scott "was eager to be liked by his companions and almost vain in seeking praise. . . . Beneath the surface, however, he was wholly different than the other men in his company. He was more sensitive, better read and less influenced by his surroundings—hence at bottom more mature."[42]

The Montgomery girls welcomed the Yankee officers, who were considered more sophisticated than the local boys. Two of the top girls were May Steiner and Zelda Sayre. The Sayre residence at 6 Pleasant Avenue was a popular calling-place among the young officers—and there were plenty, since both Camp Sheridan and Camp Taylor had recently filled up. A famous anecdote illustrates Zelda's popularity. The commander at Camp Taylor airfield supposedly issued an order against stunting planes over her house.[43] Two of the air-courting officers, Lieutenants Henry Watson and Lincoln Weaver, reportedly crashed on a nearby speedway track after attempting a tailspin above the Sayres' house.[44]

Fitzgerald dated May Steiner first and kept her photograph wrapped in an American flag in the barracks. That this was not a casual flirtation is indicated by a July entry in his ledger: "May Stiener. Zelda . . . May and I on the porch." The order was reversed in the entry in August: "Zelda & May."[45] Although Fitzgerald and Zelda first met on July 13, it was not disclosed in the ledger as love at first sight. Four days were enough for deep emotion to develop: "Fell in Love on the 17th."[46]

"Fell in Love on the 17th"

The Montgomery Country Club on Carter Hill at the head of Narrow Lane has been entertaining since its inaugural Saturday dance on May 27, 1905. *On Saturday, July 13, 1918, Zelda and Scott attend the regular*

Saturday dance. Fitzgerald wears his Brooks Brothers uniform and "cream-colored boots extending up to just below his knees."[47] *In the row of "bar-lows,"*[48] *one particular belle stands out. Underneath a thick wave of confident honey-gold hair leans a well-boned face with two intense and haunting blue eyes, intensified by the use, at the time rare, of mascara. If the somewhat beaky nose precludes a claim to classic features, this is compensated for by her thin, arousing lipsticked mouth, an embouchure inviting any male dream. An evening doll, boyish in her bodily unveiling—no one can fail to notice confidence, natural beauty, and intelligence in Zelda Sayre.*

Turnbull described Zelda as "a bucking bronco or a heap of bees."[49] Scott, if we are to trust Zelda's depiction of him in her novel *Save Me the Waltz*, gave an ambiguous impression: "There seemed to be some heavenly support beneath his shoulder blades that lifted his feet from the ground in ecstatic suspension, as if he secretly enjoyed the ability to fly but was walking as a compromise to convention."[50]

Much has been made of Fitzgerald's artistic double vision—his ability to write both immersive and distanced fiction. The grandiose description from outside the Tarleton Country Club in "The Jelly-Bean" captures the ambience of the July 13 dance:

> The Jelly-bean walked out on the porch to a deserted corner, dark between the moon on the lawn and the single lighted door of the ballroom. There he found a chair and, lighting a cigarette, drifted into the thoughtless reverie that was his usual mood. Yet now it was a reverie made sensuous by the night and by the hot smell of damp powder puffs, tucked in the fronts of low dresses and distilling a thousand rich scents to float out through the open door. The music itself, blurred by a loud trombone, became hot and shadowy, a languorous overtone to the scraping of many shoes and slippers.[51]

Zelda danced all night to that very beat, the beat of life during the war summer of 1918, which Fitzgerald emphasizes, nostalgically, in "The Last of the Belles." As Le Vot writes, "In this frantic festival atmosphere, prejudice, social barriers, all the customary restraints disappeared. People tried to fulfil the promise of a lifetime in a single summer."[52] The dog days of the Alabaman summer resonated well with the general spirit of youth—futures uncertain, death imminent, the *carpe noctem* of a fast

Country Club, Montgomery, Ala.

Country Club, Montgomery, Ala.

Montgomery Country Club, the meeting place for one of the decade's most celebrated and public love stories.

life. Fitzgerald wrote in his ledger for July: "Swimming, Watermelons, The Country Club."[53] Zelda moved her slippers through the Saturday night, but was up early the next morning rolling bandages for the Red Cross. There was still a war going on, after all, in what Scott, in a letter Zelda would open a few days later on her veranda, would call "youthful melancholy":

Zelda:

Here is the mentioned chapter . . . a document in youthful
melancholy. . . .

However . . . the heroine does resemble you in more ways than
four.[54]

Fitzgerald is referring to the "Babes in the Woods" chapter that had been
incorporated into *This Side of Paradise*. One can deduce that Zelda was
proud of both resembling and standing as model for Rosalind. "Rosalind!
I like girls like that," Zelda said in a 1923 interview. "I like their courage, their recklessness and spend-thriftness. Rosalind was the original
American flapper."[55] This was the start of intense courting on Fitzgerald's
behalf.

Scott called Zelda some days later only to be informed that her cal-
endar was full for weeks ahead. During the next Saturday dance at the
club, he was infuriated when he saw Zelda kiss a date under the "over-
hanging gas lamp of a telephone booth near the club."[56] He changed gear
and hosted a country club party on July 24 in honor of her eighteenth
birthday: "And it was a radiant night, a night of soft conspiracy and the
trees agreed that it was all going to be for the best."[57] Yet he was but one
of many of Zelda's suitors that summer.

Zelda Sayre was born in Montgomery, the youngest of six siblings.
Her mother, Minerva ("Minnie"), was known as an eccentric and artistic
person; she had declined to join the Drew-Barrymore theater company
in order to marry. Her father, Anthony Dickinson Sayre, was a judge on
the Supreme Court of Alabama and one of Alabama's leading jurists. Her
father's family had moved to Alabama shortly before the Civil War and
established themselves in society, and members of the Sayre family had
served in the U.S. Senate and edited local newspapers. In short, although
Zelda did not belong to the stratum of great plantations, she was firmly
established in upper-middle-class southern society and was a member of
what was considered one of the finest families in Alabama. While not
rich, the Sayres lived in the fashionable west side of Montgomery and
employed a small domestic staff.

Named after a gypsy queen who had appeared in one of her mother's
books, Zelda was a free spirit who disliked borders and rules. Fitzgerald
later claimed she was sexually reckless, but her friends denied this.[58] In

fact, although she was the most desired eighteen-year-old in the county, the real reason she preferred boys to girls was that they were less bound by conventions than southern girls.[59] Zelda did boyish things and pushed the limits for what was expected from a genteel girl. She rode on boys' motorcycles, smoked in public, chewed gum, danced cheek to cheek, was the first in Montgomery to bob her hair, and was happy to sneak out of her room at midnight to swim in Catoma Creek and down corn liquor and gin.[60]

Part of Scott's infatuation of Zelda can be traced to her social status. Although not comparable to Scott's first love, Ginevra King from Chicago, Zelda still moved in the air of a southern aristocracy that held a strong allure for Fitzgerald. But it would be a mistake to read social status as the sole reason for the maturation of their friendship and love. Rather, as Wilson suggested, they were kindred spirits.[61] Fitzgerald had met an equal, a girl "whose uninhibited love of life rivalled his own and whose daring, originality, and repartee would never bore him."[62] Scott and Zelda were romantics; they wanted fame, success, and glamour, and in the process of achieving them they were willing to close their eyes to some of their respective flaws. Instead, their relationship was about intensity and authenticity of life, freedom of spirit, and passion . . . passion . . . passion. As Matthew J. Bruccoli notes, they both had an exhibitionist streak, but whereas Scott wanted admiration and attention, Zelda just did not care what people thought of her.[63]

Zelda's parents opposed the couple's attachment and could not see their youngest daughter marrying a man from a middle-class Irish family; in their eyes, he had no money, no future, and too much liking for tobacco and drink.[64] During Scott and Zelda's first dinner with the Sayres, it was Zelda who was the troublemaker, though—she teased her father to such an extent that he grabbed a carving knife and chased her around the table.[65] But life at the Sayres' was typically less dramatic. The image "mellow with a romantic flare" captures these encounters: "The pair would sit out on the wide porch of the Sayres' Pleasant Street house, screened from the sun by the thick cover of clematis vines and Virginia creepers that Zelda's mother had trained up on wires."[66]

Through all the mischiefs, struggles, and tragedies that surround the most famous couple of the Jazz Age, one can always sense true love. Zelda gave Scott a silver flask with the inscription "Forget Me Not, Zelda.

9/13/18,"[67] and Fitzgerald wrote to Ruth Howard Sturtevant in early January 1919:

> Ruth
>   I
>   am
>   in
>   love![68]

In a telegram to Zelda a month later, he wrote:

> MISS SELDA SAYRE
>
> 6 PLEASANT AVE MONTGOMERY ALA
>
> DARLING HEART AMBITION ENTHUSIASM AND CONFIDENCE I
> DECLARE EVERYTHING GLORIOUS THIS WORLD IS A GAME AND
> WHITE [WHILE] I FEEL SURE OF YOU LOVE EVERYTHING IS
> POSSIBLE I AM IN THE LAND OF AMBITION AND SUCCESS AND
> MY ONLY HOPE AND FAITH IS THAT MY DARLING HEART WILL
> BE WITH ME SOON.[69]

"The Land of Ambition and Success"

Zelda was an integrated part of Scott's literary project—not only as muse, but as pure reality; without the success of a novel, she would be gone. Nowhere is this clearer than in Fitzgerald's plea to Perkins for an early publication of *This Side of Paradise* after he received the acceptance letter: "I have so many things dependent on its success—including of course a girl."[70] Fitzgerald wrote with multiple urgencies.

Fitzgerald's confidence was hit hard by the two rejections he received from Scribner's. It is possible that the cordial tone of the first rejection letter (perhaps written by Perkins), on August 19, 1918, sparked Fitzgerald to continue. Despite the rejection, Scribner's acknowledged the originality of the manuscript and stressed that the suggestions for revision should not "'conventionalize' it by any means."[71] The second rejection letter in October that same year affected him more, as is evident in a note next to the letter in his scrapbook: "The end of a dream."[72] This dream also included Zelda.

Fitzgerald's astute self-analysis illustrates his true literary talent. To Leslie, he wrote in May 1919: "That it is crude, incredibly dull in places is too true to be pleasant. . . . I have no idea why I hashed in all that monotonous drivel about childhood in the first part and would see it hacked out like an errant appendix without a murmur. . . . There are too many characters and too much local social system in the Princeton section. . . . And in all places all through, the verses are too obviously lugged in."[73] He referred to the fragmentation and lack of form as a potpourri, with poems sandwiched between "reams of autobiography and fiction."[74] Nevertheless, Fitzgerald meticulously steered his literary vessel toward the harbor of success through several important changes. Most essentially, he abandoned his first-person narration in favor of a more distanced third-person narration, which allowed for better control over the subjectivity of the narrative through the stylistic use of free indirect discourse. He renamed his hero, gave him amusing parents, cut out some biographical material, and replaced monologue with dramatic scenes.

Satisfied with his revisions in the early days of September 1919, he entrusted Thomas Daniels with delivering his typescript to New York. Daniels accidently left the script in a taxi, but it was later retrieved. This was the third occasion Fitzgerald's manuscript hovered around the Scribner's building on Forty-Second Street.

Scribner's editor in chief, William Crary Brownell, lies on a leather couch in his large office. Between chapters of the redrafted This Side of Paradise, *he spits into the brass spittoon. Upon finishing, he takes a nap. Waking up exactly an hour later, Brownell buttons his coat, caps and lights a Newman cigar, then takes a walk around the block.* Petting at Princeton. Devils. Ha! *Before returning to his desk, he has made up his mind.*[75]

The editors met, Brownell announced his opinion on the book. Charles Scribner II agreed with Brownell's assessment that the novel was frivolous—he would not put his name on a book without literary merit.[76] Perkins, agitated, stood and offered his resignation. The editorial room was silent. Perkins slowly returned to his chair and, in a calm voice, told Scribner, "If we are going to turn down the likes of Fitzgerald, I will lose all interest in publishing books."[77] This became momentous in the history of Scribner's—a clash between editors young and old. And the future won, which benefited not only Fitzgerald but also Ring Lardner, Ernest Hemingway, and other modern writers who would become Scribner's authors.

Finally published on March 26, 1920, to great acclaim, Fitzgerald's debut novel failed to impress Wilson: "*This Side of Paradise* is one of the most illiterate books of any merit ever published," he reviewed. "Not only is it ornamented with bogus ideas and faked literary references, but it is full of literary words tossed about with the most reckless inaccuracy."[78] Wilson's antagonism against *This Side of Paradise* might have come from the many proof errors that existed in the first edition, but it also echoed a larger skepticism toward his Princeton friend. Regardless of Wilson's criticism, the novel about young adult life at Princeton went on to become a generational boom novel. Burton Rascoe wrote in his review, "It is sincere, it is honest, it is intelligent, it is handled in an individual manner, it bears the impress, it seems to me, of genius. It is the only adequate study that we have had of the contemporary American in adolescence and young manhood."[79]

The novel's inherent fragmentation in form and style, its blending of genres and media types, situates it clearly in the early history of high-modernist narration. And its explicit explorations of sex and youth culture sparked a certain kind of realism that broke with earlier generations' puritan representation of life. Piper gives three very plausible explanations for its success: (1) It illustrated new freedom expressed through adolescent behavior. (2) It introduced female readership to a new kind of heroine. (3) It idealized and mythologized New York.[80] The first printing of three thousand copies sold out in three days.

The strenuous break between Scott and Zelda had truly come to an end when Scott had finished his third and final draft of the novel. Zelda wrote Scott, "Darling Heart, our fairy tale is almost ended and we're going to marry and live happily ever afterward just like the princess in her tower who worried you so much—and made me so very cross by her constant recurrence—I'm so sorry for all the times I've been mean and hateful—for all the miserable minutes I've caused you when we could have been so happy. You deserve so much—so very much—."[81] They married on April 3, 1920.

Fitzgerald summed up 1919 best: "The uncertainties of 1919 were over—there seemed little doubt about what was going to happen—America was going on the greatest, gaudiest spree in history and there was going to be plenty to tell about it. The whole golden boom was in the air—its splendid generosities, its outrageous corruptions, and the tortuous death struggle of the old America in prohibition. All the stories that came into my head had a touch of disaster in them."[82] The Jazz Age had begun.

Zelda also sensed disaster in their lives. Scott wrote to Zelda when she was hospitalized again in North Carolina in the summer of 1940: "Twenty years ago *This Side of Paradise* was a best seller and we were settled in Westport. Ten years ago Paris was having its last great American season but we had quit the gay parade and you were gone to Switzerland. Five years ago I had my first bad stroke of illness and went to Asheville. Cards began falling for us much too early."[83]

NOTES

1. John Kuehl and Jackson R. Bryer, eds., *Dear Scott / Dear Max: The F. Scott Fitzgerald—Maxwell Perkins Correspondence* (New York: Charles Scribner's Sons, 2016), 33.

2. Dave Page and John Koblas, *F. Scott Fitzgerald in Minnesota: Toward the Summit* (St. Cloud, Minn.: North Star Press, 1996), 94.

3. The Wartime Prohibition Act took effect on June 30, 1919.

4. Quoted in André Le Vot, *F. Scott Fitzgerald: A Biography*, trans. William Byron (New York: Doubleday, 1983), 70.

5. Quoted in Andrew Turnbull, *Scott Fitzgerald* (London: Bodley Head, 1962), 99.

6. Quoted in Turnbull, *Fitzgerald*, 99.

7. Andrew Scott Berg, *Max Perkins: Editor of Genius* (New York: New American Library, 2016), 14.

8. F. Scott Fitzgerald, "Early Success," in *My Lost City: Personal Essays, 1920–1940*, ed. James L. W. West III, Cambridge Edition of the Works of F. Scott Fitzgerald (Cambridge: Cambridge University Press, 2014), 185.

9. Fitzgerald, "Early Success," 185.

10. Le Vot, *Fitzgerald*, 67.

11. Fitzgerald, "Early Success," 185. The riddle is this: A farmer has a fox, a goose, and a bag of beans that he needs to ferry across a river, but the boat will only carry two things, the farmer and one other. If he leaves the fox and the goose together, the fox will eat the goose. If leaves the goose and the beans together, the goose will eat the beans. How does the farmer get all three across safely?

12. Fitzgerald, "Early Success," 185.

13. Jackson R. Bryer and Cathy W. Barks, eds., *Dear Scott, Dearest Zelda: The Love Letters of F. Scott and Zelda Fitzgerald,* with an introduction by Eleanor Lanahan (London: Bloomsbury, 2002), 18.

14. Sally Cline, author of *Zelda Fitzgerald: Her Voice in Paradise* (New York: Arcade, 2003), argues that Zelda and Scott met earlier than the dance, during a tea party. David S. Brown, *Paradise Lost: A Life of F. Scott Fitzgerald* (Cambridge, Mass: Harvard University Press, 2017), 72.

15. Bryer and Barks, *Dear Scott, Dearest Zelda,* 29.

16. Bryer and Barks, *Dear Scott, Dearest Zelda,* 35.

17. Bryer and Barks, *Dear Scott, Dearest Zelda,* 37.

18. Bryer and Barks, *Dear Scott, Dearest Zelda,* 37.

19. Le Vot, *Fitzgerald,* 67.

20. Kuehl and Bryer, *Dear Scott / Dear Max,* 33.

21. Fitzgerald, "Early Success," 186.

22. Matthew J. Bruccoli, *Some Sort of Epic Grandeur: The Life of F. Scott Fitzgerald,* 2nd ed. (Columbia: University of South Carolina Press, 2002), 99.

23. Quoted in Bruccoli, *Epic Grandeur,* 81.

24. F. Scott Fitzgerald, "F. Scott Fitzgerald's Ledger, 1919–1938," University of South Carolina Transcription, Rare Books and Special Collections, University of South Carolina, 2012, 68.

25. Henry Dan Piper, *F. Scott Fitzgerald: A Critical Portrait* (London: Bodley Head, 1966), 30.

26. Piper, *Fitzgerald,* 31.

27. F. Scott Fitzgerald, "Who's Who—and Why?" *Saturday Evening Post,* September 18, 1920, 61.

28. Turnbull, *Fitzgerald,* 87.

29. Fitzgerald, "Who's Who—and Why?" 61.

30. Quoted in Bruccoli, *Epic Grandeur,* 80.

31. Bruccoli, *Epic Grandeur,* 80.

32. James Mellow, *Invented Lives: F. Scott and Zelda Fitzgerald* (Boston: Houghton Mifflin, 1984), 63.

33. Jackson R. Bryer and Matthew J. Bruccoli, *F. Scott Fitzgerald, in His Own Time: A Miscellany* (New York: Popular Library, 1971), 116–17.

34. Quoted in Bryer and Bruccoli, *Fitzgerald in His Own Time,* 134.

35. Quoted in Bruccoli, *Epic Grandeur,* 82.

36. Quoted in Le Vot, *Fitzgerald,* 59.

37. Bruccoli, *Epic Grandeur,* 82.

38. Turnbull, *Fitzgerald,* 89–90.

39. Bruccoli, *Epic Grandeur,* 82.

40. Bruccoli, *Epic Grandeur,* 90; Le Vot, *Fitzgerald,* 61.

41. Albert E. Elmore, "Fitzgerald's High IQ: An Interview with Colonel Benjamin W. Venable, 45th Regiment, U.S. Army," *F. Scott Fitzgerald Review* 17 (2019): 10.

42. Quoted in Brown, *Paradise Lost,* 69–70.

43. Bruccoli, *Epic Grandeur,* 88.

44. Kendall Taylor, *Sometimes Madness Is Wisdom: Zelda and Scott Fitzgerald—A Marriage* (New York: Ballantine Books, 2001), 28.

45. Fitzgerald, "Ledger," 68.

46. Fitzgerald, "Ledger," 69.

47. Taylor, *Madness Is Wisdom,* 32.

48. Slang of the 1920s for "girl."

49. Turnbull, *Fitzgerald,* 92.

50. Zelda Fitzgerald, *Save Me the Waltz* (London: Vintage, 2001), 34–35.

51. F. Scott Fitzgerald, "The Jelly-Bean," in *Tales of the Jazz Age,* ed. James L. W. West III, Cambridge Edition of the Works of F. Scott Fitzgerald (Cambridge: Cambridge University Press, 2012), 20. Nancy Lamar, the heroine in "The Jelly-Bean," was

Fitzgerald's first full-fledged flapper. The *Saturday Evening Post* turned down the story because of what they considered an unhappy ending. Harold Ober managed to sell it to *Metropolitan*, the fiction-lover's magazine, instead.

52. Le Vot, *Fitzgerald*, 64.

53. Fitzgerald, "Ledger," 68.

54. Kuehl and Bryer, *Dear Scott, Dearest Zelda*, 10.

55. Quoted in Bryer and Bruccoli, *Fitzgerald in His Own Time*, 259.

56. Taylor, *Madness Is Wisdom*, 34.

57. Taylor, *Madness Is Wisdom*, 34.

58. Bruccoli, *Epic Grandeur*, 87.

59. Bruccoli, *Epic Grandeur*, 88.

60. Taylor, *Madness Is Wisdom*, 45.

61. Taylor, *Madness Is Wisdom*, 36.

62. Turnbull, *Fitzgerald*, 94.

63. Bruccoli, *Epic Grandeur*, 88–89.

64. Taylor, *Madness Is Wisdom*, 37.

65. Le Vot, *Fitzgerald*, 66.

66. Mellow, *Invented Lives*, 51.

67. Taylor, *Madness Is Wisdom*, 34.

68. F. Scott Fitzgerald, *Correspondence of F. Scott Fitzgerald*, ed. Matthew J. Bruccoli and Margaret M. Duggan (New York: Random House, 1980), 35.

69. Bryer and Barks, *Dear Scott, Dearest Zelda*, 12.

70. Bruccoli, *Epic Grandeur*, 99.

71. Fitzgerald, *Correspondence*, 31–32.

72. Bruccoli, *Epic Grandeur*, 86.

73. F. Scott Fitzgerald, *The Letters of F. Scott Fitzgerald*, ed. Andrew Turnbull (London: Penguin, 1968), 393.

74. Fitzgerald, *Letters*, 391.

75. Berg, *Max Perkins*, 11.

76. Berg, *Max Perkins*, 16.

77. Berg, *Max Perkins*, 16.

78. Quoted in Bryer and Bruccoli, *Fitzgerald in His Own Time*, 405.

79. Quoted in Bryer and Bruccoli, *Fitzgerald in His Own Time*, 305.

80. Piper, *Fitzgerald*, 60–61.

81. Quoted in Bruccoli, *Epic Grandeur*, 110.

82. Fitzgerald, "Early Success," 188.

83. Fitzgerald to Zelda, June 14, 1940, quoted in Berg, *Max Perkins*, 385.

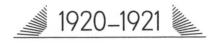

1920–1921

Walter Raubicheck

In the middle of May 1920, Scott and Zelda Fitzgerald rented a house in Westport, Connecticut, on the shores of Long Island Sound. They lived there for five months and then moved back to Manhattan, where they had been married on April 3 in the rectory of St. Patrick's Cathedral. To be married in the actual church was not permitted, for Zelda was not a Catholic. During this five-month period in Westport, which in effect constituted their honeymoon, they drank extensively, threw many weekend parties, and experienced some of the most passionate—and most difficult—weeks of their marriage. Fitzgerald wrote about these highs and lows in his second novel, *The Beautiful and Damned* (1922), which he began while they lived in what in the novel he termed "the grey house." These intense five months had a lasting effect on both of them, personally and professionally, as evidenced by their own later literary and artistic endeavors. Though they would spend significant time in New York and St. Paul during the next two years, in many ways the Westport residency established a pattern both for their marriage and for Fitzgerald's writing life for the next decade.

On March 26, 1920, Scribner's had published Fitzgerald's first novel, *This Side of Paradise,* which had the most critical and financial success upon publication of any of the four novels he completed in his lifetime. *This Side of Paradise* is very much an autobiographical novel that includes incidents from Fitzgerald's secondary school and college years, but it presents them impressionistically, the way James Joyce presented the same time span in his life in *A Portrait of the Artist as a Young Man* (1916). In addition to straightforward narrative, Fitzgerald uses poems, dramatic vignettes, and short stream-of-consciousness passages to describe Amory Blaine's coming-of-age as a person and writer. Its inclusion of scenes of adolescent romantic passion, such as a subchapter titled "Petting"—which would have been omitted from any Victorian novel—gave it some notoriety and contributed to its immediate popularity. At the end of the novel, Amory, who has lost his father figure Monsignor

Darcy to an unexpected death, is struggling to create a philosophy of life to replace the faith Darcy had represented to him: Amory and his generation have grown up to "find all Gods dead, all wars fought, all faiths in man shaken."[1] Already in his first novel Fitzgerald is presenting himself as a spokesperson for those who have come of age at the beginning of the first postwar decade: "I know myself," Amory cried, "but that is all—."[2] It is an adolescent novel, but one written from the perspective of a young artist who has left adolescence behind and is struggling to find a new code of values to live by.

Fitzgerald was suddenly a well-known author, and just as suddenly he had some money—the lack of which had prevented the couple from marrying earlier. They stayed in several Manhattan hotels for a short while; one, the Biltmore, asked them to leave because of their raucous behavior, so they moved to the Commodore Hotel a few blocks away. During these spring months the newlyweds celebrated Fitzgerald's success by attending one party after another, drinking, and spending the newfound money that came from the respectable sales of the first printing of the novel and particularly from a number of recently published short stories. Looking back from the perspective of the 1930s, Fitzgerald, remembering his state of mind riding in a taxi in New York in 1920, wrote, "I began to bawl because I had everything I wanted and knew I would never be so happy again."[3] As the summer approached, both Scott and Zelda wanted to escape the heat of the city, and Scott also wanted a quiet place to begin writing his second novel. So they bought a car and drove north, originally intending to reside at Lake Champlain for the summer, but upon being informed that Champlain was too cold to swim, they discovered Westport instead, a suburb with rural charm yet close enough to New York to please them.

Westport

During this five-month period their lives were anything but solitary: they entertained many of their Manhattan and Princeton friends and acquaintances, regularly went into Manhattan for parties, and also rode the car south to Montgomery, Alabama, on a visit to Zelda's family (a visit immortalized in Fitzgerald's subsequent 1924 magazine piece "The Cruise of the Rolling Junk"). The Westport residency was intense enough that Fitzgerald devoted almost one-third of *The Beautiful and Damned*

Scott and Zelda in front of the Westport cottage

(1922) to Anthony Patch and Gloria Gilbert's (Fitzgerald and Zelda's) stay at the grey house in Marietta (Westport). In fact, in the novel they spend three summers there, as opposed to the actual one summer, more evidence of the impact of the Westport stay on the author.

The grey house was actually known in 1920 as the Wakeman Cottage, an eighteenth-century house that still stands in Westport. It bordered on the estate of Frederick E. Lewis, a multimillionaire known for his lavish parties and whose beach the newly married couple used throughout that summer. In *The Beautiful and Damned,* when Gloria and Anthony finally leave Marietta, she thinks that the grey house had seen "the flower of their love."[4] It had also seen numerous fights and suspected betrayals. Indeed, in the novel, their relationship continues its steady decline once they arrive back in New York. The book rather presciently predicts many of the actual conflicts and dilemmas that beset Scott and Zelda's marriage beginning in 1928, in particular Scott's drinking and Zelda's desire to be an artist in her own right despite her husband's objections.

Professionally, the influence of the Westport months was felt for the next year and a half as Fitzgerald wrote and rewrote the novel that emerged from the grey house experience, first serialized in 1921 in *Metropolitan* magazine and then finally published by Scribner's in 1922.

The Westport cottage today on South Compo Road

He also wrote one of his finest early stories, "The Jelly-Bean," during the Westport months, inspired by Zelda's escapades in Montgomery, here named Tarleton.[5] After the couple moved to Great Neck on Long Island in 1922 and Fitzgerald began to conceptualize the book that would become *The Great Gatsby* (1925), the Westport experience had just as much impact on the geography of the novel as did Great Neck, a claim first put forward by Barbara Probst Solomon in a *New Yorker* article in 1996.[6] Zelda's novel *Save Me the Waltz* (1932) includes a scene that recounts a visit by the parents of Zelda-surrogate Alabama to the house in Connecticut where she and her recently successful artist husband now live.[7] Zelda based this scene on the actual visit of Zelda's parents to the grey house in August 1920.

This section of Zelda's novel echoes the disastrous visit in *The Beautiful and Damned* of Anthony's grandfather to the young couple, which results in Anthony's disinheritance, the novel's principal conflict for the remainder of the story. More evidence of the permanent impression that the Westport months had on Zelda is found in one of the decorative lampshades she was in the habit of creating: it depicts many of the

Fitzgerald residences, European and American, from their life in the 1920s, and one of the panels contains a very recognizable drawing of the Westport house. As Westport historian Richard Webb Jr., points out, the house where they lived in Great Neck on Long Island is not represented on the lampshade.[8]

Personally, the Westport months saw the beginning of the carefree but careless lifestyle the Fitzgeralds would live for the next several years, one that made them celebrities of the Jazz Age but also took an early psychological and physical toll. As one of their frequent guests, Alexander McKaig, an old classmate of Fitzgerald's, noted in his diary about the Fitzgeralds' arrival in Manhattan from Westport: "In the evening Zelda—drunk—having decided to leave Fitz & having nearly been killed walking down RR tracks, blew in. Fitz came shortly after. He had caught same train with no money or ticket. They threatened to put him off but finally let him stay on—Zelda refusing to give him any money. They continued their fight while here."[9] This incident is the basis for what is probably the most memorable scene in *The Beautiful and Damned*, Gloria's dramatic exit in the middle of the night from the grey house to the Marietta train station, pursued desperately by Anthony. In both real life and the novel, alcohol was the immediate cause of such erratic behavior on the part of both the Patches and the Fitzgeralds.

Remarkably, Fitzgerald was able to find enough quiet time and space to write his masterpiece and several of his greatest stories between 1920 and 1925 as well as his underrated, misunderstood second novel. Yet the incipient alcoholism of his undergraduate years became a full-blown addiction during 1920, one he would periodically struggle against but finally succumb to twenty years later. And though *The Beautiful and Damned* describes the ravages of alcoholism as it charts the fall of Anthony Patch, Fitzgerald was only sporadically able to apply the lessons of his fiction to his own life. As he created Anthony Patch in the serial version of the novel written in 1920 and early 1921 and in the major rewrite he did in St. Paul in the fall of 1921, the author fell prey to the same demons as his protagonist.

One of the Fitzgeralds' regular guests that summer in Westport was George Jean Nathan, America's foremost drama critic in 1920, the most prominent champion of Eugene O'Neill and the coeditor, with H. L. Mencken, of the *Smart Set*, one of the most prestigious literary journals in America. Mencken and Nathan published several of Fitzgerald's stories in 1920, in particular "May Day," an early artistic triumph, and "Benediction."[10] The *Smart Set* did not pay nearly as well as popular magazines such as the *Saturday Evening Post,* but Fitzgerald desired the literary cachet that publication in the journal brought him. Fitzgerald also became friendly with both men in 1920, but since Mencken lived in Baltimore and Nathan lived in Manhattan, he obviously spent more time with the latter, though he corresponded with Mencken and saw him when Mencken came to New York. In February 1920 Fitzgerald wrote to his editor Maxwell Perkins that "another of my discoveries is H. L. Mencken who is certainly a factor in present day literature. In fact I'm not so cocksure about things as I was last summer—this fellow Conrad seems to be pretty good after all."[11] Both Mencken and Nathan shared a caustically cynical attitude toward American bourgeois pieties, and Fitzgerald presented this attitude in both "May Day" and *The Beautiful and Damned*: in fact, Nathan served as a model for the character of the irreverent friend Maury Noble, who plays a major role in the grey house section of the novel.

Mencken, one of the most influential literary critical voices of the time, had a predilection for realistic fiction that revealed the dark side of Americans' drive for success, in particular the novels of Theodore Dreiser and Frank and Charles Norris. By introducing Fitzgerald to these authors in 1920, he influenced the overall dynamism of *The Beautiful and Damned,* which is a story of the deterioration of the protagonist, much as Dreiser had earlier depicted the decline of George Hurstwood in *Sister Carrie* (1900). In March Fitzgerald had inscribed a copy of *This Side of Paradise* to Mencken with a note that said, in part, "[as] a matter of fact, Mr. Mencken, I stuck your name in on page 224 in the last proof—partly, I suppose, as a vague bootlick and partly because I have since adopted a great many of your views."[12] Fitzgerald later referred to *The Beautiful and Damned* as "a concession to Mencken. . . . The business of creating illusion is much more to my taste and talent."[13] This admission was made as he had begun work on the story that would become *The Great Gatsby.* Clearly with *The Beautiful and Damned* he had wanted to write a novel that satisfied the critic's requirements for major literary achievement in fiction, mainly a study of "character in decay,"[14] but in doing so he had suppressed his own more romantic tendencies. Mencken remained a lifelong friend, but Fitzgerald's relationship with Nathan had soured by the end of the grey house summer because of the editor's flirtations with Zelda.

Solomon's claim that the Westport sojourn not only became the basis for the plot and setting of one-third of *The Beautiful and Damned* but also established the geography for *The Great Gatsby* has been supported and expanded on by Robert Steven Williams, a Westport filmmaker, who completed a documentary on the topic.[15] Westport native Richard Webb Jr. has also published a book, *Boats against the Current: The Honeymoon Summer of Scott and Zelda,* that explores the Westport/Gatsby thesis in depth. Essentially, both Williams and Webb argue that the locations of the Gatsby mansion and Nick Carraway's cottage bear no relation to the actual Great Neck, Long Island, home that the Fitzgeralds rented from 1922 to 1924, which was in the town and some distance from Long Island Sound. Instead, these locations replicate remarkably closely the physical relationship of the grey house in Westport to the Lewis estate next door—on the Connecticut rather than the Long Island side of Long Island Sound. They claim that the Westport experience was transplanted to Great Neck (West Egg in the novel), and the memory of Lewis's extravagant parties was transplanted to Gatsby's parties. Given Fitzgerald's penchant for creating composite characters in his fiction, characters who combine the traits of more than one person Fitzgerald knew in real life (for example, Dick Diver from *Tender Is the Night* possesses characteristics of both Fitzgerald and his friend Gerald Murphy), it is likely he did the same with two physical locations in this particular case, using the Westport "next door" proximity to a wealthy party-giving neighbor and integrating that physical arrangement into the general Long Island setting of the novel. Of course, during their two-year residence in Great Neck, Scott and Zelda were surrounded by the Gold Coast mansions that dotted the north shore of Long Island between Great Neck and Huntington in the 1910s and '20s, and no doubt they were familiar with a number of them. So the actual physical descriptions of the Gatsby house and the Buchanan house could very well have been partly derived from the extravagant homes that they visited or at least passed by. But it is equally probable that the Wakeman cottage in Westport and the Lewis mansion next door were very much on Fitzgerald's mind when he began *Gatsby.*

After Fitzgerald and his wife left the St. Patrick's Cathedral rectory as a married couple, the rituals of the Catholic Church held little attraction for Fitzgerald (although he arranged for their daughter Scottie to be christened in St. Paul, and after his death Fitzgerald was ultimately buried in the Catholic St. Mary's cemetery in Rockville, Maryland, thirty-five years after being refused such an interment because he was not a practicing Catholic). Spirituality plays almost no role in *The Beautiful and Damned* except for Maury Noble's satire on the Bible and Anthony's constant denigration of Bilphism (theosophy). Fitzgerald's relationship to Catholic culture up until 1919 may not have emerged as an active faith in his adulthood, but it did leave a mark on the moral standards that are implied in the novels when his characters suffer from having violated them. For example, Amory Blaine encounters the devil on several occasions in *This Side of Paradise* when he is in the presence of what he considers sexual corruption. And Anthony Patch plans to write a book on the Middle Ages, often referred to as the Age of Faith, though he never completes it as he descends deeper and deeper in the grip of nihilism. Certainly Fitzgerald perceived himself as a moralist in his work, despite its reputation for celebrating flappers and the new Jazz Age permissiveness. In a 1939 letter to his daughter he compares himself to the successful musical comedy writers he might have emulated, given his successes as a lyricist and book writer with the Triangle Club at Princeton: "Sometimes I wish I had gone along with that gang, but I guess I am too much a moralist at heart and want to preach at people in some acceptable form, rather than to entertain them."[16]

New York and Europe

The Fitzgeralds moved back to Manhattan in October 1920, to a home a short walk from the Plaza Hotel on 59th Street. A month earlier, Scribner's had published his first collection of short stories, *Flappers and Philosophers,* the first of what would be four volumes of his stories published in his lifetime. Often considered the weakest of the four, *Flappers* does contain two of his most enduring stories, "Bernice Bobs Her Hair" and "The Ice Palace." The first is a sly, ironic look at the new Jazz Age fashions, such as bobbed hair, and the latter is a more serious tale of a southern belle and her northern fiancé, obviously based on Scott and Zelda's own regional differences: in the story these differences doom the relationship, while the Fitzgeralds themselves had largely been able to overcome this particular obstacle to their happiness.

The following year, 1921, was highlighted by the serial publication of *The Beautiful and Damned* in *Metropolitan* and by the birth of their only child, Scottie, in St. Paul in October. But earlier there was a trip overseas, the first—and by far the least rewarding—of several European sojourns. Although they enjoyed England (in particular, Fitzgerald was enthralled by Oxford), their experiences in France and Italy left him unimpressed and xenophobic. "God damn the continent of Europe" Fitzgerald wrote to his Princeton friend Edmund Wilson. "It is of merely antiquarian interest."[17] Originally the Fitzgeralds intended for Zelda to give birth in Montgomery, but the heat drove them north, and they settled in St. Paul in August and would live there for the next year, first at a cottage north of the city near White Bear Lake and then in several locations in the prestigious Summit Avenue area. This would be the last time Fitzgerald would see his native city, and it was a distinctive visit for many reasons. The Westport months had propelled the Fitzgeralds into the 1920s; the St. Paul months gave Fitzgerald one last experience of his past, an experience that would remain a touchstone for the nostalgia that marks his best work.

St. Paul

In a speech given in 2002, St. Paul–native author and humorist Garrison Keillor said that Fitzgerald did not much like St. Paul, that New York was really his city.[18] Of course this claim contains some truth, but not all the truth: the Midwest for Fitzgerald was the embodiment of an America older and more rooted than the one that created modern New York, and of course the Midwest is where Nick Carraway returns at the end of the summer of 1922, disgusted with the moral laxity of current East Coast denizens such as Tom and Daisy Buchanan and Jordan Baker. Dick Diver returns at the end of *Tender Is the Night* to the provinciality of upstate New York (where Fitzgerald spent several of his boyhood years) after his marriage to the wealthy Nicole Warren dissolves. St. Paul and upstate New York represented nineteenth-century culture and morality for Fitzgerald, as well as his residual Catholicism, and the tension between his enthusiasm for the postwar world and his nostalgia for the world of his boyhood marked his life as well as his work. It is not surprising that his only child would be born not in New York but in the same town in which he too had been born. The Westport months in 1920 represented the beginning of his married life, his fame, and his increasingly profligate lifestyle; the St. Paul months represented traditional family life and upper-middle-class stability.

This is not to say the Fitzgeralds abstained totally from their usual carousing while in St. Paul: at one point in 1922 their antics caused them to be excluded from the White Bear Yacht Club.[19] When the Fitzgeralds left for the East Coast in 1922, what St. Paul meant to Fitzgerald was never again something he needed to experience firsthand, though it remained a permanent factor in his imagination.[20] While in St. Paul, Fitzgerald wrote one of his finest stories, "The Diamond as Big as the Ritz." It contains some of the fantasy elements he used in other stories, such as "The Curious Case of Benjamin Button," but in this story he used them to enrich his greatest satire on American materialism. The theme would be central to all of Fitzgerald's future novels, as well as *The Beautiful and Damned,* but in the story the scorn for materialism is the central idea and not connected to any personal failings of realistically drawn characters. The ego of the story's enormously wealthy, cartoonish plutocrat Braddock Washington is such that he thinks he can bribe God to spare him and restore his huge diamond mountain when his unchartered kingdom is threatened by attack from the air. He offers God the largest and most perfect diamond in the world. God declines. The moment is simultaneously funny and chilling, as it epitomizes the American worship of riches that for Fitzgerald has come to prevail in the culture. Challenging the popular impression that Fitzgerald was fascinated by the rich, this story reveals his contempt for those who live only to amass enormous wealth. Braddock Washington can be viewed as an earlier, fairy-tale version of *The Great Gatsby*'s Tom Buchanan.

Fitzgerald also kept up a steady correspondence with Maxwell Perkins, keeping him apprised of his work on revising *The Beautiful and Damned* for book publication, asking his advice about the various endings he was experimenting with, asking for money, and discussing the publication of his second book of stories, *Tales of the Jazz Age,* which would be published in 1922 after his second novel. When Scott and Zelda left St. Paul, they moved back to New York—or Long Island, as it turned out. Fitzgerald wanted to be near the theatrical center of the country largely because of a play he had begun to contemplate in St. Paul in the fall of 1921 and began to write in early 1922. Ever since his Princeton years and his musical comedy successes, he had felt particularly drawn to the theater, and he was confident his comedy/satire would bring him acclaim and a new source of income. It was not to be. *The Vegetable* would be one of Fitzgerald's few failures as a writer.

Fitzgerald's most significant endeavor artistically in the fall of 1921 was his reworking of *The Beautiful and Damned* for book publication. He found the serialization in *Metropolitan* disappointing because of the editors' cuts, so he was eager to produce a version he could control, even quarreling with Perkins over the Maury Noble episode about the Bible. The episode was finally published as Fitzgerald wanted after some minor concessions to Perkins and much vacillation as to the proper ending for the book.

The Beautiful and Damned is probably the least read of Fitzgerald's five novels. Structurally and tonally it is uneven, and its length gives it an episodic quality that undermines the consistency of his characterization of Anthony Patch and his wife Gloria Gilbert. It does contain memorable scenes, such as Maury Noble's late-night lecture on the cynicism that motivated the authors of the Bible, or Gloria's flight from the grey house, pursued by Anthony, to the Marietta train station in the scene just prior to Noble's speech. Both scenes take place during the grey house section of the book, which, together with its depiction of Anthony's courtship of Gloria in Manhattan, forms the first third of the novel and has a satisfying unity, but that quality is missing from the remainder of the novel, where we witness a lengthy collection of scenes (including a long interlude in which Anthony is drafted, leaves Gloria behind in New York, is sent to an army camp in the South, and has an affair with a local girl) that depict different stages of Anthony's decline and the deterioration of his marriage to Gloria. We witness the charm and wit of the young Anthony give way to alcoholic rage and depression, and the beauty and radiance of the young Gloria give way to physical and emotional deprivation. Yet the first third of *The Beautiful and Damned* has the lyrical charm and the precise social commentary that make the best of Fitzgerald's early short stories so successful, stories such as "May Day," "The Diamond as Big as the Ritz," and "The Ice Palace."[21]

The novel ultimately blames the couple for succumbing to the nihilism that prevailed in the new modern culture in which they had come of age: "[As] justification of his manner of living there was first, of course, The Meaninglessness of Life. As aides and ministers, pages and squires, butlers and lackeys to this great Khan there were a thousand books glowing on his shelves."[22] As for Gloria, "from her conversation it might be assumed that all her energy and vitality went into a violent affirmation of the negative principle 'Never give a damn.'"[23] One of the subchapters is titled "A Nietzschean Incident," and the spirit of the existentialist philosopher and subscribers to his ideas, such as George Bernard Shaw, pervades the intellectual atmosphere of the novel. Unlike Gatsby, who is doomed by his "romantic readiness" and his confidence in being able to reach "the green light" in a culture indifferent to idealistic dreams, Anthony and Gloria are doomed by their inability to see the point of striving for any goal whatsoever. Mencken believed the modern American novel should present "character in decay,"[24] and *The Beautiful and Damned* does just that. The conflict of the second half of the novel results from Anthony's disinheritance by his wealthy grandfather. After advice from both Zelda and Perkins, Fitzgerald settled on an ending that does not moralize directly but conveys its final message ironically. By the time Anthony and Gloria successfully contest his grandfather's will and receive the money, their marriage is in a shambles and Anthony has lost his grip on reality.

By the end of 1921, Fitzgerald had successfully completed two novels and two volumes of short stories, in addition to a number of stories that had been published in magazines but had not been collected. He had married the girl he desired more than any other, and they had had a daughter together. He was about to return to New York, "his city" as Garrison Keillor put it. He and his work were becoming more and more representative of the decade he had dubbed "The Jazz Age." Ahead of him would be his greatest achievements as an American novelist, but the seeds of these achievements were sown during the Westport months of 1920 and the final St. Paul homecoming of 1921, the future and the past.

NOTES

1. F. Scott Fitzgerald, *This Side of Paradise*, ed. James L. W. West III, Cambridge Edition of the Works of F. Scott Fitzgerald (Cambridge: Cambridge University Press, 2012), 260.

2. Fitzgerald, *This Side of Paradise*, 260.

3. F. Scott Fitzgerald, "My Lost City," in *My Lost City: Personal Essays, 1920–1940*, ed. James L. W. West III, Cambridge Edition of the Works of F. Scott Fitzgerald (Cambridge: Cambridge University Press, 2014), 111.

4. F. Scott Fitzgerald, *The Beautiful and Damned*, ed. James L. W. West III, Cambridge Edition of the Works of F. Scott Fitzgerald (Cambridge: Cambridge University Press, 2014), 235.

5. F. Scott Fitzgerald, "The Jelly-Bean," in *Tales of the Jazz Age,* ed. James L. W. West III, Cambridge Edition of the Works of F. Scott Fitzgerald (Cambridge: Cambridge University Press, 2012), 13–32.

6. Barbara P. Solomon, "Westport Wildlife," *New Yorker,* September 9, 1996, 78–85.

7. Zelda Fitzgerald, *Save Me the Waltz* (Carbondale: Southern Illinois University Press, 1967), 50–56.

8. Richard Webb Jr., *Boats against the Current: The Honeymoon Summer of Scott and Zelda* (Westport, Conn.: Prospecta Press, 2018), 57.

9. Quoted in Andrew Turnbull, *Scott Fitzgerald* (New York: Charles Scribner's Sons, 1962), 112–13.

10. See "Benediction" in *Flappers and Philosophers,* ed. James L. W. West III, Cambridge Edition of the Works of F. Scott Fitzgerald (Cambridge: Cambridge University Press, 2012); "May Day," in *Tales of the Jazz Age.*

11. F. Scott Fitzgerald, *The Letters of F. Scott Fitzgerald,* ed. Andrew Turnbull (New York: Charles Scribner's Sons, 1963), 144.

12. F. Scott Fitzgerald, *Correspondence of F. Scott Fitzgerald,* ed. Matthew J. Bruccoli and Margaret M. Duggan (New York: Random House, 1980), 55.

13. Fitzgerald, *Correspondence,* 139.

14. Henry L. Mencken, "National Letters," in *Prejudices: Second Series* (New York: Alfred A. Knopf, 1920), 40–41.

15. *Gatsby in Connecticut: The Untold Story,* directed by Robert S. Williams (Vision Films, 2020).

16. Fitzgerald, *Letters,* 63.

17. Fitzgerald, *Letters,* 326.

18. Garrison Keillor, "Speech to the F. Scott Fitzgerald Society" (St. Paul, September 2002).

19. Matthew J. Bruccoli, *Some Sort of Epic Grandeur: The Life of F. Scott Fitzgerald* (New York: Harcourt, Brace, and Jovanovich, 1981), 173.

20. Witness "Absolution," in *All the Sad Young Men,* ed. James L. W. West III, Cambridge Edition of the Works of F. Scott Fitzgerald (Cambridge: Cambridge University Press, 2014), a story with a strong Catholic and St. Paul atmosphere, and the Basil Duke Lee stories of the late 1920s, several of which draw on Fitzgerald's own boyhood and adolescence in St. Paul.

21. See "May Day" and "The Diamond as Big as the Ritz" in *Tales of the Jazz Age;* "The Ice Palace" in *Flappers and Philosophers.*

22. Fitzgerald, *The Beautiful and Damned,* 51.

23. Fitzgerald, *The Beautiful and Damned,* 172.

24. Mencken, "National Letters," 41.

1922–1923

BRYANT MANGUM

Jazz Age Echoes

For complex reasons that Fitzgerald came to understand better in the years that followed, 1922 and 1923 were pivotal years in his life. In this two-year period he continued to maintain a public profile as the flapper's historian with publication of such stories as "The Popular Girl" (1922) and "Dice, Brassknuckles and Guitar" (1923), as well as with numerous magazine and newspaper articles and interviews related to the flapper (e.g., the 1923 "What a 'Flapper Novelist' Thinks of His Wife"). However, as early as July 1922 in a letter to Maxwell Perkins he reveals that his artistic conscience was pulling him in a different direction: "I want to write something *new*—something extraordinary and beautiful and simple + intricately patterned."[1] By the end of the 1922–23 period, he had clearly taken steps in that direction: he had written "Winter Dreams" (September 1922), which he described to Perkins as "a sort of 1st draft of the Gatsby idea,"[2] and he had written "Absolution" (June 1923), which he would much later maintain he had "intended to be a picture of [Gatsby's] early life."[3] When the 1922–23 period had ended Fitzgerald was clearly well on his way to writing the "extraordinary and beautiful" work that became *The Great Gatsby*.

From the vantage point of 1931 he would look back on 1922 as the high point of the era he had named the Jazz Age.[4] In his retrospective essay "Echoes of the Jazz Age" Fitzgerald characterizes 1922 as "the peak of the younger generation,"[5] noting that "though the Jazz Age continued, it became less and less an affair of youth." Of 1923, the year he labeled "the sequel," he observed that "the younger generation was starred no longer."[6] And although reluctant to think of it in personal terms at the time, Fitzgerald understood that this was "the younger generation" of which he was part, one whose youth was fading and whose presence would soon no longer occupy center stage. In "Echoes of the Jazz Age" Fitzgerald was speaking about 1922 and 1923 in a historical rather than a personal sense, but as was frequently the case with Scott and Zelda Fitzgerald, the state of their personal lives often closely followed the state of affairs in American culture. The years Fitzgerald and others have labeled the years of his "early success," for example, coincided with the post–World War I American cultural awakening that characterized the first years of the Jazz Age. And 1929, the year of the stock market crash, came on the eve of Zelda's first mental breakdown and her hospitalization, followed by years of intermittent depression for her and years of a downward spiral into alcoholism for Scott that lasted through the Great Depression.

Early Success, Rage, and Bliss

For Fitzgerald, 1922 was the peak of his early success, and he was celebrated throughout the country—especially in his hometown of St. Paul—as the youthful voice of the Jazz Age. Although Fitzgerald never specifically defined the limits of what he considered his "early success," even in the 1937 essay with that title, the period dates at least loosely from the March 1920 publication of *This Side of Paradise* (and of "Head and Shoulders" in the *Saturday Evening Post*) through the time of publication of *The Beautiful and Damned* (March 1922) and its companion short-story volume, *Tales of the Jazz Age* (September 1922). As Andrew Turnbull noted, "Fitzgerald returned to St. Paul in triumph."[7] Adding to his public profile in 1922, midway into his time in St. Paul, the *Saturday Evening Post* published his long, two-part flapper story "The Popular Girl." The last year of his early success, 1922, was a time of celebration for Fitzgerald in the city of his youth.

The spirit of continuing celebration of Fitzgerald's popularity in the public eye was dominant at least on the surface from the time Scott and Zelda arrived in St. Paul in August 1921 until they left. In order to maintain his public success, he would need to continue to write in the midst of the celebration—perhaps even continue indefinitely to write the flapper stories for which he was now known and which, by 1922, he had grown tired of writing—in order to sustain his status as historian of the Jazz Age while also honoring his wish to write enduring works of art. This wish came into high relief regarding two stories published in 1922. As he wrote to his agent, Harold Ober: "I am rather discouraged that a cheap story like The Popular Girl written in one week while the baby was being born brings $1500.00 + a genuinely imaginative thing into which I put three weeks of enthusiasm [*sic*] like The Diamond in the Sky ["The Diamond as Big as the Ritz"] brings not a thing."[8] It is perhaps at the moment of this realization in February 1922, prompted by the relative market values of "The Popular Girl" (a gimmicky flapper story) and "The Diamond as Big as the Ritz," that Fitzgerald makes the turn toward embracing a wish he had expressed to Edmund Wilson when both were students at Princeton: a wish "to be one of the greatest writers who ever lived."[9] Fitzgerald's writing of "Diamond" is one of the most important professional and biographical events to emerge from his stay in St. Paul from summer 1921 to fall 1922.

Celebrity and Notoriety: A Diamond in the Making

"The Diamond as Big as the Ritz" is, in Matthew J. Bruccoli's words, "Fitzgerald's most brilliant fantasy,"[10] and as Fitzgerald wrote in his tongue-in-cheek table of contents for *Tales of the Jazz Age,* it "was designed utterly for my own amusement" and had grown out of a "mood characterized by a perfect craving for luxury."[11] In spite of its social criticism of the system that produced the Washingtons, "Diamond" in fact contains evidence in its descriptions of the Washington home of Fitzgerald's admiration for the sumptuous, luxurious lives that those like the Washingtons live; however, middlebrow magazines like the *Saturday Evening Post* wanted nothing to do with "Diamond" and its bitingly satirical treatment of the capitalist inhabitants of the diamond mountain.

One of the professional lessons Fitzgerald learned from this in 1922 was that in order to support himself with his writing, he had to write stories with a middlebrow audience in mind, understanding full well that such things as scathing criticism of middle-American capitalist values were not acceptable to the popular magazines of the 1920s that paid high prices for short stories. From a biographical point of view, Fitzgerald learned from the composition and marketing of "Diamond," which he knew to be artistically stunning, that serious material for his best fiction could, in fact, come from past experiences that had left indelible marks on his psyche. He had, of course, used biographical material before (e.g., for *This Side of Paradise*), but beginning with "Diamond" his appropriation of such experiences had more the mark of the artist writing for "the schoolmasters of ever afterward" than for "the youth of his own generation," to use Fitzgerald's words from "The Author's Apology" at a booksellers' convention in April 1920.[12] The biographical implications for 1922 are resonant: he will leave St. Paul only months after writing "Diamond," but before he goes he will write "Winter Dreams" (September 1922), in which he returns in imagination to 1915, an important year in his relationship with his first love, Ginevra King. The story's Judy Jones represents Ginevra, and the version of the story that appears in *All the Sad Young Men* is set in Black Bear Lake (a fictionalized White Bear Lake) and draws on his stay at the White Bear Yacht Club during the summer of 1922.

Fitzgerald's excitement over his role as visiting celebrity in St. Paul remained constant throughout the months in his hometown, thanks at least partly to the efforts of Thomas Boyd, editor of the *St. Paul Daily News,* in which Fitzgerald's name was frequently mentioned and his work often noted.[13] Boyd was also manager of Kilmarnock Books in St. Paul and had befriended the Fitzgeralds when they first arrived in St. Paul. Scott especially enjoyed the attention he received when he visited Kilmarnock Books, as he regularly did after leaving his office during the time he and Zelda lived on Goodrich Avenue. All in all, the Goodrich Avenue months appear to have been relatively uneventful, less filled with bliss and rage than most sustained periods in their lives to this point. One area of mutual agreement as the winter of 1922 set in was that both Fitzgeralds were tiring of the Minnesota weather; they were becoming restless, and both were missing life in the East, which offered greater social and intellectual stimulation than life in Minnesota. Zelda, like Sally Carrol Happer in Scott's "The Ice Palace" (1920), was especially frustrated by the heavy snow and frigid temperatures of the St. Paul winter; as she had written (with some exaggeration) to Ludlow Fowler, Scott's Princeton friend and his best man at the Fitzgeralds' wedding, "This damn place is 18 below zero."[14] Scott was also tiring of being away from the East, and after the extensive writing and revision of *The Beautiful and Damned* in 1921, he and Zelda were excitedly awaiting their trip to New York to celebrate the March 1922 publication of the novel. Both Scott and Zelda were already making plans to be in the city for the publication of the novel and for the parties that would accompany it. Both shared the excitement, and when Scott wrote Wilson in January 1922 of his anticipation of the trip to New York, he complained, "I'm bored as hell out here."[15]

The Beautiful and Damned

Fitzgerald had been working on *The Beautiful and Damned* in one form or another as early as the 1920 Westport days. It had been serialized in seven installments from September 1921 through March 1922, receiving mixed reactions. In the end, Fitzgerald had written a novel that in many ways predicted final misery for the marriage and future lives of Gloria and Anthony, which had clear overtones of Scott's thoughts about his relationship with Zelda. In Andrew Turnbull's view, *The Beautiful and Damned* seems truly to have been "a projection of what Fitzgerald had come to consider the decayed part of their lives."[16] A majority of readers and reviewers responded negatively to the book. As Jackson R. Bryer notes, "Given the response to *This Side of Paradise,* expectations for Fitzgerald's second novel were enormous—and probably impossible to satisfy."[17] And while the novel received more reviews than *This Side of Paradise,* its reception was discouraging: many of the reviews were bitingly negative, and virtually all of those that praised it did so only in a qualified way. Early royalties for the book were close to those of *This Side of Paradise,* largely because so many readers had been impressed by the first book, but they fell off quickly and were disheartening to Fitzgerald.

Another factor dampening the enthusiasm over the New York trip was that the Fitzgeralds had come East partly so Zelda could have an abortion, since she did not wish to have a second child so close on the heels of the birth of Scottie.[18] In short, the month of March in New York for Scott and Zelda was not a success. It was, from most accounts, a trip marked by drunken parties that reflected a need to mask underlying frustration and even despair. Fitzgerald's letter to Wilson after the New York trip reflects the way his hopes for the New York visit had been sabotaged: "My original plan was to contrive to have long discourses with you but that interminable party began and I couldn't seem to get sober enough to be able to tolerate being sober. In fact the whole trip was largely a failure."[19]

Back in St. Paul after the New York trip, the Fitzgeralds resumed their roles as celebrities. They remained the Golden Couple of the Jazz Age. While the Fitzgeralds were in New York, Zelda had been asked by Burton Rascoe, an influential literary editor of the *New York Herald Tribune,* to write a review of *The Beautiful and Damned.* Rascoe was an early commentator on Scott's work, and Scott felt the critic had unfairly misjudged his talent. Zelda's review reflects her sharp wit, her insight into the novel, her rebelliousness, and her seemingly offhand reaction to Scott's use of her diaries in the novel, a reaction that appears to have brought no response from Scott:

It seems to me that on one page I recognized a portion of an old diary of mine which mysteriously disappeared shortly after my marriage, and also scraps of letters which though considerably edited, sound to me vaguely familiar. In fact, Mr. Fitzgerald—I believe that is how he spells his name—seems to believe that plagiarism begins at home.[20]

Reentering the St. Paul social scene, Fitzgerald wrote a "Junior League Play," *The Flappers of Midnight,* with Zelda playing the lead role.[21] It was described in the *St. Paul Daily News,* probably with Scott's input, as "what is reported to be one of the cleverest [extravaganzas] that any author has ever written for any chapter of the Junior League."[22] All the while, Scott maintained his role as the flapper's historian, giving interviews about his opinions regarding various types of flappers to local papers. Meanwhile Zelda began writing a series of pieces for *McCall's* and *Metropolitan* on the "new woman" of the Jazz Age. The most celebrated of these essays was "Eulogy on the Flapper," in which she declared, "The Flapper is deceased. . . . It is a great bereavement to me, thinking as I do that there will never be another product of circumstance to take the place of the dear departed."[23]

"Winter Dreams"

In the summer of 1922 the Fitzgeralds moved with Scottie and her nurse to the White Bear Yacht Club, though by August their loud parties had disturbed other guests and they moved out at the club's request, spending part of the month of September in St. Paul's Commodore Hotel— their second stay at the Commodore. Fitzgerald said little in his letters or in his ledger entries about the composition of "Winter Dreams," which Bruccoli calls "the most important of the *Gatsby* cluster stories" and the one that gives "virtually a preview of *The Great Gatsby*."[24] The importance of Fitzgerald's 1922 stay in White Bear Lake and of "Winter Dreams" to *The Great Gatsby* can be concluded from known facts about the story's marketing history, from its revision history, and from comparisons of the story to the novel, which Fitzgerald would begin writing in earnest approximately a year after leaving St. Paul. "Winter Dreams" was begun while Scott and Zelda were still at the White Bear Yacht Club with ten-month-old Scottie, and Fitzgerald finished writing it in mid-September

Cover of *Metropolitan,* December 1922

in St. Paul's Commodore Hotel, shortly before the Fitzgeralds returned to New York. It was bought by *Metropolitan* for nine hundred dollars as part of a contract agreement negotiated by Ober in which *Metropolitan* agreed to purchase six Fitzgerald stories. "Winter Dreams" was the fourth of the six and, as it turns out, the last: the magazine went into receivership shortly after "Winter Dreams" was published in the December 1922 issue. The story was featured near the front of the magazine with rich illustrations by Arthur William Brown. And though the version that most readers are probably familiar with is the one Fitzgerald revised for *All the Sad Young Men* (1926), his third story collection and the one that followed *The Great Gatsby*,[25] the original 1922 *Metropolitan* version is the one whose connection to *Gatsby* is most pronounced. The strongest concrete textual evidence of Dexter Green's kinship with Jay Gatsby lies in the nearly identical passages shared by the 1922 *Metropolitan* version and the holograph manuscript of *The Great Gatsby*: a description of Judy Jones's house, and a description of Daisy's house as seen through Gatsby's eyes. The passage from "Winter Dreams" reads, in part:

> There was a feeling of mystery in it, of bedrooms up-stairs more beautiful and strange than other bedrooms, of gay and radiant activities taking place through these deep corridors and of romances that were not musty and laid already in lavender, but were fresh and breathing and set forth in rich motor cars and in great dances whose flowers were scarcely withered. They were more real because he could feel them all about him, pervading the air with the shades and echoes of still vibrant emotion.[26]

Gatsby's description of Daisy's house was clearly constructed from that earlier description of Judy's house as seen through Dexter's eyes:

> There was a ripe mystery about it, a hint of bedrooms upstairs more beautiful and cool than other bedrooms, of gay and radiant activities taking place through its corridors and of romances that were not musty and laid away already in lavender but fresh and breathing and redolent of this year's shining motor cars and of dances whose flowers were scarcely withered. . . . He felt their presence all about the house, pervading the air with the shades and echoes of still vibrant emotions.[27]

These lines are among the most beautifully lyrical passages in the *Metropolitan* version of "Winter Dreams" and in *Gatsby*. The connection between story and novel illustrated in the similarities between these two passages becomes even more dramatic when one considers that Fitzgerald seems almost certainly to have penned the description of Daisy's house in the form first contained in the manuscript of *Gatsby* with the 1922 *Metropolitan* version of "Winter Dreams" by his side, literally transcribing the passage, then revising it by replacing Daisy's name for Judy's and making only minor adjustments in the passage's diction, tone, and rhythm. The passage cited above from the holograph manuscript survived intact, with only the addition of a comma, when it was included in the published novel.

The close parallels between "Winter Dreams" and *Gatsby* are evident at virtually every turn, largely because both have biographical origins in Fitzgerald's relationship with Ginevra King, memories of which came into the foreground, for unknown reasons, during Fitzgerald's time in St. Paul and at the White Bear Yacht Club in 1922. His relationship with Ginevra began during the Christmas holidays of 1914 and ended when she threw him over two years later. Clearly the parallels between Dexter Green and Jay Gatsby are striking: Dexter falls in love with wealthy Judy Jones and devotes his life to making the money that will allow him to enter her social circle. His idealization of her is closely akin to Gatsby's feeling for Daisy Buchanan. Gatsby's idealized conception of Daisy is the motivating force that underlies his compulsion to become successful, just as Dexter's conception of Judy Jones as an important component of his "winter dreams" drives him to amass a fortune by the time he is twenty-five. The theme of commitment to an idealized dream that is at the core of "Winter Dreams" and *Gatsby* and the similarities between the two men point up the close relationship between the story and the novel. "Winter Dreams," like *The Great Gatsby,* provides a direct comment on the corrosive effects of money on human relationships.

One of the things Fitzgerald learned with the publication of the story in the middlebrow *Metropolitan*—a lesson he had not yet fully learned just months earlier with "The Diamond as Big as the Ritz"—was that indictments of wealth and comments pointing to the evils of materialism can be handled in a way that will be acceptable to the audiences of popular magazines: such remarks cannot be as bitingly satirical as they are in "Diamond," and it helps if they are woven into the fabric of a compelling love story. There can be little question that "Winter Dreams" came from genuine emotion, and the connection between Fitzgerald in 1922 and Dexter Green could scarcely be clearer. During the time of composition of "Winter Dreams," Fitzgerald, now twenty-six, had lost his youth and recognized it, as Dexter Green had lost his youth in the form of the girl of his youthful winter dreams, Judy Jones: "The dream was gone. . . . Long ago there was something in me, but now that thing is gone. Now that thing is gone. I cannot cry. I cannot care. That thing will come back no more."[28]

Tales of the Jazz Age

The year of "the peak of the younger generation" of the Jazz Age began to wind down for Fitzgerald with the completion of "Winter Dreams" and with the September 22 publication of Fitzgerald's second story collection, *Tales of the Jazz Age*. Even though *Tales* contains two of his finest stories, "May Day" and "Diamond as Big as the Ritz," reviewers often judged it largely as "popular entertainment."[29] They often singled out for comment Fitzgerald's table of contents, which provided witty comments about each of the stories. Many of the stories, in fact, either had already appeared in slick magazines (e.g., "The Camel's Back") or were leftovers from Fitzgerald's earlier writing for Princeton's *Nassau Literary Magazine* (e.g., "Jemina"). The stories in the volume that were written in Fitzgerald's college days ("Porcelain and Pink" and "Tarquin of Cheapside," for example) gave *Tales of the Jazz Age* a backward-looking quality that eerily forecast Fitzgerald's later pronouncement that by 1922 the peak of the Jazz Age—at least as it had been "starred" by youth—had arrived and was about to pass into the sequel. These were tales, the title suggested, of an era that had reached its prime. Fitzgerald dedicated *Tales of the Jazz Age* "Quite inappropriately, To My Mother." It is difficult to tell whether this dedication is sincere or ironic, though with it Fitzgerald may have been looking back with nostalgia on his lost childhood, and the book, as André Le Vot sees it, may be viewed as "a kind of farewell to his pink-and-blue, bittersweet period of tenderness and jubilation."[30] The Fitzgeralds left St. Paul in mid-September for New York, staying for their first weeks back at the Plaza Hotel.

Great Neck

In October 1922 the Fitzgeralds finally settled in what Zelda described in a letter to Xandra Kalman, a friend in St. Paul, as their "nifty little Babbit-home" at 6 Gateway Drive in Great Neck.[31] They made the acquaintance

John Held's cover for *Tales of the Jazz Age*, 1922. Regarding this dust jacket, Fitzgerald wrote to Perkins on May 13, 1922: "The jacket is wonderful, the best yet and exactly what I wanted" (*Correspondence of F. Scott Fitzgerald*, ed. Matthew J. Bruccoli and Margaret M. Duggan [New York: Random House, 1980], 106).

of their new neighbor Ring Lardner, who was a well-known sportswriter and short-story writer, as well as a serious alcoholic with whom Scott drank often. They became close friends during the Great Neck years, and Fitzgerald, with the help of Perkins, worked successfully to revive Lardner's reputation as a writer. The drinking with Lardner and others during the last months of 1922 marked the Fitzgeralds' early time in Great Neck, as Fitzgerald records simply in his ledger for December: "A series of parties."[32] The darkest parts of Fitzgerald's time in Great Neck came during the first months of 1923, which were characterized by drunken escapades of which Zelda was often a part, as she admits in a January account of New Year's to Kalman: "We saw ourselves out and the Year in between drinks at a dull party which I succeeded in ruining by throwing everybody's hat into a center bowl-shaped light."[33] Other accounts have Fitzgerald in a drunken state referring to actress Laurette Taylor as "you beautiful, beautiful egg!"—which prompted Taylor to tell her husband, "I've just seen the doom of youth. Understand? The doom of youth itself. A walking doom."[34] Taylor, more than a decade older than Fitzgerald, had apparently seen the twenty-six-year-old Fitzgerald ominously as the embodiment of the younger generation. These and stories like them present a partial picture of the Fitzgerald of 1923. He characterized the darker side of his twenty-sixth and twenty-seventh years in his ledger notations for at least much of 1923 in this way: "The repression breaks out A comfortable but dangerous and deteriorating year at Great Neck. No ground under our feet" and "The most miserable year since I was nineteen, full of terrible failures with acute miseries."[35]

"Dice, Brassknuckles and Guitar"

In the end, however, the Great Neck of 1923 had its redeeming moments for the Fitzgeralds. *Metropolitan*'s December publication of "Winter Dreams" had ushered out 1922, and in late December Fitzgerald had—with the aid of his agent, Harold Ober—negotiated a contract with *Cosmopolitan* for an option on all his 1923 stories, which would be published in *Hearst's International*.[36] The first two of the six stories eventually written and published under this contract were "Dice, Brassknuckles and Guitar" and "Hot and Cold Blood," both written and published in 1923. The single story Fitzgerald wrote in January reveals a bit of levity and hope. It also gives insight into the new year that Fitzgerald would later label "the sequel" to the Jazz Age. The story was "Dice, Brassknuckles and Guitar," which *Hearst's International* headlined as "a Typical Fitzgerald Story."[37] The story is best read as atypical in that it appears to be Fitzgerald's satirical treatment of what had come to be known as "typical" of his *Saturday Evening Post* stories about flappers, youth, and young love. The story's tone is comic: Jim Powell, a native of Tarleton, Georgia, drives with his body servant in his jalopy from Tarleton to Southampton, Long Island, to open an academy in which he, as "Jazz Master," teaches young debutantes to shoot dice, use brass knuckles, and play the guitar. Jim is an earnest, if comic, figure, and he is ultimately run out of Southampton by disapproving mothers, one of whom accuses him of running "an opium den."[38] This is of course far from what Jim's academy actually is, but he is in effect driven from the world of high society back home to Georgia. Before he leaves, a good-hearted debutante he met on the way to Southampton tells him, "You're better than all of them put together, Jim."[39] This remark suggests a connection already forming in Fitzgerald's mind to what would become *The Great Gatsby*, in which Nick tells Gatsby, "You're worth the whole damn bunch put together."[40] On one level this story could be read as Fitzgerald's signal that his focus on flappers and debutantes as subjects for his fiction was over. This, as it turned out, would not be absolutely true: Fitzgerald would continue to write occasional flapper stories after "Dice" (e.g., "Rags Martin-Jones and the Pr-nce of W-ales"), and he would write a final story about Tarleton's flapper-belle, Ailie Calhoun ("The Last of the Belles"). But the Fitzgerald of early 1923 had his sights set on breaking free of the role he had assumed in the days of his early success.

The Golden Couple Redux

Scott probably took delight in symbolically shedding for the moment his mantle of flapper's historian with the satirical "Dice," but he quickly realized he could not simply walk away from the reality that he had to fulfill his contract with *Hearst's International* magazine in order to make the money to pay his and Zelda's considerable Great Neck expenses. This contract would require him to write stories suitable for publication in a middlebrow magazine. But perhaps most important for him at this time was that writing these stories would allow him to follow through with his commitment to working on his play, *The Vegetable*, which he had begun

Alfred Cheney Johnston, *Portrait of Scott and Zelda Fitzgerald*, 1923. This photograph was published on the first page of the May 1923 issue of *Hearst's International* magazine. Scott and Zelda pasted this page into their scrapbooks, and the photograph with paratext can be seen on page 105 of *The Romantic Egoists: A Pictorial Autobiography from the Scrapbooks and Albums of Scott and Zelda Fitzgerald*, ed. Matthew J. Bruccoli, Scottie Fitzgerald Smith, and Joan P. Kerr (New York: Charles Scribner's Sons, 1974).

in St. Paul and which he planned to have ready for production later in the year. He revised the play three times during 1923, deciding "to publish it as a book before it was produced."[41] The play's opening was scheduled for November. He also wanted to work on his third novel, *The Great Gatsby*. All the while, the popular media wished to publish pictures of and articles about the couple who were still regarded as the Golden Couple of the Jazz Age. The first page of the May 1923 issue of *Hearst's International* magazine featured a flattering photograph by Alfred Cheney Johnston of Scott and Zelda beautifully dressed and with Zelda wearing what she referred to as her Elizabeth Arden face. A magazine caption identified "Mrs. F. Scott Fitzgerald" as having "started the flapper movement in this country," and her husband as "the best-loved author of the younger generation."[42]

An interview in Louisville's *Courier Journal* on Sunday, September 30, 1923, was headlined "What a 'Flapper Novelist' Thinks of His Wife," followed by an extensive article in which Scott interviews Zelda, asking her questions guaranteed to prompt clever answers showing Zelda's wit and intelligence to advantage. In the article he says of her, "She is the most charming person in the world."[43] Pictures from 1923 pasted in the Fitzgeralds' scrapbooks of Zelda holding baby Scottie depict a happy and peaceful mother and daughter. Meanwhile, Scott was also working behind the scenes with Perkins to promote Lardner's writing career, with Fitzgerald supplying the title for Lardner's first Scribner's volume, *How to Write Short Stories*. Similarly, Fitzgerald lobbied Perkins on behalf of his St. Paul friend Thomas Boyd and was instrumental in having Scribner's publish Boyd's novel *Through the Wheat* (1923).

The Vegetable, or From President to Postman

Though Scott enjoyed the attention he and Zelda received from the media and though it was satisfying to be of help to fellow writers, he was frustrated by not being able to spend time readying his play *The Vegetable, or From President to Postman* for the stage. He was convinced that the play would, as he told Ober in late 1921, "make my fortune."[44] Scribner's had brought out the play on April 27, 1923, to weak reviews, and Fitzgerald had continued, with many interruptions, to work on it. Its opening night in Atlantic City, New Jersey, was scheduled for November 19, with Ernest Truex playing the leading role of Jerry Frost and with Fitzgerald taking some part in the production during rehearsals. The Fitzgeralds,

Lardner, and his wife went to Atlantic City for the tryout night at the Apollo Theatre. The opening night was an abysmal failure; as Zelda described it to Kalman in a letter, "In brief, the show flopped as flat as one of Aunt Jemimas famous pancakes. . . . People were so obviously bored! . . . It is too terrible to contemplate."[45] Fitzgerald spent the week following opening night doing "what he could to improve the play,"[46] but it was hopeless. The play opened and closed the first week of its out-of-town tryout. No doubt its failure rested at least in part in the play's second act, which had from the beginning given Fitzgerald difficulties. The act is a baffling dream sequence in which Jerry becomes president of the United States. In the play's last act he actually becomes the postman he had always hoped to be. Zelda's is the main account we have of the audience's reaction, a negative reaction that was probably predictable to everyone except perhaps Scott.

"Absolution"

The Vegetable was a complete failure on one level, but on another level it freed Fitzgerald of his illusion that his future lay in writing plays for Broadway. While he was working on the play he was also working on what was to become his third novel, but the novel underwent many false starts, evidence of which can be found in the correspondence around his 1923 story "Absolution," published in the June 1924 issue of *American Mercury*. The story was originally intended to be a prologue to his third novel; as he told Perkins, "I'm glad you liked 'Absolution.' As you know it was to have been the prologue of the novel but it interfered with the neatness of the plan."[47] An additional bit of evidence can be found in two surviving pages of a lost false start of the draft to which "Absolution" was to have been a prologue, pages that he sent to Willa Cather in 1925.[48] The young Rudolph Miller of "Absolution" does, in fact, have a romantic temperament, as does Jay Gatsby, but Miller's Catholic background and his family circumstances render him an unlikely young Jimmy Gatz in *The Great Gatsby*. It seems likely that "Absolution" was, in fact, a prologue to a much earlier, and now lost, false start to what would become Fitzgerald's third novel. The pages that Fitzgerald sent to Cather from the lost early draft bear only a passing relationship to the novel that was to become *The Great Gatsby*. In those draft pages, the characters were named Jordan Vance, Ada, and Carraway, and this last character in the draft pages was not the narrator.[49] Fitzgerald records in his ledger for 1923 a reference to one of these false starts to his third novel: "A new schedule + more work on novel," he wrote in September. But it was not until April 1924 that he was able to add a reference to the actual start on *The Great Gatsby* as we know it in an entry that proved to be true: "Out of woods at last + starting novel."[50] This was probably Fitzgerald's first giant step toward fulfilling the wish he expressed in 1917 at Princeton to Edmund Wilson to become "one of the greatest writers who ever lived."

NOTES

1. F. Scott Fitzgerald, *Correspondence of F. Scott Fitzgerald,* ed. Matthew J. Bruccoli and Margaret M. Duggan (New York: Random House, 1980), 112.

2. John Kuehl and Jackson R. Bryer, eds., *Dear Scott / Dear Max: The Fitzgerald–Perkins Correspondence* (New York: Charles Scribner's Sons, 1971), 112.

3. F. Scott Fitzgerald, *The Letters of F. Scott Fitzgerald,* ed. Andrew Turnbull (New York: Charles Scribner's Sons, 1963), 509.

4. Kuehl and Bryer, *Dear Scott / Dear Max,* 171.

5. F. Scott Fitzgerald, "Echoes of the Jazz Age," in *My Lost City: Personal Essays, 1920–1940,* ed. James L. W. West III, Cambridge Edition of the Works of F. Scott Fitzgerald (Cambridge: Cambridge University Press, 2014), 132.

6. Fitzgerald, "Echoes of the Jazz Age," 132.

7. Andrew Turnbull, *Scott Fitzgerald* (New York: Charles Scribner's Sons, 1962), 126.

8. Matthew J. Bruccoli, ed., *As Ever, Scott Fitz—: Letters between F. Scott Fitzgerald and His Literary Agent Harold Ober, 1919–1940,* with the assistance of Jennifer McCabe Atkinson (Philadelphia: J. B. Lippincott, 1972), 36.

9. Quoted in Matthew J. Bruccoli, *Some Sort of Epic Grandeur: The Life of F. Scott Fitzgerald* (New York: Harcourt, Brace, Jovanovich, 1981), 70.

10. Bruccoli, *Epic Grandeur,* 161.

11. F. Scott Fitzgerald, *Tales of the Jazz Age,* ed. James L. W. West III, Cambridge Edition of the Works of F. Scott Fitzgerald (Cambridge: Cambridge University Press, 2012), 6.

12. F. Scott Fitzgerald, "The Author's Apology," in *Last Kiss,* ed. James L. W. West III, Cambridge Edition of the Works of F. Scott Fitzgerald (Cambridge: Cambridge University Press, 2022), 379.

13. André Le Vot, *F. Scott Fitzgerald: A Biography,* trans. William Byron (New York: Doubleday, 1983), 112.

14. Quoted in Nancy Milford, *Zelda: A Biography* (New York: Harper and Row, 1970), 85.

15. Edmund Wilson, ed., *The Crack-Up* (New York: New Directions, 1945), 257.

16. Turnbull, *Fitzgerald,* 131.

17. Jackson R. Bryer, "Contemporary Reception," in *F. Scott Fitzgerald in Context,* ed. Bryant Mangum (New York: Cambridge University Press, 2013), 70.

18. Bruccoli, *Epic Grandeur,* 163.

19. Fitzgerald, *Letters,* 334.

20. Zelda Fitzgerald, *The Collected Writings of Zelda Fitzgerald,* ed. Matthew J. Bruccoli (New York: Charles Scribner's Sons, 1991), 388.

21. Matthew J. Bruccoli, Scottie Fitzgerald Smith, and Joan P. Kerr, eds., *The Romantic Egoists: A Pictorial Autobiography from the Scrapbooks and Albums of Scott and Zelda Fitzgerald* (New York: Charles Scribner's Sons, 1974), 89.

22. David Page and John Koblas, *F. Scott Fitzgerald in Minnesota: Toward the Summit* (St. Cloud, Minn.: North Star Press, 1996), 128.

23. Z. Fitzgerald, "Eulogy on the Flapper," in *Collected Writings,* 391.

24. Bruccoli, *Epic Grandeur,* 173.

25. In the *All the Sad Young Men* version, the name of the setting is "Black Bear" (a thin disguise for "White Bear"). It was Dillard in the *Metropolitan* version. "Lake Erminie" in the *Metropolitan* version is changed to "Sherry Island" in the *All the Sad Young Men* version.

26. F. Scott Fitzgerald, "Winter Dreams," in *Best Early Stories of F. Scott Fitzgerald,* ed. Bryant Mangum (New York: Modern Library, 2005), 239.

27. F. Scott Fitzgerald, *The Great Gatsby: A Variorum Edition,* ed. James L. W. West III, Cambridge Edition of the Works of F. Scott Fitzgerald (Cambridge: Cambridge University Press, 2022), 178.

28. Fitzgerald, "Winter Dreams," 252.

29. Bruccoli, *Epic Grandeur,* 172.

30. Le Vot, *Fitzgerald,* 118.

31. Quoted in Bruccoli, *Epic Grandeur,* 176.

32. F. Scott Fitzgerald, *F. Scott Fitzgerald's Ledger: A Facsimile,* introduction by Matthew J. Bruccoli (Washington, D.C.: NCR/Microcard editions / Bruccoli Clark, 1972), 177.

33. Quoted in Turnbull, *Fitzgerald,* 134.

34. Quoted in Turnbull, *Fitzgerald,* 136.

35. Fitzgerald, *Ledger,* 177–78.

36. Bruccoli, *As Ever,* 51n.

37. Steven W. Potts, *The Price of Paradise: The Magazine Career of F. Scott Fitzgerald* (San Bernardino, Calif.: Borgo Press, 1993), 47.

38. Potts, *Price of Paradise,* 62.

39. Potts, *Price of Paradise,* 63.

40. Fitzgerald, *Great Gatsby: Variorum,* 185.

41. Bruccoli, *Epic Grandeur,* 179.

42. Bruccoli, Smith, and Kerr, *Romantic Egoists,* 105.

43. Bruccoli, Smith, and Kerr, *Romantic Egoists,* 112–13.

44. Quoted in Bruccoli, *As Ever,* 32.

45. Quoted in Bruccoli, *Epic Grandeur,* 187, 189.

46. Bruccoli, *Epic Grandeur,* 189.

47. Kuehl and Bryer, *Dear Scott / Dear Max,* 72.

48. Fitzgerald, *Great Gatsby: Variorum,* xii.

49. Bruccoli, *Epic Grandeur,* 185.

50. Fitzgerald, *Ledger,* 178.

1924–1925

Marie-Agnès Gay

"We were going to the Old World to find a new rhythm for our lives."[1]

When on May 3, 1924, the anniversary date of their first trip to Europe three years before, Scott and Zelda boarded the SS *Minnewaska*, destination Cherbourg, France, with two-and-a-half-year-old Scottie, they were not only fleeing Great Neck, where they had just spent two reckless years, but, according to Fitzgerald, they were escaping "from extravagance and clamor and from all the wild extremes among which [they] had dwelt for five hectic years."[2] Although this departure is evocative of the closing scene of *The Beautiful and Damned,* Scott and Zelda at that point had not been totally broken by dissipation; unlike the pathetic figures cut by Anthony Patch and Gloria Gilbert, they were still "striking . . . [and] beautiful"[3] and could, therefore, reasonably believe a bright future lay ahead of them: "We were going to the Old World to find a new rhythm for our lives, with a true conviction that we had left our old selves behind forever."[4] And indeed in France, on what he would later come to see as his "beloved Riviera,"[5] Scott found enough peace to complete his masterpiece, *The Great Gatsby,* within only a few months. Furthermore, in 1924–25, two important new friendships were struck: with the glamorous couple Gerald and Sara Murphy and with budding writer Ernest Hemingway. The Riviera was also the backdrop to the first serious crisis undergone by the couple, as Zelda flirted with French aviator Edouard Jozan while Scott worked on *Gatsby.* Whatever the nature of this short-lived romance, it arguably caused lasting damage, Scott being deeply shattered by it and Zelda soon showing the first serious signs of mental instability.

With this betrayal of marital love, but also with the disappointing sales of *Gatsby* and the bitter realization that the Old World would not enable the hoped-for new start, the years 1924–25 became synonymous with broken promises. The seventeen pieces of luggage that Scott and Zelda reportedly brought from the United States are an apt metaphor for the heavy baggage of old habits they would have to relinquish to reinvent themselves. Indeed, they were not long in resuming their restless drinking and partying, drifting from one place to another. Their comings and goings during those two years "read like a flutter of travel brochures": Paris, Hyères, Saint-Raphaël, Rome, Capri, Paris, Antibes, Paris, London, Paris.[6] Wherever they went, the Fitzgeralds were bound to carry their old selves along.

"Out of the woods at last"[7]

In "How to Live on $36,000 a Year," a *Saturday Evening Post* essay published in April 1924, Fitzgerald lightheartedly addresses his and Zelda's hopeless spending habits and the dire financial straits they found themselves in following the debacle of *The Vegetable* in November 1923, which left them five thousand dollars in debt.[8] As they were "too poor to economize"—Fitzgerald notes with an amusing sense of paradox[9]—the couple had to face a bare fact: "There was no help for it—I must go to work."[10] Going on the wagon and retiring to a large bare room over their garage, he went to his only sure source of financial relief: writing stories. "It took twelve hours a day for five weeks to rise from abject poverty back into the middle class," he claims in the essay.[11] However, it took him a little longer; he emerged in March with ten stories written, out of debt, and with seven thousand dollars to his name.

Only four of these stories would find their way into his next collection, *All the Sad Young Men,* which he assembled a year later: "Rags Martin-Jones and the Pr-nce of W-ales," "The Baby Party," "Gretchen's Forty Winks," and "The Sensible Thing." The last belongs to the *Gatsby* cluster of stories (alongside "Absolution," a discarded opening draft of the novel). In "The Sensible Thing," George O'Kelly, a young man who has lost a wealthy southern girl because of his poverty, returns a rich man a year later in order to win her over. But unlike Gatsby, who insists the past *can* be repeated, O'Kelly realizes as he kisses Jonquil Cary "that though he search through eternity he would never recapture those lost April hours. . . . There are all kinds of love in the world, but never the same love twice."[12] Unsurprisingly, Fitzgerald told Maxwell Perkins that the story was "about Zelda + me. All true," suggesting that Fitzgerald felt their wedded life had been marred from the very beginning by Zelda's initial refusal to marry him and had thus started on an imperfect basis.

Scott was severe about what he had written in the preceding few months. He knew that he had to economize in order not to pollute with commercial writing the time spent on his next novel, and that he had to find conditions favorable to concentration. The combination of these two imperatives led the couple to make a crucial move. In Europe, they were sure, they would find advantageous exchange rates that would stretch the value of their dollars and they would escape the vicious circle of Long Island dissipation. Like many Americans in those years, they chose France, but they would be among the first to settle on the Mediterranean coast.

"The whole French Riviera twinkling on the sea"[13]

Zelda's fictionalized account of their arrival in Europe in *Save Me the Waltz* reads: "The coast of Europe defied the Atlantic expanse; the tender slid into the friendliness of Cherbourg. . . . The train bore them down through the pink carnival of Normandy, past the delicate tracery of Paris and the high terraces of Lyon, the belfries of Dijon and the white romance of Avignon . . . into Provence."[14] Tellingly, Zelda passes over their stop in Paris, their first destination. Admittedly, they spent hardly a fortnight there, just enough to hire an English nurse for Scottie and to make a few cultural blunders: at the Hotel des Deux Mondes on the Avenue de l'Opéra, they famously mistook the bidet for a bathing tub and, lunching with Margaret and John Peale Bishop in the Bois de Boulogne, they gave Scottie a gin fizz to drink, thinking it was lemonade. John Peale Bishop was only one of several expatriate acquaintances they met in Paris. Among them was Esther Murphy, whom they had entertained in Great Neck. She introduced them to her elder brother Gerald and his wife Sara, well-off socialites and famous figures of the new Paris artistic scene. Scott and Zelda immediately took to these two elegant individuals full of charm and originality. At the time the Murphys were building a house at Cap d'Antibes, which they had discovered through their friend Cole Porter; they convinced Scott and Zelda to go south.

The Riviera was not yet the fashionable place it was soon to become; wealthy French people and expatriates usually summered in cooler Deauville on the Normandy coast. Despite its idyllic scenery, the Riviera was therefore a cheap place to visit out of season, and Scott and Zelda, eager as they were to locate someplace where they might live economically and to flee from the "boat-load of Americans pour[ing] into the boulevards" every morning,[15] boarded a train for Hyères, perhaps because they

Scott with daughter Scottie at the beach in southern France

knew Edith Wharton had a house there. In "How to Live on Practically Nothing a Year," written a few months later for the *Saturday Evening Post* as a companion piece to "How to Live on $36,000 a Year," Fitzgerald details their first days there. The Park Hotel where they settled hosted "only a superannuated dozen, a slowly decaying dozen, a solemn and dispirited dozen" and seemed to offer little more than goat's meat in "a lifeless gravy" for dinner.[16] Furthermore, it soon became obvious they would not find an affordable villa to let in Hyères. So Scott bought a Renault

6CV for $750 and, leaving Scottie under the care of her nurse, he and Zelda "combed the Riviera from Nice to Hyères."[17] Dispirited to find all the villas too expensive or unmanageable without a fleet of servants, they stopped one day in Saint-Raphaël, "a red little town . . . with gay red-roofed houses" about halfway between Hyères and Antibes.[18] There, an efficient real-estate agent found for them, report-edly in less than one hour, ex-actly what they had been look-ing for all along, "a clean cool villa set in a large garden on a hill above town," the Villa Marie.[19]

Villa Marie, Valescure, France

Scott and Zelda's life pattern in Saint-Raphaël confirms that they had not come to France as "culture-seeking expat[s]."[20] Apart from a group of French aviators stationed in nearby Fréjus, France, they mixed very little with the local population. Fitzgerald's account of the French in "How to Live on Practically Nothing a Year" is somewhat patronizing, even tinged with racialized overtones. However, as Gerald Kennedy under-lines, "the essay is not devoid of self-critical insight. Fitzgerald denounces other Americans for their avoidance of 'French life' while satirizing the Fitzgeralds' own resistance to the foreign."[21] Ironically presenting Zelda and himself as "two cultured Europeans" or quoting himself with humor ("'Je suis a stranger here,' I said in flawless French. 'Je veux aller to le best hotel dans le town'"), Fitzgerald acknowledges his limited interest in the Old World.[22] Indeed, Europe was, before anything else, a distant location from which to gain a renewed perspective on America and Americans, including through time spent with fellow expatriates.[23]

During the summer of 1924, the Murphys paid them a visit in Saint-Raphaël, which they reciprocated. In August they spent a few days at the Hôtel du Cap in Antibes, where the Murphys were staying while their

A party at Plage de la Garoupe with Gerald Murphy, in his famous sailor's jersey and white cap, in the center.

Villa America was being completed. This stay is Fitzgerald's first mention of them in his ledger.[24] In Cap d'Antibes, Scott and Zelda experienced the Murphys' stylish way of life, which the latter tuned to a Spanish adage: "Living well is the best revenge."[25] They also enjoyed the Murphys' conversation about the arts. Gerald had begun a career in painting, notably working with the Russian and Swedish ballets, and his circle of acquaintances included Igor Stravinsky, Sergei Diaghilev, Pablo Picasso, and Fernand Léger, among others. The following year the Fitzgeralds, who by then were living in Paris, spent the whole month of August at Cap d'Antibes, which had become the place to be for expatriates and artists. They whiled their time away between the beach and the Villa America: Gerald ruled graciously over the Plage de la Garoupe, entertaining his friends—and their children—with a natural talent, while Sara exercised her perfect taste as hostess, wearing her pearl necklace on the beach as a sign of sophisticated casualness. It was this idyllic atmosphere that Fitzgerald would capture in the opening chapters of *Tender Is the Night*.

Tongue-in-cheek, Fitzgerald wrote to Bishop in September 1925:

There was no one at Antibes this summer except me, Zelda, the Valentinos, the Murphys, Mistinguet, Rex Ingram, Dos Passos,

Alice Terry, the MacLeishes, Charlie Brackett, Maud Kahn, Esther Murphy, Marguerite Namara, E. Phillips Oppenheim, Mannes the violinist, Floyd Dell, Max and Crystal Eastman, ex-Premier Orlando, Etienne de Beaumont—just a real place to rough it, an escape from all the world."[26]

An expatriates' haven, the Cap d'Antibes they frequented was clearly anything but a "real place." Fitzgerald saw the Riviera as a paradise on earth, yet he was not deluded about the unreality of such a perception. Many of his depictions of the Riviera feature a stereotypical decorative moon bathing an idyllic scene: "It is twilight as I write this and out of my window [at Villa Marie the] flaming sun has collapsed behind the peaks of the Estérels and the moon already hovers over the aqueducts of Fréjus, five miles away";[27] or more strikingly, in a letter to Thomas Boyd written from Hyères: "This is the lovliest piece of earth. . . . Zelda and I are sitting in the café l'Universe writing letters (it is 10:30 P.M.) and the moon is an absolutely au fair Mediteraenean moon with a blurred silver linnen [sic] cap."[28] In "Love in the Night," a short story written just before the Fitzgeralds left Saint-Raphaël for good, a Riviera moon is the indispensable backdrop to the perfect love scene imagined by the naive, romantic young hero.

Years later, in 1931, Fitzgerald wrote in "Echoes of the Jazz Age": "One could get away with more on the summer Riviera, and whatever happened seemed to have something to do with art."[29] Indeed, Fitzgerald contributed to the artistic presence on the Riviera, as it was there that his greatest literary achievement was completed. Furthermore, it was perhaps one of his first thoughts upon discovering the Mediterranean that inspired him to create one of Gatsby's most memorable gestures: "When your eyes first fall upon the Mediterranean you know at once why it was here that man first stood erect and stretched his arms toward the sun."[30] All the more so as on Saint-Raphaël's main beachfront, idle nighttime walkers will have their eyes caught by a lighthouse's green light shining a little further away along the coast.

"I want to write something new—something extraordinary."[31]

The Villa Marie was just what Scott needed, "a quiet place to do a lot of work."[32] He had shared his good resolves with Perkins just before leaving New York: "It is only in the last four months that I've realized how much

I've, well, deteriorated. . . . I'll have to ask you to have patience about the book and trust me that at last, or at least for the first time in years, I'm doing the best I can. I've gotten in dozens of bad habits that I'm trying to get rid of."[33] That he should have embarked on the *Minnewaska* "armed with . . . a full set of the *Encyclopedia Britannica*" is also an index of his serious intent.[34] A month later, he told his friend Thomas Boyd, "I'm going to read nothing but Homer + Homeric Literature—and history 540–1200 A.D. until I finish my novel + I hope to God I don't see a soul for six months. My novel grows more + more extraordinary. . . . Well I shall write a novel better than any novel ever written in America."[35]

His resolves were indeed matched by his undeterrable confidence in the literary value of his new novel. The passage just quoted echoes the words he had used in a letter to Perkins dated June 1922 when he had first mentioned his project: "I want to write something new—something extraordinary and beautiful and simple + intricately patterned."[36] Two years later, his eagerness had not waned: "I feel I have an enormous power in me now, more than I've ever had in a way. . . . This book will be a consciously artistic achievement and must depend on that as the first books did not."[37] No doubt such aesthetic certainties account for the unflinching determination he showed in completing the novel and for the apparent lack of anxiety accompanying the writing once he was in Saint-Raphaël. His contentment shows in his words to Wilson just upon finishing the novel: "My book is wonderful, so is the air and the sea. I have got my health back—I no longer cough and itch and roll from one side of the bed to the other all night and have a hollow ache in my stomach after two cups of black coffee."[38]

Fitzgerald had seemingly been fairly advanced in the novel when he left the United States, since he initially had "every hope and plan of finishing [his] novel in June"; part of the task consisted in "approaching it from a new angle"—namely, replacing the third-person draft with a first-person final version, with Nick Carraway as the narrator, in an emulation of the masterful use of mediated perspective by Joseph Conrad, whose talent Fitzgerald had repeatedly praised since 1922. If he took more time than initially planned, it was because he couldn't "let it go out unless it ha[d] the very best [he was] capable of in it."[39] It is no surprise that Conrad's death on August 3 affected Fitzgerald; Nancy Milford reports that the morning after Gilbert Seldes and his wife arrived at Villa Marie, Gilbert, "upon opening the shutters of his window to his room, looked up and saw Scott standing on the balcony of his bedroom, which faced the sea. He was motionless as he gazed out, and then, sensing Seldes' presence, he quietly said, 'Conrad is dead.'"[40] The typescript was eventually sent on October 27. In the accompanying letter, he told Perkins, "I'm sending you my third novel, *The Great Gatsby*. (I think that at last I've done something really my own, but how good 'my own' is remains to be seen)."[41]

Perkins, who was laudatory, also gave Fitzgerald copious advice, which the latter readily accepted and acted on, putting just as much intensity into his revision of the novel as he had in the initial writing. Work on the galley proofs was concluded in Rome, where Scott and Zelda had headed just after the manuscript was sent. An earlier letter suggests Fitzgerald was planning to have Zelda help him with the revision, and he acknowledged her role in enabling him to capture the essence of Gatsby— thanks to her drawing the latter "until her fingers ache[d]."[42] She was also instrumental in convincing him that *The Great Gatsby* was the best title, as Fitzgerald continued to fret over half a dozen possibilities, with a preference for "Trimalchio" or "Trimalchio in West Egg." And finally, Fitzgerald's earnestness about his third novel was also demonstrated in his refusal to serialize it in *College Humor*, the only magazine to make an offer for it, passing up the ten thousand dollars involved just so the novel should not be cheapened in the eyes of the public.

Unsurprisingly, Fitzgerald grew more and more nervous as the date of publication—April 10—approached, and he ended a letter to Perkins "Yours in a Tremble," saying he expected a cable with news of the reception of the novel as soon as possible.[43] It was in Marseilles, on a stopover on their way back from Italy to Paris, that Scott received Perkins's first report on April 20: "Sales situation doubtful excellent reviews."[44] This was enough to have Scott sign his reply letter, "Yours in great depression."[45] The novel eventually sold a little more than twenty thousand copies in a few months, just enough to cancel his six-thousand-dollar debt to Scribner's. Income generated from the rights sold for stage and movie adaptations (thirty-five thousand dollars) somewhat compensated for these poor results. Reviews of the novel were mainly, even if not universally, positive. Several underlined Fitzgerald's artistic maturation, and Conrad Aiken perceptively remarked that *Gatsby*, "by grace of one cardinal virtue, quite escapes the company of most contemporary fiction—it has excellence of form."[46] However, a bitter Fitzgerald would later tell Wilson that even the most enthusiastic reviewers had not had "the slightest idea what the book was about,"[47] a judgment in keeping with that of Perkins, who considered that Scott was "above the heads of the multitude."[48] Fitzgerald found comfort mostly in fellow writers' personal congratulation letters, in particular those sent by Gertrude Stein, Edith Wharton, Willa Cather, and, perhaps more than any other, T. S. Eliot, who famously saw in the novel "the first step American fiction ha[d] taken since Henry James."[49]

One cannot but be struck by the confidence retained by Fitzgerald in the midst of his disappointment. He would defend his novel again and again: "*Gatsby* was far from perfect in many ways but all in all it contains such prose as has never been written in America before."[50] And "I'm much better than any of the young Americans *without exception*."[51] Such a deeply held conviction no doubt enabled him to maintain a strict writing discipline despite the marital crisis he and Zelda went through in Saint-Raphaël. The novel appeared to supersede all else: "It's been a fair summer," he wrote Perkins in late August. "I've been unhappy but my work hasn't suffered from it. I am grown at last."[52] As he would recall in a 1930 letter to Zelda, in Saint-Raphaël he had "dragged the great Gatsby out of the pit of [his] stomach in a time of misery."[53]

"That September 1924, I knew something had happened that could never be repaired."[54]

Fitzgerald's "craving for loneliness," as he put it upon his arrival in Hyères in May 1924, was central to his capacity to complete the novel.[55] But at what personal cost? As early as July 1923, Zelda had noted, "Scott has started a new novel and retired into strict seclusion and celibacy,"[56] and the summer in Saint-Raphaël confirmed that *Gatsby* was becoming synonymous with marital neglect for her. "What can I do with myself?" Zelda must have "th[ought] restlessly," like her autobiographical heroine in *Save Me the Waltz*,[57] recalling Daisy in *The Great Gatsby*: "What'll we do with ourselves this afternoon? . . . And the day after that, and the next thirty years?"[58] Zelda started spending more and more time alone with Edouard Jozan, one of the aviators she and Scott had begun socializing with: they met to swim together, play tennis, sit in the café terraces, or stroll in the nearby Estérel mountains. He was just a year older than Zelda, handsome, refined, and a born leader, as he proved by later rising to the position of vice admiral of the French navy. Tall and athletic, he contrasted with Scott, and Zelda's attraction to him is clear in her some-what clichéd portrayal of Edouard's alter ego, Jacques Chevre-Feuille, in *Save Me the Waltz*:

> She caught the outline of a broad back in the stiff white uniform of the French aviation. . . . The head of the gold of a Christmas coin nodded urgently, broad bronze hands clutched the air in the vain hope that its tropical richness held appropriate English words to convey so Latin a meaning. . . .
> "Do you think he actually *is* a god?" Alabama whispered to David. "He looks like you—except that he is full of the sun, whereas you are a moon person."[59]

A few pages later, Zelda grows more explicit: "The music stopped. He drew her body against him till she felt the blades of his bones carving her own. He was bronze and smelled of the sand and sun; she felt him naked underneath the starched linen. She didn't think of David. She hoped he hadn't seen; she didn't care."[60]

Whether Scott was too absorbed to see what was happening or whether he willfully ignored the signs of Zelda and Edouard's budding romance cannot be ascertained. The Murphys would later explain that when they visited the Fitzgeralds that summer, they immediately no-ticed what was happening. Jozan started zooming his plane just over Villa Marie, in an ostentatious display of his infatuation (a replay of 1918 Montgomery when American pilots buzzed the Sayres' house). But was this just one more example of Zelda's flirtatiousness? Or did the romance at one point turn adulterous? Although biographers have searched for evidence of what really went on that summer, consensus has it that the exact nature of this brief "affair" remains conjectural. So too are the chain of events that led Scott to note in his ledger "The Big Crisis—13th of July" and the true reasons behind Jozan's transfer first to the Hyères station, then to Indochina.[61] Did Zelda actually come to Scott asking for a divorce, as Fitzgerald reportedly told a relative years later? Did Scott in-sist that Jozan face him in Zelda's presence? Did he later keep her locked up at Villa Marie?[62] It is all but impossible to unravel fact from fiction because, as they were prone to doing, Scott and Zelda would later give varied dramatized versions of the event to different friends.

One certainty is that the showdown, whether imagined or not, became fictional material for Fitzgerald, as it found its way into chapter 7 of *The Great Gatsby* in the famous confrontation scene at the Plaza among Gatsby, Buchanan, and Daisy. Tellingly, while having Gatsby pronounce the words he must have been afraid to hear from Jozan—"Your wife doesn't love you. . . . She's never loved you. She loves me"[63]—Fitzgerald also saves face when he has Daisy refuse to yield to Gatsby's injunctions and eventually shows her shying away from leaving her husband:

> "Daisy, that's all over now," [Gatsby] said earnestly. "It doesn't matter anymore. Just tell him the truth—that you never loved him—and it's all wiped out forever."
>
> She looked at him blindly. "Why—how could I love him—possibly?"
>
> "You never loved him."
>
> She hesitated. . . .
>
> "I never loved him," she said with perceptible reluctance.[64]

Although, like Daisy, Zelda retreated, the "crisis" left an indelible mark on both Scott and Zelda. With his Catholic bend, Scott was never tolerant of sexual promiscuity, and whatever happened, Zelda and Edouard's infatuation was strong enough for Scott to have felt betrayed by his wife. The whole episode may have revived the memory of Ginevra King's having chosen a naval pilot over him.[65] On the other hand, the brutal end to the affair no doubt generated emotional strain for Zelda,[66] potentially precipitating her mental breakdown, as argued by Kendall Taylor: "The affair's wrenching conclusion . . . became a tipping point, releasing catastrophic forces and causing an emotional tailspin."[67] To be sure, friends of the Fitzgeralds soon witnessed the first serious signs of suicidal drives in her: the Seldeses, during their visit in August, noted that when they drove down to the beach together, Zelda would invariably wait until they reached the most hazardous point in the narrow, curvy road to ask Scott for a cigarette; a few days later, while at Cap d'Antibes, Scott woke up the Murphys at three o'clock in the morning, trembling with the news that Zelda had taken an overdose of sleeping pills.[68]

Although, that same month, Fitzgerald wishfully noted in his ledger, "Zelda and I close together,"[69] he also admitted in a letter to Ludlow Fowler, "I feel old, too, this summer. . . . That's the whole burden of this novel—the loss of those illusions that give such color to the world that you don't care whether things are true or false as long as they partake of the magical glory."[70] A few weeks later, the Riviera literally began to lose part of its magic as sunny weather gave way to the rainy season. When the lease on Villa Marie expired in the fall, Scott and Zelda left their lost paradise and sought warmth in Italy. The even more favorable exchange rate and Zelda's reading of Henry James's *Roderick Hudson* explain their choice of this destination, although it had left a negative impression on them on their prior trip to Europe. Once again, since the bitterness they felt could not easily be shaken off by a change of location, their stay in Rome and then Capri was to prove disastrous.

The Fitzgeralds drove down to Rome in November and settled at the Hotel des Princes in the Piazza di Spagna. *Ben-Hur* was being shot in the city. They spent time on the set, "bigger and grander papier-maché arenas than the real ones,"[71] and made friends with starring actress Carmel Myers. Scott paid attention to the cinematic technique, further sparking his interest in this new artistic medium. Real Rome, conversely, did not bring them many happy moments. The weather was unusually cold and damp, and both fell ill, Scott with the flu and Zelda with abdominal pains. This morbid atmosphere provided the background for the only story he managed to write while there, "The Adjuster." Its heroine, a flapper wife who pays a high price for her immature and undutiful behavior, reverberates almost violently with Scott's disappointment with Zelda and his still-ingrained hope of returning her to more wifely manners.[72] However, Scott's dissatisfaction was partly redirected toward others. He returned to heavy drinking as well. One night, he and Zelda were involved in a brawl with a group of taxi drivers. Scott struck out at them, knocked down a plainclothes carabiniere, and spent a night in jail, a humiliating experience he later turned into a symbolic moment of Dick Diver's inexorable decline in *Tender Is the Night*.

Driving further south, yet again, in February did not bring any magical relief. In idyllic Capri, where they settled at the Hotel Tiberio, Zelda started to paint. Her choice of a different artistic form signals her renewed need for emancipation, which would be confirmed a few months later when she turned to ballet training in Paris. Yet for the time being, she was often bedridden, having been diagnosed with colitis. Meanwhile, Scott started work on what would become one of his most acclaimed tales, "The Rich Boy." He only managed to complete another minor story, "Not in the Guidebook." And he did a lot of drinking.

Those dreary months in Italy bear out Fitzgerald's retrospective comment in his *Notebooks*: "That September 1924, I knew something had happened that could never be repaired."[73] His letter to Bishop upon leaving Capri in April indicates the violent nature of the Fitzgeralds' married life: "The cheerfulest things in my life are first Zelda and second the hope that my book has something extraordinary about it. . . . Zelda and I sometimes indulge in terrible four-day rows that always start with a drinking party but we're still enormously in love and about the only truly happily married people I know."[74] As for his literary talent, it was time to nurture it in a favorable artistic environment. Paris was the place to go.

Paris: "The Fitzgeralds were camping out there between two worlds."[75]

To avoid too long a drive, Scott and Zelda shipped their car from Naples to Marseilles and from there started driving north. They were held up in Lyon, where they needed to have the Renault repaired. But they were impatient to reach Paris, where Scott hoped to hear more about the reception of *Gatsby,* so they abandoned the car there and took a train. In mid-May they settled in a furnished fifth-floor walk-up on the Right Bank, at 14 rue de Tilsitt, just one block from the Arc de Triomphe. When he visited them, novelist Louis Bromfield noted that their apartment represented "the old aspirations and a yearning for stability, but somehow, it got only half-way. . . . The furniture was gilt Louis XVI [straight] from the Galeries Lafayette. . . . I always had the impression that the Fitzgeralds were camping out there between two worlds."[76] Indeed, while they would spend part of their time with the Left Bank literary bohemia, they chose the more conservative upper-class Right Bank as their base. And while the classical facade promised rigor to their lives, they gradually yielded to Paris's festive atmosphere, Fitzgerald later referring to "the hysteria of last May + June [1925] in Paris."[77]

Fitzgerald, however, had set foot in Paris with literature on his mind and with renewed good resolves. Scott's first move was to meet the budding writer Ernest Hemingway. The previous fall Fitzgerald had been enthusiastic about Hemingway's 1924 collection of prose vignettes, *in our time,* and had shared with Perkins his admiration for this young man with "a brilliant future," advising his editor "to look him up right away."[78] Fitzgerald would later be instrumental in facilitating Hemingway's transition to becoming a Scribner's author. However, right from their famed first encounter, the power balance between the two men was reversed. Theirs would become a sincere yet ambivalent friendship. Fitzgerald immediately stood in awe of this athletic, self-assured, and charismatic individual, with a steadfast dedication to both literature and virile outdoor sports, a reputation as a war hero, and an impressive tolerance for alcohol—in short, a man with so many of the qualities Fitzgerald felt he himself lacked.

Much of what we know about their relationship in those months comes from Hemingway's biased account in *A Moveable Feast*, written more than thirty years later. This is not to Fitzgerald's advantage, whether it be Hemingway's version of their initial encounter at the Dingo Bar (Hemingway suggests that there was a feminine touch in Scott's handsomeness, and he remembers Fitzgerald asking embarrassing questions and turning "the color of used candle wax" after a few glasses of champagne)[79] or his recollection of their trip together to Lyon to pick up the Renault (in which Scott appears as an irrational hypochondriac prone to intimate confidences). However, Hemingway acknowledges Fitzgerald's undoubtable ability: "When I had finished [Scott's] book I knew that no matter what Scott did, nor how he behaved, I must know it was like a sickness and be of any help I could to him and try to be a good friend. . . . If he could write a book as fine as *The Great Gatsby* I was sure that he could write an even better one."[80]

The two men often sat in cafés to discuss literature. Hemingway took Fitzgerald to Gertrude Stein's salon at 27 rue de Fleurus and introduced him to Sylvia Beach, a famous American expatriate who ran the bookshop Shakespeare and Company in the rue de l'Odéon and had published James Joyce's *Ulysses* in 1922. Through Hemingway, Fitzgerald came into contact with Paris's ebullient expatriate literary life, although he never actively participated in it. Though often strained, their relationship was undeniably a fecund one, important enough for Fitzgerald to write to Hemingway in December 1926: "I can't tell you how much your friendship has meant to me during this year and a half, it is the brightest thing in our trip to Europe for me."[81]

Meanwhile, Scott and Zelda went out at night and became regular patrons at Montmartre cabarets. Indulging in ever-more riotous carousing, they multiplied their drunken provocative antics, including at Cap d'Antibes, where they went back for a month in August 1925, and in

London, where they spent a few days in November. During these months, the Fitzgeralds' self-destructiveness became more conspicuous. Zelda's having to be given a shot of morphine as she experienced a bout of hysteria shows that, to use Fitzgerald's expression, they were "pay[ing] a big price" not only in physical but also in "mental hangovers."[82] Furthermore, Zelda continued to suffer from physical ailments.[83] As for Scott, his renewed interest in the Great War (which led to a trip to Verdun in the fall, a visit he would include in *Tender Is the Night*) may well have been spurred on simply by the combined proximity of Western Front battlefields and the company of war-wounded Hemingway. However, his noted fascination at that time with photographs of mutilated soldiers betrays an extremely somber mood. Indeed, what seems to have been a shared death wish was almost realized when, while in Cap d'Antibes in August, Scott and Zelda drove onto a railroad trestle, stalled their car, and, unable to restart it, went to sleep there, oblivious to the trolley due to speed through that spot in the morning. A passing French farmer saved them, but nobody, it seems, could protect them from themselves.

The miracle of the previous summer and fall had not been repeated. Fitzgerald summarized June and July 1925 in Paris as "1000 parties and no work," adding about his twenty-eighth year, "Drink, loafing."[84] During those months in Paris, Fitzgerald did little more than plan his third collection of stories, *All the Sad Young Men*, and his fourth novel, which he had originally thought would take about a year but on which he eventually spent nine long years.

"The orgastic future that year by year recede[d] before [him]"[85]

In *Save Me the Waltz*, Zelda has Alabama, her alter ego, exclaim upon arriving on the Riviera, "Oh, we are going to be so happy away from all the things that almost got us but couldn't quite because we were too smart for them!"[86] However, Europe's relative cheapness could not guard the couple against financial dissipation nor, therefore, could it free Scott from the spiral of commercial short-story "whoring."[87] That the 1924–25 span started with the epiphanic discovery of the Eden-like Riviera and all but ended with a visit to the hellish site of Verdun provides a vertiginous shortcut description of how those two years went. It is noteworthy that the mysterious character that teaches a lesson to the heroine of the short story "The Adjuster" ("You're trying to leave yourself behind but

Christmas in Paris, 1925

you can't")[88] should be called Doctor Moon, his sobering words dimming as it were the romantic moon that Fitzgerald initially, and insistently, associated with the Riviera landscapes he was so enthusiastic to discover.

One of the most famous photographs of Scott, Zelda, and Scottie from that period was taken on Christmas Day 1925 in the rue de Tilsitt apartment. Although it shows them smiling and doing a joyful kick step in front of a Christmas tree, only on the surface does the picture preserve "the insouciant image of the Fitzgeralds at the peak of his fame as the author of *The Great Gatsby*—attractive and ebullient."[89] A more somber take is that, having fled Great Neck where they had "no ground under [their] feet,"[90] Scott and Zelda lost their footing even further in Europe. The darker reality behind the glossy image was revealed only a couple of days later, circa December 27, by Scott, more than ever a very sad young man himself, in a letter written to Perkins: "Dear Max, I write to you from the depth of one of my unholy depressions. [When the new book is] finished I'm coming home for awhile anyhow though the thought revolts me as much as the thought of remaining in France." The impasse seemed total, tragic enough for him to continue: "You remember I used to say I wanted to die at thirty—well, I'm now twenty-nine and the prospect is still welcome."[91]

NOTES

1. F. Scott Fitzgerald, "How to Live on Practically Nothing a Year," in *My Lost City: Personal Essays, 1920–1940*, ed. James L. W. West III, Cambridge Edition of the Works of F. Scott Fitzgerald (Cambridge: Cambridge University Press, 2014), 41.

2. Fitzgerald, "How to Live on Practically Nothing a Year," 41.

3. Nancy Milford, *Zelda: A Biography* (New York: Harper and Row, 1970), 104.

4. Fitzgerald, "How to Live on Practically Nothing," 41.

5. F. Scott Fitzgerald, *The Letters of F. Scott Fitzgerald,* ed. Andrew Turnbull (London: Bodley Head, 1964), 200.

6. Kenneth Eble, *F. Scott Fitzgerald* (New York: Twayne Publishers, 1963), 112.

7. F. Scott Fitzgerald, "Ledger, 1919–1938," Matthew J. and Arlyn Bruccoli Collection of F. Scott Fitzgerald, Digital Collections, University of South Carolina University Libraries. https://digital.tcl.sc.edu/digital/collection/fitz/id/65/rec/1.

8. A good way to assess what these amounts meant at the time is to have a comparative landmark, such as that provided by Andrew Hook: "The average annual income of an American college teacher in l929 was $3,056." Andrew Hook, *F. Scott Fitzgerald: A Literary Life* (New York: Palgrave Macmillan, 2002), 97.

9. F. Scott Fitzgerald, "How to Live on $36,000 a Year," in *My Lost City*, 35.

10. Fitzgerald, "How to Live on $36,000," 34.

11. Fitzgerald, "How to Live on $36,000," 35.

12. F. Scott Fitzgerald, "The Sensible Thing," in *All the Sad Young Men*, ed. James L. W. West III, Cambridge Edition of the Works of F. Scott Fitzgerald (Cambridge: Cambridge University Press, 2014), 165.

13. F. Scott Fitzgerald, "Early Success," in *My Lost City*, 190.

14. Zelda Fitzgerald, *Save Me the Waltz* (London: Vintage Books, 2001), 73–74.

15. Fitzgerald, "How to Live on Practically Nothing," 43.

16. Fitzgerald, "How to Live on Practically Nothing," 46, 51.

17. Fitzgerald, "How to Live on Practically Nothing," 52.

18. Fitzgerald, "How to Live on Practically Nothing," 51.

19. Fitzgerald, "How to Live on Practically Nothing," 53.

20. David S. Brown, *Paradise Lost: A Life of F. Scott Fitzgerald* (Cambridge, Mass.: Harvard University Press, 2017), 163.

21. J. Gerald Kennedy, "Fitzgerald's Expatriate Years and the European Stories," in *The Cambridge Companion to F. Scott Fitzgerald,* ed. Ruth Progozy (Cambridge: Cambridge University Press, 2002), 120.

22. Fitzgerald, "How to Live on Practically Nothing," 55, 44.

23. As argued by Elisabeth Bouzonviller, Fitzgerald in his expatriate fiction is concerned not with "exotic Europe, but with native origins and attachments. [His] fictional French map is a palimpsest for an American one." Elisabeth Bouzonviller, "American Expatriates in France," in *F. Scott Fitzgerald in Context,* ed. Bryant Mangum (New York: Cambridge University Press, 2013), 267.

24. Matthew J. Bruccoli, *Some Sort of Epic Grandeur: The Life of F. Scott Fitzgerald,* 2nd ed. (Columbia: University of South Carolina Press, 2002), 196.

25. Bruccoli, *Epic Grandeur,* 197.

26. Fitzgerald, *Letters,* 359.

27. Fitzgerald, "How to Live on Practically Nothing," 56.

28. Quoted in Bruccoli, *Epic Grandeur,* 192.

29. F. Scott Fitzgerald, "Echoes of the Jazz Age," in *My Lost City,* 135.

30. Fitzgerald, "How to Live on Practically Nothing," 44. The sun-drenched scene in "Echoes of the Jazz Age" seems to be a negative of the moonlit scene at the end of the first chapter of *Gatsby*: "The silhouette of a moving cat wavered across the moonlight, and, turning my head to watch it, I saw that I was not alone—fifty feet away a figure had emerged from the shadow of my neighbor's mansion and was standing with his hands in his pockets regarding the silver pepper of the stars. Something in his leisurely movements and the secure position of his feet upon the lawn suggested that it was Mr. Gatsby himself, come out to determine what share was his of our local heavens. . . . I didn't call to him, for he gave a sudden intimation that he was content to be alone—he stretched out his arms toward the dark water in a curious way, and, far as I was from him, I could have sworn he was trembling. Involuntarily I glanced seaward—and distinguished nothing except a single green light, minute and far away, that might have been the end of a dock." F. Scott Fitzgerald, *The Great Gatsby: A Variorum Edition,* ed. James L. W. West III, Cambridge Edition of the Works of F. Scott Fitzgerald (Cambridge: Cambridge University Press, 2022), 25–26.

31. F. Scott Fitzgerald, *A Life in Letters,* ed. Matthew J. Bruccoli (New York: Charles Scribner's Sons, 1994), iv.

32. Fitzgerald, "How to Live on Practically Nothing," 48.

33. Fitzgerald, *Letters,* 162–63.

34. Sarah Churchwell, *Careless People: Murder, Mayhem, and the Invention of the Great Gatsby* (London: Virago Press, 2013), 15.

35. Quoted in Bruccoli, *Epic Grandeur,* 192.

36. Fitzgerald, *Life in Letters,* iv.

37. Fitzgerald, *Letters,* 163.

38. Fitzgerald, *Letters,* 341.

39. Fitzgerald, *Letters,* 162.

40. Milford, *Zelda,* 110.

41. Fitzgerald, *Letters,* 168.

42. Fitzgerald, *Letters,* 173.

43. Fitzgerald, *Letters,* 178.

44. Quoted in Bruccoli, *Epic Grandeur,* 217.

45. Fitzgerald, *Letters,* 181.

46. Quoted in Edward J. Rielly, *F. Scott Fitzgerald: A Biography* (Westport, Conn.: Greenwood Press, 2005), 50.

47. Quoted in Eble, *Fitzgerald,* 101.

48. Quoted in Bruccoli, *Epic Grandeur,* 218.

49. Quoted in Bruccoli, *Epic Grandeur,* 218.

50. Fitzgerald, *Life in Letters,* 112.

51. Quoted in Andrew Turnbull, *Scott Fitzgerald* (New York: Charles Scribner's Sons, 1962), 151.

52. Fitzgerald, *Letters,* 166.

53. Jackson R. Bryer and Cathy W. Barks, eds., *Dear Scott, Dearest Zelda: The Love Letters of F. Scott and Zelda Fitzgerald,* with an introduction by Eleanor Lanahan (London: Bloomsbury, 2002), 63.

54. Fitzgerald in his *Notebooks,* quoted in Bruccoli, *Epic Grandeur,* 195.

55. Bruccoli, *Epic Grandeur,* 192.

56. Quoted in Eble, *Fitzgerald,* 100.

57. Z. Fitzgerald, *Save Me the Waltz,* 92.

58. Fitzgerald, *Great Gatsby: Variorum,* 141.

59. Z. Fitzgerald, *Save Me the Waltz,* 84–86.

60. Z. Fitzgerald, *Save Me the Waltz,* 91.

61. Fitzgerald, "Ledger," https://digital.tcl.sc.edu/digital/collection/fitz/id/65/rec/1.

62. Milford, *Zelda,* 112; Kendall Taylor, *The Gatsby Affair: Scott, Zelda, and the Betrayal That Shaped an American Classic* (London: Rowman and Littlefield, 2018), 75; Linda Wagner-Martin, *Zelda Sayre Fitzgerald: An American Woman's Life* (New York: Palgrave Macmillan, 2004), 83.

63. Fitzgerald, *Great Gatsby,* 156.

64. Fitzgerald, *Great Gatsby,* 158–59.

65. Ginevra King was a beautiful and rich sixteen-year-old girl from Lake Forest, Illinois, whom Fitzgerald met when he was eighteen. A passionate courtship ensued, but the young heiress put an end to their relationship after two years.

66. "Still only twenty-four, still beautiful and vivacious but with an increasing sense of her inferiority to the woman Scott had thought he was marrying in 1920, Zelda was suffering in part from the loss of what she had assumed was the great love of her life [Edouard Jozan]. She was also suffering from her own sense of anomie: for a girl who thought life was such a promise, in so many exciting areas, she had ended up . . . with an increasingly bitter life." Wagner-Martin, *Zelda Sayre Fitzgerald,* 84.

67. Taylor, *Gatsby Affair,* 79.

68. Most biographers of Scott and Zelda link Zelda's attempted suicide to her ill-

fated affair with Jozan. See, for instance, André Le Vot, *Scott Fitzgerald: Biographie* (Paris: Julliard, 1979), 228; Milford, *Zelda*, 111; Taylor, *Gatsby Affair*, xiii, 79; Brown, *Paradise Lost*, 184.

69. Fitzgerald, "Ledger," https://digital.tcl.sc.edu/digital/collection/fitz/id/65/rec/1.

70. Fitzgerald, *Life in Letters*, 78.

71. F. Scott Fitzgerald and Zelda Fitzgerald, "Auction—Model 1934," in *My Lost City*, 159.

72. As argued by Alice Hall Petry, "Substitute 'Scott' for 'Charles,' and 'Zelda' for 'Luella,' and it seems possible that in 'The Adjuster' Fitzgerald is offering a remarkably astute appraisal of the psychological components of his relationship with his own wife." Alice Hall Petry, *Fitzgerald's Craft of Short Fiction: The Collected Stories 1920–1935* (Ann Arbor, Mich.: UMI Research Press, 1989), 113. In the story, Luella, who is bored by marital life and motherhood, goes through a series of domestic ordeals in the wake of her husband's nervous collapse, and the narrative tragically climaxes with the unexpected death of their baby son Chuck. As she is ready to run away from her marriage, the mysterious Doctor Moon—who has been a sort of ghostly figure throughout the story—stops her in the hall. "The more you try to run from yourself, the more you'll have yourself with you," he chastens her. F. Scott Fitzgerald, "The Adjuster," in *All the Sad Young Men*, 131. Doctor Moon's words seemingly work a miracle as Luella returns to her husband, and the two spouses in an epilogue-like happy ending are shown to have achieved relative peace and felicity with their two newly born children.

73. Fitzgerald in his *Notebooks*, quoted in Bruccoli, *Epic Grandeur*, 195.

74. Fitzgerald, *Letters*, 357.

75. Louis Bromfield, quoted in Brown, *Paradise Lost*, 187.

76. Louis Bromfield, quoted in Brown, *Paradise Lost*, 187.

77. Quoted in Bruccoli, *Epic Grandeur*, 238.

78. Quoted in Bruccoli, *Epic Grandeur*, 204.

79. Ernest Hemingway, *A Moveable Feast* (New York: Charles Scribner's Sons, 1964), 152.

80. Hemingway, *Moveable Feast*, 176.

81. Fitzgerald, *Letters*, 298.

82. Fitzgerald, *Letters*, 193.

83. Zelda suffered from colitis but also from ovarian problems and asthma. She seemed not to be properly medicated, and years later she remembered that period as one when she was always sick. Wagner-Martin, *Zelda Sayre Fitzgerald*, 89–90.

84. Fitzgerald, "Ledger," https://digital.tcl.sc.edu/digital/collection/fitz/id/66/rec/1.

85. Fitzgerald, *Great Gatsby*, 218.

86. Z. Fitzgerald, *Save Me the Waltz*, 81.

87. Hemingway, *Moveable Feast*, 155.

88. Fitzgerald, "The Adjuster," 131.

89. Bruccoli, *Epic Grandeur*, 244.

90. Fitzgerald, "Ledger," https://digital.tcl.sc.edu/digital/collection/fitz/id/64/rec/1.

91. Fitzgerald, *Letters*, 193.

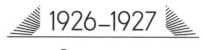

1926–1927

JADE BROUGHTON ADAMS

On January 17, 1926, the *New York Times* reported that Scott Fitzgerald was "critically ill in Paris this week," leaving his friends "greatly worried over his condition."[1] This was untrue, however, and a few days later Fitzgerald wired his concerned agent, Harold Ober, "RUMOR UNFOUNDED."[2] Fitzgerald speculated about the rumor's provenance in a letter to his editor, Maxwell Perkins, suggesting that "perhaps Zelda [was] using an imaginary illness as a protection against the many transients who demand our time."[3] In fact, Fitzgerald gave his time freely, enjoying a social life that was both lively and physically draining.

Fitzgerald produced comparatively little finished work during this two-year period, although it was his most lucrative to date because *The Great Gatsby* was adapted for Broadway and again for the silver screen. Despite the lack of sustained work on his new novel, provisionally titled "The World's Fair," several experiences during this time—notably the deepening of his friendship with Ernest Hemingway, the souring of his Riviera expat idyll, and his first foray into Hollywood—had a profound influence on him, infusing ideas that were gestating during this period, eventually to emerge in *Tender Is the Night* (1934) and *The Last Tycoon* (1941).

1926: France

Fitzgerald greeted the advent of 1926 with a New Year's resolution of sorts. He wrote to Perkins from Paris: "The more I get for my trash the less I can bring myself to write. However this year is going to be different."[4] Fitzgerald's prediction that he was going to write more short stories (what he referred to as "trash") in 1926 than he had written in 1925 did not come to pass. In fact, in 1926 he wrote only two short stories, a career low that remained unchallenged until 1938, when his short-story output dropped to zero.

The pained declaration with which Scott opened 1926 was countered by Zelda's actual and persistent abdominal pain. She would be "delivered of an unwelcome appendix" in June, but in January 1926 her doctor in Paris sent her to southwestern France for a rest cure at the health resort of Salies-de-Béarn, renowned for its salt baths and Pyrenean mountain air.[5] Fitzgerald described Salies-de-Béarn as a "desolate hole," a place sufficiently free of distractions to enable him to write two stories and an essay during a brief stay of a few weeks. "The Dance" was written in January and appeared in *Red Book Magazine* in June 1926. The story reflects Fitzgerald's sense of claustrophobia in the sleepy resort, opening with "All my life I have had a rather curious horror of small towns."[6] At this point, *Red Book* served as an outlet for Fitzgerald's more "serious," "experimental," or "gloomy" stories that were difficult to sell elsewhere.[7] Unlike the *Smart Set,* his previous venue for such stories, *Red Book* paid Fitzgerald well for his work. During the Fitzgeralds' stay in Salies, *Red Book* published "The Rich Boy," which Fitzgerald considered "one of the best things I have ever [d]one."[8]

At Salies, Fitzgerald channeled his enthusiasm over a new friendship into his writing. "How to Waste Material: A Note on My Generation," published in May 1926, was an essay-review of Hemingway's *In Our Time* (1925) in which Fitzgerald critiqued a "literary gold rush" among certain contemporary writers, who he said were "running through our material like spendthrifts" and then "doctor[ing]" said material "to give it a literary flavor." Fitzgerald contrasts these attempts with *In Our Time,* which he commends for its economy and for being "something temperamentally new."[9] Though Fitzgerald and Hemingway had known each other for only a year, they had developed a close friendship. In early May, Hemingway wrote to Fitzgerald, "I wish to hell you had come up [to Paris] with [the] Murphys."[10] A few weeks after writing this letter, the Hemingways would join the Fitzgeralds on the Riviera. The friendship with Hemingway intensified over the following eighteen months, before reaching its climax and changing irrevocably. But in March 1927, Hemingway called Fitzgerald "the best damn friend I have."[11]

On February 2, 1926, good news reached the stranded Fitzgeralds: an adaptation of *The Great Gatsby* had opened at the Ambassador Theatre on Broadway, starring James Rennie and written by Owen Davis. Perkins wrote to Fitzgerald telling him that "the cast is excellent" and the adaptation "distinctly well done."[12] The adaptation was generally faithful to the book, save for minor changes: a prologue was added depicting Gatsby and Daisy's prewar courtship in Louisville, George Wilson's job was transposed to the Buchanan household as a chauffeur, and the drunken apartment scene in New York City was replaced by two acts taking place in Gatsby's library.

Not only was the cast widely praised (in particular Rennie's Gatsby and Florence Eldridge's Daisy), but the production was hailed by the majority of critics. The achievement of *The Great Gatsby* as a novel was reinforced by these enthusiastic reviews of the play. Several reviews comment on the way the novel "seemed at once to invite and to defy dramatization."[13] Even criticism of the play served to affirm the high opinion of the source material. J. Brooks Atkinson in the *New York Times* concluded that "the novelist's lightness of touch, the detachment of the 'first person singular,' and the art of deft suggestion cannot endure the glare of the footlights."[14] Fitzgerald was stoically businesslike in the face of the nearly unanimous praise. He wrote to Perkins, "I hope to God it will make some money for me at last."[15] It did: Fitzgerald made $6,864.21 in his share of the receipts, after commissions. The play ran in New York until May 8, 1926, and reportedly prompted the opening of three new speakeasies in the theater's vicinity.[16]

The encouraging reviews of the play were followed at the end of February by the success of Fitzgerald's third collection of short stories, *All the Sad Young Men,* which had a print run of 16,200 copies. The reception of the collection was generally very positive. Many commentators noted what they viewed as Fitzgerald's maturation into a serious and disciplined artist who had entered a second phase of his career with the publication of *The Great Gatsby.* Multiple reviewers, among them R. Ellsworth Larsson in the *New York Sun,* delighted in the prospect of Fitzgerald proving naysayers wrong: "Previous to the publication of that stimulating novel 'Gatsby' it was the custom to dispose of Fitzgerald as one who would amass a considerable amount of money by the writing of short-lived sensations."[17] Fitzgerald was also praised for his poetic qualities (notably in the *New York Times Book Review* and in the *New York Herald Tribune* books section), and many reviewers picked out Fitzgerald's deft use of satire and irony for praise.[18]

One sour note mixed among the praise was an advertisement promoting the book that included a rather severe sketch of the author. Fitzgerald was furious, writing to Perkins, "I suppose this sounds vain and unpleasant but if you knew how it has taken the joy out of the press on my book to have that leering, puffy distortion reach me at the head of almost every review, you'd know the way I've gotten worked up over it."[19]

Fitzgerald was profoundly aware of the tightrope walk between art and commerce, and despite denigrating his short fiction as "trash" on multiple occasions, he was also proud of much of it, not just because of the high fees it commanded but for the literary craftsmanship itself. Reviews like Larsson's in the *New York Sun* must have served to further complicate Fitzgerald's conception of the value of his output: "Fitzgerald is even now at work on a novel which he admits, without remorse, won't sell at all. . . . This novel that is in progress one hopes will compensate him, in satisfaction if not in money, for having risked the loss of a very profitable following."[20]

Satisfaction wasn't enough to pay the bills, however, and Fitzgerald's "profitable following" was on his mind during this period. He desperately hoped that 1926 would mark a turning point in terms of both earnings and productivity. Short-story writing gained him as close to a regular monthly income as was possible for Fitzgerald, who was unusual among his con-

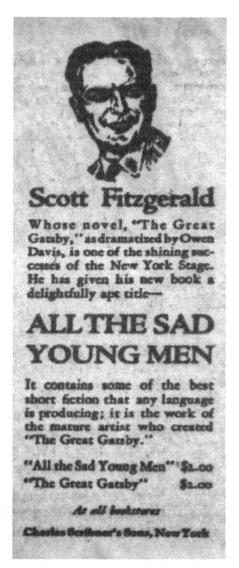

An advertisement for *All the Sad Young Men,* February 1926

temporaries for supporting himself solely through his writing. Fitzgerald began 1926 fixated on his debts and his route out of debt. From Salies, he wrote to Ober, "I must owe you thousands. . . . From now till March 1st will be a steady stream of $2500 stories—five more of them. . . . I honestly think I cause you more trouble and bring you less business than any of your clients. How you tolerate it I don't know—but thank God you do. And 1926 is going to be a different story."[21] Fitzgerald's five $2,500 stories did not materialize: only one more story was written between this letter and June 1927.

The Riviera

In late February 1926, the Fitzgeralds moved into Villa Paquita, Juan-les-Pins, sixteen miles southwest of Nice on the French Riviera. Fitzgerald's relationship with this part of the world was complex: on the one hand, he wrote *The Great Gatsby* there during his summer 1924 stay; on the other hand, it was the setting for Zelda's emotional (and possibly sexual) betrayal of him with the aviator Edouard Jozan that same summer. But at this point, in spring 1926, Davis's adaptation of *The Great Gatsby* was appearing on Broadway, Fitzgerald's new collection of short stories was garnering better-than-predicted sales, both the volume of stories and the lucrative stage version of *Gatsby* were helping Fitzgerald clear his debts, and the path to writing his next novel lay open before him.

In mid-March, Fitzgerald wrote to Perkins:

> In fact with the play going well + my new novel growing absorb-
> ing + with our being back in a nice villa on my beloved Riviera
> (between Cannes and Nice) I'm happier than I've been for years.
> It's one of those strange, precious and all too transitory moments
> when everything in one's life seems to be going well.[22]

A month later, the *New Yorker* featured a profile on Fitzgerald, and he was offered $16,666 for the movie rights to *Gatsby*. Though external circumstances were in his favor, it turned out that revisiting the locale where *Gatsby* had been written didn't boost Fitzgerald's productivity: he couldn't "repeat the past" after all.

The April 1926 *New Yorker* profile by John C. Mosher reported that Fitzgerald was in fine physical form that spring: "superbly preserved, so stocky, muscular, clear-skinned, ... with no lines of worry or senility, no saggings anywhere." But the piece goes on to concede that Fitzgerald's carefree, "fresh" demeanor sits in contrast with the labor of writing: "The popular picture of a blond boy scribbling off best sellers in odd moments between parties is nonsense. He's a very grave, hardworking man, and shows it. In fact there is definitely the touch of melancholy often obvious upon him."[23] This "touch of melancholy" was to develop as spring turned into summer. Writing for a primarily American audience from a villa in the south of France presented several challenges ranging beyond the midmorning sherry on the Plage de la Garoupe.

On top of an eleven-day delay between letters being sent and reaching their addressee, the magazines often exerted a level of editorial pressure that frustrated Fitzgerald on both an artistic and a practical level.[24] In March 1926, Fitzgerald let off some steam to Ober over the *Saturday Evening Post* editors' "silly cutting" of the story "The Adolescent Marriage":

> They have a right to be silly at 2500. a story but when two very
> clever paragraphs disappear of which I have no duplicate or record
> it makes me angry. Could you get me the ms. or an uncut proof of it
> so I can clip the pps. for my files? Especialy the one about a church
> with car-cards in the pews or something.[25]

"The Adolescent Marriage" was written in December 1925 and was published in the *Post* on March 6, 1926. It was a happily-ever-after story about an architect and his young sweetheart in which love conquers all, even immaturity.[26] In his edition of *All the Sad Young Men,* which includes additional tales written between April 1925 and April 1928, James L. W. West III has restored the "car-cards" paragraph Fitzgerald so lamented losing, by careful collation of an unmarked carbon typescript (the ribbon copy is not extant) with the serial text as it appeared in the *Post.* Fitzgerald wrote: "He would want Garnett to plan a church— one of these modern churches with a cabaret on the twentieth floor, car-cards in every pew and a soda-fountain in the sanctuary." The *Post* cut the details, rendering the description far less vivid: "He would want Garnett to plan one of these modern churches, perhaps."[27] The second of the two paragraphs Fitzgerald refers to in his letter remains a mystery.

Fitzgerald was deeply familiar with the practicalities of short-story writing and marketing stories for different audiences. In February 1926, in Salies, he wrote "Your Way and Mine." Fitzgerald called it "one of the lowsiest stories I've ever written." He had tried to write a compelling story fitting within "a business plot," complete with moralistic comment on ambition, but the rushed denouement and clunky splicing on of a second storyline set decades later was, as Fitzgerald rightly identified, devoid "of my usual spirit." Fitzgerald asked Ober to bury the story in a magazine with a smaller circulation than the *Post* or *Red Book*: "I'd rather have $1,000 for it from some obscure place than thrice that + have it seen."[28] Ober duly obliged, and the story was published in May in *Woman's Home Companion.*

After moving to another villa, Villa St. Louis, closer to the casino in Juan-les-Pins, Fitzgerald advised Ober in early May 1926 that his novel was a quarter complete and that he was intending for it to be serialized in *Liberty* in spring 1927, which necessitated an ambitious goal of delivering the manuscript at the beginning of the year.[29] Fitzgerald's progress on his own novel was in fact stalled, but he happily invested time and effort in helping Hemingway with his novel in progress, which was published in October 1926 as *The Sun Also Rises.* Although in *A Moveable Feast* Hemingway conspicuously fails to recall Fitzgerald's impact on the editing process for *The Sun Also Rises,* in early June 1926 he asked Fitzgerald to read the typescript. Reading the novel immediately, Fitzgerald wrote Hemingway a frank and thorough letter in which he suggested cutting parts of the novel's opening, with its biography of Brett Ashley and series of anecdotes about the Latin Quarter of Paris. Hemingway carefully considered Fitzgerald's advice and decided to cut the first sixteen pages of the manuscript in their entirety. He wrote to Perkins, "I think it will move much faster from the start that way. Scott agrees with me."[30] The framing of the cuts as his own idea is a little disingenuous, but the evidence is clear that Hemingway acted on Fitzgerald's suggestions.

The night before Hemingway asked Fitzgerald to read his typescript was an eventful one. The Murphys had given a party to welcome Hemingway to the Riviera. Half-infatuated with Sara Murphy at the best of times, Fitzgerald got drunk and disgraced himself, showing signs of jealousy when Sara paid attention to Hemingway and crawling around on the floor moaning, "Sara's being mean to me."[31] The summer was full of such drink-fueled incidents. Fitzgerald flirted with fifty-year-old retired dancer Isadora Duncan at a restaurant, prompting Zelda to throw herself down a flight of stone steps. At a party hosted by the Murphys he unsubtly interrogated the couple about their relationship and whether they had slept together before they were married, to such an insistent degree that it led Gerald to leave his own party.[32] This produced an angry

Zelda and Scott at Villa St. Louis, Juan-les-Pins, French Riviera, 1926

letter from Sara the next day, admonishing Scott for his impertinence: "You can't expect anyone to like or stand a *Continual* feeling of analysis + sub-analysis, + criticism—on the whole unfriendly—Such as we have felt for quite awhile."[33] On another occasion, Fitzgerald purposefully smashed three of Sara's cherished gold-flecked Venetian wineglasses and was banished from Villa America for three weeks.[34] In July 1926, the Murphys had joined the Hemingways on a trip to Pamplona to attend the San Fermín Fiesta. The Fitzgeralds did not join them, perhaps because Zelda had spent a fortnight in Paris for an appendectomy in June.[35] It is easy to see why the Murphys had begun to tire of Scott's reckless behavior and believed Hemingway to be the more dedicated friend as well as the more talented writer. "The one we took seriously was Ernest, not Scott," Gerald Murphy explained.[36]

By September, when the Riviera season ended, Fitzgerald was furious with himself. In his ledger he wrote, "Futile, shameful useless but the $30,000 rewards of 1924 work. Self disgust. Health gone."[37] Fitzgerald recorded his earnings for the year as $25,686.05. Of this, the income generated from the *Gatsby* play and film was $19,464.21; his book royalties were $2,033.20; and new work written in 1926 (two stories and an article) earned him $3,465. He had completed just four of a projected twelve chapters on his novel by the time he sailed home in December.

1927: Hollywood

After arriving in New York, the Fitzgeralds visited Scott's parents in Washington, D.C., and spent Christmas in Montgomery with Zelda's parents. Leaving Scottie with Scott's parents and her nanny, the Fitzgeralds accepted a lucrative invitation to travel to Hollywood for a two-week stay working on a flapper film treatment for Constance Talmadge. Fitzgerald was contracted by John W. Considine Jr. of United Artists to receive $3,500 initially, with a further $8,500 upon acceptance of the story. Two weeks turned into eight, and the trip ended up costing the Fitzgeralds money when they discovered that the film treatment had been rejected and would not be filmed.

Their impressions of Hollywood were mixed. Initially enchanted with the "long avenues of palm trees and Eucalyptus," Zelda soon became homesick for Paris and the Riviera but said she would settle for New York.[38] She began a scrapbook on architecture and interior design and asked Scottie to make a drawing of her ideal home so they could start looking for one to buy. After such a transient few years, the concept of home was clearly on Zelda's mind, and the artifice of Hollywood didn't help with her yearning for authentic roots. Comparing Hollywood with the many other cities they had lived in, Scott and Zelda were surprised by the lack of nightlife and by how early the restaurants closed. They began making their own fun, taking the liberty of introducing themselves to Lillian Gish and turning up uninvited at a party hosted by Samuel Goldwyn for the Talmadge sisters.

Compounding their sense of disappointment in Hollywood, Zelda wrote to Scottie to tell her that they went to see the film adaptation of *The Great Gatsby,* directed by Herbert Brenon, but reported, "It's ROTTEN and awful and terrible and we left."[39] The *New York Times* film critic Mordaunt Hall hesitantly called it "quite good entertainment" but said that "it would have benefitted by more imaginative direction."[40] Starring Warner Baxter as Gatsby, Lois Wilson as Daisy, and a scene-stealing William Powell as Wilson, the film (which, sadly, is now lost) had opened in November 1926, a few weeks before the Fitzgeralds' visit.

Fitzgerald's assignment, as reported in the press, was to write "one of the hectic flapper comedies, in which Constance Talmadge has specialized for years" and for which Fitzgerald had complimented her as early as 1921.[41] Talmadge was often described, including by Fitzgerald, as "sparkling" and "witty," and, while her roles always included physical humor, she deliberately avoided outright slapstick.[42] Anita Loos and John Emerson had written a series of twelve treatments and screenplays for Talmadge between 1919 and 1925. The formula they consolidated, according to film historian Jeanine Basinger, was "a fun loving, witty woman in a contemporary setting, with a good wardrobe and a handsome costar . . . romp[ing] through a plot that contained a little bit of farcical misunderstanding, a solid battle of the sexes, and a good deal of romance."[43] In his film treatment, "Lipstick," Fitzgerald incorporated elements of this formula: a fur coat and a luxury limo, a charming male lead, and a farcical sequence in which the silverware goes missing from a dinner. He wisely avoided depicting the heroine as a seductress but neglected to create a particularly "witty" or "sparkling" protagonist, and the battle-of-the-sexes element is entirely absent from Fitzgerald's treatment.

This is particularly perplexing given that Fitzgerald was clearly familiar with Talmadge's screen persona. During his time in Hollywood

in winter 1927, Fitzgerald gave an interview in which he taxonomizes the
flapper by type. His verdict on Constance Talmadge reads:

> [Talmadge] is the epitome of young sophistication. She is the deft
> princess of lingerie—and love—plus humor. She is Fifth Avenue
> and diamonds and Catalya orchids and Europe every year. She is
> sparkling and witty and as gracefully familiar with the new books
> as with the new dances. I have an idea that Connie appeals every bit
> as strongly to the girls in the audience as to the men. Her dash—her
> zest for things—is compelling. She is the flapper *de luxe*.[44]

Yet the story Fitzgerald wrote for Talmadge does not reflect this assessment of her talents. Talmadge was to star as Dolly Carrol, a flapper who
had nobly taken the blame for an errant uncle's corporate espionage and
served two years in prison. She meets and falls in love with an Ivy League
university student, who is initially judgmental of her but eventually falls
in love with her. However, the inclusion of a magic lipstick destabilizes
the integrity of the narrative: this lipstick makes the wearer irresistible,
although the story establishes that Dolly and the Princeton student, Ben,
would fall in love without its enchantments.

Even though Fitzgerald was identified in popular culture with the
fringed-dress-wearing flapper that populated films throughout the decade, he had declared the flapper "passé" as early as 1923, "[at least] in
the East."[45] Manufactured on the West Coast by the time the Fitzgeralds
visited, the Hollywood incarnation of the flapper flourished throughout
the 1920s, as Ruth Prigozy has established. In his essay "Echoes of the
Jazz Age" (1931), Fitzgerald differentiates between his flappers and movie
flappers, stating, "The social attitude of the producers [of flapper films]
was timid, behind the times and banal."[46] He had first identified this
"timid[ity]" in an interview given during his stay in Hollywood in early
1927, asserting, "The flappers today are perhaps less defiant, since their
freedom is taken for granted and they are sure of it."[47]

Fitzgerald's flapper heroines of the early 1920s shared aesthetic traits
with the film flappers of the mid-1920s—namely, svelte figures and magnetic beauty—but their personalities differed. In contrast to the somewhat generic screen flappers, Fitzgerald's literary flappers were "individuals, often troubled, generally courageous, frequently in conflict with
themselves, and never predictable."[48] Whereas Fitzgerald's literary flap-

per characters were complex, the film flapper archetype relied on stylish clothes and makeup and on aspirational architecture and decor; on the screen, flappers were infused with the individual screen personalities of the actresses who played them.[49] Most important, "beneath the surface" they remained "pure, conventional, and decidedly moral."[50] Fitzgerald was conscious of these traits when he was writing his film treatment for Talmadge.

In "Lipstick," Fitzgerald makes an effort to think filmically, rather than literarily, including with a prom scene anticipating a Busby Berkeley–style kaleidoscopic overhead shot (three years before Berkeley came to Hollywood):

> Looked at from above the prom resolved itself into a central circle of closely packed stags around which hub revolved the varicolored wheel of dancers. Outside the wheel was a further ring of stags, flanked at each end by a celebrated orchestra from New York. The slow revolution of the wheel and the flashes of black darting out to dance with pink or blue or gold, kept the whole scene in constant, colorful motion.[51]

The introductions of Dolly and Ben occur in parallel scholastic settings that would lend themselves well to crosscutting, and Fitzgerald introduces a secondary character, Ben's fiancée, through clippings taped on the wall of Dolly's prison cell—a scene that would find better form in a montage. Ultimately, the treatment was not successful, and Considine told Fitzgerald the film would not be made because "everyone thinks the beginning or premise contains exceptionally fine material but the rest of the story is weak."[52] Even for the increasingly hackneyed genre of flapper films, there was too much farce, and Dolly was neither fun loving, feisty, nor rebellious.

In 1937, en route to Hollywood for a third and final time, Fitzgerald wrote to his daughter, giving a clear-eyed assessment of his previous visits to Hollywood. He remembered his 1927 self as "confidant to the point of conceit." He went on: "I honestly believed that <u>with no effort on my part</u> I was a sort of magician with words—an odd delusion on my part when I had worked so desperately hard to develop a hard, colourful prose style. Total result—a great time + no work."[53] Fitzgerald's first visit to Hollywood was mainly significant for his meeting two people who would have a great impact on his writing: seventeen-year-old actress Lois Moran and twenty-seven-year-old Metro-Goldwyn-Mayer production head Irving Thalberg.

Twelve years after his Hollywood visit, when he was compiling notes for *The Last Tycoon,* Fitzgerald recalled meeting the latter and remembered an anecdote Thalberg had charismatically told him about finding a route through a mountain as a metaphor for leadership: "I was very much impressed by the shrewdness of what he said—something more than shrewdness—by the largeness of what he thought and how he reached it at the age of 26 which he was then."[54] Thalberg was a seminal inspiration for the character of Monroe Stahr in *The Last Tycoon.*

Moran was probably introduced to Scott and Zelda through their mutual acquaintance Carl Van Vechten in January 1927. She had entered the public eye in the melodrama *Stella Dallas* (1925) and was just seventeen when they met her. At thirty, Scott was secure in his reputation as an accomplished writer, regardless of the lack of output at the time. Moran's attentions certainly flattered him, and he even took a screen test, at her suggestion, in order to see whether he could join her on the silver screen. The test was unsuccessful, and the episode was later used in *Tender Is the Night.*

Biographers have long speculated over the nature of Fitzgerald and Moran's relationship. The earliest assessment, when Moran was still alive to speak for herself, was from Arthur Mizener, who described them as "fascinated" by each other, noting that Moran "was important to his imagination" while emphasizing that "there is no evidence that his feeling for her was ever so mixed up with personal exhaustion as was Dick's for Rosemary."[55] Other biographers insist that the relationship never progressed beyond friendship, among them Matthew J. Bruccoli, who notes, "Fitzgerald was never alone with Moran."[56] But Scott Donaldson reports a story claiming that Fitzgerald supposedly burst into Arthur W. Brown's hotel room in the early hours, with Lois on his arm, asking Brown to provide an alibi for his whereabouts that day.[57] The anecdote was told by Brown to Mizener, but the latter chose not to include it in his biography. In a letter to Zelda's psychiatrist in 1932, Scott refers to his relationship with Moran as an "affair" and equates it with Zelda's transgression with Edouard Jozan: "Her affair with Edward Josaune in 1925 (and mine with Lois Moran in 1927, which was a sort of revenge) shook something out of us."[58]

Moran consistently denied the relationship was sexual, though according to her biographer Richard Buller, "that they were indeed sexually involved is virtually inescapable," and her son believed "Fitzgerald took her virginity."[59] Whether or not this is true, Fitzgerald clearly remained an important part of her life, as Moran telephoned Fitzgerald on the morning of her wedding in 1935 (after the ceremony, as she was keen to point out to Mizener).[60] Whatever the exact nature of Scott and Lois's relationship, it had an impact on Zelda: one night when Scott and Lois were at a dinner together in Hollywood, Zelda is reputed to have collected a bundle of clothes she had made for herself and burned them in the hotel bathtub. This self-destructive statement was followed up on the train back east by a powerful rejection of Scott's earned wealth: she threw the platinum and diamond wristwatch he had given her out the train window.[61]

Ellerslie, Delaware

In April 1927, the Fitzgeralds leased a nineteenth-century Greek revival mansion named Ellerslie, at Edgemoor, on the Delaware River near Wilmington. Fitzgerald's college roommate and future executor John Biggs Jr. lived nearby, and Perkins thought a slower pace of life would create a fecund environment, free from distraction, in which Fitzgerald could make progress on the novel. In May 1927, Moran and her mother were invited to visit Ellerslie. It was the weekend Charles Lindbergh flew the Atlantic to land in Paris. In "Echoes of the Jazz Age," Fitzgerald fondly recalled that moment:

> In the spring of '27, something bright and alien flashed across the sky. A young Minnesotan who seemed to have had nothing to do with his generation did a heroic thing, and for a moment people set down their glasses in country clubs and thought of their old best dreams.[62]

During the weekend visit, the group had a picnic on the banks of the Delaware River and took snapshots of each other outside the house. In her correspondence with Mizener, Moran revealed she had kept a couple of these pictures as mementoes of the weekend, and on one of them, a photograph of Lois and Scottie, Scott had written, "My two golden girls."[63]

Guest of Honor

Scott Fitzgerald and Lois Moran at Ellerslie, May 1927

His original golden girl, however, was increasingly unhappy. Despite her impeccable manners in hosting Moran at Ellerslie, Zelda had been deeply hurt by Scott's admiration of Moran's hard work and self-sufficiency, feeling that Scott viewed her, by contrast, as a useless social-ite. This galvanized Zelda into a remarkably productive period: she wrote four essays, seriously resumed ballet training, painted an exquisite lampshade depicting places the Fitzgeralds had lived, and constructed an intricate dollhouse for Scottie. As the Fitzgeralds' relationship grew more strained, glimpses of their previous, happier selves were occasionally visible. On their way back to the Plaza Hotel after a party in New York, they saw a newsboy standing in the rain and Scott stopped their cab in order to buy all the sodden boy's papers. His ledger contains three cryptic references to experiencing "stoppies" during August and September 1927, which Bruccoli has suggested relate to "a series of nervous ailments."[64] In September, Perkins visited Fitzgerald at Ellerslie and left concerned that Fitzgerald was in real danger of a nervous breakdown; he was terribly worried at Scott's inability to complete any steady or consistent work on his novel.

Fitzgerald's retrospective summary of the past year in his ledger that September, as he turned thirty-one, reflected the lows of the year as well as his tentative optimism: "Total loss at beginning. A lot of fun. Work begins again."[65] The work really did begin to flow again in summer 1927, when he capitalized on his frequent visits to his alma mater to write the essay "Princeton" in early June. Moran was still very much on his mind as he composed his first short story in fifteen months, "Jacob's Ladder." Drawing on his experiences in Hollywood, the story involves a shopgirl-to-movie-star Cinderella arc and also incorporates a latently romantic interest between an older man and a teenage girl—a theme that permeated other contemporary stories, such as "The Love Boat" (written in August 1927) and "Magnetism" (written in December 1927), as well as the evolving plot of his novel in progress. The new novel was provisionally titled "The World's Fair"; in June 1927 he considered renaming it "The Boy Who Killed His Mother," but it would eventually emerge (after major revisions to plotting and characterization) as *Tender Is the Night* in 1934, nine years after the publication of *The Great Gatsby*.

Despite the fact that Fitzgerald was writing salable fiction again, his professional life was in some disarray, and he requested a cash advance from Ober every single week during September. In October, he wrote frankly to Hemingway, admitting

No work this summer but lots this fall. Hope to finish the novel by 1st December. Have got nervous as hell lately—purely physical but scared me somewhat—to the point of putting me on the wagon and smoking denicotinized cigarettes. . . . The Post now pays me $3500. . . . I can't tell you how I miss you.[66]

Hemingway wrote the beginnings of a reply, in which he asked whether Fitzgerald was sleeping well and said, "I'm sorry as hell you've been nervous—it is a hell of a business but imagine that laying off liqor and smoking these coughless carloads will fix it up," but the letter was never sent.[67]

Having sold his last two stories to the *Post,* Fitzgerald offered the ghost story "A Short Trip Home" to them first, with half an expectation that they would reject it.[68] The *Post* wrote to Ober, explaining, "Ghosts are rather difficult to handle in the Post, but the story is so well done that we have not been able to resist it."[69] Fitzgerald was at a low ebb personally, trying to juggle advances from publishers and mounting debts amid interminable delays delivering promised stories. Yet the *Post* "[couldn't] resist" a story they wouldn't usually consider publishing, *College Humor* was desperate for Fitzgerald to provide them with something to publish, and earlier in the year *Liberty* had been trying to poach him from his usual home in the *Post* with a price raise.

The last of the Moran-inspired stories was "Magnetism," written in December 1927 and published in the *Post* in March 1928. Fitzgerald used "Magnetism" to rehearse the love-triangle plot at the heart of what would become *Tender Is the Night.* An actor with Dick Diveresque charm, George Hannaford, becomes infatuated with a costar, Helen Avery. Hannaford's wife, Kay, retaliates with a dalliance with an old flame. Avery, at eighteen years old, is described as a "dark, pretty girl with a figure that would be full-blown sooner than she wished."[70] The story dramatizes the ultimately unstable foundations of celebrity and theatrical identity.

Fitzgerald sent the manuscript of "Magnetism" to Ober in mid-December as the family prepared for Christmas. Fitzgerald wrote to Hemingway to declare ominously, "I've tasted no alcohol for a month but Xmas is coming."[71] The Fitzgeralds' Christmas of 1927 was not a happy one. Scottie spent the next morning in tears after a Christmas Day during which her father was most certainly not "on the wagon." Contrary to their plans for a relatively quiet celebration, the house had filled with guests wreaking an all-too-familiar variety of drunken havoc, the intricately constructed neatness of Scottie's dollhouse throwing into stark relief the chaos of post-Christmas-festivities Ellerslie. According to James Mellow, "Fitzgerald, with some nonchalance and evidently a considerable hangover, surveyed the wreckage and said, 'Just think—it's like this now all over the country.'"[72] It was a sad end to a financially successful year: Fitzgerald's ledger records his total earnings for 1927 as a career high of

$29,737.87. This included $15,300 from selling five stories to the *Post*, four of which were paid at his raised fee of $3,500. It also included an advance against his forthcoming novel of $5,752.06.[73]

The Fitzgeralds traveled a great deal, but the period of 1926–27 was particularly peripatetic, even by their standards. Regardless of where they were, whether in the United States or Europe, money worries continued to plague them, just as a permanent home proved elusive. Progress on his novel had been inconsistent, but Fitzgerald had made headway in the character study of Rosemary, who would lie at the heart of the eventual marital conflict between Dick and Nicole Diver in *Tender Is the Night*. Fitzgerald tasted success, both commercially and critically, with the dramatization of *The Great Gatsby* and the publication of *All the Sad Young Men*, but the period also saw the beginnings of Zelda's mental anguish that led to her 1930 breakdown.

The year 1927 was Fitzgerald's highest-earning year to date, but he ended it in debt once more. He had begun 1926 faced by a false report that friends were "greatly worried over his condition." By the end of 1927, indeed they were.

NOTES

1. "Scott Fitzgerald Ill in France," *New York Times*, January 17, 1926.

2. Matthew J. Bruccoli, ed., *As Ever, Scott Fitz—: Letters between F. Scott Fitzgerald and His Literary Agent Harold Ober, 1919–1940*, with the assistance of Jennifer McCabe Atkinson (London: Woburn Press 1973), 84.

3. F. Scott Fitzgerald, *The Letters of F. Scott Fitzgerald*, ed. Andrew Turnbull (London: Bodley Head, 1964), 197.

4. F. Scott Fitzgerald, *A Life in Letters*, ed. Matthew J. Bruccoli (London: Penguin, 1998), 133.

5. Bruccoli, *As Ever*, 91.

6. F. Scott Fitzgerald, "The Dance," in *All the Sad Young Men*, ed. James L. W. West III, Cambridge Edition of the Works of F. Scott Fitzgerald (Cambridge: Cambridge University Press, 2014), 297.

7. Bryant Mangum, *A Fortune Yet: Money in the Art of F. Scott Fitzgerald's Short Stories* (New York: Garland, 1991), 67–68.

8. F. Scott Fitzgerald, *Correspondence of F. Scott Fitzgerald*, ed. Matthew J. Bruccoli and Margaret M. Duggan (New York: Random House, 1980), 152.

9. F. Scott Fitzgerald, "How to Waste Material: A Note on My Generation," in *My Lost City: Personal Essays, 1920–1940*, ed. James L. W. West III, Cambridge Edition of the Works of F. Scott Fitzgerald (Cambridge: Cambridge University Press, 2014), 77–78, 80.

10. Ernest Hemingway, *The Letters of Ernest Hemingway*, vol. 3, 1926–1929, ed.

Rena Sanderson, Sandra Spanier, Robert W. Trogdon (Cambridge: Cambridge University Press, 2015), 70–71.

11. Hemingway, *Letters*, 222.

12. John Kuehl and Jackson R. Bryer, eds., *Dear Scott / Dear Max: The Fitzgerald–Perkins Correspondence* (London: Cassell, 1973), 131.

13. See, for example, Arthur Pollock, "Plays and Things," *Brooklyn Daily Eagle*, February 3, 1926.

14. J. Brooks Atkinson, "Drama for Adults," *New York Times*, February 7, 1926.

15. Kuehl and Bryer, *Dear Scott / Dear Max*, 132.

16. Karl K. Kitchen, "Up and Down Broadway," *Tampa Bay Times*, March 14, 1926.

17. Quoted in Jackson R. Bryer, ed., *F. Scott Fitzgerald: The Critical Reception* (New York: Burt Franklin, 1978), 263.

18. Bryer, *Fitzgerald*, 257–58, 270–71.

19. Kuehl and Bryer, *Dear Scott / Dear Max*, 137.

20. Quoted in Bryer, *Fitzgerald*, 265.

21. Bruccoli, *As Ever*, 85.

22. Fitzgerald, *Life in Letters*, 139.

23. John C. Mosher, "That Sad Young Man," *New Yorker*, April 17, 1926, 20–21.

24. Fitzgerald, *Life in Letters*, 136.

25. Bruccoli, *As Ever*, 87–88.

26. Mangum, *A Fortune Yet*, 104.

27. F. Scott Fitzgerald, "The Adolescent Marriage," in *All the Sad Young Men*, 279–80.

28. Fitzgerald, *Life in Letters*, 139.

29. Fitzgerald, *Life in Letters*, 140.

30. Quoted in Scott Donaldson, *Hemingway vs. Fitzgerald: The Rise and Fall of a Literary Friendship* (London: John Murray, 2000), 96.

31. Amanda Vaill, *Everybody Was So Young. Gerald and Sara Murphy: A Lost Generation Love Story* (New York: Broadway Books, 1999), 177.

32. Matthew J. Bruccoli, *Some Sort of Epic Grandeur: The Life of F. Scott Fitzgerald,* 2nd ed. (Columbia: University of South Carolina Press, 2002), 251–52.

33. Fitzgerald, *Correspondence*, 196.

34. Bruccoli, *Epic Grandeur*, 251.

35. Bruccoli, *As Ever*, 91.

36. Quoted in Calvin Tomkins, *Living Well Is the Best Revenge: Two Americans in Paris, 1921–1933* (London: André Deutsch, 1972), 102.

37. F. Scott Fitzgerald, *F. Scott Fitzgerald's Ledger: A Facsimile,* introduction by Matthew J. Bruccoli (Washington, D.C.: NCR/Microcard Editions / Bruccoli Clark, 1972), 180.

38. Quoted in Nancy Milford, *Zelda: A Biography* (New York: Harper and Row, 1970), 127.

39. Quoted in James R. Mellow, *Invented Lives: F. Scott and Zelda Fitzgerald* (London: Souvenir Press, 1985), 281.

40. Mordaunt Hall, "The Screen," *New York Times*, November 22, 1926.

41. Arthur Mizener, *The Far Side of Paradise: A Biography of F. Scott Fitzgerald* (Cambridge, Mass.: Riverside Press, 1951), 203; Matthew J. Bruccoli and Jackson R. Bryer, eds., *F. Scott Fitzgerald in His Own Time: A Miscellany* (Kent, Ohio: Kent State University Press, 1971), 245.

42. Matthew J. Bruccoli, Scottie Fitzgerald Smith, and Joan P. Kerr, eds., *The Romantic Egoists: A Pictorial Autobiography from the Scrapbooks and Albums of F. Scott and Zelda Fitzgerald* (New York: Charles Scribner's Sons, 1974), 149.

43. Jeanine Basinger, *Silent Stars* (Middletown, Conn.: Wesleyan University Press, 2000), 163.

44. Bruccoli, Smith, and Kerr, *Romantic Egoists*, 149.

45. F. Scott Fitzgerald, "My Lost City," in *My Lost City*, 112.

46. F. Scott Fitzgerald, "Echoes of the Jazz Age," in *My Lost City*, 134.

47. Bruccoli, Smith, and Kerr, *Romantic Egoists*, 149.

48. Ruth Prigozy, "Fitzgerald's Flappers and Flapper Films of the Jazz Age: Behind the Morality," in *A Historical Guide to F. Scott Fitzgerald*, ed. Kirk Curnutt (Oxford: Oxford University Press, 2004), 135.

49. F. Scott Fitzgerald, "Lipstick," *Fitzgerald/Hemingway Annual*, 1978: 34.

50. Prigozy, "Fitzgerald's Flappers and Flapper Films," 132.

51. Fitzgerald, "Lipstick," 28.

52. Fitzgerald, "Lipstick," 35.

53. Fitzgerald, *Life in Letters*, 330.

54. F. Scott Fitzgerald, *The Love of the Last Tycoon: A Western*, ed. Matthew J. Bruccoli, Cambridge Edition of the Works of F. Scott Fitzgerald (Cambridge: Cambridge University Press, 2014), xviii.

55. Mizener, *Far Side of Paradise*, 204.

56. Bruccoli, *Epic Grandeur*, 255.

57. Scott Donaldson, *Fool for Love: F. Scott Fitzgerald* (Minneapolis: University of Minnesota Press, 2012), 54.

58. Fitzgerald, *Life in Letters*, 210.

59. Richard Buller, *A Beautiful Fairy Tale: The Life of Actress Lois Moran* (Pompton Plains, N.J.: Limelight Editions, 2005), 132.

60. Buller, *Beautiful Fairy Tale*, 126.

61. Bruccoli, *Epic Grandeur*, 256–57.

62. Fitzgerald, "Echoes of the Jazz Age," 136.

63. Buller, *Beautiful Fairy Tale*, 118.

64. Bruccoli, *Epic Grandeur*, 261.

65. Fitzgerald, *Ledger*, 181.

66. Fitzgerald, *Life in Letters*, 152.

67. Hemingway, *Letters*, 323.

68. In "A Short Trip Home," references to a Lois-like character appear in the *Post* serial version but not in the *Taps at Reveille* version, in keeping with Fitzgerald's revisions for the collection. See West's Record of Variants in F. Scott Fitzgerald, "A Short Trip Home," in *Taps at Reveille*, ed. James L. W. West III, Cambridge Edition of the Works of F. Scott Fitzgerald (Cambridge: Cambridge University Press, 2014), 348–49.

69. Bruccoli, *As Ever*, 103.

70. F. Scott Fitzgerald, "Magnetism," in *All the Sad Young Men*, 411.

71. Fitzgerald, *Life in Letters*, 154.

72. Mellow, *Invented Lives*, 307.

73. Fitzgerald, *Ledger*, 61–63.

1928–1929

CATHERINE DELESALLE-NANCEY

1928: The Pouilly with Bouillabaisse at Prunier's in a time of discouragement.

1929: A feeling that all liquor has been drunk and all it can do for one has been experienced, and yet—"Garçon Chablis-Mouton 1902, et pour commencer, une petite carafe de vin rose. C'est tout. Merci."

This is what Francis Scott Fitzgerald, with playful clear-sightedness, reduces 1928 and 1929 to in his "Short Autobiography."[1] The joyful inebriation of the 1920s has turned into the irrepressible intoxication and hangover of the '30s. "All liquor has been drunk," all emotions experienced, all money spent, and Zelda and Scott Fitzgerald, the enfants terribles of the Jazz Age, embrace the fate of their generation, experiencing their own private great depression.

In the two-year interval 1928–29, the life of the Fitzgeralds was but a dizzying succession of trips and moves. Frustrated with Ellerslie, their palatial rented home just outside Wilmington, Delaware, Zelda expressed in a letter to Carl Van Vechten: "Wilmington has turned out to be the dark hole of Calcutta and I simply must have some Chablis and curry and fraises des bois with peaches in champagne for dessert. Also I want to feel a sense of intrigue which is only in Paris, and, maybe, in Monte Negro"—they decided to move to Paris, where they arrived in April 1928.[2] But soon dissatisfied with Paris, they went back to their American home in September 1928, taking with them Scottie's French nanny and Philippe, a former boxer who acted as butler–chauffeur and drinking companion for Scott, only to cross the Atlantic again when their two-year lease in Ellerslie was up in March 1929. This time, they landed in Genoa and spent a month on the Riviera before going up to Paris again, staying first in a cheap hotel that they loathed and then in an apartment in the rue Palatine. In July, they were back in Cannes, in the Villa Fleur des Bois,

Scott's and Zelda's French identity cards, 1929

which they left at the end of the season in October to head north through Arles, Vichy, and Tours before moving into yet another apartment in Paris, 10 rue Pergolèse. But the whirlwind of trips and alcohol could not conceal that they were stalled, as were the sprightly 1920s.

Going Bankrupt

Although the Fitzgeralds, with no money invested in the stock market, were not financially hit by the 1929 stock market crash, the crisis came to symbolize what Scott was later to call their own "emotional bankruptcy," an idea that pervades Fitzgerald's introspective essays posthumously collected in *The Crack-Up*.[3] On October 24, 1929, they were staying in a hotel in Saint-Raphaël en route to Paris after a five-month stay on the French Riviera. It is Zelda this time who registers the dark mood and the ominous signs of their own downfall:

> The night of the stock-market crash, we stayed at the Beau Rivage in St Raphaël in the room Ring Lardner had occupied another year. We got out as soon as we could because we had been there so many times before—it is sadder to find the past again and find it inadequate to the present than it is to have it elude you and remain forever a harmonious conception of memory.[4]

Ring Lardner, a dear friend of the Fitzgeralds, was a gifted sports journalist and short story writer, a notoriously heavy drinker with a self-destructive bent and a kind of cynical indifference to his own talent.[5] Sleeping in Lardner's room on the night of the crash seems to encapsulate all the tragedy of wasted talent and self-destructive behaviors, which robs the past of any rose-colored aura. David Brown writes:

> To what extent did Fitzgerald's alcoholism and its attendant confusions, anxieties and insecurities contribute to Zelda's declining health? Scott habitually deflected such accusations, elevating his wife's breakdown to a grand morality play on par with the collapse of the country's financial markets. Depression took on a dual meaning for Fitzgerald, whose *Ledger* entry above the calendar year September 1929–September 1930 read, "The Crash! Zelda + America."[6]

As America sank into depression, it was easy for Scott to draw a parallel with Zelda's psychological collapse, signs of which had been accumulating for years. Brown also notes that Scott "sens[ed] history in the making and [saw] himself on its front line."[7] Scott felt he was part of the new postwar generation who had been banking on their infinite potential and who were now drained. "I began to realize that for two years my life had been a drawing on resources that I did not possess, that I had been mortgaging myself physically and spiritually up to the hilt," we read in *The Crack-Up*, and a few pages further: "The question became one of finding why and where I had changed, where was the leak through which, unknown to myself, my enthusiasm and my vitality had been steadily and prematurely trickling away."[8]

The celebrated author of *The Great Gatsby*, whose fame enabled him in 1929 to be paid four thousand dollars for each short story published in the *Saturday Evening Post* and whose substantial earnings reached $25,732.96 in 1928 and $32,448.18 in 1929,[9] was spending recklessly, as he and Zelda were living on a grand scale.[10] Had it not been for the *Post* short stories, he would hardly have managed; his only other income was Scribner's advance against his next novel, a novel he was finding it increasingly difficult to write. Scott's drinking, always a problem, was now getting totally out of control: until now, he had always written sober, but he said he started mixing work and liquor in 1928 in Ellerslie.[11] Alcohol had turned from an extravagance supposedly meant to enhance life into a means to forget his own felt inadequacy. Along with having difficulty writing, Scott was becoming obnoxious and his social behavior was growing increasingly erratic—smashing a stranger's hat in a bar, insulting people, trying to get attention by any means possible—resulting in his being jailed twice in Paris in 1928. Of course, his marital relationship was also impaired, for which Zelda was later to reproach him:

> You made no advances toward me and complained that I was unresponsive. You were literally eternally drunk the whole summer. I got so I couldn't sleep and I had asthma again. . . . You didn't want me. Twice you left my bed saying 'I can't. Don't you understand'! I didn't.[12]

Scott's drinking probably contributed to Zelda's growing madness. Drinking had definitely become a manifestation of the death drive, condemning the couple to an inescapable downward spiral. As he noted in "Echoes of the Jazz Age" (1931), the Fitzgeralds were but mirrors of an entire generation:

> By this time contemporaries of mine had begun to disappear into the dark maw of violence. A classmate killed his wife and himself on Long Island, another tumbled "accidentally" from a skyscraper in Philadelphia, another purposefully from a skyscraper in New York. One was killed in a speakeasy in Chicago; another was beaten to death in a speakeasy in New York and crawled home to the Princeton club to die; still another had his skull crushed by a maniac's axe in an insane asylum where he was confined. These are not catastrophes that I went out of my way to look for—these were my friends; moreover these things happened not during the depression but during the boom.[13]

The couple's flamboyant performances, which had been accepted as part and parcel of their youth and fame in the mid-1920s when they were in Paris or on the Riviera—partying among the artistic and literary circles and being regular customers of such popular places as Brasserie Lipp, Prunier, the Dingo Bar, and many others—became increasingly rash and reckless, embarrassing their friends and the artists they met.

When they arrived in Paris in April 1928, hoping to recapture the inspiration and artistic excitement that had enabled Scott to write *The Great Gatsby*, the Fitzgeralds rented an apartment on rue de Vaugirard near the Luxembourg Gardens so that Scottie might play with the Murphys' children. But the glamour was gone: Scott and Zelda came to refer to this apartment as "Hôtel de la Morgue," and Zelda thought it would have been a fit setting for Mme Tussaud's wax figures. Although they went out a lot to escape from the dreariness of the apartment and met famous people such as Cole Porter, Fernand Léger, Thornton Wilder (the Murphys' friends) or King Vidor (the film director), Scott drank too much and often ended up going out alone at night, vainly looking for ghosts of the past, while Zelda was involved in her dancing practice. They could no longer attune themselves to Scottie's excitement at the Paris sights, and as summer came and the Murphys moved to the Riviera, taking in their wake a good many of their artist friends, Paris felt more and more deserted or, alternately, too full of plain Americans and foreigners. Shiploads of tourists landed, spoiling the enthusiasm of feeling part of a privileged elite. Yet in that summer 1928, thanks to two librarians, Adrienne Monnier (owner of La Maison des Amis des Livres) and Sylvia Beach (an American who owned the Shakespeare and Company bookshop), the Fitzgeralds met two new literary figures: the French writer André Chamson and James Joyce.

In both instances, Fitzgerald acted foolishly. Invited by the two women to a dinner with Joyce, an inebriated Scott sank down on one knee and kissed the great writer's hands, as if he were a bishop. Leaping on the parapet, he then poured out compliments on Nora Joyce's beauty and threatened to jump if she did not say she loved him. The rather shy James Joyce could not but be perplexed. Likewise, when he visited Chamson, who lived in a small sixth-floor apartment, Fitzgerald perilously climbed on the iron window railing, screaming out, "I am Voltaire! I am Rousseau!" On another occasion, as he was bringing champagne in an enormous ice bucket, he stopped halfway up the stairs and started to undress to prove he could swim in the bucket, and was only narrowly stopped from doing so by an embarrassed Chamson. Yet Chamson always kept good memories of Fitzgerald and his good-natured generosity, even when the latter, rather tactlessly, displayed to him, Gatsby-like, his drawers full of silk ties, monogrammed handkerchiefs, and golden lighters and urged him to choose one as a gift. Chamson, at the time a young writer of restricted fame, was very poor, but he was to refer to the incident humorously as "an early Marshall plan, liberal aid to under-developed friends."[14] He considered it on a par with Fitzgerald's recommending him to Maxwell Perkins and making it possible for his novel *Les Hommes de la route* to be translated and published in the United States, or with his introducing him to King Vidor to work on a film adaptation of the novel. Although the two men wrote in completely different styles (Chamson wrote about rural life in the Cévennes), they immediately took to each other, and Fitzgerald, however eccentric and awkward his behavior could be, showed his natural desire to promote his friends' work.

But not everybody had Chamson's equanimity, and with time friends got tired of Scott's lack of any restraint; his generosity could no longer make up for the nastiness and violence of some of his remarks. Scott's entry in the ledger for July 1928 reads: "Drinking and general unpleasantness" and in August he writes: "General aimlessness and boredom."[15] On his thirty-second birthday, he encapsulated the year in a few words whose truth was later to be confirmed: "Ominous. No real progress in any way and wrecked myself with dozens of people."[16] Indeed, when back on the Riviera in summer 1929, the Fitzgeralds were no longer welcome at parties and were left very much to themselves, Scott's alcoholism and Zelda's increasingly strange behavior barring them from guest lists. The charm of the Riviera had also worn off, as floods of American tourists were spoiling their paradise, and it seems everybody (in their set) was spending more time in bars than on the beach. Their second stay in Paris in fall 1929 was no more successful than the first. France could no longer be a place of inspiration and regeneration.

In their restless to-and-fros across the Atlantic, the Fitzgeralds were actually trying to escape from themselves. The last transatlantic crossing in 1929 gave Scott further material for a short story, "The Rough Crossing," in which a husband and wife each get involved in vain flirtations that jeopardize their illusory hope of recovering their lost intimacy and starting anew together in a little villa in Brittany.[17] The story somehow encapsulates the forever-rekindled and forever-disenchanted quest for youth, beauty, and happiness. Another short story, published in 1929, "The Swimmers," captures the mood of disenchantment felt by the Fitzgeralds as America, a young country, failed to live up to its promises and as the romantic aura and spirit of the avant-garde that used to surround France and Europe turned into dissipation and corruption.

The Fitzgeralds aboard a ship for Europe

"The Swimmers" indeed features Henry Marston, an American married to an unfaithful French woman, Choupette, and a young unnamed American girl who teaches him how to swim; the girl obviously stands for the freshness and regenerative power of young America as set against the decadence of Europe. Though eventually triumphant, the values of America are shown to be threatened with corruption both from the outside (Europe's dissipation) and from the inside, as money supersedes the ideals of the young nation. The contrast between Europe and America, clearly evinced in the story, is also one between age and youth. In their endless trips between America and Europe, the Fitzgeralds sought their irrecoverable youth and faced the tragedy of aging, be it at the national or personal level.

A Vain Attempt to Settle

The year 1928, which had started in Ellerslie, attested this tragedy. The family's settling in 1927 in a ducal 1842 Greek revival mansion alongside the Delaware River (after an aborted stay in Hollywood) indicated their desire to come of age gracefully. Scott was determined to complete his next novel, alternately called "The World's Fair," "The Boy Who Killed His Mother," or again "Our Type," two chapters of which he read to Edmund Wilson and Gilbert Seldes, trusted readers whose advice he requested in early 1928. In January, Scott and Zelda were invited to Quebec by the Canadian Transportation Agency, which hoped they would write a chronicle of their stay. They visited Montreal, made an abortive attempt at skiing, and spent most of their time in Château Frontenac, playing

Ellerslie, Edgemoor, Delaware

cards and sending fanciful postcards to Scottie. They were back at the end of January, and Scott was invited to deliver a speech on the art of writing at the Cottage Club in Princeton, the very club he had been evicted from in 1920. What could have been a form of rehabilitation turned into a fiasco as an awed and sober Scott was only able to mumble a few sentences, drinking his humiliation away in the party that followed.

Attempts to play the social game were soon shattered as weekend parties organized by the Fitzgeralds turned increasingly wild, being even more extravagant than the wasteful revelries and dissipation of the early 1920s in Great Neck: playing polo on the lawn with croquet mallets and plow horses, or shooting dinner plates for target practice. (In February 1928 the latter led to a life-threatening incident when Scott invited Thornton Wilder to the attic and, waving around a gun, accidentally fired, narrowly missing him.) Though meant to keep up or revive friendships, the parties became unpleasant even for their most reckless friends, who would receive letters of apology from their hosts in the days following a party. But these could not dispel the embarrassment felt, such as when, in February 1928, Scott asked the chauffeur to report on what the guests had said about him on the way to the train station, or when, back at Ellerslie in November after their stay in France, he made, in the presence of Ernest Hemingway, sexually offensive remarks to the attractive black maid who was serving dinner. Indeed, although they had left Ellerslie in April 1928 for Paris, nothing changed when they came back in September 1928, except for the presence of Philippe, the French chauffeur, who got sent to jail with Fitzgerald several times and had to be bailed out by John Biggs. Zelda disliked Philippe, and when the French nanny fell in love with him, Zelda took an aversion to her as well, avoiding her presence (and in consequence Scottie's company) and concentrating more and more on her dancing. The dream of domestic bliss, landed-gentry respectability, and an atmosphere conducive to work never existed but as a fantasy.

Cracks Within: The Amateur versus the Professional

Achieving success as artists was essential to both Scott and Zelda, but as each suffered from a lack of self-confidence, proving their own worth was carried out at the expense of the other. The atmosphere was one of aggressive competition. Hemingway thought he could observe a strange smile on Zelda's face whenever she saw Scott drink, knowing well how disabling that would be to his writing. When Zelda took to dancing at Ellerslie, attending Catherine Littlefield's ballet classes in Philadelphia three times a week, it was first as a reaction to Scott's flirting with Lois Moran, a young actress he met in Hollywood and probably a model for Rosemary Hoyt in *Tender Is the Night*; Lois was praised for her youth and dedication to work while Zelda was not working at anything professionally. Zelda began feverishly practicing at home, converting the living room into a dance studio with a ballet bar placed in front of a gigantic, heavily decorated gilt mirror that had once belonged to a brothel. Scott referred to it as "the Whorehouse Mirror."[18] Zelda was making a determined effort to become, at twenty-seven, a professional ballet dancer. She practiced all day, regardless of the friends that came for dinner or tea, playing Tchaikovsky's "March of the Wooden Soldiers" on a loop—an apt symbol for her military-like discipline and an index of her growing mania. Her obsessive behavior arguably encouraged Scott's drinking, all the more so as he could easily compare her dedication with his own dissipation that was preventing work on his novel.

He expressed his frustration in a short story, "Two Wrongs," in which a Broadway film producer's declining health, a result of alcoholism and tuberculosis, is offset by his wife's success in ballet. This hints at Scott's deep anxiety, even though he considered that, because of her age, Zelda was doomed to remain an amateur. In Zelda's autobiographical novel *Save Me the Waltz*, David Knight—the heroine's husband and Scott's alter ego—seems to voice Scott's opinion when he tells Alabama Beggs, his wife, "I hope you realize that the biggest difference in the world is between the amateur and the professional in the arts." She answers: "You might mean yourself and me."[19] But Zelda persevered, and when they moved to Paris in April 1928, Gerald Murphy introduced her to Madame Lubov Egorova, head of the ballet group for the Sergei Diaghilev troupe and former teacher of Catherine Littlefield. Under her demanding supervision, Zelda practiced eight hours a day and ate little, for she wanted to keep the lithe figure of a ballerina. Her asceticism again contrasted with Scott's overindulgence as he spent his nights in cafés while an exhausted Zelda preferred to stay home. Zelda wanted to prove, at all costs, her own worth and her capacity to exist as herself, not in Scott's shadow as the wife of a famous author. To Sara Mayfield, who urged her to believe in herself, Zelda answered, "I want to but Scott won't let me. He doesn't want me to believe in anything but him. I try to, but I can't—."[20] She once invited the Murphys, who were supportive of her, to come and see her practice at Madame Egorova's studio, but they felt very uncomfortable watching Zelda's exertions and almost grotesque intensity. In spite of her complete dedication to this art and the incredible progress she made considering she had started so late, she was offered the opportunity to dance not in the Diaghilev troupe but only for the Folies Bergères as an American shimmy girl. Her dream of dancing for Diaghilev was definitely buried with his death in 1929.

The dance lessons were expensive, and Fitzgerald had to pay the lease for Ellerslie; Zelda also wanted to reach some measure of financial independence and be able to pay for the lessons. To do so, she wrote two articles for *Harper's Bazaar,* which were published in 1928 under both their names, although Scott credited them to Zelda. Such apparent joint authorship was the only means for Zelda to be published and paid a decent amount of money. The same strategy was repeated late in 1928 and in 1929 when Zelda started working on a set of six short stories about different types of girls—southern belles, debutantes, and young married women—for *College Humor*. Although Scott only revised them, five of these stories appeared in *College Humor* as "written by F. Scott and Zelda Fitzgerald," while the sixth, "A Millionaire's Girl," published in the *Saturday Evening Post*, was credited solely to Scott. Harold Ober, their agent, feeling guilty about this, explained he had had to drop Zelda's name for fear that, jointly authored, the story should be considered as part of the *College Humor* girls series and get the *Post* into contractual trouble. Thus Zelda, in her very attempt at independence, was reminded that she could not but rely on her husband's fame.

Worse still, by choosing artistic expression not only through ballet dancing but also through writing, she was trespassing on Scott's artistic territory, using, as he would often reproach her, *his* material. In October 1929, he told Ober that in the *College Humor* series Zelda was drawing on their "common store of material" and that the originals of the types of girls she had described, "[he] had in [his] notebook to use."[21] Himself insecure, unhappy with his inability to produce the great novel he wanted to write, and feeling he was wasting his talent in writing short stories for the *Post*, Scott could not but resent Zelda's artistic ambitions; he was indeed very sensitive to anything concerning his work and considered his significant output of potboilers (in 1929 alone, he wrote no less than seven short stories, some of them highly praised by Ober) as whoring. He bitterly wrote to Hemingway in September 1929: "The *Post* now pays the old whore $4000 a screw."[22] In the destructive competition in their marriage, the other was but an evil mirror.[23] Scott admitted, "I found myself saying hateful things to her. I couldn't stop. I was at war with myself."[24]

For Scott, fighting with himself through others in a combination of self-deprecation and fierce competition was characteristic of those years, and the story of the relationship between Fitzgerald and Hemingway is a case in point. Their relationship, which started when Fitzgerald was the famous author giving advice to Hemingway and introducing him to Perkins at Scribner's, was now reversed; now Hemingway and Perkins discussed Fitzgerald's difficulties and his inability to produce the novel he had been promising ever since *Gatsby*'s publication. Hemingway's theory was that *Gatsby*'s succès d'estime paralyzed Fitzgerald, who kept procrastinating, daunted by the task of writing the great novel he wanted to author.[25] Perkins was despairing of Fitzgerald, who did not seem to have written a word of the novel since arriving in Paris in April 1928, and he wished he would come back to Ellerslie and settle down to work. Fitzgerald eventually sent Perkins two chapters of his projected novel in November 1928, promising the next two parts for December, but when he left again for Genoa in the spring of 1929, he hadn't sent anything and promised, once more, he would finish the novel on the ship, then that he would finish in Genoa, then in Paris—but it all came to naught. Fitzgerald was caught in a vicious circle: his inability to recover his creative inspiration made him increasingly despondent and hence unable to get seriously down to work.

Yet he remained active, writing short stories and promoting the works of other writers. Having received a copy of *A Farewell to Arms* from Scribner's, he wrote a detailed nine-page report, both laudatory and critical, which did not go down well with Hemingway. Even though Hemingway did take some of Fitzgerald's suggestions, he later derided the misguided advice of his once-friend and mentor.[26] Fitzgerald was well aware his words might offend Hemingway: "Our poor old friendship probably won't survive this, but there you are—better me than some nobody in the *Literary Review* that does not care about you + your future."[27] That year, 1929, marked a breaking point in their relationship. Pauline and Ernest Hemingway avoided the Fitzgeralds in Paris: although they rented an apartment in the same area, they did not want the Fitzgeralds to find out their address, fearing one of their uncalled-for and noisy visits at any time of day or night. At Fitzgerald's insistence, Hemingway did eventually agree to meet him in the spring of 1929.

The famous incident of the boxing match between Canadian author Morley Callaghan and Hemingway in the summer of 1929 is emblematic of the competitive and increasingly tense relationship between Hemingway and Fitzgerald. Invited to act as timekeeper, Fitzgerald, caught up in the fight, forgot to call time at the end of the round, causing Hemingway to go down. Fitzgerald was apologetic and Hemingway furious, accusing Scott of having done it on purpose. Callaghan in his book *That Summer in Paris* reports that the incident made him recognize the deep animosity between the two men, the violence remaining all the time latent, hidden behind a veil of politeness and courtesy:

> Yet now my two friends began to behave splendidly. . . . We were all suddenly polite, agreeable, friendly and talkative. I knew how Scott felt; he had told me. He felt bitter, insulted, disillusioned in the sense that he had been aware of an antagonism in Ernest. Only one thing could have saved him for Ernest. An apology. A restoration of respect, a lifting of the accusation. But Ernest had no intention of apologizing. He obviously saw no reason why he should. So we all behaved splendidly. We struck up graceful camaraderie. Ernest was jovial with Scott. We were all jovial. We went out and walked out to the Falstaff. And no one watching us sitting at the bar could have imagined that Scott's pride had been shattered.[28]

The incident assumed even more importance when a distorted account of it appeared in the *New York Herald Tribune* in November 1929, turning Hemingway into a bragging cock who had taken a beating. Infuriated, Hemingway summoned Fitzgerald to cable Callaghan asking him to correct the story. But Callaghan, who had already sent a correction to the *Herald Tribune* and was not responsible for the circulation of the story, was so furious with Fitzgerald's request that Hemingway later had to confess that it was he who had asked Scott to send the cable. The whole incident, fraught with misunderstandings, was damaging to the three writers' relationship.

Many of Fitzgerald's relationships became tense during this period, mostly because of Scott's bitter and nasty remarks to friends, or even to strangers. The Murphys, once close friends, became upset with Scott's increasingly unsociable behavior. Sara Murphy once remarked to Scott in an undated letter:

> Why—for instance should you trample on other people's feelings continually with things you permit yourself to say and do—owing partly to the self-indulgence of drinking too much and becoming someone else (uninvited) instead of the Scott we know and love and more—unless from the greatest egotism and sureness that you are righter than anyone else. I called it "manners" but it is more serious—it is that you are only thinking of yourself.[29]

The break with the Murphys came to a head in the summer of 1929 in Cannes, when Scott had resumed "serious" work on his novel. He decided to drop the matricide story to focus on a hero very much modeled on Gerald Murphy and himself. He thus became inquisitive, using the Murphys as objects of psychological and sociological observation, eliciting a hurt and angry reaction from Sara, who wrote to tell him how unpleasant it was to be constantly analyzed and criticized in such an unfriendly manner.

Shunned by old friends, the Fitzgeralds, as of 1928, started seeing other people, and were introduced to Parisian lesbian circles that gathered many artists and fostered feminine creation.[30] They attended Natalie Barney's literary salon and were once invited to the studio of painter Romaine Brooks. André Le Vot described Brooks's studio as "a hotspot of inversion, a gallery of sacred monsters from Sodom and Gomorrah."[31] The portraits represented some notorious gay men, such as Jean Cocteau or Reynaldo Hahn, but most were of famous lesbian women dressed as men: Radclyffe Hall, Renée Vivien, Natalie Barney—the Amazon—portrayed with a whip in her hand. Spending time in circles with shifting gender identities paralleled the Fitzgeralds' complex relationship to sexuality, with its lethal cocktail of frustration, jealousy, and homoerotic desires. Zelda indeed complained about Scott's lack of sexual interest in her and about his physical inadequacy, and, resenting the closeness between Scott and Hemingway, accused them of having a homosexual relationship. On her side, she felt attracted to Egorova, admiring her and buying her expensive flowers every day, much to Scott's discontent. She confessed later to her psychiatrists that she had fallen in love with Egorova. But weren't Scott and Zelda, also, each in love with idealized projections of their professionally successful selves? As writer or ballerina?

Stepping Back and Aside: The Basil and Josephine Stories

Competition, frustration, narcissistic infatuations—they provided the atmospheric background to the writing of the Basil and Josephine series of short stories, started by Scott in January 1928. Although he found it impossible to make progress on his novel, he was prolific in writing what he considered potboilers for the *Post*, and no fewer than thirteen Basil and Josephine stories were published between April 1928 and August 1931.[32] The first series was about Basil Lee, Scott's alter ego as a young boy in prep school and Princeton, and the second about Josephine Perry, Basil's feminine counterpart, modeled on Scott's first love, the socialite Ginevra King. He later adamantly resisted Ober's and Perkins's entreaties that he publish these stories as a book, arguing that they would damage his reputation as a serious writer and forever turn him in the public eye into a writer of lighter fiction, a second-rate writer. But however uneven their quality, the writing of those short stories—at a time when his life, his marriage, his ambition seemed to be falling apart—indicates that Fitzgerald needed to return to his youth. This was no nostalgic move back to an idyllic past but, rather, an attempt to go back to the root and understand where things had gone wrong.

The stories, with their irony toward a younger self, are evidence of Fitzgerald's famous double vision. Basil appears as a young man swinging back and forth between success and humiliation, a failed hero who eventually learns from his mistakes and understands that the girl is not the ultimate prize, that what matters is creation. At the end of "He Thinks He's Wonderful," Basil reflects:

> Time after time, the same vitality that had led his spirit to a
> scourging made him able to shake off the blood like water, not to
> forget, but to carry his wounds with him to new disasters and new
> atonements—toward his unknown destiny.[33]

Was that how Fitzgerald found the strength to believe in his own worth despite present setbacks? In the later Josephine stories, Basil's feminine alter ego is granted neither such self-awareness nor the possibility of a bright future. Unlike Basil, Josephine starts with the gifts of wealth and beauty, but these are bound to go, and she makes the most of what she has in the time of adolescence, collecting flirtations, until she proves unable to form true relationships and give love anymore. "One cannot both spend and have," Fitzgerald writes in the last story of the cycle, "Emotional Bankruptcy."[34] Experiencing parallel yet reverse destinies, Basil and Josephine never meet but, taken together, the stories, with their pattern of rise and fall, give a sense of tragicomedy. Josephine is modeled on Ginevra King, yet the reverse fall-and-rise pattern somehow foreshadows the destinies of Dick and Nicole Diver in *Tender Is the Night,* with this time Dick faring better than Nicole. Even though, according to many of their friends, a self-absorbed Scott seemed to ignore the signs of Zelda's mental deterioration, he must have known their fates were irrevocably intermingled.

La Despedida

"Once we were one person and always it will be a little that way," Scott was later to write to Zelda.[35] In *Under the Volcano,* Malcolm Lowry has Yvonne, the wife of the British consul Geoffrey Firmin, reflect on a picture, *La Despedida,* representing a rock split by forest fires:

La Despedida, she thought. The Parting! After the damp and detritus had done their work both severed halves of that blasted rock would crumble to earth. It was inevitable, so it said on the picture. . . . Was it really? . . . But granted it had been split, was there no way before total disintegration should set in of at least saving the severed halves? There was no way. The violence of fire which split the rock apart had also incited the destruction of each separate rock, canceling the power that might have held them as unities. Oh but why—by some fanciful geologic thaumaturgy, couldn't the pieces be welded together again! She longed to heal the cleft rock. She was one of the rocks and she yearned to save the other, that both might be saved. . . . The other rock stood unmoved, "That's all very well," it said, "but it happens to be your fault, and as for myself, I propose to disintegrate as I please!"[36]

In the case of Scott and Zelda, it seems both halves at once longed to heal the other and "propose[d] to disintegrate as [they pleased]," both burning with an inward fire they could not control. The incident that happened in Ellerslie in February 1928 while Zelda's sister Rosalind and her husband, Newman Smith, were visiting appears symbolically meaningful. On coming back home late at night, very drunk, from the Cottage Club in Princeton, Scott began to argue with Zelda and hurled her favorite blue vase into the fireplace; she called his father an Irish cop and he slapped her, making her nose bleed. Newman tried to step in and Rosalind told her sister she had to ask for a divorce. But Zelda adamantly refused and quarreled with her sister, saying the Sayre family had no right to interfere in her relationship with Scott. The destruction of a beautiful domestic object chosen by Zelda, its being hurled into the hearth/heart of the home, seems to stand for the definite cracking of their relationship.

When Zelda, in September 1929, was eventually invited to be part of the San Carlo Opera Ballet Company in Naples and to dance a solo in the opera *Aida,* she did not go. According to Elizabeth Waites:

> Zelda declined the opportunity for reasons never clear. Given subsequent developments, both her refusal of the Naples offer and the psychotic break that followed seem to have been related to her inability to separate from Scott, no matter how chaotic their lives became.[37]

We may also imagine that Scott would not let her go, the two being irredeemably bound to each other, both impelled by a death drive. This was made obvious when Zelda, in September 1929, driving on the Grande Corniche, deliberately veered toward a cliff, what would have been a fatal accident only averted by Scott's last-minute intervention; conversely, on another occasion, when Zelda lay down in front of the car and challenged Scott to drive over her, he was only narrowly stopped from doing so. But their personal tragedy was indivisible from their aesthetic lives; even though Zelda's breakdown deeply affected Scott and his writing ability, she was yet indisputably an inspiration. As he eventually wrote to her: "We ruined ourselves—I never thought that we ruined each other."[38] Though the rock of Zelda and Scott's life had already started cracking, after the split of 1928–29 the two disintegrating halves were soon to be set apart physically, though remaining kindred and doomed spirits, each radiating creative light.

NOTES

1. F. Scott Fitzgerald, "A Short Autobiography," ed. James L. W. West III (New York: Charles Scribner's Sons, 2001), 97.

2. Quoted in Kendall Taylor, *Sometimes Madness Is Wisdom: Zelda and Scott Fitzgerald; A Marriage* (London: Robson Books, 2002), 201.

3. "Emotional Bankruptcy" is the title of the last of the Josephine Perry stories.

4. F. Scott Fitzgerald and Zelda Fitzgerald, "Show Mr. and Mrs. F. to Number —," in *The Crack-Up*, ed. Edmund Wilson (New York: New Directions, 2009), 50.

5. Lardner is said to have been the inspiration for the character of Abe North in *Tender Is the Night*.

6. David S. Brown, *Paradise Lost: A Life of F. Scott Fitzgerald* (Cambridge, Mass.: Harvard University Press, 2017), 209.

7. Brown, *Paradise Lost,* 209.

8. Fitzgerald, *The Crack-Up*, 72, 80.

9. Andrew Hook, *F. Scott Fitzgerald: A Literary Life* (New York: Palgrave Macmillan, 2002), 93, 97.

10. By comparison, as Andrew Hook notes, "An index of just how vast a sum this was is given by the statistic that the average annual income of an American college teacher in 1929 was $3,056." Hook, *Fitzgerald*, 97.

11. Andrew Turnbull, *Scott Fitzgerald* (New York: Charles Scribner's Sons, 1962), 186.

12. Jackson R. Bryer and Cathy W. Barks, eds., *Dear Scott, Dearest Zelda: The Love Letters of F. Scott and Zelda Fitzgerald,* with an introduction by Eleanor Lanahan (London: Bloomsbury, 2002), 71.

13. F. Scott Fitzgerald, "Echoes of the Jazz Age," in *The Crack-Up,* 20.

14. Quoted in André Le Vot, *Scott Fitzgerald: Biographie* (Paris: Julliard, 1979), 292.

15. F. Scott Fitzgerald, "F. Scott Fitzgerald's Ledger, 1919–1938," 182, Matthew J. and Arlyn Bruccoli Collection of F. Scott Fitzgerald, Digital Collections, University of South Carolina University Libraries, https://digital.tcl.sc.edu/digital/collection/fitz/id/69/rec/1.

16. Fitzgerald, "Ledger," 183.

17. "The Rough Crossing" actually seems to telescope several transatlantic crossings: the 1924 crossing to Cherbourg and Zelda's flirting with Bunny Burgess (Sarah Churchwell, *Careless People: Murder, Mayhem, and the Invention of the Great Gatsby* [London: Virago Press, 2013], 298), the 1928 crossing back to the States (Mary Jo Tate, *F. Scott Fitzgerald A to Z: The Essential Reference to His Life and Work* [New York: Checkmark Books, 1998]), and the 1929 crossing to Genoa (Malcolm Cowley, introduction to *The Stories of F. Scott Fitzgerald: A Selection of 28 Stories* [New York: Charles Scribner's Sons, 1951], 175).

18. Nancy Milford, *Zelda: A Biography* (New York: Harper and Row, 1970), 143.

19. Zelda Fitzgerald, *Save Me the Waltz* (London: Vintage, 2001), 152–53.

20. Sara Mayfield, *Exiles from Paradise: Zelda and Scott Fitzgerald* (New York: Delacorte Press, 1971), 127.

21. Quoted in Hook, *Fitzgerald*, 94.

22. Quoted in Hook, *Fitzgerald*, 94.

23. One cannot but note the echoes between the reproaches Scott made to Zelda and his own self-doubts: Zelda's "whoring mirror" and Scott's remark to Hemingway; his taunting Zelda with amateurism and his comment to John Biggs that he felt he could never be a first-rate writer, only "the top of the second class." Quoted in Turnbull, *Fitzgerald*, 187.

24. Quoted in Taylor, *Madness Is Wisdom*, 218.

25. Although *The Great Gatsby* was highly praised by the intelligentsia, the sales were poor and the critical reception mixed.

26. Notably, Hemingway suppressed the long passage on Frederic Henry's dreaming and took into account Fitzgerald's idea for the ending of the novel. Scott Donaldson, *Hemingway vs. Fitzgerald: The Rise and Fall of a Literary Friendship* (London: John Murray, 2000), 128.

27. F. Scott Fitzgerald, *A Life in Letters*, ed. Matthew J. Bruccoli (New York: Charles Scribner's Sons, 1994), 165, letter dated June 1929.

28. Morley Callaghan, *That Summer in Paris* (London: C. Nicholls, 1953), 134–35.

29. Quoted in Taylor, *Madness Is Wisdom*, 206. The letter was probably written in 1934 after a call paid by Scott to the Murphys, then in New York, as he was visiting Zelda in a sanatorium in upstate New York.

30. In a letter to Hemingway, dated August 23, 1929, Scott wrote, "It's been gay here but we are, thank God, desperately unpopular and not invited anywhere." Quoted in Turnbull, *Fitzgerald*, 305.

31. Le Vot, *Fitzgerald*, 297.

32. In addition to the thirteen Basil and Josephine stories, in those same years Fitzgerald also wrote many other stories, an incredible feat considering the crisis he was going through during this period.

33. F. Scott Fitzgerald, "He Thinks He's Wonderful," in *The Basil, Josephine, and Gwen Stories*, ed. James L. W. West III, Cambridge Edition of the Works of F. Scott Fitzgerald (Cambridge: Cambridge University Press, 2022), 98.

34. F. Scott Fitzgerald, "Emotional Bankruptcy," in *Basil, Josephine, and Gwen Stories*, 286.

35. Fitzgerald, *Life in Letters*, 355.

36. Malcolm Lowry, *Under the Volcano* (London: Penguin, 2000), 59–60. Although they never met, we may consider Fitzgerald and Lowry soulmates, and not only on account of their addictions. Lowry was very impressed with *Tender Is the Night*, and two years after the publication of *Under the Volcano* he started to work on a movie script of Fitzgerald's novel.

37. Waites, "The Princess in the Tower: Zelda Fitzgerald's Creative Impasse," quoted in Linda Wagner-Martin, *Zelda Sayre Fitzgerald: An American Woman's Life* (New York: Palgrave Macmillan, 2004), 125.

38. Quoted in Turnbull, *Fitzgerald*, 173.

1930–1931

Kirk Curnutt

A writer embodying the profligate Roaring Twenties could only view the stock market collapse that ignited the Great Depression as a symbol of his own fleeting fortunes. As Matthew J. Bruccoli notes, the tumultuous five days between Black Thursday and Black Tuesday (October 24–29, 1929) when the Dow Jones Industrial Average dropped 25 percent, losing investors $30 billion, did not initially affect F. Scott Fitzgerald; like 85 percent of Americans, he "owned no securities and had never played the market."[1] Yet twelve months later he summarized his thirty-third year in four stark words: "The Crash! Zelda + America."[2] The parallels were almost too perfect. In the same way that four thousand American banks collapsed in 1930–31, unemployment rose to 16 percent, and wages deflated by 40 percent, seemingly insurmountable reversals besieged the Fitzgeralds.[3] Most notably, Zelda suffered a breakdown in April 1930 that hospitalized her for sixteen months, irrevocably altering their relationship. Paying for treatment at a leading Swiss sanitarium forced Fitzgerald into a frenzy of short-story writing that in 1931 earned him, paradoxically, peak earnings of $37,600 ($635,000 in today's dollars)—an astronomical amount when the per capita American income was $526. Yet after Zelda was released in September 1931, the couple returned to the United States to live austerely, grimly sensing that neither they nor the economy had yet hit rock bottom.

Within the fifteen *Saturday Evening Post* stories published in these two years, the crash demands accounting for Jazz Age excesses, sometimes literally, other times figuratively. August 1930's "The Bridal Party" dramatizes the market volatility of the Depression's earliest months. Inspired by the lavish May 1930 wedding of Virginia Megear and Thomas Powell Fowler, the brother of Fitzgerald's Princeton classmate Ludlow Fowler (the inspiration for 1926's "The Rich Boy"), the story pits nemesis Hamilton Rutherford, who loses his liquidity to the plummeting oil market, against a cash-poor hero, Michael Curly, who unexpectedly inherits a fortune. Curly hopes Caroline Dandy will abandon Rutherford for him, yet she insists, broke or not, her fiancé is her true soulmate. Her commitment to Rutherford is rewarded when he suddenly receives a fifty-thousand-a-year job offer. Although Curly's and Rutherford's convenient windfalls defy credulity, Fitzgerald captures Wall Street anxieties about economic stability. As Curly realizes, the rich live "at a different pace now," stripped of their insulating entitlement and "nervous as a ticker-tape."[4]

Several of these stories attempt to soothe bourgeois nerves by depicting market fluctuations—the Dow Jones did not bottom out until July 1932—as refortifying core American values. In "A Change of Class" (September 1931), barber Earl Johnson scores a six-figure fortune during the boom through a stock tip from a customer, Philip Jadwin. Earl acquires a house, a car, and a spendthrift wife, then loses all but two thousand dollars. Chastened, he realizes that stock speculation "was something I oughtn't to have meddled with."[5] Unbeknownst to him, Jadwin plays a charitable role in enabling Earl to purchase his own shop after his wife and her lover steal his last cash. The patronage rewards the barber for having the wisdom to save even a fraction of his ephemeral wealth, a fantasy of a cross-class safety net that insists the rich actually care about the working class. The story insists that readers, too, should admire Earl's work ethic, which the bull market corrupted. Fitzgerald concludes that "the Marxian" would say Earl has "the soul of a slave," but he dismisses proletarian calls for class revolution (an anathema to the conservative *Post*). Rather, the "sort of a soul that Earl has" cherishes humility, "and he's pretty happy with it. I like Earl."[6]

"A Change of Class" offers a patently roseate view of the Depression. Fitzgerald interrogated the moral consequences of the crash with far greater nuance in the story that posthumously proved his most famous, "Babylon Revisited" (February 1931). After a breakdown, stockbroker Charlie Wales must confront the moral dissipation that inadvertently led to the death of his wife, Helen. Visiting former haunts in expatriate Paris, Charlie blames the overvaluation of the market for the drunken profligacy that in a jealous fit led him to lock Helen out of their apartment on a snowy night, causing her to catch a fatal case of pneumonia. "The snow of twenty-nine wasn't real snow," he confesses, describing the irrational exuberance afforded by the inflated exchange rate. "If you didn't want it to be snow you just paid some money." After Charlie inadvertently ruins his chance to reclaim his daughter, Honoria, from his bitter in-laws, he confesses to "selling short" the value of family. "I heard you lost a lot in the crash," a Ritz Hotel bartender greets him. "I did," admits Charlie, "but I lost everything I wanted in the boom."[7]

Financial metaphors abound even in works set before the crash. Five 1930–31 stories make up a companion series to the eight coming-of-age tales about Basil Duke Lee that Fitzgerald produced in 1928–29. Set in Chicago of the 1910s, "First Blood," "A Nice Quiet Place," "A Woman with a Past," and "A Snobbish Story" feature debutante Josephine Perry, "an unconscious pioneer in the generation that was destined to get 'out of hand,'" based on the writer's adolescent flame, Ginevra King.[8] Josephine's initiation experiences involve the same popularity contests and courtship rituals as the frothy flapper tales Fitzgerald had patented a decade earlier, only now depicted somberly instead of farcically. The culminating story, "Emotional Bankruptcy," forces Josephine to acknowledge in the language of fiscal responsibility that her coquetry has squandered her capacity for authentic feeling: "One cannot both spend and have," she recognizes after a beau dumps her. "The love of her life had come by, and looking in her empty basket, she had found not a flower left for him—not one."[9] Just as Charlie Wales has wasted his moral capital, Josephine has "sold short" her passions.

Although these stories testify to Fitzgerald's undiminished craftsmanship, the Depression transformed perceptions of his relevance. Walter Winchell still reported on his long-gestating work in progress, insisting in August 1930 that "Scribner's probably will kiss us for informing them that the novel on which F. Scott Fitzgerald has been sweating for three years will be delivered within three months"—a premature prediction, as events proved.[10] Yet that same month the *Davenport (Iowa) Daily Times* wondered, "Whatever has become of F. Scott Fitzgerald[?] . . . One wonders what sort of going *[This Side of Paradise]* would be now. And would it be like some beautiful gown that is outmoded—lovely in material, perfect in workmanship, but having a sad, dejected appearance? . . . Yesterday's generation is like yesterday's champagne."[11] The syndicated columnist Charles B. Driscoll was even blunter: "He is not yet in the prime of life, and he is forgotten."[12]

Fitzgerald was far from forgotten, of course. His short stories received prestigious accolades, with Edward J. O'Brien selecting "Babylon Revisited" for his *Best Short Stories* anthology. Yet alongside such up-and-comers as William Faulkner, Kay Boyle, and Erskine Caldwell, he and Dorothy Parker, the only other contributor eking out as long a career as his, couldn't help but seem to be representatives of an era suddenly as remote as the Belle Epoque. Cementing this perception was Frederick Lewis Allen's best-selling *Only Yesterday: An Informal History of the 1920s* (1931). Repeatedly citing *This Side of Paradise* with nary a mention of *The Great Gatsby,* Allen treated Fitzgerald as a fad as disposable as mah-jongg, flagpole sitting, and, inevitably, the petting parties *Paradise* scandalously dramatized. As the glib chronicler of "the Problem of the Younger Generation," Fitzgerald made disillusionment fashionable but offered few ethical solutions: "Uncomfortable as it was to be harassed by prohibition agents and dictated to by chambers of commerce, it was hardly less comfortable in the long run to have [his] freedom and not know what to do with it," Allen decided.[13]

Unfortunately, Fitzgerald abetted the perception that he was unfashionable—although, ironically, he did so in a genre in which he produced his most mature writing of the 1930s. Before the crash, his nonfiction had consisted of lightweight generational commentary (1924's "Wait Till You Have Children of Your Own!")[14] or satires of the boom's money madness (1924's "How to Live on $36,000 a Year" and "How to Live on Practically Nothing a Year"). In "Echoes of the Jazz Age," however, he melded historical reflection and confessional autobiography to establish a genre of alternately intimate and evasive soul baring that culminated with 1936's controversial "Crack-Up" essays. "It was an age of miracles, it was an age of art, it was an age of excess, and it was an age of satire," begins "Echoes" before concluding, "Now once more the belt is tight and we summon the proper expression of horror as we look back at our wasted youth. . . . [Yet] we will never feel quite so intensely about our surroundings any more."[15] The essay raked over the same coals as *Only Yesterday* but with a more pining nostalgia and a sharper epigrammatical precision that later historians found irresistibly quotable:

> Scarcely had the staider citizens of the republic caught their breaths when the wildest of all generations, the generation which had been adolescent during the confusion of the War, brusquely shouldered my contemporaries out of the way and danced into the limelight. . . . A whole race [was] going hedonistic, deciding on pleasure. . . .
>
> But it was not to be. Somebody had blundered and the most expensive orgy in history was over.[16]

Yet thanks to its postmortem lyricism, "Echoes of the Jazz Age" implied Fitzgerald could only look back, never forward. Columnists who bid the Roaring Twenties adieu without fanfare or regret chuckled that the "minnesinger of the Great Jazz–Gin Epoch" had become "the doctor . . . who signed the death certificate."[17] Even George Gershwin commented on "Echoes," declaring that, while the crash had killed the Jazz Age, jazz *music* was thriving: "I can best explain why I take issue with Mr. Fitzgerald's statement by citing from my own musical experience," Gershwin announced. "My feeling for the music I am writing today is essentially no different from what it was for the pieces I composed seven or more years ago."[18] With "Ain't We Got Fun" replaced by "Brother, Can You Spare a Dime?" artists had to assure audiences that popular culture wasn't a luxury item.

Given the tumult engulfing Fitzgerald in this period, it is remarkable that he was at all prolific. The year 1930 began with his fourth novel—already five years in the making—stalled after a spurt of reinvention the previous year. With the Lew and Nicole Kelly draft of *Tender Is the Night* fizzling out by New Year's Day, he attempted to resuscitate the four original chapters with Francis Melarky, tentatively titled "The Boy Who Killed His Mother," that he had intermittently toiled over since 1925. After Zelda's collapse in April, however, he would not return to the book for two years. "Because I don't mention my novel it isn't because it isn't finishing up or that I'm neglecting it," Fitzgerald fibbed to Maxwell Perkins on January 21. "[It's] only that I'm weary of setting dates for it till the moment when it is in the Post Office Box."[19]

Zelda had published three stories of her own by late spring: "The Girl the Prince Liked" (January), "The Girl with Talent" (April), and "A Millionaire's Girl" (May). When the first two appeared in *College Humor* under the byline "Scott and Zelda Fitzgerald" and the *Post* credited "A Millionaire's Girl" solely to Scott, she saw that his fame would always overshadow her work. Since 1928, ballet had given her a métier all her own. Beginning in fall 1929, Zelda practiced obsessively with former Ballets Russes ballerina Lubov Egorova in the Sergei Diaghilev discipline's Right Bank studio above the Olympia theater.

To relieve mounting tensions at the couple's 10 rue Pergolèse apartment, Scott booked a guided tour of Algeria. The itinerary took the Fitzgeralds from Bou Saâda to Algiers, but Zelda grew distressed missing her ballet training, and the strain etched into her features. As Nancy

Scott and Zelda tour North Africa, early 1930. The vacation was a desperate—
and unsuccessful—attempt to stabilize their marriage on the brink of Zelda's
breakdown.

Milford writes, "They took a series of snapshots which they carefully saved
in one of their scrapbooks. . . . Scott was tanned and his hair was thinner,
but Zelda looked ravaged in the harsh and telling light. It was characteristic of her to appear entirely different in each of her pictures, but in these
the effect was eerie; she is wraithlike, as if haunted. Her shoulders are
hunched, deep lines surround her eyes, her mouth is unsmiling always.
She looks furtive and distracted."[20] In the 1934 essay (written in collaboration with Scott) "Show Mr. and Mrs. F to Number —," Zelda con-

veys her perturbation through images of colonialism and Third World exoticism:

> The world crumbled to pieces in Biskra; the streets crept through the town like streams of hot white lava. Arabs sold nougat and cakes of poisonous pink under the flare of open gas jets. Since *The Garden of Allah* and *The Sheik* the town has been filled with frustrated women. In the steep cobbled alleys we flinched at the brightness of mutton carcasses swung from the butchers' booths.[21]

The excursion's one positive byproduct was Scott's "One Trip Abroad," which the *Post* published that October. Salvaging the Kellys from his second abandoned version of *Tender* (with Lew renamed Nelson), Fitzgerald melds expatriate dissolution and marital disharmony with a supernatural twist harkening back to his O. Henry–esque "The Cut-Glass Bowl" of 1920. As newlyweds Nelson and Nicole wander North Africa and Central Europe, they encounter another couple who appear to be their cheap obverses, with weak chins, wan complexions, and a certain flabby "unwholesomeness." A chance encounter in the Swiss mountains above Lake Geneva disabuses the Kellys of their superiority: "They're us! They're us! Don't you see?" cries Nicole as a lightning blast reveals the strangers are doppelgängers mirroring her and Nelson's exhausted vitality.[22] Even more than "Babylon Revisited," "One Trip Abroad" satirizes expatriate life as aimless and bigoted. "Every place is the same," a cynical American assures Nicole. "New scenery is fine for a half an hour, but after that you want your own kind to see."[23]

The story's raciest moment critiques cultural voyeurism. In Bou Saâda, the Kellys attend a performance by the Ouled Naïl, a Berber tribe long exoticized in Western eyes for their colorful costumes and sensual dancing.[24] Invited to watch native women writhe "in more or less—ah—Oriental style" (in the nude), Nelson enthusiastically agrees, but Nicole walks out when she discovers the performers are "two pale brown children of perhaps fourteen."[25] The incident is the first marital fracture that leads to adultery and domestic violence, with Nelson eventually blackening Nicole's eye. But while "One Trip Abroad" dissects domestic disenchantment as clinically as either *The Beautiful and Damned* or *Tender Is the Night,* it also holds out hope. Shortly before their climactic encounter with their doubles, Nicole insists the Kellys can revivify their bond: "It's just we don't understand what's the matter. . . . Why did we lose peace and love and health, one after the other? If we knew, if there was anyone to tell us, I believe we could try. I'd try so hard."[26] Ultimately, the story blames the duo's estrangement on both their wayward lifestyle *and* the inherently adversarial nature of marriage. Either way, reading Nicole's plea as anything but Scott and Zelda's autobiographical prayer to save their relationship is almost impossible. Although Fitzgerald declined to republish "One Trip Abroad" after recycling memorable phrases and images in *Tender Is the Night,* it remains second only to "Babylon Revisited" among his 1930–31 stories.

Far from relieving Zelda's stress, the North Africa vacation accelerated her erratic behavior. Accounts from the early 1930s struggle for euphemisms to characterize her actions. According to André Le Vot, in Paris she rushed back to her ballet lessons "like a junkie to her fix." To her husband, her "eccentric" demeanor exhibited "definite, though intermittent irrationalities." Arthur Mizener describes her as "frighteningly tensed up" and "overwrought." Andrew Turnbull says her obsessiveness bordered on "fury." Nancy Milford uses the adjective "peculiar" twice in three paragraphs, noting that her paranoia alarmed friends. To Sara Mayfield, she was "nervous" and, echoing Mizener, "overwrought." Linda Wagner-Martin pictures her as "distraught" and prone to "breathless, disordered" rambling. Kendall Taylor portrays her as "dazed" and "agitated over the smallest things."[27]

As Jeffrey Meyers writes, "Zelda's first breakdown was so sudden" that "the warning signs only became clear retrospectively."[28] In truth, "breakdown" is a misnomer; instead of a single collapse, there were escalating incidents that made ignoring her deterioration impossible. Mizener describes Zelda growing so despondent with an "old friend" when her cab was stuck in traffic—threatening to make her late for her lesson with Egorova—that she changed into her dancewear in the back seat and dashed off through traffic.[29] Turnbull first identified that friend as Oscar Kalman, whose wife, Xandra, had known Scott from childhood.[30] Milford adds two anecdotes to illustrate Zelda's decline. Drawing from a 1964 interview with Gerald Murphy, she depicts a "surprisingly quiet" Zelda suddenly demanding of Scott and John Peale Bishop, "Were you talking about me?" As Murphy reflected, "Can you imagine suspecting they were talking about her? I mean, she was sitting right there with them!"[31] In a second incident, Zelda threw herself at Egorova's feet during

When Scribner's previewed Fitzgerald's postmortem on the 1920s in "Echoes of the Jazz Age" in the months before the essay's November 1931 publication, columnists took issue with his melancholy tone, anticipating the negative response to his "Crack-Up" essays five years later. Here, syndicated columnist Hyman Sandow turned to George Gershwin to rebut Fitzgerald's insistence that the jazz vogue had passed.

an afternoon tea, declaring her love for her teacher, an event Egorova re-counted to Milford in 1968.[32] According to Taylor's biography, this epi-sode occurred the same night as the taxicab incident, although Taylor offers no corroboration for that timing.[33]

What facts remain are largely found in surviving documents. Turnbull was the first to translate the admission report for Zelda's late April entry into Paris's Malmaison Clinic, exactly "ten years and twenty days after her wedding," as Bruccoli notes in his 1981 biography of Scott Fitzgerald, *Some Sort of Epic Grandeur*. Bruccoli excerpts the case file at length:

> Mrs. FITZ-GERALD entered on 23 April 1930 in a state of acute anxiety, restlessness, continually repeating: "This is dreadful, this is horrible, what is going to become of me, I have to work, and I will no longer be able to, I must die, and yet I have to work. I will never be cured, let me leave. I have to go to see 'Madame' (dance teacher), she has given me the greatest joy that can exist, it is comparable to the light of the sun that falls on a block of crystal, to a symphony of perfume, the most perfect chord from the greatest composer in music."

As the report concluded, the "slightly tipsy" patient, "exhausted from work in an environment of professional dancers," was fixated on "some obsessive ideas," including "her fear of becoming a homosexual. She thinks she is in love with her dance teacher."[34] For two weeks doctors urged her to eat healthily and avoid liquor. The treatment did so little to soothe her agitation that she checked herself out of Malmaison on May 2.

The timing couldn't have been worse. The Fowler wedding festivities that inspired "The Bridal Party" were under way, with old friends luring Scott to all-night fetes. Objecting to the omnipresent alcohol, Zelda fer-vently resumed her ballet lessons. By late May, "she was dazed and inco-herent. She heard voices that terrified her, and her dreams, both waking and sleeping, were peopled with phantoms of indescribable horror. She had fainting fits and the menacing nature of her hallucinations drove her into an attempted suicide. Only an injection of morphine could comfort her."[35] Frantic, Scott accepted a referral to the Valmont Clinic in Glion, Switzerland. According to a report by a clinic doctor, H. A. Trutman, Zelda complained of being "brought under duress."[36] She suffered "no visible signs of mental illness"; her main stressor was "the husband's visits" that occasioned "violent arguments, provoked especially by the husband's attempts to reason with the patient."[37] Because Valmont was not a psychiatric clinic (it treated gastrointestinal disorders), Trutman consulted psychiatrist Oscar Forel, who recommended transferring Zelda to his newly opened clinic, Les Rives de Prangins, in nearby Nyon. On June 5, Scott convinced his wife to submit to Dr. Forel's care.

"Then Switzerland and another life," Zelda remembered cryptically in "Show Mr. and Mrs. F to Number —."[38] Forel's first step was to quarantine the ailing wife from her husband for three months. Commuting between Lake Geneva and Paris (where the Fitzgeralds' daughter, Scottie, remained), Scott cranked out a *Post* story on average every six weeks to finance the price tag at Prangins, which exceeded one thousand dollars a month (fifteen thousand dollars today). For the first time since their courtship, the couple's relationship became epistolary. Zelda sent Scott three dozen letters that are remarkable for alternating "between the deepest, most tender affection for him and absolute scorn—between relying on him exclusively for kindness and understanding and accusing him of abandoning her, even to the point of demanding a divorce."[39] Zelda's anger lay in her conviction that she deserved a professional identity of her own: "If I had work or something," she insisted in her first dispatch, "it would be so much decenter to try to help each other and make at least a stirrup cup out of this bloody mess."[40]

Yet Forel's second step in treatment, heartily endorsed by Fitzgerald, was to break her obsession with ballet. At his recommendation, Scott petitioned Egorova for an unvarnished opinion of his wife's talent, which she harshly supplied: Zelda was competent but undistinguished, in part because she hadn't begun training seriously until her midtwenties. A modest career as a company dancer was possible, but not eminence. Faced with Egorova's assessment, Zelda passively accepted the prescription that regaining her mental health meant relinquishing her ambition. Letting go sparked a painful flare-up of eczema that lasted deep into September. "Please," begs one anguished letter to Scott, "out of charity write to Dr. Forel to let me off this cure. . . . For a month and a week I've lived in my room under bandages, my head and neck on fire. I haven't slept in weeks. The last two days I've had bromides and morphine but it doesn't do any good."[41]

As Sharon Kim notes, Forel was a leading proponent of "combining Freudian theory with the clinical advances of scientific psychiatry," but the doctor soon doubted the value of psychotherapy because he considered Zelda's "mental anomalies . . . constitutional, making social adaptation impossible."[42] Convinced psychoanalysis would do more harm than good, he could only treat Zelda chemically, with endocrines, morphine, belladonna, and luminal, along with "purges of seidlitz water, wet packs and hydrotherapy."[43] Although he encouraged her to write about her childhood and marriage to deduce the emotional triggers of her trauma—art therapy was also encouraged at Prangins—his greatest success was hypnosis: during one fall session, he induced Zelda into a thirteen-hour sleep that, for a few short weeks at least, cleared her eczema.[44]

Other aspects of Forel's treatment are equally questionable. If Zelda rebelled against her therapy (early on she attempted to escape Prangins), she was confined in the Villa Eglantine, a secured building on the clinic grounds where unrulier patients were restrained in bed. Yet she was often cagier rather than defiant with the doctor. As Forel perceived, she intuited his expectations and parroted them back. He also noted that she played up her childlike qualities, as if performing the dependency on her husband, a dependency she resented.

Her evasiveness eventually led Forel to question his diagnosis of schizophrenia. In November, at Scott's request, he solicited a second opinion from Paul Eugen Bleuler, the psychiatrist who in 1912 first defined that condition. The consultation cost five hundred dollars, which Zelda found ludicrous, especially after Bleuler rather tautologically reconfirmed his colleague's assessment. The consensus today is that Zelda suffered from bipolar disorder, but schizophrenia was the diagnosis du jour, especially among psychiatrists of the so-called Zurich school to which both doctors belonged. Feeling trapped in their definitions, Zelda railed against Forel's "Teutonic sophistries" and addressed Bleuler as if he were a "giant imbecile," as Forel reported to Scott.[45] In the end, though, she was given little input into her treatment; her letters correspondingly resonate with images of imprisonment and suffocation. "The whole vicinity of my room," she wrote her sister, "is covered with grease and bandages and powder and antiseptic."[46]

Scott alternated among his own moods. To friends, he exaggerated Zelda's prospects for recovery. With his parents and in-laws, he disavowed blame. Specifically, he denied that his alcoholism exacerbated his wife's instability, even though her correspondence refers constantly to his excessive drinking and the marital disharmony it caused. When

Forel told him Zelda's health depended upon his sobriety, Scott's response was defiant:

> Give up strong drink permanently I will. Bind myself to forswear wine forever I cannot. My vision of the world at its brightest is such that life without the use of its amenities is impossible. I have lived hard and ruined the essential innocence in myself that could make it that possible, and the fact that I have abused liquor is something to be paid for with suffering and death perhaps but not with renunciation. For me it would be as illogical as permanently giving up sex because I caught a disease (which I hasten to assure you I never have).[47]

His behavior inspires little sympathy. His one surviving letter to Zelda at Prangins, probably unsent, is self-pitying rather than compassionate. He accuses his wife of "megalomaniacal selfishness" and indifference toward his literary reputation. "The nearest I ever came to leaving you," he wrote with wounded pride, "was when you told me you thot I was a fairy in the Rue Palatine," a reference to the taunts Zelda was prone to hurl at Scott's masculinity.[48] Proving his manhood grew paramount. Throughout Zelda's earliest months at Prangins he pressed Forel for permission to visit so the couple could resume sexual relations, even though his wife exhibited little erotic interest in him (or anyone). Forel was appalled.

Meanwhile, as Scott shuttled between hotels in Caux, Vevey, and Lausanne, Switzerland became a pivotal setting in his fiction. A passage in "One Trip Abroad" describes the Alpine country as a kind of limbo where picturesque tranquility masks a paralyzing stasis: "Switzerland is a place where very few things begin but many things end."[49]

The line presages his most quoted statement on the effect Zelda's hospitalization bore on his worldview, a beautifully cadenced admission that inverts the sublime, salubrious appeal of Swiss geography to convey the dreary asceticism of the country's "clinic culture," which insisted on cloistering and immobilizing patients within the spectacular landscapes: "I left my capacity for hoping on the little roads that led to Zelda's sanatorium," he wrote.[50] "One Trip Abroad" alludes to darker currents beneath this "background of mountains and waters of postcard blue," describing "waters that are a little sinister beneath the surface with all the misery that has dragged itself here from every corner of Europe."[51] A subsequent story, "The Hotel Child," dives even deeper into the undertow. Here an eighteen-year-old Jewish–American expatriate, Fifi Schwartz—innocent but not, like Henry James's Daisy Miller, naive—fends off advances from two European grifters sporting dubious aristocratic titles, Count Stanislas Borowki and Marquis Bopes Kinkallow. "This corner of Europe does not draw people," Fitzgerald writes of Switzerland. "Rather, it accepts them without too many inconvenient questions." Some travelers may come for the "private *cliniques* or for tuberculosis resorts," but those like the count and the marquis gather because they are "no longer *persona grata* in Italy or France."[52] "The Hotel Child" is Fitzgerald's most decadent *Post* story. The manuscript even included bold references to cocaine and hashish, which were predictably cut—in the hashish's case because it is fed in pill form to an addled Pekingese.

Fitzgerald based the owner of that dog, Lady Capps-Karr, on British socialite Bijou O'Connor, with whom he began an affair in autumn 1930. Decades later the colorful O'Connor claimed she accompanied Scott to visit Zelda and the other "loonies" at Prangins.[53] If true, Fitzgerald seems to have capitalized on his allure with other women to undermine his wife's self-confidence, just as he had with Lois Moran in 1927. Another lover, Margaret Egloff, inspired a more sympathetic character, Emily Elliot in May 1931's "Indecision." Fitzgerald met Egloff, a student of Carl Jung, in Gstaad, Switzerland, while on a Christmas skiing holiday; she influenced his understanding of the power dynamics of psychoanalysis, which *Tender Is the Night* would soon explore. As Scott Donaldson notes, "Indecision" suggests that despite his flagrant extramarital dalliances, Scott felt guilty for abandoning at least the platonic idea of his and Zelda's union. Here a Scott-styled hero, Tommy McLain, must choose between a flirtatious southern belle and a reliable but staid divorcée: "In the end Tommy asks Rosemary (the Zelda of 1918, not 1931) to marry him and as he does so the image of Emily 'faded from his mind forever.'"[54]

Although Fitzgerald wrote "Indecision" on the heels of "Babylon Revisited," it marks a major downturn in the quality of his short fiction. With the exception of "Emotional Bankruptcy," his 1931 stories are formulaic and forced. When the *Post* reluctantly accepted "Flight and Pursuit," Fitzgerald's agent Harold Ober warned that his submissions were not up to snuff: "[The editors] think it might be a good idea for you to write some American stories," Ober reported. "They feel the last stories have been lacking in plot." While "Flight and Pursuit," "Indecision," and other stories of the period (such as "A New Leaf," "Six of One—," and "On Your Own") might contain "very vivid bits of life," they "failed to make the reader care about any one of the characters."[55] Like "A Change of Class," some of these efforts treated the Depression too sanguinely: the *Post* even rejected July's "Six of One—" when its narrative of poor boys making good amid adverse circumstances strained plausibility. Although *Redbook* eventually printed "Six of One—," a half dozen leading periodicals passed on "On Your Own," which remained unpublished for forty-eight years.

The strain of paying Zelda's medicals bills only partly explains the eroding quality of Fitzgerald's work. His work routine was interrupted when his father died unexpectedly on January 26, 1931. Never a dutiful son, Scott nevertheless journeyed to Rockville for the funeral. He attempted to reflect on Edward Fitzgerald's failures but stopped in self-doubt: "I don't see how all this could possibly interest anyone but me," the posthumously published "The Death of My Father" reads.[56] At least he finished "On Your Own," which cites the failed traditions Edward embodied, culminating in an adieu later resuscitated, slightly tweaked, in *Tender Is the Night*: "Goodbye then, Father, all my fathers."[57] The story's heroine, Evelyn Lovejoy, suggests writing wasn't Fitzgerald's only consolation: she was based on Bertha Goldstein, the wife of a Brooklyn judge. Scott met her aboard ship while she traveled under the alias Bert Barr. The pair enjoyed their own brief affair that, like those with O'Connor and Egloff, reveals Scott's enduring need for female succor.

Perhaps not surprisingly, Scott's departure for America occasioned a sharp improvement in Zelda's condition. Throughout the winter she resumed writing, eventually publishing the Montgomery-set "Miss Ella" in *Scribner's Magazine*. At Forel's encouragement, old friends such as Gerald and Sara Murphy visited, and Zelda was permitted unsupervised day trips to Geneva and Lausanne. By July 1931, she could even accompany her family on a two-week vacation to Annecy, France: "[We] said at the end that we'd never go there again because those weeks had been perfect," she remembered, "and no other time would match them."[58] The Fitzgeralds would never again visit Annecy or Europe together, but for reasons far less romantic.

Finally, on September 15, 1931, Forel discharged Zelda from Prangins. The Fitzgeralds returned to the States to settle in Montgomery, renting a boxy house at 819 Felder Avenue that fifty years later became home to

Zelda posing, at the couple's rental home in Montgomery, Alabama, in the costume of the art form her husband and doctors had forced her to abandon. Since 1987 the house has been open to the public as the Scott and Zelda Fitzgerald Museum. In late 1931 Zelda appeared far healthier than she had just months earlier while in treatment at Prangins in Switzerland. Her demeanor was deceiving, however: a relapse was imminent.

the Scott and Zelda Fitzgerald Museum. In the sunroom Zelda donned a tutu and posed for a photography session atop her travel trunks. In one portrait she adjusts her ballet slipper; in another she smiles and holds the family cat. In both she appears healthy and full-bodied, a far cry from her haggard mien in North Africa and at Prangins. No sooner were Scott and Zelda unpacked than the hometown newspaper, the *Montgomery Advertiser,* requested an interview, euphemistically noting that the duo had spent the previous two years abroad "gathering color for their writing."[59] When another *Advertiser* contributor knocked at her door, Mont-

gomery's most famous daughter admitted she still hungered for recognition in a métier of her own: "I'm no celebrity," she told Frances Pitts. "I
wish I were."[60]

Zelda's family worried about her stability when her seventy-three-
year-old father, Alabama State Supreme Court justice Anthony Sayre,
died on November 17, 1931. Yet she weathered the funeral with moder-
ate though concerning bouts of eczema and asthma. The judge's burial
in Oakwood Cemetery—the setting of Scott's early short story "The Ice
Palace" (1920)—inspired a moving scene in her novel, *Save Me the Waltz*,
in which heroine Alabama Beggs realizes her father encouraged her ex-
troversion despite his stern, disapproving exterior: "Once he had said,
'If you want to choose, you must be a goddess.' That was when she had
wanted her own way about things. It wasn't easy to be a goddess away
from Olympus."[61]

Scott did not attend the funeral. A week before the judge died, Metro-
Goldwyn-Mayer (MGM) had unexpectedly offered him six thousand dollars for five weeks of screenwriting work on a Jean Harlow movie called
Red-Headed Woman. This was his second attempt at a side career in
Hollywood; it proved no more successful than the two-month foray in
1927 when he met Lois Moran. This time, after Fitzgerald flaunted his
contempt for films and insulted his assigned collaborator, his script was
junked for one by Anita Loos (author of the 1925 novel *Gentlemen Prefer
Blondes*). The two trips proved important for his future fiction, however.
In his first trip to Hollywood Fitzgerald had met studio wunderkind
Irving Thalberg, whose managerial approach to film production both
fascinated and antagonized the writer; the fascination continued during
his second foray into Hollywood. Invited to a party at the home Thalberg
shared with wife Norma Shearer, an intoxicated Fitzgerald performed
an embarrassing comedic skit, an incident he transcribed into "Crazy
Sunday" (1932), the best of his Hollywood stories. After Thalberg died
prematurely in 1936, his mystique steepened for Fitzgerald, eventually in-
spiring the magnetic producer Monroe Stahr in his final, uncompleted
novel, *The Love of the Last Tycoon*.[62]

Scott and Zelda had reunited in Montgomery by the holiday season.
They briefly enjoyed a moment's optimism, even as the Depression showed
no signs of bottoming out. On the last day of the year the *Advertiser* reported that in Washington, D.C., demonstrators had descended on Congress "to make it damn uncomfortable for those who won't feed the

unemployed." Herbert Hoover loyalist William Green, head of the American Federation of Labor, lambasted the protesters as shovel-leaners. Spending federal funds to help the jobless and homeless, he said, would put the United States on the "dole" and sap the American entrepreneurial spirit needed to save the economy.[63]

With his MGM paycheck, Fitzgerald faced no such money worries. For the first time in two years, his earnings topped his expenses, and his savings could finance work on *Gatsby*'s long-delayed follow-up, for which 1932 was do-or-die time. Zelda, too, was preparing to tell her story in novel form. The atmosphere at Felder Avenue was comfortable, though far from indulgent.

Alas, the peace would not hold. Not even one full month into 1932 Zelda relapsed, and the Fitzgeralds' world crashed anew.

NOTES

1. Matthew J. Bruccoli, *Some Sort of Epic Grandeur: The Life of F. Scott Fitzgerald*, 1st rev. ed. (New York: Carroll and Graf, 1991), 339.

2. F. Scott Fitzgerald, "F Scott Fitzgerald's Ledger, 1919–1938," Matthew J. and Arlyn Bruccoli Collection of F. Scott Fitzgerald, Digital Collection Department, University of South Carolina, 184. https://digital.library.sc.edu/collections/f-scott -fitzgeralds-ledger-1919-1938/.

3. The unemployment rate peaked in 1933 at 25 percent.

4. F. Scott Fitzgerald, "The Rich Boy," in *Taps at Reveille*, ed. James L. W. West III, Cambridge Edition of the Works of F. Scott Fitzgerald (Cambridge: Cambridge University Press, 2014), 262.

5. F. Scott Fitzgerald, "A Change of Class," in *A Change of Class*, ed. James L. W. West III, Cambridge Edition of the Works of F. Scott Fitzgerald (Cambridge: Cambridge University Press, 2016), 19.

6. Fitzgerald, "Change of Class," 34.

7. F. Scott Fitzgerald, "Babylon Revisited," in *Taps at Reveille*, 177.

8. F. Scott Fitzgerald, "First Blood," in *The Basil, Josephine, and Gwen Stories*, ed. James L. W. West III, Cambridge Edition of the Works of F. Scott Fitzgerald (Cambridge: Cambridge University Press, 2009), 188.

9. F. Scott Fitzgerald, "Emotional Bankruptcy," in *Basil, Josephine, and Gwen Stories*, 286.

10. Walter Winchell, "On Broadway," *Wisconsin State Journal*, August 30, 1930, 3.

11. Addie May Swan, Book Reviews, *Davenport (Iowa) Daily Times*, August 30, 1930, 3.

12. Charles B. Driscoll, "The World and All," *Lansing (Mich.) State Journal*, February 14, 1931, 6.

13. Allen Frederick Lewis, *Only Yesterday: An Informal History of the 1920s* (New York: Harper and Brothers, 1931), 239–40.

14. F. Scott Fitzgerald, "Wait Till You Have Children of Your Own," in *My Lost City: Personal Essays, 1920–1940,* ed. James L. W. West III, Cambridge Edition of the Works of F. Scott Fitzgerald (Cambridge: Cambridge University Press, 2005), 66–76.

15. F. Scott Fitzgerald, "Echoes of the Jazz Age," in *My Lost City,* 131, 138.

16. Fitzgerald, "Echoes of the Jazz Age," 132, 137.

17. Jerome Coignard, "Of the Making of Books—,"*Brooklyn Daily Eagle,* November 1, 1931, 64.

18. Quoted in Hyman Sandow, "Latest Argument about the Jazz Age," *Montana Standard,* August 30, 1931, 56.

19. F. Scott Fitzgerald, *F. Scott Fitzgerald: A Life in Letters,* ed. Matthew J. Bruccoli (New York: Charles Scribner's Sons, 1994), 173.

20. Nancy Milford, *Zelda: A Biography* (New York: Harper and Row, 1970), 157.

21. F. Scott Fitzgerald and Zelda Fitzgerald, "Show Mr. and Mrs. F. to Number —," in *The Collected Writings of Zelda Fitzgerald,* ed. Matthew J. Bruccoli (New York: Charles Scribner's Sons, 1991), 428.

22. Fitzgerald, "One Trip Abroad," in *Taps at Reveille,* 285, 287.

23. Fitzgerald, "One Trip Abroad," 266.

24. For an overview of how the Ouled Naïl were depicted in Western art from the late nineteenth century up to the postcolonial era, see Roger Benjamin, *Orientalist Aesthetics: Art, Colonialism, and French North Africa, 1880–1930* (Berkeley: University of California Press, 2003), 160–70.

25. Fitzgerald, "One Trip Abroad," 267–68.

26. Fitzgerald, "One Trip Abroad," 286.

27. André Le Vot, *F. Scott Fitzgerald: A Biography,* trans. William Byron (New York: Warner Books, 1984), 249; Fitzgerald to Dr. Mildred Squires, April 4, 1932, Princeton University Library, quoted in Linda Wagner-Martin, *Zelda Sayre Fitzgerald: An American Woman's Life* (New York: Palgrave Macmillan, 2004), 126–27; Arthur Mizener, *The Far Side of Paradise: A Biography of F. Scott Fitzgerald* (Boston: Houghton Mifflin, 1949), 239; Andrew Turnbull, *Scott Fitzgerald* (New York: Charles Scribner's Sons, 1962), 199; Milford, *Zelda,* 157–58; Sara Mayfield, *Exiles from Paradise* (New York: Delacorte Press, 1971), 148; Wagner-Martin, *Zelda Sayre Fitzgerald,* 127–28; Kendall Taylor, *Sometimes Madness Is Wisdom: Zelda and Scott Fitzgerald; A Marriage* (New York, Ballantine, 2001), 222.

28. Jeffrey Meyers, *Scott Fitzgerald: A Biography* (New York: HarperCollins, 1994), 193.

29. Mizener, *Far Side of Paradise,* 239.

30. Turnbull, *Fitzgerald,* 199.

31. Milford, *Zelda,* 157.

32. Milford, *Zelda,* 158.

33. Taylor, *Madness Is Wisdom,* 224.

34. Quoted in Bruccoli, *Epic Grandeur,* 342–43.

35. Milford, *Zelda,* 159.

36. Quoted in Meyers, *Fitzgerald,* 194.

37. Quoted in Wagner-Martin, *Zelda Sayre Fitzgerald,* 130.

38. Fitzgerald and Fitzgerald, "Show Mr. and Mrs. F to Number —," 468.

39. Jackson R. Bryer and Cathy W. Barks, eds., *Dear Scott, Dearest Zelda: The*

Love Letters of F. Scott Fitzgerald and Zelda Fitzgerald, with an introduction by Eleanor Lanahan (New York: St. Martin's Press, 2002), 78.

40. Bryer and Barks, *Dear Scott, Dearest Zelda*, 80.

41. Bryer and Barks, *Dear Scott, Dearest Zelda*, 96.

42. Sharon Kim, "Posttraumatic Healing in *Caesar's Things*," *F. Scott Fitzgerald Review* 17 (2019): 125–26.

43. Sally Cline, *Zelda Fitzgerald: Her Voice in Paradise* (New York: Arcade, 2003), 130.

44. Milford, *Zelda*, 177.

45. Bryer and Barks, *Dear Scott, Dearest Zelda*, 97; quoted in Milford, *Zelda*, 179.

46. Zelda Fitzgerald to Rosalind, n.d., Princeton University Library, quoted in Wagner-Martin, *Zelda Sayre Fitzgerald*, 132.

47. Fitzgerald, *Life in Letters*, 197.

48. Fitzgerald, *Life in Letters*, 189.

49. Fitzgerald, "One Trip Abroad," 283.

50. F. Scott Fitzgerald, *The Notebooks of F. Scott Fitzgerald*, ed. Matthew J. Bruccoli (New York: Harcourt Brace Jovanovich / Bruccoli Clark, 1978), 204.

51. Fitzgerald, "One Trip Abroad," 283.

52. F. Scott Fitzgerald, "The Hotel Child," in *Taps at Reveille*, 288.

53. Bijou O'Connor, "Audio Arts: Bijou O'Connor Remembers F. Scott Fitzgerald," Tate Gallery. https://www.tate.org.uk/art/archive/items/tga-200414-7-3-2-6/audio-arts-published-supplement-bijou-oconnor-remembers-f-scott-fitzgerald.

54. Scott Donaldson, *Fool for Love: F. Scott Fitzgerald* (Minneapolis: University of Minnesota Press, 2012), 58.

55. Matthew J. Bruccoli *As Ever, Scott Fitz—: Letters between F. Scott Fitzgerald and His Literary Agent Harold Ober, 1919–1940*, with the assistance of Jennifer McCabe Atkinson (Philadelphia: J. B. Lippincott, 1972), 176.

56. F. Scott Fitzgerald, "The Death of My Father," in *Last Kiss*, ed. James L. W. West III, Cambridge Edition of the Works of F. Scott Fitzgerald (Cambridge: Cambridge University Press, 2017), 419.

57. F. Scott Fitzgerald, "On Your Own," in *Last Kiss*, 176. The line reappears in the novel as "Good-by, my father—good-by, all my fathers." Fitzgerald, *Tender Is the Night: A Romance*, ed. James L. W. West III, Cambridge Edition of the Works of F. Scott Fitzgerald (Cambridge: Cambridge University Press, 2012), 233.

58. Fitzgerald and Fitzgerald, "Show Mr. and Mrs. F. to Number —," 429.

59. Keith Walling, "Scott Fitzgeralds to Spend Winter Here Writing Books: Author Finds Montgomery Less Preoccupied with 'Depression' Than East," *Montgomery Advertiser*, October 8, 1931.

60. Frances Pitts, "The World Is Going to the Dogs," *Montgomery Advertiser*, December 11, 1931.

61. Zelda Fitzgerald, *Save Me the Waltz*, in *Collected Writings*, 189.

62. The novel was originally published posthumously in 1941 under the title *The Last Tycoon*; since the 1993 Cambridge Edition edited by Bruccoli it has been known by the longer title.

63. "Jobless Leader Warns Country to Help Needy," *Montgomery Advertiser*, December 31, 1931.

1932–1933

SCOTT DONALDSON

F. Scott Fitzgerald fought through a critical period in the years 1932–33. His marriage was on the verge of ending, and not well, owing to Zelda's worsening schizophrenia and his own out-of-control drinking. Husband and wife clashed in a personal and literary rivalry that left both angry and embittered.

Nineteen thirty-one ended with a downbeat. On the plus side, Zelda was judged to be well enough to leave her care at Les Rives de Prangins. She and Scott returned to her hometown of Montgomery, Alabama, rented a house there, and prepared to settle down. But Metro-Goldwyn-Mayer made Scott an offer of $1,200 a week to work on a script for *Red-Headed Woman* (studio boss Irving Thalberg wanted him), and inasmuch as his annual income was shrinking, he accepted. He finished his script—it was not used—but Fitzgerald salvaged "Crazy Sunday," one of his best stories, out of the experience, and got $6,000 ahead—so he wrote his editor Maxwell Perkins—to finance "five consecutive months" on his long-delayed novel *Tender Is the Night.*[1]

During Scott's absence Zelda's father, Judge Anthony Sayre, died, and Zelda, suffering from asthma attacks, traveled to Florida to escape the damp Alabama weather. Fitzgerald was back for Christmas and early in January accompanied his wife on a second trip to Florida. During the return to Montgomery, she conceived a delusion that "terrible things were being done to her" and insisted that she needed hospital care.[2]

Scott got in touch with Oscar Forel, the doctor who had overseen Zelda's treatment in Switzerland. Forel recommended that the Fitzgeralds come back to Prangins, but that did not fit in with their desire to remain in their home country. They decided instead to send Zelda to the Henry Phipps Psychiatric Clinic in Baltimore's Johns Hopkins University Hospital. Adolf Meyer, head of the Phipps Clinic, did not get along well with either Zelda or Scott. Zelda thought Meyer dull and humorless, and Scott was persistently annoyed by Meyer's disapproval of his drinking and accompanying unwillingness to regard him as a reliable

Henry Phipps Psychiatric Clinic at Johns Hopkins Hospital

professional. Fortunately, Zelda was placed under the care of Mildred Squires at Phipps, who encouraged her to finish the novel she had started in Alabama. In the remarkably short period of four weeks (February 12 to March 6, 1932), she completed the first draft of what would become *Save Me the Waltz*, and—without telling her husband—put the manuscript in the mail to Perkins at Scribner's. Scott was resentful about this show of independence, yet once he'd had the opportunity to read the draft, he re-asserted his control by demanding changes and taking over all contact with Perkins during the process of revision.

Life at La Paix

The Turnbulls' La Paix estate, with a sign over the front door reading "Pax Vobiscum," was peaceful all right, but also somewhat antiquated and rundown. The Turnbull family—parents Bayard and Margaret, and children Andrew (at eleven just about the same age as Scottie Fitzgerald), Eleanor, and Frances—abandoned that house and built a newer and "happier," more modern, less dreary one to live in.[3] So the original place was up for rent. Fitzgerald heard about it from a Baltimore lawyer named

Edgar Allan Poe he had known at Princeton and moved there in May 1932 for a stay that lasted until near the end of 1933.

The most interesting account of that period is embedded in *Scott Fitzgerald,* the 1962 biography that Andrew Turnbull published thirty years later. The visiting author manifestly took a shine to young Andrew and involved him in a number of sports—Princeton football above all—that both of them were interested in. Andrew, then attending the Gilman preparatory school, particularly admired Gilman's "smashing" fullback Pepper Constable, and Fitzgerald—who preferred smaller and more cerebral players—eventually came to share Andrew's enthusiasm for Constable, who captained Princeton's undefeated 1935 team.

Fitzgerald took Andrew—himself slightly undersized—to Princeton games and orchestrated the boy's boxing match with a neighbor lad named Sammy Green, "a little tough" who lived just outside the Turnbulls' twenty-eight-acre estate. Andrew was not eager to fight, and neither, he later came to suspect, was Sammy. After several rounds of "grunting and sweating and flailing of skinny arms,"[4] Fitzgerald called the bout a draw: an altogether more satisfactory result than that of his lapse as timekeeper in the Ernest Hemingway–Morley Callaghan match in Paris in the summer of 1929, when a time-keeping blunder by Fitzgerald generated significant resentment from Hemingway.[5] With Zelda more or less incapacitated, Scott supervised daughter Scottie's development. He was proud of Scottie and expected her to excel in everything. He was outraged when he discovered that Scottie and Eleanor were exchanging notes about what little they knew of sex, concealing them in a soggy shoebox hidden in a forsythia bush. But Scottie's natural buoyancy survived such misadventures. "A golden little girl," she accepted and even welcomed her father's supervision. According to Andrew, her every other word was "Daddy" or "Daddy says." He remembered one evening at La Paix when father and daughter, in winsome solidarity, waved goodbye from their porch, Fitzgerald weakly singing "Goodnight, Sweetheart" and breaking into a foxtrot shuffle.[6]

Andrew described Fitzgerald, then thirty-six, with admiration. At times he looked "a trifle worn and seedy," yet in his saddle shoes and pink shirt he resembled "a college athlete home for vacation." He was both "delicate and compact," with a nervous precision about his movements and something scrappy "and even a little belligerent" in his swagger of a walk. Though clearly unskilled, and paunchy in his white flannels, he moved about the tennis court gracefully and managed "to look like a good player." Under the influence of this "charming, unpredictable man," Andrew reported, life on the Turnbull estate vibrated to a faster rhythm.[7]

Scott liked all the Turnbull children and kept up-to-date with their development. Andrew followed Fitzgerald's precedent by attending Princeton, and the novelist wrote a laudatory letter recommending him to the Cottage Club "as a brilliant kid and fearless, despite his small stature."[8] He thought of Andrew's younger sister Eleanor as an aspiring actress, and observed that his older sister Frances looked "like a trinket."[9] Years later, when Frances sent him a story she'd written, he told her that she hadn't put her whole self into the piece and that to do so was the obligation of the literary artist.

And where was Zelda? Not often in sight, according to Andrew's book. At first she was hospitalized at Phipps, but in June she was discharged, not "cured," to join her husband and daughter at La Paix. Andrew recalled her arrival, alone in the back seat of a taxicab. "That's Mrs. Fitzgerald. She's sick," he was told. She struck him as an odd and rather pathetic figure, with everything organized for her benefit, "a boyish wraith of a woman" in ballet slippers and sleeveless dresses. She continually played "Valencia" on the Victrola and sometimes sang along or danced to it. "There was something not wholesome about her," Andrew thought.[10]

His mother, Margaret—the reader in the Turnbull family—had heard about F. Scott Fitzgerald but only began to read his work after he rented La Paix. Like her son, but for different reasons, Mrs. Turnbull thought Fitzgerald charming. He was "the only man" she had ever known "who would ask a woman a direct question about herself" and listen attentively to her response. He "had this extraordinary quality of giving you his undivided attention." She also was impressed by his attitude toward Zelda. She was "his invalid," and he sought to exert control over her behavior, but he spoke only of her charm, her appeal for men, and her brilliance.[11]

When T. S. Eliot came to Baltimore to lecture at Johns Hopkins, the Turnbulls invited Fitzgerald to a dinner in the visitor's honor and asked him to read some of the poet's work. Fitzgerald, who had been pleased by Eliot's judgment that *The Great Gatsby* represented the first step forward since Henry James, was happy to comply. "I read him some of his poems," he told Edmund Wilson, "and he seemed to think they were pretty good."[12]

Zelda's Case, and Scott's

From the beginning, Fitzgerald was at odds with Adolf Meyer. Meyer looked on the Fitzgeralds as a dual case, with Scott's drinking a parallel to Zelda's mental illness. Even worse, Meyer did not seem to value Scott's accomplishments as a writer. There were a number of meetings of the principals at Johns Hopkins, with each Fitzgerald vying for an advantage over the other. Zelda wanted a relationship that allowed her to decide her own life pattern. Scott wanted to assert his authority by establishing a strict daily regimen, and when she was released from Phipps to La Paix as an outpatient, it was on that basis.

Fitzgerald regarded it as his duty to make sure that Zelda followed the schedule that he and the doctors at Phipps had agreed on, including daily exercise and an evening work period. But she resisted Scott's authority and his role as dominant parent to Scottie. There were occasional shouting matches, and before quarrels were resolved, Zelda sometimes retreated to her room and locked the door. As Nancy Milford reconstructed one such occasion in her landmark biography *Zelda,* Scott tried to coax Zelda downstairs and, failing in that, slipped this note under the door:

> Darling when you shut yourself away for twenty four hours it is not only very bad for you but it casts a pall of gloom and disquiet over the people who love you. To spend any reasonable time in your room has been agreed upon as all right, but this shouldn't be so exaggerated that you can't manage the social side any further than sitting at table. It would help if you could enter a little into Scotty's life here on the place, and your reluctance to play tennis and swim is a rather reckless withdrawal; for whatever of the normal you subtract from your life will be filled up with brooding and fantasy. If I know that there is exercise scheduled for morning and afternoon and a medical bath in the afternoon & that you have half an hour for us after supper and you stop work at ten, my not very exigent list, *insisted upon by Dr. Meyer,* is complete. When you throw it out of joint I can only sit and wait for the explosion that will follow. . . .
> We can't afford scenes—the best protection is the schedule and then the schedule and again the schedule, and you'll get strong without knowing it.[13]

If he didn't love her so much, he added, her moods wouldn't affect him so deeply. With Scott both in charge of administering the schedule and also drinking to excess, Zelda rebelled against his authority. Both of them and her doctors were agreed that his role was *"not to be that of a doctor,"* she maintained. Her case had been taken over at Phipps by Thomas A. C. Rennie, a young psychiatrist she preferred to Meyer. On August 29, 1932, after an unusually fierce husband–wife dispute, she telephoned Rennie asking that she be sent to the nearby Sheppard and Enoch Pratt Hospital. Rennie did not consent to that. It was the goal of her present therapy, he explained, to keep her *out of* hospitals and functioning on her own.[14]

Literary Rivalry

The most serious difference between the Fitzgeralds involved Zelda's writing. The rift began in the first years of their marriage, when Scott freely borrowed from Zelda's letters and diaries for his own fiction. As Zelda humorously commented in connection with *The Beautiful and Damned* (1922), Scott's second novel, "Mr. Fitzgerald—I believe that is how he spells his name—seems to believe that plagiarism begins at home."[15] By 1923 she was writing sketches of her own that Scott's agent, Harold Ober, was able to sell to *College Humor* for five hundred to eight hundred dollars apiece. To jack up the prices, these were marketed as the joint efforts of F. Scott and Zelda Fitzgerald. In one extreme case, Ober sent her story "A Millionaire's Girl" to the *Saturday Evening Post* (May 17, 1930) as solely *Scott's* work, not hers, and was able to get four thousand dollars (the absolute top price for his stories) for it.[16] Scott also sent Perkins three "haunting and evocative" stories Zelda had written in Switzerland during the depths of her "nervous breakdown" for possible publication in *Scribner's Magazine.*[17]

When her illness forced her to abandon a possible career as a ballet dancer, Zelda turned to writing as a way of establishing her creative independence. She angered her husband by sending the manuscript of *Save Me the Waltz* to Perkins on March 9, 1932, without telling him. She did so because she feared Scott's "scathing criticism" of her work, she told him in a letter of apology. Zelda also confessed that she "was afraid we might have touched [on] the same material."[18] In fact, she incorporated several incidents from their past in her book, events he felt belonged to him alone as the professional writer in the family.

Zelda's use of these subjects was not a complete surprise to Scott, for earlier in the composition process she had predicted that he would like her novel as "distinctly École Fitzgerald, though more ecstatic" than his work.[19] Her story is indeed highly autobiographical, with a protagonist named Alabama Beggs, in tribute to her origins in Montgomery, and a philandering husband called Amory Blaine, the name of the principal character in Scott's autobiographical first novel *This Side of Paradise* (1920).

"Amory Blaine" would have to go, Scott demanded, and Zelda changed it to David Knight, a probable reference to a New York lawyer, Dick Knight, who admired her and aroused Scott's jealousy. It was but one of many changes they made in her manuscript as he placed himself in charge of *Save Me the Waltz*, communicating directly with Perkins about it and even telling the editor what he should say to her. Scott tried hard to salvage Zelda's book, despite its occasional fevered prose and wild metaphors. In mid-May he sent the revised script to Perkins with a strong endorsement. "It's a good novel now, perhaps a very good novel—I am too close to it to tell."[20] Scribner's accepted her "novel of showy brilliance,"[21] and it was brought out in October to unfavorable reviews and negligible sales. Fitzgerald negotiated with Scribner's to apply half the royalties up to five thousand dollars against his borrowed debt with the publisher, but *Save Me the Waltz*'s earnings for 1932 came to a paltry $120.73. Critics deplored the "ludicrous lushness" of its prose and the publisher's failure—never Perkins's strong point—to give the book even elementary proofreading.[22]

Zelda was not devastated by the fate of her novel. She still had high hopes for a career of her own as a writer. Behind locked doors she began to write another book, also autobiographical, dealing with her struggles with insanity—a subject that her doctors warned her against and that her husband regarded as an outright invasion of his long-delayed *Tender Is the Night*: the tale of a promising young psychologist sacrificing himself through marriage to and simultaneous treatment of an attractive and wealthy patient suffering from schizophrenia.

In August 1932 Fitzgerald noted in his ledger that *Tender Is the Night* was now plotted and planned, "never more to be permanently interrupted," and supplemented this burst of optimism with sixteen pages of a "General Plan" outlining the background of his major characters—Dick Diver, for example, as a "communist-liberal-idealist" with a drinking problem who falls disastrously in love with his patient.[23] The novel was

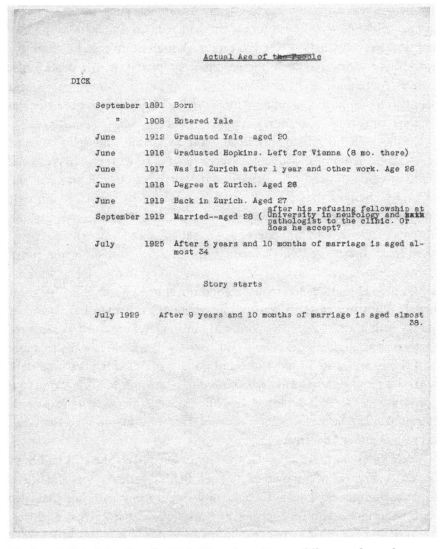

The biographical timeline for Dick Diver from Fitzgerald's reconfigured 1932 plan for *Tender Is the Night*.

by that time in its fourth or fifth stage of development, with Fitzgerald repeatedly promising Perkins and Ober from 1925 onward that next year, next month, any day now he would buckle down and deliver the manuscript in short order. The August 1932 statement fell into that pattern, for he was not yet ready or able to devote himself fully to the novel.

Part of the difficulty had to do with his financial situation. His earn-

Fitzgerald's earnings in 1933 were only marginally better than those of the previous year.

ings for 1932 came to $15,832.40, the lowest figure since 1919, and rose only slightly to $16,328.03 in 1933.[24] Meanwhile his expenses were rising, with Zelda's medical costs and Scottie's school fees. To come close to breaking even, he cranked out stories for the *Saturday Evening Post,* three in the spring of 1932, three in the middle of 1933, and two more late in that year. But the *Post's* advertising revenue was declining in the bottom of the Great Depression, and its editors complained that Fitzgerald's new stories did not reach his usual standard. They cut his payments from $4,000 to $3,500 to $3,000 to $2,500 and rejected some of his efforts altogether. He was finding it increasingly difficult to write stories of young love gone wrong but in the end made right. In "One Hundred False Starts," a March 1933 essay, Scott admitted that there was necessarily a certain similarity among his works:

> Mostly we authors must repeat ourselves—that's the truth. We
> have two or three great and moving experiences in our lives—
> experiences so great and moving that it doesn't seem at the time
> that anyone else has been so caught up and pounded and dazzled

and astonished and beaten and broken and rescued and illuminated and rewarded and humbled in just that way ever before.[25]

Then, he added, authors learned their craft and told their two or three stories, "each time in a new disguise," perhaps ten times, perhaps a hundred, as long as people would listen.[26] Scott's single greatest story had to do with a poor—actually middle-class—boy falling in love with a rich girl. Sometimes it ended happily, as in most of his *Saturday Evening Post* stories. Sometimes it did not, as in most of his novels. Eventually, he feared, people might stop listening.

The Crisis: May 28, 1933

The tension in the Fitzgerald household increased over time and was only exacerbated by the abject failure of Zelda's play *Scandalabra*, staged in the spring of 1933 by the Vagabond Players, a Baltimore little-theater group. After its dismal opening night, Scott held court in the greenroom, reading the script to the cast line by line and trimming anything that did not advance the plot. But this "radical surgery" did not work, and the play was simply abandoned.[27]

Scott became increasingly convinced that he was sacrificing his own future in order to provide for Zelda's. He made that point in correspondence with her doctors and in private memoranda. "Perhaps she would have been a genius if we had never met," he wrote Meyer in April 1933,[28] but as matters stood she was hurting him by invading his territory in her own writing—most particularly in the book she had begun about her mental illness, material she knew he was exploring in *Tender Is the Night*. Zelda, on the other hand, desired freedom to write whatever she wanted.

These quite opposite views were uncovered in a long interview that Rennie supervised at La Paix on May 28, 1933, with a stenographer on hand to record a 114-page transcription of their conversation. Rennie hoped that the couple could talk out their differences in such a meeting. Scott wanted to stop Zelda's fictional ventures from drawing on material from their marriage, and he wanted her to channel her energies in some other direction. Zelda wanted freedom from his control. The session with Rennie, Scott recognized in advance, would amount to a confrontation between them, and he set down notes about how to approach the day.

Prepare physically, he reminded himself, and added seven points of debater's notes, including two alternatives for Zelda to pursue:

> to try to write instead of self-justification (& working always on sched-
> ule) a series of short observations on things & facts, *observed things*
> which she can sell & make money [on] if she wants that to go to art
> school or to learn commercial design & try to combine talent for art
> with etc. into some unit? like cartooning & leave my field to me.[29]

In another memorandum to himself, he spelled out how the differences
between himself and Zelda were nearly insoluble. They were no longer
partners but enemies, locked into an adversarial relationship only one of
them would survive.

> As I got feeling worse Zelda got mentally better, but it seemed to me
> that as she did she was also coming to the conclusion she had it on
> me, if I broke down it justified her whole life—not a very healthy
> thought to live with about your own wife. . . . Finally four days ago
> told her frankly & furiously that had got and was getting rotten
> deal trading my health for her sanity and from now on I was going
> to look out for myself & Scotty exclusively, and let her go to Bedlam
> for all I cared.[30]

"KEEP COOL BUT FIRM," he advised himself in red capitals on this document, but when the confrontation before Rennie began, he spoke dis-
paragingly of Zelda's artistic accomplishments. She was "a third-rate
writer and a third-rate ballet dancer," he said, while he was "a professional writer with a huge following" and "the highest paid short story
writer in the world,"[31] a reference to his former four-thousand-dollar-
per-publication rate at the *Saturday Evening Post.*

If so, Zelda responded, it seemed to her that he "was making a rather
violent attack on a third-rate talent."[32] Why should he care what she was
writing? Because she was always encroaching on his material, picking
up crumbs at the dinner table and putting them into books, he maintained.[33] This had been bad enough with *Save Me the Waltz.* It would be
even worse with her venture into a psychiatric novel in competition with
Tender Is the Night.

He was the professional writer in the family, Scott insisted, and she the amateur. The difference was vast and hard to define, but Fitzgerald gave it a try. To become a professional required "the keen equipment . . . a scent, a smell of the future in one line." And above all it required having something important to say, as he thought Zelda did not, and that was "a question of sleepless nights and worry and endless ratiocination of a subject—of endless trying to dig out the essential truth, the essential justice."[34] Talent wasn't enough. You had to have a conscience operating in your work.

By way of counterattack, Zelda focused on Scott's eight-year procrastination with *Tender Is the Night*. If he ever managed to finish that novel, she said, he wouldn't feel "so miserable and suspicious and mean towards everybody else." He was so "full of self-reproach" that he had stooped to accusations against her. She also emphasized his excessive drinking, a point that the doctors had warned against.[35]

Things were said in that interview that could not easily be forgotten. Both Scott and Zelda insisted that there had to be a change in their relationship if their marriage was to survive. Zelda cited her husband's behavior after a trip to New York the previous fall during which, manifestly drunk, he had managed to alienate both Edmund Wilson and Ernest Hemingway, two of the men he most valued. He was still under the influence of alcohol when he got back to La Paix. "You sat down and cried," Zelda recalled. "You said I had ruined your life and you did not love me and you were sick of me and wished you could get away."[36] She could not live under such conditions, she said. He had to stop drinking.

But this was a step Scott refused to take. To do so, he believed, would only confirm to the Sayre family their conviction that he and his alcoholic lifestyle were responsible for Zelda's illness. In the coming summer, it became clear that there were other psychologically disturbed people among Zelda's relatives when her brother Anthony committed suicide by leaping to his death from a hospital window. Scott immediately relayed this news to Margaret Turnbull: she had to see now, he said, that Zelda's inherited disease was at fault, not anything he had said or done.

Lacking this news in the Rennie interview, Scott took a hard line against his wife. There hadn't been any sex for three or four months, he revealed, though before that their relations were "pleasant enough." Zelda responded ironically that she was glad he had found them "satisfactory." He finally asked her whether she would like to "go to law" to settle their differences, and he may have been surprised by her answer that yes, in fact, divorce might be the only answer "because there is nothing except ill will on [his] part and suspicion."[37]

Scott plunged ahead with an ultimatum that she had to cease and desist writing about their lives in any form, including drama. If she was writing a play, it could not be about psychiatry or located in Switzerland, and whatever she was writing had to be submitted to him for approval. Reluctantly she agreed to these provisions, but only until he finished *Tender Is the Night*. After that, they'd "better get a divorce" because she could not accept living on those terms.[38]

Scott took that comment literally, and he met with the lawyer Poe to learn about the varying state laws governing divorce from a mentally ill partner. In another of his private communications he went further, sketching out a plan to drive Zelda certifiably insane. This brief document, located among his papers at Princeton's Harry S. Firestone Memorial Library, is reprinted here:

> Plan—To attack on all grounds
> Play (suppress), novel (delay), pictures (suppress),
> character (showers???), child (detach), schedule
> (disorient to cause trouble) no typing
> Probably result—new breakdow
> Danger to Scotty (?)
> " " herself (?)
> All this in secret

There is no evidence that Fitzgerald carried out this diabolical scheme, but its existence testifies to his belief at the time that he and Zelda were locked in mortal combat.[39]

Last Months

In any event, Zelda's condition did not improve over time. In June 1933 she started a fire by attempting to "burn something" in a long-unused second-story fireplace at La Paix. Firemen had to be summoned to put it out. That event marked a turning point in the Fitzgeralds' stay.[40] Scott withdrew into work on his novel and was able to write Perkins on September 25 that he would appear at Scribner's the following month to deliver the years-delayed manuscript, a deadline he actually kept. He told Perkins, half sarcastically, not to have a band for the occasion for he didn't really care for music.[41]

He had not stopped drinking. If anything, his consumption of alcohol went up, and he later lamented that he had written the third part of *Tender Is the Night* "entirely on stimulant." A short story could be written on a bottle, but not a novel, where you needed "the mental speed . . . to keep the whole process in your head." Twice in the fall of 1933 he admitted himself to Johns Hopkins Hospital for three or four days to dry out, and having established that pattern he returned six more times in succeeding years.[42]

Ring Lardner, Scott's friend and drinking companion during his days in Great Neck, New York, died in September from a combination of tuberculosis and alcoholism. His death inspired Fitzgerald to write a reminiscence that appeared in the October 11, 1933, issue of *New Republic*, an article that Dorothy Parker regarded as "the finest and most moving thing" she had ever read.[43] In it, Fitzgerald lamented that Lardner, despite his talent, had "got less of himself" down on paper, less of what was in his mind and heart, than any other American writer "of the first flight." The piece served as a warning to himself as well for neglecting his work during long periods of partying, but at least he was soon to produce a second great novel in *Tender Is the Night*.[44]

It was also in Baltimore that Fitzgerald became most seriously concerned with the communist movement. His interest in Marxist doctrine was stimulated by reading in late 1931 a Book of the Month primer on Russia's Five-Year Plan—a book that he passed on to Zelda and that she discussed with Scottie during his eight weeks in Hollywood. Zelda did not share his doubts about the future of capitalism, though. As she commented in the summer of 1932, "Scott reads Karl Marx—I read the cosmological philosophers. The brightest moments of our day are when we get them mixed up."[45]

Then, too, Scott was influenced by Edmund Wilson's communist sentiments. To Margaret Turnbull he deplored any politician who had not bothered to school himself in Marxist doctrine. He read some if not all of *Das Kapital* and was moved by the injustices under capitalism described in the chapter "The Working Day." He had occasional meetings with "the Community Communist" (Zelda's phrase) while at La Paix. That person was probably V. F. Calverton, the brilliant young editor of the *Modern Monthly*. Scott loaned out La Paix for meetings of local communists and even spoke at an antiwar rally sponsored by the Johns Hopkins Liberal Club and the Baltimore chapter of the National Student League (probably a communist front organization), where he minimized his commitment to the cause by addressing the audience as "fellow cranks." "Political worries, almost neurosis," Fitzgerald noted in his November 1932 ledger entry.[46] These found their way into his novel, too, most conspicuously in the dialogue between socialist Albert McKisco and professional warrior Tommy Barban.

Yet despite his early-1930s Depression belief that capitalism was doomed, Fitzgerald never joined the Communist Party. He lacked the discipline and devotion required of members and was disturbed by the communists' exploitation of African Americans in their antiwar campaign. He indulged in at least one racial maneuver of his own during a lunch that Zelda organized for a party of four women at La Paix, an incident that Andrew Turnbull included as an example of Scott's capacity to be cruel to his wife. Zelda's guests were Margaret Turnbull and two others Turnbull did not identify by name—Zelda's sister Rosalind Smith, who tried to liberate Zelda and Scottie from his supervision (the model for Marion, the woman who keeps Charles Wales from his daughter Honoria in "Babylon Revisited") and another Baltimore matron "who was an old friend from Montgomery."[47]

Scott tried hard to ruin this gathering. He rattled chains and issued sepulchral growls from the bedrooms above and then, dressed in a Roman robe, began striding across the porch, visible from the dining room through French windows, while reciting passages from Shakespeare's *Julius Caesar*. The ladies ignored him, but then an unsuspecting intruder happened upon the scene, "a Negro clergyman" who twice a year came to the Turnbull estate to solicit funds for an orphanage. Fitzgerald seized the opportunity and escorted the bewildered visitor into the dining room, introducing him as a distinguished figure from equatorial Africa and requesting that he be invited to join the meal. The polite and "elderly" fellow escaped as soon as possible, and Scott resumed his solemn march before finally giving up his "prank." Zelda kept her dignity throughout, and the other ladies did their best to ignore his performance.[48]

But this strange, cruel, and undoubtedly liquor-assisted incident was hardly typical of Scott, who genuinely cared for Zelda. When she suffered another relapse in 1934, "his gallantry refused to contemplate" divorce proceedings.[49]

NOTES

1. Matthew J. Bruccoli, *Some Sort of Epic Grandeur: The Life of F. Scott Fitzgerald* (New York: Harcourt Brace Jovanovich, 1981), 324.

2. Linda Wagner-Martin, *Zelda Sayre Fitzgerald: An American Woman's Life* (London: Palgrave Macmillan, 2004), 153.

3. Andrew Turnbull, *Scott Fitzgerald* (New York: Charles Scribner's Sons, 1962), 209.

4. Turnbull, *Fitzgerald*, 215.

5. The Hemingway–Callaghan fight is described in Catherine Delesalle-Nancey's essay on 1928–1929 in this book.

6. Turnbull, *Fitzgerald*, 223–24.

7. Turnbull, *Fitzgerald*, 211–13.

8. Quoted in Scott Donaldson, *Fool for Love: F. Scott Fitzgerald* (New York: Congdon and Weed, 1983), 30–31.

9. Turnbull, *Fitzgerald*, 230.

10. Turnbull, *Fitzgerald*, 230.

11. Nancy Milford, *Zelda: A Biography* (New York: Harper and Row, 1970), 258–59.

12. Quoted in Turnbull, *Fitzgerald*, 229–30.

13. Milford, *Zelda*, 259–60.

14. Milford, *Zelda*, 261.

15. Quoted in Donaldson, *Fool for Love*, 81.

16. Donaldson, *Fool for Love*, 81.

17. Turnbull, *Fitzgerald*, 194.

18. Milford, *Zelda*, 220.

19. Quoted in Donaldson, *Fool for Love*, 82.

20. Quoted in Donaldson, *Fool for Love*, 83.

21. James R. Mellow, *Invented Lives: F. Scott and Zelda Fitzgerald* (Boston: Houghton Mifflin, 1984), 400.

22. Mellow, *Invented Lives*, 406–7.

23. Quoted in Bruccoli, *Epic Grandeur*, 335–40.

24. Bruccoli, *Epic Grandeur*, 331, 356.

25. F. Scott Fitzgerald, "One Hundred False Starts," in *My Lost City: Personal Essays, 1920–1940*, ed. James L. W. West III, Cambridge Edition of the Works of F. Scott Fitzgerald (Cambridge: Cambridge University Press, 2014), 86–87.

26. Fitzgerald, "One Hundred False Starts," 87.

27. Turnbull, *Fitzgerald*, 232.

28. Quoted in Donaldson, *Fool for Love*, 84.

29. Quoted in Donaldson, *Fool for Love*, 87.

30. Quoted in Donaldson, *Fool for Love*, 86.

31. Quoted in Donaldson, *Fool for Love,* 84.

32. Quoted in Donaldson, *Fool for Love,* 84.

33. Donaldson, *Fool for Love,* 84.

34. Quoted in Turnbull, *Fitzgerald,* 233–34.

35. Quoted in Donaldson, *Fool for Love,* 85.

36. Quoted in Donaldson, *Fool for Love,* 85.

37. Quoted in Donaldson, *Fool for Love,* 85.

38. Quoted in Donaldson, *Fool for Love,* 85. On this meeting, see also Milford, *Zelda,* 272–75; Bruccoli, *Epic Grandeur,* 348–55; and Mellow, *Invented Lives,* 410–12.

39. Donaldson, *Fool for Love,* 86.

40. Turnbull, *Fitzgerald,* 237–38.

41. Bruccoli, *Epic Grandeur,* 360.

42. Bruccoli, *Epic Grandeur,* 346, 360.

43. F. Scott Fitzgerald, *Correspondence of F. Scott Fitzgerald,* ed. Matthew J. Bruccoli and Margaret M. Duggan (New York: Random House, 1980), 318.

44. Bruccoli, *Epic Grandeur,* 359–60.

45. Quoted in Scott Donaldson, "The Political Development of F. Scott Fitzgerald," ed. Jack Salzman, *Prospects* 6 (1981): 324.

46. Quoted in Donaldson, "Political Development," 323–25, 332–35.

47. The third guest was probably Sara Haardt, married to H. L. Mencken.

48. Turnbull, *Fitzgerald,* 231–32.

49. Turnbull, *Fitzgerald,* 235.

1934–1935

William Blazek

From *Tender Is the Night* to "The Crack-Up"

The year 1934 began in expectation and hope for F. Scott Fitzgerald. His fourth novel was in the first installment of its monthly serialization in *Scribner's Magazine,* and he was reworking proofs for the book, which would be published on April 12. Although he anticipated *Tender Is the Night* would be difficult to sell in the harsh economic climate of the fifth year of the Great Depression, he nevertheless felt it could gradually find a readership to appreciate its nuanced complexities in structure, meaning, and cultural critique. "The novel will certainly have *success d'estime,*" he predicted to his editor at Scribner's, Maxwell Perkins, "but it may be slow in coming—alas, I may again have written a novel for novelists with little chance of its lining anybody's pockets with gold."[1] Fitzgerald certainly needed the money in this period, though, because he was paying for Zelda's medical treatment at expensive psychiatric institutions, for the raising and educating of his daughter, Scottie, and for an overly indulgent lifestyle that outstripped his publisher's advances, agent's loans, and income, derived mainly from selling short stories to the popular-magazine market. Ultimately, the heavy pressures on him over the next two years to deal with the conclusiveness of Zelda's mental illness, to earn money from professional writing while debts mounted, and to maintain his core integrity as a craftsman and artist all conspired to damage his physical and mental health and to exacerbate his alcoholism. He was forced to confront his identity as a "writer only," stripped of much of his personal dignity but facing his despair by writing about and through it. By the end of 1935, Fitzgerald was struggling to draw on the reserves of creative imagination that had made him the most highly paid short-story writer in America. As his income from magazines plummeted and his personal tribulations mounted, he nevertheless was able to reinvest his writerly skills, to survive through language. He often turned to nostalgia in this period as a means to alleviate an unsettling present, and he finally resorted to sly defiance with the first "Crack-Up" essays.

In his 1933 essay "One Hundred False Starts," Fitzgerald explains, "The decision as to when to quit, as to when one is merely floundering around and causing other people trouble, has to be made frequently in a lifetime."[2] Writing *Tender Is the Night* posed such decisions for him frequently over the nine years after his first succès d'estime, *The Great Gatsby*, in the summer of 1925. "My new novel is marvellous," he reported to a friend from Paris in October 1925. "I'm in the first chapter. You may recognize certain things and people in it."[3] The new novel would evolve through seventeen drafts involving three major versions—beginning with the Francis Melarky narrative, first titled "Our Type," which was reworked in first person with the indicative title "The Boy Who Killed His Mother," followed by drafts with the tentative titles "The Melarky Case" and "The World's Fair" and finally by one without the first-person narrator. Fitzgerald abandoned the matricide plot in his second version, introducing the characters Nicole, Rosemary, and Lew Kelly, who would appear in different guises in the finished text. The third iteration, used in the first part of *Tender Is the Night,* focused on Dick Diver, but Fitzgerald composed most of Books 2 and 3 of the final text over an eighteen-month period from mid-1932 at La Paix, the fifteen-room manor house he rented for his family in Towson, Maryland, less than ten miles north of central Baltimore. They then moved to a less expensive, four-bedroom town house at 1307 Park Avenue in midtown Baltimore, where he finished the novel's proofs. In January 1934 Fitzgerald predicted the novel's fate yet tried to assure Perkins of its quality and the effort given to write it: "It is a book that only gives its full effect on its second reading. Almost every part of it has been revised and thought out from three to six times."[4]

Scribner's pressed Fitzgerald to finish the book manuscript, with Perkins anxiously writing on February 14, 1934: "I hope you can get through the book proof pretty fast. We are mighty crowded for time."[5] A month before the novel's publication and still dealing with errors in the printer's proofs, Fitzgerald wrote to Perkins, "After all, Max, I am a plodder. . . . When I decided to be a serious man, I tried to struggle over every point until I made myself into a slow moving Behemoth . . . and so there I am for the rest of my life." He added, "I have lived so long within the circle of this book and with these characters that often it seems to me that the real world does not exist but that only these characters exist, . . .—so much so that their glees and woes are as important to me as what happens in life."[6] He would have cause to reflect on this concept as his life

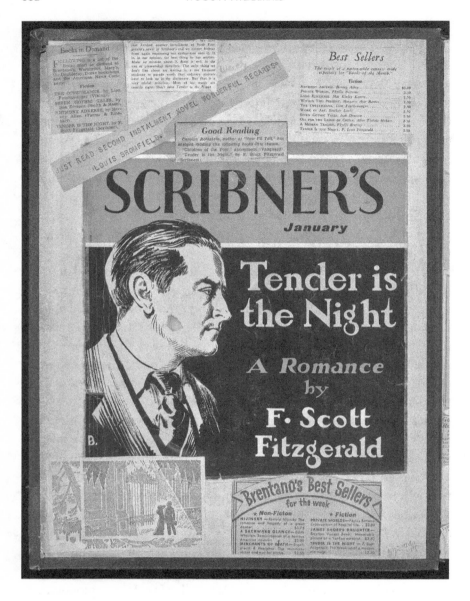

and writing melded together over the next two years and as his friends
and fellow writers considered the importance of his accomplishment.
Tender Is the Night is dedicated to Gerald and Sara Murphy, the wealthy
American expatriates who served as models for the protagonists, Dick
and Nicole Diver. Gerald wrote to him on New Year's Eve 1935: "I know
now that what you said in 'Tender Is the Night' is true. Only the invented
part of our life,—the unreal part—has had any scheme any beauty."[7]

F. Scott Fitzgerald scrapbook entries for *Tender Is the Night*: serialization
in *Scribner's Magazine,* January–April 1934 *(opposite)* and book publication,
April 12, 1934 *(above).*

While Fitzgerald's highest artistic endeavors provided existential
worth, they yielded inadequate financial compensation. *Tender Is the
Night* sold just under 15,200 copies over three printings, earning the author
about $5,100, little more than half his compensation from the magazine

serialization.[8] The author might have contracted the serialization with *Cosmopolitan* for thirty thousand to forty thousand dollars but decided that *Scribner's* would disguise his hiatus from novel publication, lend a semblance of continuity, and thus create potential for larger book sales. His biographer Matthew J. Bruccoli ascribes the low sales figures to the dire publishing market of 1934, when the novel reached fifth-bestseller status for fiction in the United States, although he acknowledges that in both the United States and the United Kingdom, "Fitzgerald's wastrel reputation impeded the recognition of his best work." Bruccoli also notes that there were twice as many favorable as unfavorable reviews, and he dismisses the notion that the novel's 1920s settings and European focus were at odds with the prominence of American proletarian fiction in the mid-1930s, for in fact historical romance and escapist adventure novels dominated the year's bestseller lists.[9]

Fitzgerald's fellow writers seemed to be as impressed that the author had actually completed the novel as by its content and achievement. John Dos Passos epitomized one side of the reaction, praising Fitzgerald for fighting through bad luck, illness, and depression: "Scott was meeting adversity with a consistency of purpose that I found admirable. He was trying to raise Scottie, to do the best possible for Zelda, to handle his drinking and to keep a flow of stories into the magazines to raise the enormous sums Zelda's illness cost. At the same time he was determined to continue writing firstrate novels."[10] Ernest Hemingway had to be prompted indirectly by Perkins and frustratedly by Fitzgerald himself to give an initial response. It focused mainly on chastising his one-time advocate for using the Murphys as character fodder and for abusing his true talent. Fitzgerald's carefully measured response was to explain his employment of composite characters from life. He also recalled the writers' agreement about ending novels, both *A Farewell to Arms* and *Tender Is the Night*, with a "dying fall," derived from the work of Joseph Conrad and David Garnett, in order to appeal to "the lingering after-effects in the reader's mind."[11] Defending *Tender Is the Night* to his former Princeton classmate John Peale Bishop, who was turning from poetry to novel writing, Fitzgerald declared, "I believe that the important thing about a work of fiction is that the essential reaction shall be profound and enduring."[12] Hemingway later conceded to Perkins, who was serving as intermediary in the one-time close friends' increasingly distanced association, that his appreciation of *Tender Is the Night* greatly improved on rereading. Yet while Fitzgerald was grateful to hear this, he replied to Perkins, "I always think of my friendship with him as being one of the high spots of life. But I still believe such things have a mortality, perhaps in relation to their very excessive life," before turning his attention back to his novel: "Things happen all the time which make me think that it is not destined to die quite as easily as the boys-in-a-hurry prophesied."[13]

Zelda Fitzgerald consistently boosted her husband's belief in the lasting value of the novel's artistic merits. In April 1934, directly following its publication, she wrote about it to Scott on four separate occasions: "It makes me very sad—largely because of the beautiful, beautiful writing." "The book is grand." "It is a swell evocation of an epoch and a very masterly presentation of tragedies sprung from the beliefs (or lack of them) of those times." And "the chief function of the artist was to inspire *feeling* and certainly 'Tender' did that. . . . There may be a tremendous revision of aesthetic judgments and responses."[14] The fact that she was writing these encouragements just two months after her third mental breakdown reflects the strength of both her emotional and her critical faculties, as well as the severely difficult conditions under which Scott worked to complete the book and his increasingly desperate reliance on his writing to earn money to pay for Zelda's medical care.

Upon her relapse on February 12, 1934, Zelda was readmitted to the Henry Phipps Psychiatric Clinic of Johns Hopkins University Hospital, where she had been undergoing treatment as a weekday outpatient. With no signs of improvement, she was transferred on March 8 to Craig House, an expensive convalescent hospital located on the Hudson River, a ninety-minute drive northwest of New York City. Scott stayed with friends in New York for an exhibition of Zelda's artwork and remained there for several days to promote the publication of the novel, a sojourn that became an excuse for excessive drinking. Concerned about the pressures he was under, Zelda repeatedly told Scott that although she liked Craig House ("my room is the nicest room I've ever had, any place") she would be happy to move to a less expensive, even state-run institution. "You must realize," she explained, "that to one as ill as I am, one place is not very different from another and that I would appreciate your working whatever adjustments would rend[er] your life less difficult—."[15] That concern for his work and welfare rings true in their other correspondence in 1934, and while a certain self-serving element can sometimes be detected, in that she was almost entirely dependent on his financial support, nevertheless their long-standing bonds are reaffirmed time and again.

Reading their letters from that year and the next is a torturous experience, both heart-breaking and disturbing in the emotional turns they take. Clearly dependent on each other, the couple mirror each other's weaknesses and virtues as they reflect different facets of their psychological states and seek outlets for their financial and emotional needs. From Craig House a month before the publication of *Tender Is the Night*, Zelda encouraged and scolded Scott: "Work, and don't drink, and the accomplished effort will perhaps open unexpected sources of happiness, or contentment, or whatever it is you are looking for—certainly a sense of security—."[16] Two weeks after the novel's appearance, his response to her contains a mixture of anxious concern and forced optimism: "You and I have had wonderful times in the past, and the future is still brilliant with possibilities if you will keep up your morale, and try to think that way. . . . We are certainly on some upsurging wave, even if we don't yet know exactly where it's heading. . . . You and I have been happy; we haven't been happy just once, we've been happy a thousand times."[17] He also contradicts himself in a revolving sequence of references to their shared past and a wrenching desire for rebalance. "Forget the past—what you can of it," he begged, but then recalled good times in Montgomery two years before, drawing on memory as a foundation for hope.

Those notes of nostalgia and increasingly unlikely promise dominate their correspondence after May 19, 1934, when Zelda was transferred to the Sheppard and Enoch Pratt psychiatric hospital in Towson, near the Fitzgeralds' former home La Paix.[18] Her illness had become more acute, marked by apathy, silence, depression, and aural hallucinations. Suicidal at times, she reported in early June, "I am miserable in thinking of the unhappiness my illness has caused you," and she promised to cooperate with the doctors and try to recover quickly. In her unstable mental state, she continued, "Darling—I feel very disoriented and lonely. I love you, dearheart. Please try to love me some in spite of these stultifying years of sickness—and I will compensate you some way for your love and faithfulness."[19] But the compensation of living together again would never materialize. Zelda remained at Sheppard Pratt until April 1936, when she was moved to the Highland Hospital in Asheville, North Carolina. The summer of 1934 was particularly difficult for the couple, with Scott focused on writing and plans for writing, visiting Zelda when allowed to, but confused about what to expect of his life and theirs. Their letters exhibit the uncertainties—wishing to spend time traveling together, considering a project to publish a collection of her writings, dreaming of better days, yet enmeshed in the illusive reality of their situation. "I am so glad your letter sounded so well and cheerful," Zelda wrote. "It made me very homesick—your sweet buoyancy always holds so much promise of bright and happy things in such a vital world." Nevertheless, she had to confess, "Life is idle. Yesterday we took a long ride around familiar roads and it seemed so unreal not to be going home to La Paix—." In the autumn, she declared simply "I am lonesome," and amid wishes and thoughts of escape she wrote, "The Sheppard Pratt hospital is located somewhere in the hinterlands of the human consciousness and I can be located any time between the dawn of consciousness and the beginning of old age."[20] Scott's ledger summary for the twelve months ending in September 1934 reads: "Zelda breaks, the novel finished. Hard times for me, slow but sure. Ill health throughout."[21]

If all optimism for Zelda's return to a normal life had vanished, within that acceptance they found channels of consideration for each other. Among Zelda's fears was that Scott's talent was being spoiled for her sake: "You have not got the right, for Scottie's sake, and for the sake of letters to make a drudge of yourself for me."[22] "I am sorry that there should be nothing to greet you but an empty shell," Zelda wrote in a poignant letter of June 1935, reminiscing about their past, expressing dreamy wishes, but showing concern for his own: "I want you to be happy—if there were justice you would be happy—maybe you will be anyway—."[23] A few weeks later, she continued, "There is no way to ask you to forgive me for the misery and pain which I have caused you. I can only ask you to believe that I have done the best I could and that since we first met I have loved you with whatever I had to love you with," before ending with a plea to "please get well and love Scottie and find something to fill up your life—."[24] A year before, she had expressed that desire in an elliptic yet emphatic manner: "So, in the words of Ernest Hemingway, save yourself. This is what I want you to do."[25] The tone of their letters toward the end of 1935 has a terminal ring, but there were some compensations for Scott even as he endured his own mental and physical exhaustion. "It was wonderful to sit with her head on my shoulder for hours and feel as I always have, even now, closer to her than to any other human being," he revealed in September to Laura Guthrie, his secretary, although he added,

"This is not a denial of other emotions—oh, you understand,"[26] for the letter also candidly tells of his ending an affair with Beatrice Dance, a married woman he pursued while recuperating in Asheville from illness and fatigue.[27]

Understanding the trials of Scott Fitzgerald in extremis must take into account the severe financial and emotional strains he was under. He felt a deep regret for lost happiness, often blamed Zelda, found faults in her personality and amateurish ambitions, and sought outlets in sexual affairs and alcoholic binges.[28] Yet what he owed to money and loyalty, he fought to reconcile through writing. "How I ever got so deep in debt I don't know unless it's been this clinic business," he wrote to Perkins in late June 1934, "because I've written regularly a story a month since finishing the last proof of 'Tender' and they have been sold. I've also fixed up some of Zelda's little articles besides. Debt is an odd thing and it seems if you ever get started in it is very difficult to get disentangled."[29] He anticipated the problem before the publication of the novel's serialization: "What worries me is the possibility of being condemned to go back to the Saturday Evening Post grind at the exact moment when the book is finished" instead of having a well-earned rest.[30] Even with the *Post* and *Redbook* still able to pay him $3,600 for a short story, he explored various other ways to capitalize on his writings—pursuing film and theater rights and a republication contract for *Tender Is the Night,* meeting with Clark Gable to encourage a sound-picture remake of *The Great Gatsby,* collaborating on a movie treatment for *Tender Is the Night,* writing radio scripts, and searching for a new line of short stories, like the earlier Basil and Josephine series, that could be marketed individually to magazines and collected in a new book.[31] This last was one of four prospects he sent to Perkins, a list that included an omnibus edition of short stories and a collection of personal essays, but decided for expediency on what became Fitzgerald's final collection of stories, *Taps at Reveille.* "You are in a position where you are compelled to think of immediate financial return beyond anything else," Perkins acknowledged, while encouraging Fitzgerald to review the book proofs for the new collection as quickly as possible for an autumn 1934 release.[32]

Fitzgerald's drinking and concurrent ill health slowed his progress: "I am not in the proper condition either physically or financially to put over the kind of rush job that this would be," the author exclaimed. "I

have got to get myself out of this morass of debt," and that meant returning to writing for popular magazines.[33] In a long letter that November,
he explained to Perkins: "I should have known perfectly well that, in
debt as I was to the tune of about $12,000 on finishing 'Tender,' I should
have to devote the summer and most of the fall to getting out of it."[34]
Complaining of mental tiredness, he reasoned, "I know you have the
sense that I have loafed lately but that is absolutely not so. I have drunk
too much and that is certainly slowing me up. On the other hand, without drink I do not know whether I could have survived this time." He
then adds the kind of list that a schoolboy would use to demonstrate his
worth: "In actual work since I finished the last proof of the novel in the
middle of March, eight months ago, I have . . . ," and then he itemizes
over a dozen and a half writing projects, about half of them aborted but
the rest successfully completed.[35]

Taps at Reveille was published on March 10, 1935. Fitzgerald did not
expect it to be "a money book," and the 5,100 copies of the first printing
did not sell out during his lifetime.[36] He was more concerned about the
artistic integrity of the work, a theme that runs through his final two
completed books, although in the case of the story collection the ambition proved greater than the product. "Babylon Revisited" is the one
acknowledged classic in the collection, and "The Last of the Belles" and
"Crazy Sunday" have their critical advocates. But all three texts were
republications, and the quality of the newer pieces falls below the standards that the author set himself. In correspondence with his literary
agent, Harold Ober, about paying back $6,500 in loans to him, Fitzgerald
explained, "There is no use of me trying to rush things," for even in the
author's most productive years he could produce at most eight or nine
high-quality stories a year. "It is simply impossible—," he exclaimed; "all
my stories are conceived like novels, require a special emotion, a special
experience—." Writing "pattern stories" would be easier, he added, "but
the pencil just goes dead on me. I wish I could think of a line of stories like the Josephine or Basil ones which could go faster + pay $3000.
But no luck yet."[37] Nevertheless, he tested his luck with patterned lines to
develop, including a group of medieval-era stories about a hero named
Philippe that he imagined might be turned into a novel, and further efforts modeled on a sequence of Gwen Bowers stories, based on behavioral
observations of his teenage daughter.

In an analysis of Fitzgerald's career as a professional writer, James L. W. West III concludes in part that the author "was at his most productive when he worked under financial pressure, not when he had money in hand. Fitzgerald seems to have needed the prodding of debt, with an attendant dose of guilt, to move him to his writing table."[38] The pressures, not only financial, were indeed high for Fitzgerald in 1934–35; emotional and physical concerns increased also, and the quality of his work under those conditions declined to the extent that he became for a time his own nemesis, a hack writer.

The Philippe stories illustrate the fall. Three were published between October 1934 and August 1935 under contract with *Redbook*; a fourth was scheduled to appear in the September 1935 issue, but by then the publisher had decided to end what must be considered an embarrassing experiment.[39] "Am so fascinated with the medieval series that my problem is making them into proper butcher's cuts for monthly publication," he reported to Perkins. The meat-cleaving metaphor would prove apt: "I have thought of the subject so long that the actual fertility of invention has become even a liability."[40] He researched extensively and created a "histomap" covering his study wall with a graphic medieval time line.[41] Both despite and in some ways because of his fascination with the medieval subject, Fitzgerald's efforts turned into an odd goulash of exciting adventure story (with fairly well paced action about a ninth-century French count reclaiming his ancestral lands from Viking invaders), flawed plotting, and often hilariously anachronistic dialogue.

In the opening story, "In the Darkest Hour," Philippe fails in his first attempts at communication with the locals, so he tries pigeon-phrasing: "No speak Lingua Franca?"[42] A common language is difficult to discern in the dialogue between him and what might be considered hybrid peasants of an ill-bred and illiterate southern-sharecropper type; "I heard tell of a thing up to Tours last market day," one says. Philippe attempts to adapt, with "Howdy, . . . God save you!," although using a less promising approach to a young maiden: "You're a pretty little parcel." In gangster mode, he asserts authority and explains his plans to his new people: "Well, men . . . here's the line-up."[43]

Fitzgerald wanted to use the thirty thousand words he had written of the Philippe stories and expand them into a novel titled "Philippe, Count of Darkness" or "The Tower" but decided not to build on the initiative, mainly because of the time it would take to complete the structure, at the cost of further lost income. One can understand the attraction of the project for him. The narrator of "In the Darkest Hour" explains that in the center of the Dark Ages "were two hundred years so brutal, so ignorant, so savage, so dark, that little is known about them," when Europe "had fallen into a state of helpless and sub-bestial degradation."[44] From his own devastated personal life, here was a chance to escape through a story of reclamation, in which he could imagine himself, like Philippe, as master of his destiny, resurrecting his past authority. Each of the published stories earned him less money than a *Saturday Evening Post* story would have, "but I can do them faster because of the feeling of enthusiasm," he told Perkins, "probably the feeling of escape from the modern world."[45] Fitzgerald later revived the hope of publishing the stories as a whole in *Scribner's Magazine* and of expanding them into a full novel.[46]

Fitzgerald sold seven short stories in 1935, two each to the *Post* and *McCall's,* and single submissions to *American, Liberty,* and *Esquire.*[47] Founded in 1933, *Esquire* was a new outlet for him. Its publisher, Arnold Gingrich, was willing to take most anything from well-known authors as the magazine established itself, but he paid only a tenth or less than the major popular magazines. Gingrich accepted "Shaggy's Morning," written from the perspective of the eponymous canine narrator, describing his encounters with other dogs on his neighborhood streets and showing his relationship with his owners, a wife and husband identified as the Brain and the Beard. It may be the only Fitzgerald story that the majority of his readers will feel that they could have written better.[48] Increasingly desperate for new subject matter, Fitzgerald drew on his friendship with the wealthy celebrity couple Nora and Maurice "Lefty" Flynn for the *McCall's* story "The Intimate Strangers" to examine the compromises of marriage.[49] He used his secretary's interest in fortune-telling as a gimmick in "Fate in Her Hands" for *American* magazine. "Zone of Accident" in the *Post* draws on his memory of Zelda's treatment at Johns Hopkins Hospital, including an image of the imposing statue *Christus Consolator* in its entrance hall.[50] (Fitzgerald also used hospital settings for two 1934 *Post* stories, "New Types" and "Her Last Case," as well as for the last story he sold to the *Post,* "Trouble," in 1937.) Returning elsewhere to themes about conflict between generations, the lasting socio-psychological effects of war, and the need for fulfilling work, he also dug up the hurtful jealousies of Zelda's flirtation in 1924 with the French aviator Edouard Jozan and applied them to the story "Image on the Heart." With their sometimes halfhearted efforts to investigate Depression-era concerns about austerity, unemployment, and generational shifts, the stories are too often marred by unconvincing plots, narratives that are either too compact or too drawn-out, and underdeveloped characters.

The composition flaws and Fitzgerald's increasing unreliability in delivering manuscripts on time led to rejections.[51] Two Gwen short stories, the first begun in December 1935, were accepted by the *Post,* but a third, "Lo, the Poor Peacock," was declined by both the *Post* and *Ladies' Home Journal.*[52] Other manuscripts, including "Travel Together," "The Legend of Lake Lure," "The Pearl and the Fur," and "Make Yourself at Home," were either delayed by initial refusals or not accepted at all. "I'd Die for You" was turned down by seven magazines.[53] Etiolated by financial and health worries, Fitzgerald grew increasingly frustrated by his inability to recapture the spark of talent and concentrated discipline that had driven his professional career.[54] A recurrence of active tuberculosis caused him further anxiety, and beginning in April 1935 he spent less time in Baltimore, traveling regularly to Asheville, North Carolina, for specialist treatment and to rest. Writing to Perkins in late June, he revealed, "As to the health business, I was given what amounted to a death sentence about three months ago."[55]

Alcoholism added to the threat. Most commonly a persistent drinker but prone to frequent bouts of heavy binge drinking, Fitzgerald repeatedly stresses in his letters the normality of his recourse to alcohol for consolation or inspiration, but in this period he also righteously trumpets his stretches of sobriety. "I am, of course, on the wagon as always," he claimed to Perkins in April,[56] and in May he wrote to John Peale Bishop, "Haven't had a drink this year—not even wine or beer—are you surprised?"[57] He informed the playwright Zöe Akins, "No news from me except that I don't drink any more, many moons now since liquor of any kind has touched these lips."[58] "Decided to quit drinking for a few years (which has honestly been no trouble so far)," he declared to Gingrich, conscientiously trying to overcome the addiction because "I was doing my stuff on gin, cigarettes, bromides, and hope."[59] However, his summer stay in North Carolina at the Grove Park Inn diverted him from abstemiousness and had the added distraction of his awkward liaison with Beatrice Dance. Guilt and renunciation again of alcohol then followed, and in September Laura Guthrie read, "I have stopped all con-

Skyland Hotel, Hendersonville, North Carolina

nections with M. Barleycorn."[60] Yet there were frequent lapses, and even Fitzgerald's declarations of how much he had cut down on his intake ring hollow, such as the justification that he had reduced his alcoholic consumption by drinking only beer—a mere nine bottles one day but thirty-seven on another.[61] The reduced quality of his short fiction and the failure to begin a fifth novel belie the rationalization he presented to Perkins: "A short story can be written on a bottle, but for a novel you need the mental speed that enables you to keep the whole pattern in your head and ruthlessly sacrifice the sideshows."[62]

Fitzgerald's physical and mental descent through 1935 is reflected in the peripatetic nature of his life that year. Though still based at the town house on Park Avenue in Baltimore, he spent two weeks in February at the Oak Hall Hotel in Tryon, North Carolina, to counter his recurring tuberculosis. In the spring and summer he was mainly resident at the Grove Park Inn in Asheville, with an interim stay at the grand Hotel Stafford back in Baltimore. He spent part of September drying out from alcoholism in an Asheville hospital, returning to the Hotel Stafford later that month. November would find him in a cheap room at the Skyland Hotel in Hendersonville, North Carolina, twenty-two miles south of Asheville. He closed the year back in Baltimore, renting an apartment at the Cambridge Arms, across the street from Johns Hopkins University (today the university's Wolman Hall). He simultaneously leased an apartment a block and a half away at 3300 St. Paul Avenue.[63]

By November in Hendersonville he had reached financial and emotional lows, bemoaning to Ober that his writing since late August had yielded less than two thousand dollars. His health was weak, and he was drinking intemperately. He exclaimed, "I am living here at a $2.00 a day hotel, utterly alone, thank God!" in order to finish writing "Too Cute for Words" (the first of the short-lived Gwen series), which he sent to Ober a month later. The author also noted that he had, for two hundred dollars in emergency cash, completed an article for *Esquire,* almost certainly "The Crack-Up."[64] A year later, wondering if he could embark on a new novel, Fitzgerald estimated to Ober that it would require an eighteen-thousand-dollar investment for him to cover his expenses if he were to take a year off from magazine writing.[65] In 1934 the average net income from all tax returns to the Internal Revenue Service was $3,125, and in 1935 it was $3,259.[66] The U.S. per capita income in 1935 was $472.[67] Fitzgerald earned $20,032 in 1934, $16,845 in 1935, and $10,181 in 1936.[68] These are substantial sums, especially relative to the lives of most Americans, but the pattern of decline, combined with ongoing medical expenses for Zelda and school fees and upkeep for Scottie, signaled the full collapse that the author describes in "The Crack-Up." Yet rather than finding despair and failure in that text, an admission of defeat at the end of 1935 after the hopeful start of 1934 and *Tender Is the Night,* one might look for signs of artistic recovery and personal fortitude.

"Of course all life is a process of breaking down," "The Crack-Up" begins, reiterating a theme of dissipation and entropy that he had written into many of his short stories, essays, and novels after *This Side of Paradise.* Then, after giving examples showing that "the test of a first-rate intelligence is the ability to hold two opposed ideas in the mind at the same time"—in particular the ability "to see that things are hopeless and yet be determined to make them otherwise"—the author confesses that "ten years this side of forty-nine, I suddenly realized that I had prematurely cracked."[69] What follows next appears to be a delineation of reasons for that physical and spiritual fracture, leading to snarling misanthropy and permanent loss of vitality; then the essay turns to a strange dialogue with "a person whose life makes other people's lives seem like death—," conceived perhaps as one of the female Fates or Muses. Rather than finding pathos or embarrassment in the essay, therefore, readers might well feel a growing suspicion that it forms an ironic commentary on Fitzgerald's personal life, presented as a written performance for a public audience.[70] The persona of the text, rather than succumbing to his pathetic condition, conversely in a witty and sardonic mode, reassures the reader that "vitality never 'takes.' You have it or you haven't, like health or brown eyes or honor or a baritone voice."[71] That disparate sequence contains incorruptible elements as well as mutable ones, and Fitzgerald cunningly declares his intention to use his restorative talent, to draw on reserves of energy that regenerate each time he puts pencil to paper. The years 1934–35 were among the most difficult of his life, with the de facto end of his marriage, financial and health crises, and the decline of his productivity. The next two years would lead him into deeper depression and further anxieties over financial debts and the direction of his literary career. But *Tender Is the Night* remains as testimony to his extraordinary talent, and even during the nightmare years of "waste and horror," as he recounted in his 1934 essay "Sleeping and Waking," Fitzgerald retained an adamantine belief in his ability to recapture and renew through writing, for "irresistible, iridescent—here is Aurora—here is another day."[72]

NOTES

1. John Kuehl and Jackson R. Bryer, eds., *Dear Scott / Dear Max: The Fitzgerald–Perkins Correspondence* (New York: Charles Scribner's Sons, 1971), 189.

2. F. Scott Fitzgerald, "One Hundred False Starts," in *My Lost City: Personal Essays, 1920–1940*, ed. James L. W. West III, Cambridge Edition of the Works of F. Scott Fitzgerald (Cambridge: Cambridge University Press, 2014), 89.

3. F. Scott Fitzgerald, *The Letters of F. Scott Fitzgerald*, ed. Andrew Turnbull (New York: Charles Scribner's Sons, 1963), 488.

4. Kuehl and Bryer, *Dear Scott / Dear Max*, 189.

5. Kuehl and Bryer, *Dear Scott / Dear Max*, 193.

6. Kuehl and Bryer, *Dear Scott / Dear Max*, 193, 194.

7. Linda P. Miller, ed., *Letters from the Lost Generation: Gerald and Sara Murphy and Friends*, expanded ed. (Gainesville: University Press of Florida, 2002), 151.

8. Matthew J. Bruccoli, *Some Sort of Epic Grandeur: The Life of F. Scott Fitzgerald*, 2nd ed. (Columbia: University of South Carolina Press, 2002), 363.

9. Bruccoli, *Epic Grandeur*, 366, 363–64.

10. John Dos Passos, *The Best Times: An Informal Memoir* (New York: New American Library, 1966), 209–10.

11. F. Scott Fitzgerald, *A Life in Letters*, ed. Matthew J. Bruccoli (New York: Charles Scribner's Sons, 1994), 262–64.

12. Fitzgerald, *Letters*, 362.

13. Fitzgerald, *Life in Letters*, 279.

14. Jackson R. Bryer and Cathy W. Barks, eds., *Dear Scott, Dearest Zelda: The Love Letters of F. Scott and Zelda Fitzgerald*, with an introduction by Eleanor Lanahan (London: Bloomsbury, 2002), 184–85, 188, 190.

15. Bryer and Barks, *Dear Scott, Dearest Zelda*, 179, 196.

16. Bryer and Barks, *Dear Scott, Dearest Zelda*, 179.

17. Bryer and Barks, *Dear Scott, Dearest Zelda*, 196.

18. Bryer and Barks note two gaps in the Fitzgeralds' correspondence during 1934–35: "first from the fall of 1934 until February of 1935, during which Scott was allowed to make frequent visits to the hospital and Zelda was able to spend Christmas at home with Scott and Scottie, making letters unnecessary; and then again from the fall of 1935 to April 1936, when Zelda began alternating between a religious mania, during which she was often incoherent, and a depressive silence in which she spoke to no one." Bryer and Barks, *Dear Scott, Dearest Zelda*, 198.

19. Bryer and Barks, *Dear Scott, Dearest Zelda*, 200.

20. Bryer and Barks, *Dear Scott, Dearest Zelda*, 208, 208, 210.

21. "F. Scott Fitzgerald's Ledger, 1919–1938," Matthew J. and Arlyn Bruccoli Collection of F. Scott Fitzgerald, Irvin Department of Rare Books and Special Collections, University of South Carolina, 188. https://digital.library.sc.edu/collections/f-scott -fitzgeralds-ledger-1919-1938.

22. Bryer and Barks, *Dear Scott, Dearest Zelda*, 195.

23. Bryer and Barks, *Dear Scott, Dearest Zelda*, 212.

24. Bryer and Barks, *Dear Scott, Dearest Zelda*, 214.

25. Bryer and Barks, *Dear Scott, Dearest Zelda*, 197.

26. Fitzgerald, *Life in Letters*, 290–91.

27. See Laura Guthrie Hearne's diary account of this episode in the period June to September 1935: Hearne, "A Summer with F. Scott Fitzgerald," *Esquire*, December 1, 1964,

28. Besides the summer dalliance with Beatrice Dance, Fitzgerald is reported to have sought out a prostitute in Asheville. Tony Buttitta, *The Lost Summer: A Personal Memoir of F. Scott Fitzgerald* (London: Robson Books, 1974), 111–16. And he wrote to both Perkins and Ober about visiting a woman in New York: "—it's a long peculiar story (. . . —one of the curious series of relationships that run thru a man's life)." Kuehl and Bryer, *Dear Scott / Dear Max*, 224; Fitzgerald, *Letters*, 398; Scott Donaldson, *Fool for Love: F. Scott Fitzgerald* (New York: St. Martin's Press, 1983), chapter. 10.

29. Kuehl and Bryer, *Dear Scott / Dear Max*, 202.

30. Kuehl and Bryer, *Dear Scott / Dear Max*, 183.

31. Kuehl and Bryer, *Dear Scott / Dear Max*, 210; Bruccoli, *Epic Grandeur*, 386–88.

32. Kuehl and Bryer, *Dear Scott / Dear Max*, 205–6.

33. Kuehl and Bryer, *Dear Scott / Dear Max*, 206.

34. Kuehl and Bryer, *Dear Scott / Dear Max*, 206. In an August 23, 1934, letter to Perkins, Fitzgerald claimed to have reduced his debts from twenty thousand dollars during the final work on *Tender Is the Night* to two or three thousand dollars.

35. Kuehl and Bryer, *Dear Scott / Dear Max*, 210.

36. Kuehl and Bryer, *Dear Scott / Dear Max*, 207; James L. West III, introduction

to *Taps at Reveille,* ed. James L. W. West III, Cambridge Edition of the Works of F. Scott Fitzgerald (Cambridge: Cambridge University Press, 2014), xv.

37. Fitzgerald, *Life in Letters,* 284.

38. James L. West III, "F. Scott Fitzgerald, Professional Author," in *A Historical Guide to F. Scott Fitzgerald,* ed. Kirk Curnutt (Oxford: Oxford University Press, 2004), 59.

39. The three first published were "In the Darkest Hour" (October 1934), "The Count of Darkness" (June 1935), and "The Kingdom of the Dark" (August 1935). The fourth story, "Gods of Darkness," was published posthumously by *Redbook* in November 1941.

40. Kuehl and Bryer, *Dear Scott / Dear Max,* 214.

41. Bruccoli, *Epic Grandeur,* 383.

42. F. Scott Fitzgerald, "In the Darkest Hour," in *The Price Was High: The Last Uncollected Stories of F. Scott Fitzgerald,* ed. Matthew J. Bruccoli (New York: Harcourt Brace Jovanovich / Bruccoli Clark, 1979), 514.

43. Fitzgerald, "In the Darkest Hour," 516, 517, 518.

44. Fitzgerald, "In the Darkest Hour," 514.

45. Kuehl and Bryer, *Dear Scott / Dear Max,* 209.

46. Kuehl and Bryer, *Dear Scott / Dear Max,* 225, 229–30, 251, 253–54.

47. Bruccoli, *Epic Grandeur,* 397.

48. "*Esquire* holds up beautifully but my dog story was rotten," he admitted to Gingrich. Fitzgerald, *Letters,* 524. Bruccoli suggests that the story could have been a parody of Hemingway. Bruccoli, *Epic Grandeur,* 397. Fitzgerald would have known of other literary canines, such as Virginia Woolf's *Flush* (1933), a biography of Elizabeth Barrett Browning's cocker spaniel, and Edith Wharton's short story "Kerfol" (published in *Scribner's Magazine,* 1916), involving some ghost dogs.

49. "The Intimate Strangers" is the only text from 1934–35 that Ruth Prigozy references in her study of Fitzgerald's short stories of the 1930s. While sympathetic to its focus on marriage and individual selfhood, she also criticizes the unexciting narrative, uninteresting settings, confused plot, wooden characters, and clichéd expression. Ruth Prigozy, "Fitzgerald's Short Stories and the Depression: An Artistic Crisis," in *The Short Stories of F. Scott Fitzgerald: New Approaches in Criticism,* ed. Jackson R. Bryer (Madison: University of Wisconsin Press, 1982), 115.

50. *Christus Consolator* ("Divine Healer") is a copy of the 1833 work by the Danish sculptor Bertel Thorvaldsen.

51. A year earlier, Ober had complained, "Lately when you have wired me that a story would be sent on a certain date I have no faith at all that it will come." Matthew J. Bruccoli, ed., *As Ever, Scott Fitz—: Letters between F. Scott Fitzgerald and His Literary Agent Harold Ober, 1919–1940,* with the assistance of Jennifer McCabe Atkinson (Philadelphia: J. B. Lippincott, 1972), 206.

52. A fourth Gwen story, "A Full Life," was written in 1937 but not published until 2017.

53. Many of Fitzgerald's previously unpublished or difficult-to-find short stories were recently collected in Fitzgerald, *A Change of Class,* ed. James L. W. West III, Cambridge Edition of the Works of F. Scott Fitzgerald (Cambridge: Cambridge University Press, 2022); Fitzgerald, *Last Kiss,* ed. James L. W. West III, Cambridge Edition of the Works of F. Scott Fitzgerald (Cambridge: Cambridge University

Press, 2022); and Fitzgerald, *I'd Die for You, and Other Lost Stories,* edited by Anne Margaret Daniel (New York: Charles Scribner's Sons, 2017).

54. West succinctly describes the situation: "He tried to manufacture stories in his old bright manner for dependable outlets like the *Post* but found, to his dismay, that his knack for writing this kind of short fiction had deserted him." West, "Professional Author," 61.

55. Kuehl and Bryer, *Dear Scott / Dear Max,* 224.

56. Kuehl and Bryer, *Dear Scott / Dear Max,* 220.

57. Fitzgerald, *Life in Letters,* 283.

58. Fitzgerald, *Letters,* 521.

59. Fitzgerald, *Letters,* 523.

60. Fitzgerald, *Life in Letters,* 291.

61. Fitzgerald, *Letters,* 526. Julie M. Irwin, among others, notes the excessive beer intake, and she tabulates "between the years 1933 and 1937, Fitzgerald was hospitalized eight times for alcoholism and was arrested at least as often." Julie M. Irwin, "F. Scott Fitzgerald's Little Drinking Problem," *American Scholar* 56, no. 3 (Summer 1987): 426–27. See also Donaldson, *Fool for Love,* chapter 10, "Demon Drink." John T. Irwin theorizes that Fitzgerald developed a social persona that could excuse his behavior when drunk, a persona that allowed him to gather material for his real self, "the serious writer with high artistic standards whose genre was the modern novel of manners." Irwin, *F. Scott Fitzgerald's Fiction: "An Almost Theatrical Innocence"* (Baltimore: The Johns Hopkins University Press, 2014), 122.

62. Fitzgerald, *Letters,* 259.

63. Bruccoli, *Epic Grandeur,* 398.

64. Bruccoli uses "possibly" in his note for this letter in Fitzgerald, *Life in Letters* (292n1), but in his biography he concludes, "Here he wrote 'The Crack-Up.'" Bruccoli, *Epic Grandeur,* 400.

65. Fitzgerald, *Life in Letters,* 312.

66. U.S. Treasury Department, Bureau of Internal Revenue, *Statistics of Income for 1934,* part 1 (U.S. Government Printing Office, 1936), 59, www.irs.gov/pub/irs-soi/34soireppt1ar.pdf; U.S. Treasury Department, Bureau of Internal Revenue, *Statistics of Income for 1935,* part 1 (U.S. Government Printing Office, 1938), 73, www.irs.gov/pub/irs-soi/35soireppt1ar.pdf.

67. Simon Kuznets, *National Income, 1919–1935,* National Bureau of Economic Research, Bulletin 66, September 27, 1937, 2. Actually the amount was about $379 because the source has adjusted the figure in pre-Depression 1929 prices.

68. Bruccoli, *Epic Grandeur,* 387, 402, 412.

69. F. Scott Fitzgerald, "The Crack-Up," in *My Lost City,* 139–40.

70. Edward Gillin examines the ironic mode in the three "Crack-Up" essays, in contrast with earlier critical interpretations. Gillin, "Telling Truth Slant in the 'Crack-Up' Essays," *F. Scott Fitzgerald Review* 1 (2002): 158–76.

71. Fitzgerald, "The Crack-Up," 144.

72. F. Scott Fitzgerald, "Sleeping and Waking," in *My Lost City,* 167.

1936–1937

ELISABETH BOUZONVILLER

A Crack-Up in Life and Letters

The Fitzgeralds' life seemed to parallel the nation's postwar history of boom and depression. A fashionable couple in the spotlight during the 1920s after Scott's "early success," they approached the following decade in a much darker condition due to Zelda's nervous collapse and Scott's alcoholism, poor health, and financial and literary troubles. Nevertheless, in 1936–37, he still managed, despite adversity, to show signs of his "epic grandeur," whether through his writing, his caring for Zelda and Scottie, his working for Metro-Goldwyn-Mayer (MGM), or his relationship with Sheilah Graham.[1]

After some of his dark stories from 1935 had been repeatedly rejected by the magazines that had previously published him, Fitzgerald applied to *Esquire* for financial help, but the magazine's editor Arnold Gingrich answered that the accountants required proof of some kind of writing, and he advised Fitzgerald to

> put down anything that came into his head, as automatic writing in the Gertrude Stein manner, or that, if even that was beyond his powers of concentration, he simply copy out the same couple of sentences over and over, often enough to fill eight or ten pages, if only to say I can't write stories about young love for *The Saturday Evening Post*.[2]

This advice led to the "Crack-Up" series, which Romanian philosopher and essayist Emil Cioran has deemed the best achievement in Fitzgerald's literary career:

> Thus, Fitzgerald's admirers wish he had not dwelt at length on his failure and spoiled his literary career by insistently focusing on it and brooding over it. We, on the contrary, wish he had devoted himself more to it, we wish he had gone deeper into it to make the

most of it. Only second-rate minds cannot choose between literature and the "real dark night of the soul."[3]

Having fled cold Baltimore in November 1935, Fitzgerald settled at the Skyland Hotel in Hendersonville, North Carolina, where he started to write
the "Crack-Up" series, which was eventually published in the February,
March, and April 1936 issues of *Esquire*. From personal, literary, and financial despair there came three moving and thought-provoking essays,
"The Crack-Up," "Pasting It Together," and "Handle with Care," which,
in a letter to Gerald and Sara Murphy, he described as his "little trilogy."[4]

In mid-December 1935, he left Hendersonville and was back in Baltimore trying to sort out his financial trouble and find new literary projects. On January 21, 1936, he wrote cautiously to his agent Harold Ober
about "The Crack-Up," which the latter had not seen before publication:
"If you read my piece in Esquire remember it was written last November
when things seemed at their very blackest."[5] Ober and editor Maxwell
Perkins considered at the time that this publication had damaged his
reputation. Fellow writers reacted even more negatively to this publication. In a letter, John Dos Passos exclaimed:

> Christ, man, how do you find time in the middle of the general
> conflagration to worry about all that stuff? If you don't want to
> do stuff on your own, why not get a reporting job somewhere. . . .
> We're living in one of the damndest tragic moments in history—
> if you want to go to pieces I think its absolutely o.k. but I think you
> ought to write a first rate novel about it (and you probably will)
> instead of spilling it in little pieces for Arnold Gingrich—.[6]

Hemingway did not get in touch with Fitzgerald; his last located letter to Fitzgerald dates back to December 21, 1935.[7] His comment on the
"Crack-Up" articles came indirectly in a letter from February 7, 1936, to
their common editor:

> Feel awfully about Scott. I tried to write to him once (wrote him
> several times) to cheer him up but he seems to almost take pride
> in his shamelessness of defeat. The Esquire pieces seem to me to be
> so miserable. There is another one comeing too. I always knew he

couldn't think—he never could—but he had a marvelous talent and the thing is to use it—not whine in public.[8]

In addition to this criticism, in August 1936 Hemingway included this notorious scornful remark in his short story "The Snows of Kilimanjaro":

The rich were dull and they drank too much or they played too much backgammon. They were dull and they were repetitious. He remembered poor Scott Fitzgerald and his romantic awe of them and how he had started a story once that began, "The very rich are different from you and me." And how someone had said to Scott, Yes they have more money. But that was not humorous to Scott. He thought they were a special glamorous race and when he found they weren't it wrecked him just as much as any other thing that wrecked him.[9]

As regards this scoffing episode (with its erroneous reference to Fitzgerald's "The Rich Boy"),[10] Perkins definitely supported Fitzgerald, as shown by a letter the former sent to the novelist from September 23, 1936:

As for what Ernest did, I resented it, and when it comes to book publication, I shall have it out with him. It is odd about it too because I was present when the reference was made to the rich, and the retort given, and you [Fitzgerald] were many miles away.[11]

Bruccoli explains, indeed, how Hemingway was actually the one who was silenced, by Mary Colum, in front of Perkins in 1936 with the sarcastic reply that was eventually used at Fitzgerald's expense in the short story.[12]

Aggrieved by this taunt and by the general reception of the "Crack-Up" series, Fitzgerald reacted with bitter humor in an August 1936 letter to Hemingway that clearly refers to the "trilogy": "Please lay off me in print. If I choose to write *de profundis* sometimes it doesn't mean I want friends praying aloud over my corpse."[13] Written in the first person and referring to Fitzgerald's "emotional bankruptcy,"[14] the "trilogy" was an autobiographical undertaking that drew harsh criticism from those who disliked what they considered an exercise in self-pity. Fitzgerald had anticipated that reaction in "Pasting It Together," where he remarked, "There are always those to whom all self-revelation is contemptible."[15]

In addition to his personal collapse due to a mixture of illness, alcoholism, and depression, the "Crack-Up" articles focus on his inability to write, a crucial topic to Fitzgerald during these years and one that he also dealt with in his following *Esquire* publications: "Author's House" in July 1936, "Afternoon of an Author" in August 1936, and, eventually, "Financing Finnegan" in January 1938, after it had been refused by the *Saturday Evening Post*.[16] All three stories could be summed up by his autobiographical comment from "Who's Who and Why": "The history of my life is the history of the struggle between an overwhelming urge to write and a combination of circumstances bent on keeping me from it."[17]

Apart from making lists, "hundreds of lists,"[18] the narrator from "The Crack-Up" does not write any more; he can only moan the fading "power of the written word subordinate to another power, a more glittering, a grosser power"[19]—Hollywood's, which would nevertheless provide him with a solution to his financial problems in July 1937. This loss of writing skills is even more emphasized in the short stories, although their autobiographical aspect is subtler. Unlike the essays of the "Crack-Up" trilogy, "Afternoon of an Author" relies on a third-person narrator, but the internal focalizer is the "author" of the title. Mary Jo Tate notices that "Fitzgerald was undecided as to whether [to] classify this piece as nonfiction or a story," which implies that there is an autobiographical aspect mixed with fiction.[20] In "Author's House," the narrator interviews "the author" and follows him in his house, from cellar to attic and tower, an allegorical reference to everything that influenced Fitzgerald from infancy to adulthood and success. The writer makes it clear that he does not live at the top of the house any longer, and so one feels the sense of a fall. In "Afternoon of an Author," the time reference of the title is obviously a metaphor for the writer's declining career, and one of the last direct-speech passages of the story is imbued with humorous self-deprecation, as the narrator (who is actually Fitzgerald's double) has been unable to write anything lately:

> "The residence of the successful writer," he said to himself. "I wonder what marvelous books he's tearing off up there. It must be great to have a gift like that—just sit down with pencil and paper. Work when you want—go where you please."[21]

From the beginning to the end, the narrative evokes the author's past writing, contrasting it with his present absence of results. Even the projects that are mentioned seem to be doomed to failure, given his lack of energy. During the one-day time frame of the story, he wanders aimlessly in town between two scenes displaying his lying down at home, he remembers his past literary success, and he hopes to find new inspiration, but the narrative clearly stages his inability to write:

> The problem was a magazine story that had become so thin in the middle that it was about to blow away. The plot was like climbing endless stairs, he had no element of surprise in reserve, and the characters who started so bravely day-before-yesterday couldn't have qualified for a newspaper serial.[22]

In "Financing Finnegan," the narrator, a failed writer, is witness to Finnegan's literary collapse, the onomastic Joycean connotation conjuring up an idea of disintegration and death.[23] Once again, the story is tainted with autobiographical overtones, and it can even be read as a short roman à clef with an imaginary twist at the end since the narrator's and Finnegan's common agent and publisher (Cannon and Jaggers) are obviously doubles of Harold Ober and Maxwell Perkins, while the initial of the writer's name points to Fitzgerald.[24] The recurring references to Finnegan's financial trouble and the broken shoulder due to a diving accident are also clear allusions to Fitzgerald's life.

The Phoenix of American Letters

Zelda's condition did not improve at the Sheppard and Enoch Pratt Hospital in Towson, Maryland, outside Baltimore. She seemed to become increasingly religious, so Fitzgerald had her transferred to Highland Hospital in Asheville, North Carolina, on April 8, 1936, and he stayed in Asheville from July to December at the Grove Park Inn. He broke his right shoulder in July in a diving accident (claiming, like the narrator in "Financing Finnegan," that his shoulder had broken before he hit the water).[25] He was placed in a body cast with his right arm elevated. This forced him to either dictate his texts or write on an overhead board. While in his cast, he also fell in the bathroom and developed arthritis from lying on the floor. Moreover, because his heavy drinking was troublesome to the other guests (reaching a climax when Fitzgerald fired a gun in a suicide attempt), the hotel required he stay with a nurse, Dorothy Richardson, who provided both company and drinking control. He also hired Martha Marie Shank, the owner of a local secretarial service, as a business manager to help with his work. During that time, among other texts, he dictated "Thumbs Up,"[26] a Civil War story inspired by his father's memories that would develop into "The End of Hate," which was published by *Collier's* in 1940 after thirteen refusals from other magazines and various requests for revision from *Collier's*.

In "Financing Finnegan," the author's decline is emphasized through the spectral flavor given to the character, who is never seen—he is only discussed by others as if he were already a ghost of himself. Throughout the story, the narrator hears about the author's literary potential and financial trouble, but he is also a recurrent witness to the latter's unfulfilled promises to their common agent and publisher. In "Afternoon of an Author," the writer's past literary success is mentioned, but he is now just recovering from a nameless illness echoing the nervous "crack" of the 1936 trilogy. Even if the sustained cracked-plate image conveys the writer's disintegration and self-centered pity, it is not devoid of self-irony. In fact, all these texts seem to offer what could be called an ironical *mise en abyme* of the writer's inability to write, since they ponder a difficulty that is precisely overcome by the creation of the texts themselves. Moreover, Finnegan may no longer write anything marketable, yet his life story itself, like Fitzgerald's, remains a source of interest and speculation, a narrative of its own. Eventually, his North Pole expedition is the climax of irony, as his agent and his editor, who thought they might profit by the money from his life insurance, see their expectations brought to naught by the sudden reappearance of Finnegan. His cablegram, sending his "greetings from the dead,"[27] is therefore the final ironical touch that contradicts the whole story's impression of faded glory. In the end, it is also proof that despite his own personal collapse and his friends' criticisms, Fitzgerald, like Finnegan, remained talented and keen on exploiting his literary skills.

After having harbored many reasons to despise Finnegan and dismiss him as hopeless, the narrator eventually reads one of his manuscripts and surrenders utterly to his writing power, which can be interpreted as wishful-thinking by Fitzgerald for himself:

It was a short story. I began it in a mood of disgust but before I'd
read five minutes I was completely immersed in it, utterly charmed,
utterly convinced and wishing to God I could write like that. When
Cannon finished his phone call I kept him waiting while I finished it
and when I did there were tears in these hard old professional eyes.
Any magazine in the country would have run it first in any issue.[28]

Thus, in these stories, the writers are not at the ends of their careers. The
North Pole, with its "snowstorm" and "ice and snow," seems to operate as
a kind of revitalizer for Finnegan, who reappears "from the dead."[29] It is
also a metaphor for the blank page, whose paralyzing powers may not last
forever. On this blank page of the Arctic North, Finnegan, Fitzgerald's
doppelgänger, defeats adversity and leaves his own marks, eventually re-
appearing with a written text, if only an ironical cablegram, followed by
a single "love story."[30]

Despite its pessimistic mood, one should remember that the "Crack-Up"
trilogy includes an article titled "Pasting It Together," which not only suggests recovery but insists, above all, on the writer's power to overcome
personal disaster through his literary activity, which is actually what was
taking place with the writing of the trilogy itself:

I must continue to be a writer because that was my only way of
life. . . . I have now at last become a writer only.[31]

With the "Crack-Up" articles and the following stories, Fitzgerald rose
from his literary ashes, "bringing back plenty greetings from the dead"
in the manner of Finnegan.[32] Thus, even if Fitzgerald dramatized his deteriorating emotional and literary condition, the "power of the written
word" was definitely back by early 1936,[33] even though it did not necessarily mean the end of his financial trouble.

"Hampered by So Many False Starts"[34]

Inspired by Zelda's ballet experience, Fitzgerald became involved in
writing a screenplay, "Ballet Shoes" or "Ballet Slippers," for ballerina
Olga Spessivtseva, as he had met her manager, L. G. Braun, in North
Africa in early 1930. In 1936, Braun was in the United States to arrange a

contract for her with Samuel Goldwyn. Ober was skeptical, as his letter to Fitzgerald from February 14, 1936, proves: "Now regarding this idea for a ballet picture. I read Mr. Braun's letter over carefully and it doesn't seem to me that he has anything very definite to offer you."[35] Eventually the project fell through, and only a two-page synopsis remains,[36] but the idea that Hollywood could be a way out of financial trouble was in the air. However, Fitzgerald was not ready yet for another stay in Hollywood after his last failed attempt there in 1931.

He considered various other projects, which would eventually be dropped. After the interest stirred by "The Crack-Up," in March 1936, he was approached by Simon and Schuster, who were interested in a volume of his *Esquire* autobiographical articles. Perkins, instead, suggested a "reminiscent book,—not autobiographical, but reminiscent" for Scribner's.[37] However, by June, both these projects were forgotten. In a letter from October 16, 1936, to Perkins, Fitzgerald evoked "a novel planned or rather . . . conceived," but he also had the foresight to conclude, "It may have to remain among the unwritten books of this world," and it was apparently forsaken indeed.[38]

Unlike his protagonist from "Afternoon of an Author," Fitzgerald was still writing fiction, but the *Saturday Evening Post* was reluctant to accept stories dealing with "dark and stark" topics.[39] He was adamant that his texts were not to be corrected against his will and that topics were not to be imposed on him, as had often been the case previously. In 1935 and 1936, he tried to launch the Gwen Bowers series of stories based on Scottie. The *Saturday Evening Post* published two of them, "Too Cute for Words" on April 18, 1936, and "Inside the House" on June 13, but it declined "The Pearl and the Fur" and "Make Yourself at Home," which were sold to the New York women's magazine *Pictorial Review* after revision. When *Pictorial Review* went out of business in 1939, neither story had yet been published. Eventually "Make Yourself at Home" was resold to *Liberty* and published as "Strange Sanctuary" on December 9, 1939.

In May 1936, Fitzgerald also imagined a series of stories based on the character of a nurse nicknamed Trouble, but the first one, "Cyclone in Silent Land," was refused by the *Saturday Evening Post* and had to wait eighty-one years to be published in the 2017 volume edited by Anne Margaret Daniel, *I'd Die for You, and Other Lost Stories*. The *Saturday Evening Post* reluctantly accepted the second nurse story, "Trouble," for which Fitzgerald was still paid the high price of two thousand dollars. Written in June 1936, it belatedly appeared in the issue of March 6, 1937, and would be Fitzgerald's last collaboration with the magazine. By the end of 1936, the *Post*'s editor George Horace Lorimer had retired and his successor, Wesley W. Stout, had no particular connection with Fitzgerald. Hence, seventeen years of collaboration, which had started with "Head and Shoulders" in the issue of February 21, 1920, and included the publication of sixty-five stories, came to an end. Fitzgerald's letter of June 5, 1936, to the *Post*'s fiction editor Adelaide W. Neall heralded the break and his new unyielding attitude after years of submission to the public's and editors' tastes in stories:

> I've decided to go on with the series of medical stories hoping to unearth something new—and as a beginning have decided to rewrite this story with the original as a skeleton. . . . I don't need criticism a bit—the critics are always wrong (including you!) but they are always right in the sense they make one re-examine one's artistic conscience.[40]

Thus, in 1936, three stories were sold to the *Saturday Evening Post,* and "Fate in Her Hands" and "Image on the Heart" were both published in April by, respectively, the *American* magazine and *McCall's,* but now Fitzgerald dealt mainly with *Esquire*: "Three Acts of Music," was published in May 1936, "The Ants at Princeton" in June, "An Author's Mother" in September, "I Didn't Get Over" in October, "Send Me In, Coach" in November, "An Alcoholic Case" in February 1937, "The Honor of the Goon" in June, "The Long Way Out" in September, "The Guest in Room Nineteen" in October, and "In the Holidays" in December.

Death and Despair in the Family

Between April and July 1936, having settled Zelda at Highland Hospital, Fitzgerald went back to Baltimore, partly because of his mother's poor health. Mollie McQuillan Fitzgerald suffered a stroke in June, and after painfully "going thru her things," Fitzgerald had to move her from the hotel where she had been living for "fifteen years" to a nursing home, as he explained to his sister Annabel.[41] When Mollie died in early September, he was unable to attend her funeral because of his broken shoulder. His filial love had always been discreet; however, Jeffrey Meyers quotes a few moving words supposedly addressed by Fitzgerald to his St. Paul friend Oscar Kalman, words that testify to a sense of loss more acute than he generally expressed:

> A most surprising thing in the death of a parent is not how little it affects you, but how much. When your Father or Mother has been morbidly perched on the edge of life, when they are gone, even though you have long ceased to have any dependence on them, there is a sense of being deserted.[42]

"An Author's Mother" was written shortly before Mollie's death and was published in *Esquire* in September. Just as in the case of "Afternoon of an Author," Fitzgerald failed to classify it as either a story or an article.[43] The fictional mother's son is "a successful author,"[44] but she is critical of his choice of a profession and of his literary style, which probably echoes Mollie's lack of understanding of Scott's achievements. Her ridiculous look is also a reminder of Mollie's careless, eccentric way of dressing, which embarrassed Scott, but her sudden lonely death seems to suggest a son's sense of guilt and effort at bridging the generational and intellectual gap. Bruccoli, in his introduction to the story in *The Price Was High,* mentions that Fitzgerald's mother "was proud of her only son, but it is doubtful whether she understood a word of what must have seemed to her his shockingly modern writing,"[45] hence Fitzgerald's declaration: "Mother and I never had anything in common except a relentless stubborn quality."[46] The story adopts the old mother's point of view and, without resorting to melodrama, presents her mixed feelings of attachment and solitude as she dwindles on the verge of death and fails to acknowledge any interest in her son's modernist writing. Fitzgerald's relationship with his mother had always been ambiguous, and his paradoxical feelings can be perceived in his semi-ironic remark in a letter from September 15, 1936, to Beatrice Dance (whom he had met in 1935 at the Grove Park Inn):

> By an irony which quite fits into the picture, the legacy which I received from my mother's death (after being too ill to go to her death bed or her funeral) is the luckiest event of some time. She was a

defiant old woman, defiant in her love for me in spite of my neglect of her, and it would have been quite within her character to have died that I might live.[47]

Despite his sometimes disordered life and shattered health, he remained committed to providing his family with the best, as he mentioned to Perkins in a letter dated October 16, 1936:

> Such stray ideas as sending my daughter to a public school, putting my wife in a public insane asylum, have been proposed to me by intimate friends, but it would break something in me that would shatter the very delicate pencil end of a point of view.[48]

His mother's death meant temporary financial relief, although, under Maryland law, he had to wait six months for his inheritance, which meant that in the meantime he was indebted to Scribner's, Ober, or Kalman. By the time he received his inheritance, he was left with only five thousand dollars, of which he spent seventy-five dollars on a 1927 Packard roadster that he kept in Asheville. In September 1936, he managed to obtain a reduction in the tuition fees at Ethel Walker School in Simsbury, Connecticut, so that Scottie could enter the school. This would be the end of their family life as, from then on, she would be mainly taken care of at schools and by friends during holidays. The Obers, in particular, would welcome her like foster parents in their home in Scarsdale, New York. Fitzgerald kept a keen eye on her education and behavior, providing endless advice, mostly through their correspondence, until the end of his life.

After the various blows to his morale in 1936, there came another one from the press. On his fortieth birthday, while he was sick and drinking, he had been interviewed at the Grove Park Inn by Michel Mok for the *New York Post*. The front-page article was published on September 25 under the title "The Other Side of Paradise, Scott Fitzgerald, 40, Engulfed in Despair, Broken in Health, He Spends Birthday Regretting That He Has Lost Faith in His Star." The portrait was dreadful, and when Fitzgerald learned that the story had been picked up by *Time* magazine, he greatly feared that Scottie might see it and be shocked. This disastrous publicity led him to swallow an overdose of morphine, which he vomited up immediately, as he explained in an early October letter of distress to Ober: "When that thing came it seemed about the end."[49]

Perkins was worried about Fitzgerald's depressive state and asked novelist Marjorie Kinnan Rawlings, who would become the 1938 Pulitzer
Prize winner for *The Yearling* and had herself fought depression, to see
him while she was in North Carolina. They met in Asheville and she
reported about their meeting in a letter to Perkins on October 26, 1936.
Later she wrote to Arthur Mizener on March 18, 1948:

> He was exhilarated. He talked of his own work. He was modest,
> but he was *sure*. He said that he had made an ass of himself, that his
> broken bone was the result of his having tried to "show off" in front
> of "debutantes" when he dived proudly into a swimming-pool, that
> he had gone astray with his writing, but was ready to go back to it
> in full force.[50]

They had a pleasant evening, although apparently Fitzgerald ordered quite
a lot of alcohol to be up to the situation. His drinking was certainly not
under control when he went back to Baltimore in December to give a tea
dance for Scottie, at which he was drunk and unpleasant. This led him to
spend the Christmas holidays at the Johns Hopkins Hospital to sober up
and cure his flu.

In January 1937, he stayed at the Oak Hall Hotel in Tryon, North
Carolina, trying to write and get published to earn a living. But the
high-paying magazines were no longer interested in him. Apart from
the stories mentioned above, he sold the autobiographical article "Early
Success" to *American Cavalcade,* where it was published in October.
It is a very fine nostalgic analysis of his early literary career entangled
with his personal life in the national frame of the gorgeous Roaring
Twenties that were doomed to be succeeded by the Great Depression of
the 1930s.

The year 1936 had ended poorly in terms of health and finances for
Fitzgerald, and his prospects were no better at the dawn of 1937. In his
letter of October 16, 1936, to Perkins, he had raised two alternatives:

> The present plan as near as I have formulated it, seems to go on
> with this endless Post writing or else go to Hollywood again. Each
> time I have gone to Hollywood, in spite of the enormous salary,
> has really set me back financially and artistically.[51]

F. Scott Fitzgerald,
June 4, 1937.
Photograph by
Carl Van Vechten.

Since publishing with the *Post* came to an end with "Trouble," the remaining alternative was the dream factory, or rather, in Fitzgerald's words, the "mining town in lotus land,"[52] with its good salaries and pitiless treatment of screenwriters, who felt they worked at "the salt mines," as William Faulkner complained.[53]

"En Route to Hollywood"[54]

MGM story editor Edwin Knopf had met Fitzgerald in France; he had even written the plot for King Vidor's *The Wedding Night* (1935), initially entitled "Broken Soil," a movie starring Gary Cooper and Anna Sten, inspired by Fitzgerald's novelist life. Hearing about the latter's personal and financial trouble, Knopf was keen on hiring him at MGM. In a letter from August 26, 1936, Ober explained:

> I had a long talk today with Knopf who is interested in having you go to Hollywood for Metro and I think I have convinced him that you would do a good job and that they need not worry about you. Knopf is going back to Hollywood tomorrow and will go into the matter again and let me know what is decided.[55]

Knopf had to convince Louis B. Mayer, Sam Katz, and Eddie Mannix, the studio executives, which was not easy because they were not impressed by, or even aware of, Fitzgerald's literary reputation.[56]

In May 1937 Fitzgerald took Zelda to Myrtle Beach, South Carolina, on a holiday, and then he met Hemingway briefly on June 4 in Carnegie Hall in New York at the American Writers' Congress when Hemingway gave a speech against fascism. He was back in New York later in June to be interviewed by Knopf, as MGM recalled his former unproductive stay and feared his alcoholism. The executives had made an offer, which H. N. Swanson, Ober's associate in Hollywood, had considered far too low to forward, but in his financial distress, Fitzgerald accepted the thousand-dollar-a-week contract (which was actually a good one compared to Faulkner's three hundred dollars a week in the 1940s, for example). His July letter to Scottie is headed "[En route to Hollywood]," as he had been hired for six months. The letter reveals his hopes and fears: "I feel a certain excitement. The third Hollywood venture. Two failures behind me though one no fault of mine."[57]

Ober had organized his accommodation at the Garden of Allah, 8152 Sunset Boulevard, where he shared a two-story stucco bungalow with screenwriter Edwin Justus Mayer. Other friends and well-known figures lived close by: John O'Hara, Dorothy Parker and her husband Alan Campbell, Marc Connelly and Robert Benchley. Fitzgerald bought a 1934 Ford coupe to drive to the MGM studios in Culver City. He started his new job on July 12, in an office on the third floor of the Thalberg building, where working days lasted from around 9 a.m. until 6 p.m. On that same day, he also went to Fredric March's place to see *The Spanish Earth,* a film written by Hemingway and Dos Passos to support the Republican cause, but Fitzgerald and Hemingway do not seem to have actually talked, and this was the last time Fitzgerald saw him. The following day, Fitzgerald sent him a wire to praise the movie.

Irving Thalberg, who had hired Fitzgerald in 1931 as a screenwriter for the film *Red-Headed Woman,* had died in 1936, but the studios retained his style, which involved expensive, high-quality movies but also mass-produced scripts at the expense of screenwriters who were used simultaneously or successively on one project for better results. Fitzgerald's first assignment was *A Yank at Oxford,* a comedy starring Robert Taylor and Maureen O'Sullivan. A veteran MGM screenwriter, Frank "Spig" Wead, had been first on the project, which fell to Fitzgerald on his arrival, as he was considered an expert on students, given the success of *This Side of Paradise.* He was lucky not to be assigned a collaborator, but eventually the scenario was entrusted to Malcolm Stuart Boylan and Walter Ferris, and George Oppenheimer put the finishing touch to it. His work did not earn him a screen credit, as would often be the case in the years to come.

Relying heavily on Coca-Cola during the day, chloral and Nembutal before sleep, to which he added digitalin for his heart later on, he tried to do seriously a job that was intended to help him out of his financial difficulty but that had never been his first choice. In an early July letter to Perkins, he wrote, "Everyone is very nice to me, surprised and rather relieved that I don't drink. I am happier than I've been for several years."[58] However, on July 26, 1937, despite the glamour of the place, he complained to Ober's wife:

> I have seen Hollywood—talked with Taylor, dined with March,
> danced with Ginger Rogers (this will burn Scottie up but it's
> true), been in Rosalind Russel's dressing room, wise-cracked with
> Montgomery, drunk (ginger-ale) with Zukor and Lasky, lunched
> alone with Maureen O'Sullivan, watched Crawford act, and lost
> my heart to a beautiful half-caste Chinese girl whose name I have
> forgotten. . . . And this is to say I'm through. From now on I go
> nowhere and see no one because the work is hard as hell, at least
> for me, and I've lost ten pounds.[59]

Sheilah Graham, "A Woman with a Past"[60]

Nevertheless, Fitzgerald's stay in Hollywood was not only hard, frustrating work. Shortly after his arrival, on July 14, 1937, Robert Benchley organized

Sheilah Graham in 1936

a party at his bungalow to celebrate the engagement of twenty-eight-year-old movie columnist Sheilah Graham and the Marquess of Donegall. Born Lily Shiel in Leeds, England, Graham had been placed at age six in the Jews Hospital and Orphan Asylum in London by her poor, widowed mother, and at eighteen she had married John Graham Gillam. A showgirl and freelance writer in London, she had eventually emigrated to the United States in 1933 and divorced in June 1937. That year, she earned $160 a week for her daily "Hollywood Today" columns and her Saturday article. Fitzgerald first saw her at Benchley's, although they did not have the opportunity to speak. To her, he embodied the already faded Roaring Twenties and their flappers: "In SHEILAH GRAHAM SAYS, when I wanted to chide women for silly behavior, I described them as passé, as old-fashioned F. Scott Fitzgerald types, though I had never read anything he wrote."[61] In *Beloved Infidel*, she romantically recalls a first fugitive vision of the novelist,[62] in the style of Nick Carraway's description of Gatsby's evanescent apparition at the end of chapter 1.[63] To him, she resembled Zelda in her young days and he first mistook her for an actress. After this visual encounter, which inspired Kathleen Moore and Monroe Stahr's first meeting in *The Last Tycoon*, a mix-up occurred that also found echoes in the novel.[64] Fitzgerald, who had left the party, was induced to come back after a phone conversation with Benchley, who had said a blonde actress was still there, but when he arrived, Fitzgerald discovered this actress was Tala Birell; Sheilah had already left.

Scott and Sheilah met briefly a second time at the Screen Writers' Guild dinner dance on July 22 at the Ambassador Hotel where he was Dorothy Parker's guest, while she had been invited by Marc Connolly. In *Beloved Infidel*, Graham recalls their first exchange: "Then he leaned forward and said, smiling across the two tables 'I like you.' I was pleased. Smiling, I said to him, 'I like you, too.'"[65] In *Intimate Lies*, reporting this conversation, Graham's son speculates that this must have felt bold to Fitzgerald as she was publicly engaged to Donegall.[66] Graham then describes a "smile that suddenly transfigured his face,"[67] and once again, this seems borrowed from *The Great Gatsby*.[68] They met next on July 24 when Eddie Mayer invited them for dinner. Since she was due to spend the evening with Jonah Ruddy, a correspondent for British papers, they made a party of four and went to the Clover Club. This time, they danced most of the evening together. Under the romantic effect of memory, Graham seems inspired again by Fitzgerald's third novel, as she becomes a kind of seductive Daisy for a mysterious Gatsby:

> It is hard to put into words how Scott Fitzgerald worked this magic, but he made me feel that to dance with me was the most

Scottie with Fred Astaire and Helen Hayes in 1937

extraordinary privilege for him. . . . He gave me the delightful feeling that hundreds of attractive men were just waiting for the chance to cut in on him and to snatch me away because I was so irresistible.[69]

They were supposed to have dinner together three days later, but he sent a telegram to cancel since Scottie was coming for a short visit with Helen Hayes, who was one of the Fitzgeralds' friends. Disappointed at the cancellation, Graham offered to join them anyway. The evening at the Cafe Trocadero, which also included two boys Scottie had known in the East, was uncomfortable for Fitzgerald, caught between his position as a father and his budding relationship with Graham, but once the young ones had been dropped off, he followed her to her apartment on Kings Road in Hollywood Hills, and presumably their intimacy started that night. Graham's recollections in her various autobiographies are in conflict with certain dates ascertained by Bruccoli;[70] nevertheless, whatever the date, it seems that they became involved after the Trocadero evening. As for teenage Scottie, she had an exciting Hollywood visit, as her father, despite regular lectures about her behavior, organized meetings for her with stars like Fred Astaire, Joan Crawford, and Norma Shearer.

Graham gave up on the idea of marrying Lord Donegall, although he had sent a cablegram from England to announce that his mother had finally agreed to the match. Graham and Fitzgerald were now involved in a relationship that led her to confess her past, which, to her surprise, did not put him off. He would even enthusiastically devise the "college of one" program to help her catch up with her limited educational background. Since he was still on the wagon, she did not imagine his own weaknesses at first. They met daily after work, when he visited in his coupe, as they kept their own separate accommodations.

Dream Factory or "Mining Town in Lotus Land"?

After *A Yank at Oxford,* Fitzgerald's new assignment was the screenplay for *Three Comrades,* a movie inspired by Erich Maria Remarque's war novel of the same name and produced by Joseph Mankiewicz, which would result, in 1938, in Fitzgerald's only screen credit. He managed to submit two-thirds of the script by the first week of September, when he left to visit Zelda and take her to Charleston with Scottie. On his return he was assigned a collaborator, E. E. Paramore, who was supposed to curb his novelistic tendencies and adapt his writing to Hollywood standards. By February 1, 1938, they had submitted six drafts, only to see Mankiewicz rewrite lines that did not suit him; "Joe thinks he's Shakespeare," Oppenheimer commented.[71] Correcting Fitzgerald was no sacrilege to him because he thought "Scott's dialogue lacked bite, color, rhythm."[72] What with the responsibility for Zelda's and Scottie's care, the anxieties linked to his new relationship with Graham, and a visit to California by now-divorced Ginevra King, Fitzgerald could not hold on to his sobriety resolutions and fell off the wagon by October.

Despite disappointments and tensions, in December his MGM contract was renewed and his salary increased by $250. He left in January for holidays with Zelda, which he sadly described to Scottie: "Your mother was better than ever I expected and our trip would have been fun except that I was tired. We went to Miami and Palm Beach, flew to Montgomery, all of which sounds very gay and glamorous but wasn't particularly."[73] Back in Hollywood in early 1938, he had yet to transform his studio experience into the Pat Hobby stories and *The Last Tycoon,* calling on his knowledge of Hollywood and on his deepest emotions: "Taking things hard—from Genevra to Joe Mank—That's stamp that goes into my books so that people can read it blind like brail."[74]

NOTES

1. F. Scott Fitzgerald, *The Letters of F. Scott Fitzgerald*, ed. Andrew Turnbull (London: Bodley Head, 1964), 62.

2. Quoted in Matthew J. Bruccoli, *Some Sort of Epic Grandeur: The Life of F. Scott Fitzgerald* (London: Cardinal, 1991), 476.

3. Translated by the author from the original French: "Ainsi, les admirateurs de Fitzgerald déplorent qu'il se soit appesanti sur son échec, et qu'il ait, à force de s'y pencher et de le ruminer, gâché sa carrière littéraire. Nous déplorons, au contraire, qu'il ne lui ait pas voué assez de fidélité, qu'il ne l'ait pas suffisamment approfondi ni exploité. C'est d'un esprit de second ordre que de ne pouvoir choisir entre la littérature et la 'vraie nuit de l'âme.'" Emil Cioran, *Œuvres, exercices d'admiration* (Paris: Gallimard, 1995), 1618–19.

4. Fitzgerald, *Letters*, 425.

5. Matthew J. Bruccoli, *As Ever, Scott Fitz—: Letters between F. Scott Fitzgerald and His Literary Agent Harold Ober, 1919-1940*, with the assistance of Jennifer McCabe Atkinson (London: Woburn Press, 1973), 244.

6. Quoted in Bruccoli, *Epic Grandeur*, 478.

7. Matthew J. Bruccoli, *Fitzgerald and Hemingway: A Dangerous Friendship* (London: André Deutsch, 1995), 186–89.

8. Quoted in Bruccoli, *Fitzgerald and Hemingway*, 189.

9. Quoted in Bruccoli, *Epic Grandeur*, 486. Fitzgerald was mentioned in "The Snows of Kilimanjaro" in the August 1936 *Esquire* issue. He then put pressure on Perkins to have the text amended and his name removed. Thus, "Poor Scott Fitzgerald" became "poor Julian." Bruccoli, *Fitzgerald and Hemingway*, 199-200.

10. Actually, "The Rich Boy" does not begin with this sentence; we find it in the last paragraph of part one of the story: "Let me tell you about the very rich. They are different from you and me." "The Rich Boy," *Taps at Reveille*, ed. James L. W. West III, Cambridge Edition of the Works of F. Scott Fitzgerald (Cambridge: Cambridge University Press, 2014), 5.

11. John Kuehl and Jackson R. Bryer, eds., *Dear Scott / Dear Max: The Fitzgerald-Perkins Correspondence* (New York: Charles Scribner's Sons, 1971), 232.

12. Bruccoli, *Fitzgerald and Hemingway*, 191–92.

13. Fitzgerald, *Letters*, 311.

14. "Emotional Bankruptcy" is the title of a Fitzgerald short story published on August 15, 1931, in the *Saturday Evening Post*. See F. Scott Fitzgerald, "Emotional Bankruptcy," in *The Basil, Josephine, and Gwen Stories*, ed. James L. W. West III, Cambridge Edition of the Works of F. Scott Fitzgerald (Cambridge: Cambridge University Press, 2022).

15. F. Scott Fitzgerald, "Pasting It Together," in *My Lost City: Personal Essays, 1920-1940*, ed. James L. W. West III, Cambridge Edition of the Works of F. Scott Fitzgerald (Cambridge: Cambridge University Press, 2014), 145.

16. According to Philippe Jaworski, it is "an irony of fate" that "Afternoon of an Author" was published in the same August 1936 issue of *Esquire* as Hemingway's "The Snows of Kilimanjaro," which deals with "a dying writer's loss of integrity" and mocks Fitzgerald's statement in "The Rich Boy." F. Scott Fitzgerald, *Romans, nouvelles et récits de F. Scott Fitzgerald*, ed. and trans. Philippe Jaworski (Paris: Gallimard, Bibliothèque de la Pléiade, 2012), 1780.

17. F. Scott Fitzgerald, "Who's Who—and Why?," in *My Lost City*, 3.

18. F. Scott Fitzgerald, "The Crack-Up," in *My Lost City*, 141.

19. Fitzgerald, "Pasting It Together," 148.

20. Mary Jo Tate, *F. Scott Fitzgerald A to Z: The Essential Reference to His Life and Work* (New York: Facts on File, 1998), 2.

21. F. Scott Fitzgerald, "Afternoon of an Author," in *My Lost City*, 180.

22. Fitzgerald, "Afternoon of an Author," 176.

23. See F. Scott Fitzgerald, "Financing Finnegan," in *The Lost Decade: Short Stories from "Esquire," 1936–1941*, ed. James L. W. West III, Cambridge Edition of the Works of F. Scott Fitzgerald (Cambridge: Cambridge University Press, 2014), 50–58.

24. *F* for both Finnegan and Fitzgerald.

25. "You ought to hear Finnegan on the subject. . . . It seems he was in a run-down condition and just diving from the side of the pool . . . and he saw some young girls diving from the fifteen-foot board. He says he thought of his lost youth and went up to do the same and made a beautiful swan dive-but his shoulder broke while he was still in the air." Fitzgerald, "Financing Finnegan," 740–41.

26. F. Scott Fitzgerald, "Thumbs Up," in *I'd Die for You, and Other Lost Stories*, ed. Anne Margaret Daniel (New York, Charles Scribner's Sons, 2017), 159–86.

27. Fitzgerald, "Financing Finnegan," 58.

28. Fitzgerald, "Financing Finnegan," 54.

29. Fitzgerald, "Financing Finnegan," 55, 56, 58.

30. Fitzgerald, "Financing Finnegan," 58.

31. F. Scott Fitzgerald, "Handle with Care," in *My Lost City*, 151–53.

32. Fitzgerald, "Financing Finnegan," 58.

33. Fitzgerald, "Pasting It Together," 148.

34. F. Scott Fitzgerald, "One Hundred False Starts," in *My Lost City*, 90. In "One Hundred False Starts," published in the *Saturday Evening Post* on March 4, 1933, Fitzgerald portrays his experience as a writer struggling for results and relying on personal emotions as a starting point.

35. Bruccoli, *As Ever*, 253.

36. Fitzgerald, "Explanatory Notes," in *My Lost City*, 281.

37. Kuehl and Bryer, *Dear Scott / Dear Max*, 228.

38. Kuehl and Bryer, *Dear Scott / Dear Max*, 233, 234.

39. Fitzgerald, *I'd Die for You*, 119–36.

40. Quoted in Bruccoli, *Epic Grandeur*, 481.

41. Fitzgerald, *Letters*, 535.

42. Quoted in Jeffrey Meyers, *Scott Fitzgerald: A Biography* (London: Macmillan, 1994), 276.

43. Bruccoli, *Epic Grandeur*, 483.

44. F. Scott Fitzgerald, *The Price Was High: The Last Uncollected Stories of F. Scott Fitzgerald*, ed. Matthew J. Bruccoli (London: Pan Books, 1979), 736; Fitzgerald, "An Author's Mother," in *My Lost City*, 181.

45. Matthew J. Bruccoli, introduction to Fitzgerald, *Price Was High*, 360.

46. F. Scott Fitzgerald, *A Life in Letters*, ed. Matthew J. Bruccoli (New York: Charles Scribner's Sons, 1994), 306.

47. Fitzgerald, *Letters*, 541.

48. Kuehl and Bryer, *Dear Scott / Dear Max*, 234.

49. Bruccoli, *As Ever*, 282.

50. Quoted in Arthur Mizener, *The Far Side of Paradise: A Biography of F. Scott Fitzgerald* (New York: Avon Books, 1974), 287.

51. Kuehl and Bryer, *Dear Scott / Dear Max*, 233.

52. F. Scott Fitzgerald, "Selected Fitzgerald Working Notes: Facsimiles," in *The Love of the Last Tycoon: A Western*, ed. Matthew J. Bruccoli, Cambridge Edition of the Works of F. Scott Fitzgerald (Cambridge: Cambridge University Press, 1993), 199.

53. André Bleikasten, *William Faulkner: Une Vie en romans* (Paris: Aden, 2007), 340.

54. Fitzgerald, *Letters*, 16.

55. Bruccoli, *As Ever*, 279.

56. Aaron Latham, *Crazy Sundays: F. Scott Fitzgerald in Hollywood* (New York: Simon and Schuster, 1975), 99.

57. Fitzgerald, *Letters*, 16.

58. Fitzgerald, *Letters*, 274.

59. Fitzgerald, *Letters*, 552–53.

60. This is the title for one of Fitzgerald's short stories published on September 6, 1930, in the *Saturday Evening Post* (Fitzgerald, "A Woman with a Past," in *Basil, Josephine, and Gwen Stories*, 264–84).

61. Sheilah Graham and Gerold Frank, *Beloved Infidel* (New York: Bantam Books, 1962), 131.

62. Graham and Frank, *Beloved Infidel*, 131.

63. F. Scott Fitzgerald, *The Great Gatsby*, ed. Matthew J. Bruccoli, Cambridge Edition of the Works of F. Scott Fitzgerald (Cambridge: Cambridge University Press, 1991), 20.

64. Fitzgerald, *Love of the Last Tycoon*, chaps. 2, 3, and 4.

65. Graham and Frank, *Beloved Infidel*, 132.

66. Robert Westbrook, *Intimate Lies: F. Scott Fitzgerald and Sheilah Graham* (New York: HarperCollins, 1995), 98.

67. Graham and Frank, *Beloved Infidel*, 132.

68. Fitzgerald, *Great Gatsby*, 40.

69. Graham and Frank, *Beloved Infidel*, 133–34.

70. Bruccoli, *Epic Grandeur*, 509.

71. Quoted in Latham, *Crazy Sundays*, 118.

72. Quoted in Latham, *Crazy Sundays*, 121.

73. Fitzgerald, *Letters*, 22.

74. F. Scott Fitzgerald, *The Notebooks of F. Scott Fitzgerald*, ed. Matthew J. Bruccoli (New York: Harcourt Brace Jovanovich / Bruccoli Clark, 1978), 163.

# 1938–1939

Arne Lunde

Writers are just schmucks with Underwoods.

—Jack Warner

Fitzgerald made me think of a great sculptor who was hired to do a plumbing job. He did not know how to connect the fucking pipes.

—Billy Wilder

In the public imagination, Fitzgerald's final years in Hollywood (1937–40) have long been a cautionary fable about the destruction of a great and gifted artist by a crushing, profit-driven commercial system. From his heights of literary celebrity and wealth in the Jazz Age 1920s, Fitzgerald legendarily sank into financial desperation and the grind of studio hackwork in the Depression-era '30s in Los Angeles, ultimately dying broke and broken of a heart attack in Hollywood at age forty-four. Yet the arc of Fitzgerald's Hollywood period is a more complex one than the reigning mythology would have it.

Fitzgerald had two brief interludes in Hollywood before the late 1930s when Los Angeles became his adopted home city. In 1927, at the tail end of the silent era, he briefly stayed in Hollywood (along with Zelda) to write an original screenplay for a movie to be called "Lipstick." Although Fitzgerald was paid well by the First National Studio in Burbank, the project was subsequently canceled and never realized as a film. Following the Hollywood studios' conversion from silent to talking pictures (1927–30), he returned to Los Angeles in 1931. Fitzgerald worked at the Metro-Goldwyn-Mayer (MGM) studio in Culver City together with Marcel de Sano on a screenplay based on the Katharine Brush novel *Red-Headed Woman*. Although production head Irving Thalberg respected Fitzgerald's talent and standing, he ultimately replaced him on the project. Fitzgerald's drinking also became an embarrassment at a Sunday

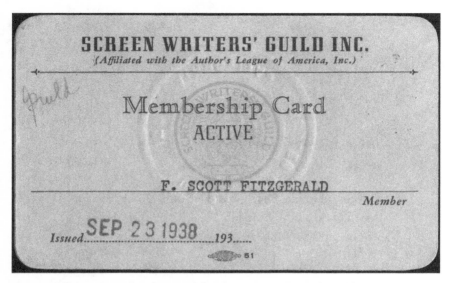

Fitzgerald's 1938 membership card for the Screen Writers' Guild

afternoon gathering of Hollywood royalty at the beach mansion of Thalberg and his movie-star wife, Norma Shearer. After a drink or two too many, the shy author from the East spontaneously plunked down at the piano and sang an amusing doggerel about a dog, a performance met with silent disbelief. Fitzgerald later recycled elements of the humiliating experience in his short story "Crazy Sunday."

His third and final sojourn in Hollywood lasted from 1937 until his death in December 1940. Deeply in debt, Fitzgerald accepted a lucrative six-month contract with MGM at one thousand dollars per week. Starting in July 1937, he lived at the fabled Garden of Allah bungalow colony on Sunset Boulevard near Crescent Heights Boulevard. The retired silent-era diva Alla Nazimova had subdivided her original estate into upscale courtyard bungalows clustered around a large swimming pool in the shape of the Russian-born actress's native Black Sea. Fitzgerald's neighbors included fellow literary luminaries from the East Coast such as Dorothy Parker, Robert Benchley, S. J. Perelman, and Ogden Nash. The Garden of Allah complex was demolished in 1959; a bank and its parking lot currently occupy the site.

Beginning in July 1937, Fitzgerald started work at MGM, the most prestigious studio in Hollywood but unfortunately the least amenable to screenwriters who were literary artists. Irving Thalberg (whom Fitzgerald would valorize as Monroe Stahr in *The Last Tycoon*) had died at age thirty-seven in September 1936. Any protection that Fitzgerald's talent and independence might have had under Thalberg was gone. MGM cofounder and studio chief Louis B. Mayer assumed full dominion over the studio. He and his closest associates doubled down on producer-driven, top-down control of this most corporate of Hollywood factory systems. Signing with MGM, Fitzgerald received a huge salary and the prestige of working at the Tiffany's of 1930s studios but, as he quickly came to learn, he would have virtually no freedom or independence as a writer.

Fitzgerald bought a used 1934 Ford to drive to work at MGM in Culver City. He also brought a briefcase full of bottles of Coca-Cola to work every day. His initial assignment was to revise and punch up dialogue for *A Yank at Oxford* (1938), starring Robert Taylor, Maureen O'Sullivan, and Vivien Leigh. The script had been nearly completed by Frank "Spig" Wead; the studio assigned Fitzgerald to add "collegiate gloss," and some of his dialogue remains in the finished film.

In July 1937, Fitzgerald first met Sheilah Graham, the woman who would famously become Fitzgerald's lover and muse until his death three and a half years later. Born Lily Shiel, the daughter of Ukrainian Jewish immigrants to Leeds, England, she was brought up in poverty in London's East End. A showgirl and then a journalist on Fleet Street, she reinvented herself as a British-accented high-society gossip columnist for the North American Newspaper Alliance. Graham's "Hollywood Today" column competed with Louella Parsons and Hedda Hopper in America's newspapers, with an added hint of British wit, snobbery, and snark. Robert Benchley had arranged an engagement party for her and her British noble fiancé the Marquess of Donegall on Bastille Day, July 14, 1937: this was when she first met Scott. The party began at her house high in the Hollywood Hills, and then moved down to the Garden of Allah on Sunset Boulevard. Needless to say, Sheilah never married the marquess.

Fitzgerald's second MGM assignment was *Three Comrades* (1938), the only film for which he received a writing credit on screen. The producer of *Three Comrades* was Joseph L. Mankiewicz. Mankiewicz was one of the most important writer–director–producers in studio-era Hollywood, winning multiple Oscars at his zenith for *A Letter to Three Wives* (1949) and *All about Eve* (1950) at Twentieth Century–Fox. When Fitzgerald arrived at MGM, Mankiewicz was one of Mayer's top lieutenants, a producer with a great deal of experience and knowledge of how the corporate

Fitzgerald and Sheilah Graham in Los Angeles

factory system model worked most efficiently. At this point, the major studios (MGM, Paramount Pictures, Warner Bros., Twentieth Century–Fox, and RKO Pictures) were releasing a new feature film nearly every week. This assembly-line system, rivaled only by General Motors and Ford and the auto industry in Detroit, was a hugely popular and lucrative American industry, selling celluloid dreams and global stars to the world.

Among a number of projects at MGM that Mankiewicz was supervising as a producer that year was an adaptation of Erich Maria Remarque's 1937 antiwar novel *Three Comrades*. Remarque, a German veteran of the horrors of trench warfare, had written the best-selling novel *All Quiet on the Western Front* (1929; translated from the original German text *Im Westen nichts Neues*). Carl Laemmle's Universal Pictures made a powerful film adaption of the novel in 1930, winning only the third Academy Award for Best Picture. Both the novel and the film were attacked savagely by Hitler's Brownshirt hooligans and propagandists, just a few years before the Third Reich came to power in January 1933.

The MGM screen adaptation of *Three Comrades* stars Robert Taylor, Franchot Tone, and Robert Young as three friends, veterans of World War I, now struggling to survive Germany's dire economy and the rise of the Nazis. Margaret Sullavan (who was Oscar-nominated for Best Actress) plays Taylor's tubercular wife. Fitzgerald's initial screenplay draft included several fanciful ideas, including inserting St. Peter and an

Movie poster for *Three Comrades*, 1938

angel into the grimly realistic narrative. Sullavan also complained that a great deal of her dialogue was unspeakable—that is, that it was awkwardly literary prose and not naturalistic speech. Mankiewicz assigned Edward E. Paramore, a more experienced screenwriter, to collaborate, an intrusion into Fitzgerald's creative independence that he resented bitterly. Mankiewicz, who also oversaw MGM's writing program for young writers (a program that included Waldo Salt) worked further on the

Fitzgerald's only screen credit

screenplay, as did his apprentices. While this multiple author / multiple draft process was intrinsic to the studio system of factory filmmaking, Fitzgerald perceived it as a personal and professional affront to his loner romanticism as the singular author of his writing and work.

When Mankiewicz starting rewriting some of Fitzgerald's dialogue and story ideas, the author poured his anger and frustrations into a letter to the producer that has been widely reproduced over the decades since. It reads in part:

> I guess all these years I've been kidding myself about being a good writer. . . . To say I'm disillusioned is putting it mildly. I had an entirely different conception of you. For nineteen years, with two years out for sickness, I've written best-selling entertainment, and my dialogue is supposedly right up at the top. But I learn from the script that you've suddenly decided it isn't good dialogue and you can take a few hours off and do much better.
>
> I think you now have a flop on your hands—as thoroughly naïve as "The Bride Wore Red" but utterly inexcusable because this time you *had* something and you arbitrarily and carelessly tore it to

pieces. . . . My God, Joe, you must be intelligent enough to see what you've done. . . . Oh, Joe, can't producers ever be wrong? I'm a good writer—honest. I thought you were going to play fair. Joan Crawford might as well play the part now, for the thing is as groggy with sentimentality as The Bride Wore Red, but the true emotion is gone.[1]

In letters to friends, Fitzgerald also privately nicknamed Mankiewicz "Monkeybitch." Mankiewicz also once commented, "If I go down at all in literary history in a footnote, it will be as the swine who rewrote F. Scott Fitzgerald."[2] As late as a 1969 interview Mankiewicz (on the set while directing *There Was a Crooked Man*) stated, "When I rewrote Scott's dialogue, people thought I was spitting on the flag."[3]

Mankiewicz and MGM were also dealing with fraught censorship, political, and financial issues with the *Three Comrades* project. Slowly, the anti-Nazi bite of the original novel was being compromised and watered down in efforts to protect the studio's crucial German export market. Fitzgerald had been adamant about preserving the source material of the original novel. As Kenneth Geist has written, "Fitzgerald was unwilling to relinquish the amiable whores, the futilely patriotic German Jews and the vicious proto-Nazis that populate Remarque's depression-era Berlin."[4] Much of the seedier material of the novel also had to be eliminated because of Hollywood's puritanical Production Code—self-censorship that had gone into effect July 1, 1934. Meanwhile, MGM was leery of offending Nazi Germany's export market and would not make a film critical of the Third Reich until 1940 (with *The Mortal Storm*) after that market was gone because of the outbreak in Europe of World War II.

Despite all the compromises Fitzgerald had endured, he had been given a coveted screen credit for *Three Comrades,* and the film was a commercial and critical success. He earned a renewal of this contract and a raise to $1,250 per week. His next project was "Infidelity," a screenplay based on an Ursula Parrot short story. The project (with Hunt Stromberg as producer) was intended as a vehicle for MGM star Joan Crawford, but the film's controversial adultery themes and censorship challenges led to its being dropped in May. Fitzgerald also worked on *Marie Antoinette* (1938) but received no screen credit. In April 1938, he rented a bungalow on the beach in Malibu, and then in October 1938 he moved to the San Fernando Valley, to a cottage on the Encino estate nicknamed "Belly

Acres" by its owner, character actor Edward Everett Horton. Fitzgerald paid two hundred dollars a month in rent. His home address was 5521 Amestoy Avenue—a site now occupied by the U.S. 101 freeway.

During the second half of 1938 Fitzgerald was assigned to work with director Sidney Franklin on Donald Ogden Stewart's script of *The Women,* based on Clare Boothe's play of the same name. Fitzgerald's dialogue was apparently not catty enough, and the studio replaced him with Anita Loos (the author of *Gentlemen Prefer Blondes*). In December, Scott's MGM contract was not renewed, although he had lasted eighteen months. In that time at MGM, he earned about eighty-five thousand dollars, but most of it went to pay Zelda's hospital bills, Scottie's Vassar tuition, and debts to friends. By all accounts, Fitzgerald took screenwriting very seriously and studiously. Writing longhand in pencil, he would create backstories for characters and produce copious treatments, drafts, and sketches before final polishes on dialogue. Yet Fitzgerald never quite mastered the art of screenwriting by committee inside such a formulaic popular-genre system, any more than the Coen brothers' Barton Fink could write a Wallace Beery wrestling picture. As Billy Wilder once quipped in 1930s Hollywood, "Fitzgerald made me think of a great sculptor who was hired to do a plumbing job. He did not know how to connect the fucking pipes."[5]

Following his release from MGM, Fitzgerald was a freelance writer again. In January 1939, he worked briefly for two weeks on David O. Selznick's *Gone with the Wind,* polishing one of the myriad versions of the script. Then, calamitously, in February he traveled east with screenwriter Budd Schulberg to do research at the Dartmouth Winter Carnival for a film project. Schulberg was born into the elite of silent-era Hollywood as the son of Paramount Pictures producer B. P. Schulberg. He later wrote the most cynically satirical of Hollywood novels, *What Makes Sammy Run?* (1941); was the Oscar-winning screenwriter of *On the Waterfront* (1954); and wrote the screenplay for Elia Kazan's *A Face in the Crowd* (1957). Schulberg was a recent Dartmouth alumnus, and producer Walter Wanger assigned Fitzgerald and Schulberg to develop a script based on the college's traditional Winter Carnival, insisting they both visit the real location and event. Fitzgerald, who was on the wagon, did not want to leave Los Angeles, but Wanger insisted he accompany Schulberg. To complicate matters, B. P. Schulberg presented his son and

Scott with two bottles of Mumm's champagne for the plane journey from Burbank to New York City.

It was the beginning of a drunken lost weekend. Fitzgerald sneaked out to a bar in New York, and more drinks were consumed on the Winter Carnival special train from Manhattan to Hanover. Fitzgerald's and Schulberg's drunken antics scandalized the college town and its festivities, ending with both of them being fired by Wanger. Scott had to be hospitalized in New York City, and news of the debacle further damaged Fitzgerald's name and employability in Hollywood. Following the Dartmouth fiasco in the spring of 1939, Fitzgerald drank heavily, fought with Sheilah, and took an ill-advised vacation trip with Zelda to Cuba, where he was beaten up for trying to stop a cockfight. That trip was also the last time he would ever see Zelda. More than a decade after Scott's death, Schulberg wrote a roman à clef, *The Disenchanted* (1951), with Fitzgerald as Manley Halliday and Budd as the twenty-five-year-old Shep. The novel gives us a psychological portrait of the beautiful wreck that was Fitzgerald in his final years in Los Angeles. Sheilah Graham was incensed by Schulberg's merciless portrayal, and she wrote her own mythologizing memoir about Scott's final years in *Beloved Infidel: The Education of a Woman* (1958), which was adapted by Twentieth Century–Fox into *Beloved Infidel* (1959), starring a badly miscast Gregory Peck as Scott and the always reliable Deborah Kerr as his dear "Sheilo."

In late 1938, while Fitzgerald was renting the white guest cottage down from the manor house on the Horton estate in the San Fernando Valley, he hired as a secretary-assistant the young Frances Kroll Ring, whose 1985 memoir *Against the Current: As I Remember F. Scott Fitzgerald* is one of the rare and intimate firsthand accounts of Fitzgerald in Hollywood. Kroll served as his secretary and confidante during the last twenty months of his life. She was only twenty years old (almost the same age as Scottie, who was at Vassar) when Scott hired her through Rusty's Employment Agency on Hollywood Boulevard. He was looking for a secretary who was not a Hollywood person or working for the studios in any capacity. He told her he was starting a new novel about the motion picture industry and wanted no word to leak out. Fitzgerald had a bed desk built for his antique bed, where he could write and edit with a thick pencil that he sharpened with a knife. Kroll recollects Scott's nonstop consumption of Gordon's gin and filtered Raleigh cigarettes. She also made weekly drives up to Sepulveda Canyon, where she dumped burlap sacks filled with his empty gin bottles into a ravine. She noted that among his other few indulgences were books and records.

After the guaranteed MGM contract lapsed, Fitzgerald was always on short-term contracts and piecework writing assignments from other studios. In August 1939, he took a one-week assignment at the Samuel Goldwyn Studios in Hollywood to rewrite some stale dialogue for *Raffles,* a David Niven film. He later had a stint at Twentieth Century–Fox to work on *The Light of Heart.*

In October 1939, Fitzgerald began work on his unfinished master-piece *The Love of the Last Tycoon: A Western.* And between November 1939 and July 1941, his seventeen Pat Hobby stories were published by Arnold Gingrich in *Esquire* magazine. In May 1940, Fitzgerald moved to Hollywood, to 1403 North Laurel Avenue, to avoid the long trek from the San Fernando Valley and to live only a block from Graham. In October 1940, he had his first heart attack, outside Schwab's Pharmacy on Sunset Boulevard (famously later used as a location in Billy Wilder's 1950 noir classic *Sunset Blvd.*). On December 21, 1940, Fitzgerald died of a second heart attack at Graham's apartment at 1443 North Hayworth Avenue. Allegedly, his last meal was at the nearby Greenblatt's Deli on Sunset. Fitzgerald's close friend Nathanael West died the very next day in a car crash.

Although Jackson R. Bryer covers Fitzgerald in 1940 in this volume expertly and thoroughly, I wish to add some final musings on Scott in Los Angeles beyond the 1938–39 time frame of this chapter. Fitzgerald's twin literary projects reveal the Hollywood studio system from the top down in *The Last Tycoon* and from the bottom up in the Pat Hobby stories. The unfinished *Tycoon* remains as tantalizing as Charles Dickens's partial and fragmentary last work *The Mystery of Edwin Drood.* What might have been had the author lived to complete it? The Hobby stories meantime chart the huge fissures between the silent-era Roaring Twenties and Depression-era talking thirties. Fitzgerald's semi-autobiographical Pat Hobby is a middle-aged, washed-up screenwriter whose heyday is a decade or more gone. Paralleling his fictional creation to an extent, Fitzgerald was accepting B-grade studio hackwork at Universal while also cranking out the Hobby stories for survival money.

The tight monthly deadlines for *Esquire* meant the stories were produced under duress, yet they coalesce into a larger collective literary work. These brilliant, martini-dry, satirical vignettes of the Hollywood studio system of the 1920s and '30s from the inside are as witty as the prose of Dorothy Parker and Robert Benchley, his friends and neighbors at the Garden of Allah.

With both Pat Hobby, Monroe Stahr, and the strange insular world they inhabit, Fitzgerald deconstructs the Hollywood system, particularly as personified by his main employer, MGM. Through Hobby's shameless (and somewhat misanthropic) audacity as a lowly writer and mere cog in the factory-system machine, Fitzgerald's stories expose and ridicule the fraught hierarchies of gender and class privilege and the way the most absurd gradations of status and importance are institutionally and socially policed at every moment. He reveals every minor locus of the dream-factory studio infrastructure—the main administration building (clearly modeled on the Thalberg building at MGM), the studio commissary (power-ranked tables and seating signaling everything), the barber shop, the shoeshine stand: the enclosed city within a city.

Yet beyond their satirical barbs and comic invention, the stories also show us a Pat Hobby in 1940 Hollywood now age forty-nine, looking backward nostalgically and mournfully to a lost glorious past, when he was a top writer in 1920s Hollywood. Pat remembers his Beverly Hills mansion, swimming pool, and big salary, all of it long gone for a writer now struggling week to week for any meager studio assignment at all. Hobby is often drunk at work or taking naps at his desk. He avoids real writing at any cost while inventing half-baked schemes to make a fast buck at the lot (or at the track), forever angling to scam another screen credit and renewed contract—delusional gambits always doomed to fail and boomerang back at this pathetic middle-aged wreck.

It is impossible to know if Billy Wilder was partly inspired by Fitzgerald and the Pat Hobby stories when he cowrote and directed *Sunset Blvd.* ten years later. Hobby anticipates in eerie ways Joe Gillis (William Holden), the sardonic out-of-work screenwriter whose better days are far behind him. To keep his car from being repossessed, Gillis hustles, grifts, and begs for studio writing work. Not unlike Gatsby, Gillis ultimately ends up full of bullet holes and floating dead in the swimming pool of Norma Desmond, a ghostly survivor of the fabulous, legendary lost 1920s of Hollywood.

Fitzgerald explored throughout his time in Hollywood and Los Angeles the question of whether or not creating art was possible within this commercial, industrial, star-based system of making movies. In the Hobby stories and in *The Last Tycoon* manuscripts, he exposes the 1930s Hollywood industry (with MGM as Exhibit A) as a profit-driven, hierarchical, corrupt American factory system. Fitzgerald shows Hollywood as just as powerful and prestigious as General Motors and Ford in Detroit, their rivals in producing mass-market dreams and commodities for America and the world. His American literary rivals had better luck in that system. William Faulkner mostly wrote collaboratively and under the protection of Howard Hawks as a producer–director, working on such screenplays as *The Big Sleep* (1945). Ernest Hemingway made a fortune selling book rights on his novels and short stories to Hollywood but never actually played the game of studio screenwriting. As his lower-tier screenwriter friend Nathanael West did with his own dark, corrosive, no-irish Hollywood novel *The Day of the Locust* (1939), Fitzgerald used his experiences in Los Angeles as the genesis of final acts of creation and redemption as a great writer. The Pat Hobby stories and *The Last Tycoon* (both executed as Scott was slowly dying in his early forties) remain testaments to his literary genius, his astonishing resilience, and his poetic gifts.

NOTES

1. F. Scott Fitzgerald to Joseph Mankiewicz, January 20, 1938, quoted in Matthew J. Bruccoli, afterword to *F. Scott Fitzgerald's Screenplay for* Three Comrades *by Erich Maria Remarque*, ed., with an afterword, by Matthew J. Bruccoli (Carbondale: Southern Illinois University Press, 1978), 263–64.

2. Quoted in John Wakeman, ed., "Mankiewicz, Joseph L.," *World Film Directors*, vol. 1, *1890–1945* (New York: H. W. Wilson, 1987), 716.

3. Quoted in Aaron Latham, *Crazy Sundays: F. Scott Fitzgerald in Hollywood* (New York: Viking, 1971), 123.

4. Kenneth L. Geist, *Pictures Will Talk: The Life and Films of Joseph L. Mankiewicz* (New York: Charles Scribner's Sons, 1978), 91.

5. Quoted in Gene D. Phillips, *Some Like It Wilder: The Life and Controversial Films of Billy Wilder* (Lexington: University Press of Kentucky, 2010), 16.

1940

Jackson R. Bryer

As F. Scott Fitzgerald entered the fifth decade of the twentieth century, and what would prove to be his final year, both his personal and professional lives were in turmoil. In the fall of 1939, he had completed an extensive synopsis and a draft of the first chapter of his new novel about Hollywood, centered on Monroe Stahr, a producer–director modeled on Irving Thalberg; but Kenneth Littauer of *Collier's* had declined to offer him an advance based on the synopsis and was dissatisfied with the six-thousand-word first chapter the author subsequently sent him, finding it "PRETTY CRYPTIC THEREFORE DISAPPOINTING."[1] Upon receiving Littauer's rejection, Fitzgerald told Maxwell Perkins to send the sample chapter to the *Saturday Evening Post*, but the *Post*, which had been so willing to publish his short fiction in the 1920s and early 1930s, "considered [it] too strong for the magazine," according to Matthew J. Bruccoli.[2] Earlier in the year, in July 1939, Fitzgerald had ended his almost twenty-year relationship with his literary agent, Harold Ober, because of Ober's refusal to continue advancing him money, and in December 1939, he also dismissed H. N. Swanson, Ober's associate who had been his Hollywood agent.

Arresting a Downward Spiral

The split with Swanson was largely due to Swanson's inability to get Fitzgerald the screenwriting work that had brought him to Hollywood in 1937, which had begun to diminish markedly, especially after his disastrous experience on *Winter Carnival* with Budd Schulberg in February 1939. He subsequently hired Leland Hayward to represent him in Hollywood. Fitzgerald had worked for a week on Samuel Goldwyn's *Raffles* in September 1939 before he was dismissed because of a disagreement with Goldwyn and director Sam Wood. Bouts of ill health, exacerbated by heavy drinking, further incapacitated him; and then, late in the year, depressed by his inability to make any progress on his novel and drinking heavily, he fought violently with Sheilah Graham, who terminated their relationship, plunging him further into a downward spiral.[3] As the new year began, Fitzgerald was at one of the lowest points in his life. He was without a meaningful romantic relationship; he was deeply in debt to his publisher and unable to obtain advances from his agent (his only source of income from his writing was the $250 per story he was receiving from *Esquire,* to which he was sending a series of short stories about Pat Hobby, an unsuccessful Hollywood scriptwriter); and, without any appreciable income source, he was having great difficulty providing much-needed financial support for his wife Zelda, who was institutionalized in North Carolina, and his daughter Scottie, who was at Vassar College in New York.

Although Matthew J. Bruccoli and Margaret M. Duggan date two apologetic letters Fitzgerald wrote to Graham to December 2, 1939, and "Early December 1939,"[4] according to Graham, her split from Fitzgerald lasted into early 1940. "It was pleasant, those first days of 1940," she writes in her autobiography, "to go out again with young men, to be once more a part of the movie colony."[5] Then, one night after she had been out with friends "for an evening of fun," Fitzgerald called and asked to see her the following day. The next day they drove to the top of Laurel Canyon and he declared, "I am going to stop drinking. I have made a promise to myself. Whether you come back to me or not, I will stop drinking. But I want you back—very much." She replied, "How do I know I can believe you. *Can* you stop drinking? Do you really mean it?" But after he assured her that he meant it and that she could "test" him, she "went back to him, and everything fell into place once more."[6] Graham maintains that Fitzgerald kept his pledge of abstinence; in *The Real F. Scott Fitzgerald: Thirty-Five Years Later,* she asserts that "from the end of November 1939 to December 21, 1940," he "stopped drinking."[7] Frances Kroll Ring, who had become his secretary-assistant in April 1939, later wrote that "the drinking was under control"; he "hadn't stopped completely" but "his consumption appeared to be minimal."[8]

After they were reconciled, in Graham's account:

> We lived very quietly. . . . At noon each day . . . Scott would come down to the pool and give me swimming lessons. While I floundered in the water, Scott, in a sweater and hat, coached me from the side, careful to keep out of the sun no matter how exasperated he grew. After lunch, we each went to our own rooms, Scott to

work . . . I to read steadily whatever book he had assigned me. . . .
After dinner we took long walks and Scott discussed with me in
detail what I had read. Or, in the evening, we sat like an old married couple on his balcony, sometimes not exchanging a word for
a long time.[9]

Also during this period, Graham says that she and Fitzgerald "drove
down to Tijuana for a day and, on an impulse, had a picture snapped of
us by a sidewalk photographer." It was, she adds, "the only photograph
we had ever had taken together."[10]

Fitzgerald's domestic life was now restored to normalcy, but his health
and professional life remained unsettled. According to Ring, "Early in
1940," he "suffered his first mild heart seizure. While trying to open a window, he raised his arms and felt a sharp stab of pain that took his breath
away. It was followed by a stiffness in the arms." Although his doctor assured him that it was not a heart attack, he "did worry about a recurrence."[11] He did not refer to this episode in any of his frequent letters to
his wife or daughter, probably because he did not want to worry the two
people who depended on him so completely for financial support. The
heart scare did, in Ring's words, intensify Fitzgerald's "hypochondria,"
demonstrated by the fact that he was "a chronic taker of temperature."[12]
This was evident in a spring 1940 letter to Gerald and Sara Murphy in
which he reported, "There were months with a high of 99.8, months at
99.6 and then up and down and a stabilization at 99.2 every afternoon
when I would write in bed."[13]

From Screenwriting to Short Stories and Back

Professionally, Fitzgerald's screenwriting career was at a standstill. In a
plaintive letter to Leland Hayward on January 16, after a deal to work on
the movie *Kitty Foyle* had not materialized, he asked Hayward to "find out
why I am in the doghouse," adding, "I have a strong intuition that all is
not well with my reputation and I'd like to know what is being said or not
said."[14] A little more than a month later, with no film work in sight, he left
Hayward's agency and went to the Berg–Allenberg Agency, where he was
thereafter represented by William Dozier, head of their story department.[15]

After he was unable to raise any advance money for his novel, Fitzgerald stopped working on it and concentrated on writing short stories

Graham and Fitzgerald in Tijuana in 1940

for *Esquire* and its editor Arnold Gingrich. In the first three months of 1940, he sent Gingrich six Pat Hobby stories, all of which *Esquire* eventually published, as well as two other stories, "Dearly Beloved" and "The Woman from 21," and a poem, "Beloved Infidel."[16] Fitzgerald was concerned that although *Esquire* was publishing so many of his stories, he nonetheless badly needed to continue to sell Gingrich additional pieces, so in a February 23 letter he proposed sending material to *Esquire* under "my nom de plume John Darcy."[17] When film and stage actor Edward Everett Horton approached Fitzgerald "with the idea of making the Pat Hobbys into a theatrical vehicle for him,"[18] Fitzgerald responded in a March 1 letter, "I'd be delighted if your eastern managers can hit on a playwrite who would be interested."[19] (At the time Fitzgerald was living in a rented cottage on Horton's Encino estate, nicknamed "Belly Acres.") When that didn't work out because "Horton's man . . . has gone on some other job and abandoned the notion," he convinced Frances Kroll's brother Nathan Kroll to try to dramatize the series, explaining in a May 6 letter that the stories were "characterized by a really bitter humor and only the explosive situations and the fact that Pat is a figure almost incapable of real tragedy or damage saves it from downright unpleasantness" and suggesting that a play "should attempt to preserve some of this flavor."[20] Kroll's efforts were not successful, but by this time Fitzgerald had, somewhat unexpectedly, received an offer to write a screenplay.

Unlike earlier assignments, this screenplay was to be based on one of his own stories. As early as January 25 he had written his daughter Scottie, "You have earned some money for me this week because I sold 'Babylon Revisited,' in which you are a character, to the pictures (the sum received wasn't worthy of the magnificent story—neither of you nor of me—however, I am accepting it)."[21] The sale had been to independent producer Lester Cowan, who bought the rights to Fitzgerald's story for one thousand dollars and paid him five hundred dollars a week to write the screenplay, which brought the total he was to receive to five thousand dollars.[22] From mid-April until late May or early June, he worked very hard and quite happily on this project,[23] writing Scottie on April 11 that he foresaw "three months of intense toil" and calling it "a swell flicker piece" in a May 4 letter to her and "a really brilliant continuity" in a May 11 letter to his wife;[24] he titled it "Cosmopolitan." Ring told Aaron Latham that "Cowan had intelligence . . . and Fitzgerald respected that. Cowan was very respectful, too; he had a sense of respect for Fitzgerald's talent."

Frances Kroll (Ring)

Most important, Fitzgerald "had complete control" over the screenplay, and because Cowan "always let him work at home," it "was very different from going to the studios."[25] Ring has described how Fitzgerald and Cowan worked together:

> Cowan would come over . . . every few days to thrash out the development of the scenario. They would talk for a couple of hours.

I would fix them a simple lunch—soup and a ham and cheese sandwich on toast—while they conferred. Then Cowan would leave and we would get to work.

The screenplay was an area of writing for which Scott abandoned his customary pencils. He preferred to dictate. Scott was the writer, the actor, the director. And he was a one-man show. He paced back and forth—more of a shuffle in his backless slippers. . . . As he paced, he talked, gave directions, grew animated, intense, sad, nervous.[26] . . .

. . . As soon as a segment was finished he would go over it and if he liked it would phone Cowan and read it to him. He would wave me over to the phone to watch his performance. Scott, looking like a matinee idol who had seen better days, would give such a touching portrayal Cowan would dissolve in tears at the other end of the line and Scott would cry at his end. After he hung up the phone, he would turn to me in a diabolical change of mood and tell me how good it felt to have wrung some tears out of a producer who was underpaying him.[27]

Personal and Professional Good News

About the time he began working on "Cosmopolitan," Fitzgerald received very good news from Asheville, North Carolina, where Zelda was institutionalized at Highland Hospital. Early in March, he received a letter from Robert S. Carroll, the psychiatrist in charge of her care, telling him that because Zelda had had an uneventful stay at her mother's home in Montgomery, Alabama, in December 1939, she would soon be released from Highland and allowed to live with her mother. On March 8, Fitzgerald informed his wife of Carroll's decision: "You can go to Montgomery the first of April and remain there indefinitely or as long as you seem able to carry on under your own esteem."[28] In her reply, she promised to "be very meticulous in my social conduct and . . . not to cause any trouble."[29] Zelda did well enough in Montgomery that she was able to have Scottie visit her there in June and September.

On May 26, Fitzgerald wrote Zelda, "This is the last day of the script and I'm pretty much all in";[30] on May 28, he wrote Cowan, telling him he was "going to lie up in Santa Barbara or Carmel for a week or ten days" and that "this is the best and final version of the 1st draft" of the screenplay, which he was then calling "Honoria" after the little girl in the story modeled on Scottie.[31] He also recommended movie actors that Cowan should consider for the lead roles in the film.[32] On June 7, he wrote Scottie, "I finished the picture and am doing a short story. Had intended to rest for a week, but there wasn't a chance," and on June 25, he sent Gingrich another Pat Hobby story, "Fun in an Artist's Studio."[33] Also in early June, he left Encino and moved to an apartment in Hollywood at 1403 North Laurel Avenue. He told both Zelda and Scottie that the move was so he could be "near my work,"[34] but the real reason probably was to be closer to Graham, who lived on the next street.[35] According to Graham, the apartment was on the third floor, "some of the neighbors were noisy, which harassed him, and the furniture was rather dreary— vomit green as he described the settee—but it was new and clean and there was a small open balcony adjoining the living room." Among his neighbors were actress Joyce Mathews—later to marry Milton Berle and then Billy Rose—and Lucille Ball, at the time being wooed by Desi Arnaz.[36] Also, at this time, *Collier's* published Fitzgerald's short story "The End of Hate" in its June 22 issue; as he pointed out in a letter to Scottie, he had actually started it in 1936 and "wrote it in intervals over the next couple of years," submitting the final version in June 1939.[37] "It seemed terrible to me," he told his daughter.[38]

Attempting to Get "Cosmopolitan" Produced

Although the screenplay was finished, there was no assurance that the film would be made unless stars could be found, especially for the role of the little girl. In a July letter to Zelda, Fitzgerald said that Cowan bought the rights to "Babylon Revisited" because he wanted to star Shirley Temple in "a romantic drama," since her most recent movies, in which they had "put everything . . .—song, dance, sleight of hand, etc.," had "fail[ed] to hold the crowd" and had been "rather nauseous" in their "sentimental- ity."[39] Accordingly, on July 11, he went to visit Temple and her mother in an attempt to interest her in doing the film. The next day, he reported on the meeting in a letter written to his wife:

> I spent a silly day yesterday with Shirley Temple and her family.
> They want to do the picture and they don't want to do the picture,
> but that's really the producer's worry and not mine. She's a lovely
> little girl, beautifully brought up and she hasn't quite reached the

difficult age yet—figuring the difficult age at twelve. She reminds me so much of Scottie in the last days at La Paix, just before she entered Bryn Mawr.[40]

An August letter to Cowan read in part:

> I was very impressed with the Temple kid—no trace of coyness or cuteness, yet a real dignity and gentleness. . . . If the personality that she has in private life could be carried *almost without heightening* over into the picture, I believe she would be perfect. . . . She is a perfect thing now in her way, and I would like to see that exquisite glow and tranquility carried intact through a sustained dramatic action. Whoever you get for the part would have to forget such old dodges as talking with tears in her voice, something that a well brought-up child wouldn't.[41]

Years later, Temple remembered Fitzgerald "as a kindly, thin and pale man, who was recovering from an illness. The thing that impressed me the most as an eleven or twelve-year-old was that he drank six or eight Coca-Colas during his visit. As a young girl, I thought this to be a stunning accomplishment—in fact I *still* do."[42] As negotiations continued, Fitzgerald tried to interest Garson Kanin at RKO Pictures (who had apparently read and admired the screenplay) in directing the film, writing him on August 23, "Your work is so fresh and new that I hope you will uncover material worthy of it."[43] Meanwhile, he kept revising, assuring Zelda on July 29, "If and when [Cowan] sells Mrs. Temple and Paramount the script there'll be a little more money," and telling her on August 10, "I'm finishing the Temple script tomorrow."[44] By September 14, he was writing her, "Paramount doesn't want to star Shirley Temple alone on the . . . picture and the producer can't find any big star who will play with her so we are temporarily held up."[45] As Latham puts it, although Fitzgerald's screenplay was never used, "Scott was spared knowing that he had failed once again" because he "died believing that his picture had a chance."[46]

While Fitzgerald was awaiting word from Cowan, he received an offer from Darryl F. Zanuck, the head of Twentieth Century–Fox. He wrote Zelda on August 24: "I think I have a pretty good job coming up next week—a possibility of ten weeks work and a fairly nice price."[47] The assignment, for which Latham says Fitzgerald was paid seven thousand dollars, was an adaptation of British dramatist Emlyn Williams's recent play *The Light of Heart*.[48] On August 30, he wrote Zelda, "It seems odd to be back in the studio again," adding, "There's a couch in my office and while they insist on your physical presence in the studio there are no peepholes they can look into and see whether I am lying down or not."[49] By September 21, he was telling her, "I don't know how this job is going. It may last two months—it may end in another week,"[50] but Latham contends that "the Zanuck people thought Scott's story was too gloomy" and the assignment was transferred to Nunnally Johnson, a writer whom, two years before, Fitzgerald had told, "Get out of Hollywood. It will ruin you. You have a talent—you'll kill it here."[51] Johnson's script was filmed and released as *Life Begins at Eight-Thirty* in 1942.[52] By October 11, after having attended a late September tea at Dorothy Parker's home, where, among others, he encountered actress Fay Wray and composer Deems Taylor, as well as "a younger generation" who made him feel "very passé," he was telling Zelda, "I expect to be back on my novel any day."[53]

The Novelist Returns to *The Last Tycoon*

It had been almost ten months since Fitzgerald had stopped working on his novel, but now he returned to it with as much energy as his precarious health permitted. On October 11, admitting to "weeks of fever and coughing," he wrote Zelda, "I don't suppose anyone will be much interested in what I have to say this time and it may be the last novel I'll ever write, but it must be done now because after fifty one is different." Determined to "finish my novel by the middle of December . . . I think of nothing else," he wrote her on October 19, adding, "My room is covered with charts like it used to be for 'Tender is the Night' telling the different movements of the characters and their histories." And on October 23, again to Zelda, "I am deep in the novel, living in it, and it makes me happy."[54] Throughout the rest of October and November, in his weekly letters to Zelda, he reported positively on his progress: October 26: "No news except I'm working hard, if that is news"; November 2: "The novel is hard as pulling teeth. . . . But later it should go faster"; November 9: "I'm still absorbed in the novel which is growing under my hand—not as deft a hand as I'd like but growing"; November 23: "It will . . . be nothing like anything else as I'm digging it out of myself like uranium—one ounce to the cubic ton of rejected ideas."[55]

Frances Kroll Ring described working with Fitzgerald during this period: "We established a routine. He turned out pages every day and I typed—first in triple-spaced drafts giving him ample room for making corrections, then retyping in double-space and then, likely as not, another retyping for the possible 'first' draft."[56] Sheilah Graham outlined in detail how he used material from her life with Fitzgerald in his new work, recalling that "it became a delightful game for me, waiting each night to hear more of the story Scott wove from us into the novel he hoped would restore him to his rightful place among his contemporaries."[57]

In late October, Fitzgerald received a copy of Ernest Hemingway's new novel, *For Whom the Bell Tolls,* inscribed, "To Scott with affection and esteem Ernest."[58] Fitzgerald's response depended on whom he was addressing. "It's a fine novel, better than anybody else writing can do," he wrote Hemingway on November 8, adding, "I read it with intense interest, participating in a lot of the writing problems as they came along and often quite unable to discover how you brought off some of the effects, but you always did."[59] But on October 26, he had written Zelda that he was "in the middle" of the book, noting, "It is not as good as the 'Farewell to Arms.' It doesn't seem to have the tensity or the freshness nor has it the inspired poetic moments. But I imagine it would please the average type of reader, the mind who used to enjoy Sinclair Lewis, more than anything he has written."[60] In his notebook, he wrote, "It is a thoroughly superficial book which has all the profundity of Rebecca."[61] And in a telephone conversation with Budd Schulberg, he "talked 'for anyway forty minutes' about the 'dreadful' depiction of Maria and the love interest" in it.[62]

Health Problems Recur

Fitzgerald's health continued to decline; he wrote Zelda that he often spent most of his time "in bed where I write on a wooden desk that I had made a year and a half ago."[63] Ring recalled that "just when Scott was working at his best, he began to have warnings—recurrent spells of dizziness. I never witnessed them, but he would describe to me how he would stand up and suddenly have to grab for some support."[64] After his doctor prescribed bed rest and because his apartment required climbing stairs, he moved in with Graham in her first-floor apartment. It was, according to Ring, "a temporary arrangement" because Graham "used her apartment for an office, and had a full-time secretary"—so "the household was busier than Scott was accustomed to." He asked Ring to find him another place in the neighborhood, and she found him "a charming walk-in bungalow on Fountain Avenue, nicely furnished, that would be available after the first of the year." He signed the lease, and they began to pack his books and papers for the move.[65]

Another reason for the move to Graham's apartment was an incident that occurred in late November. Fitzgerald had gone to Schwab's Pharmacy for cigarettes, and when he returned, as Graham describes, he was "gray and trembling" as he lowered "himself slowly into his easy chair." When she asked what had happened, he replied, "I almost fainted at Schwab's. Everything started to fade. I think I'd better see Dr. Wilson in the morning." The next morning he drove to the doctor's office and reported on his return that he had had "a cardiac spasm" rather than a heart attack. While Dr. Wilson had apparently recommended bed rest, Fitzgerald lied and told Graham that he had only been advised to "take it easy."[66] In a December 6 letter to Zelda, he admitted, "I'm angry that this little illness has slowed me up. I've had trouble with my heart before but never anything organic. This is not a major attack but seems to have come on gradually and luckily a cardiogram showed it up in time." A week later, he wrote her, "The cardiogram shows that my heart is repairing itself but it will be a gradual process that will take some months. It is odd that the heart is one of the organs that does repair itself."[67]

By mid-December, Fitzgerald was estimating in a letter to his wife that his novel was "about three-quarters through and I think I can go on till January 12 without doing any stories or going back to the studio."[68] To Perkins, on December 13, he wrote, "The novel progresses—in fact progresses fast. I'm not going to stop now till I finish a first draft which will be some time after the 15th of January." In that same letter, he reported that he'd read Budd Schulberg's forthcoming novel about Hollywood, *What Makes Sammy Run?* He admitted, "It's not bad" and said, "It doesn't cut into my material at all."[69] On that same day, he wrote Bennett Cerf of Random House, who was publishing Schulberg's novel, praising the book as "utterly fearless and with a great deal of beauty side by side with the most bitter satire," which "gets the feeling of Hollywood with extraordinary vividness." He gave Cerf permission to use any portion of his letter as a blurb for the book;[70] when *What Makes Sammy Run?* was published early in 1941, Fitzgerald's entire letter was printed on the back of the dust jacket, along with a much briefer blurb from John O'Hara.

TWO LETTERS CONCERNING

Budd Schulberg's

WHAT MAKES SAMMY RUN?

1. A letter written by F. Scott Fitzgerald, author of *This Side of Paradise*, *The Great Gatsby*, etc., just a few days before his untimely death:

December 13, 1940

DEAR BENNETT CERF:

I told Budd I was going to write you a word about his novel with permission to quote if you wanted. I read it through in one night. It is a grand book, utterly fearless and with a great deal of beauty side by side with the most bitter satire. Such things *are* in Hollywood—and Budd reports them with fine detachment. Except for its freshness and the inevitable challenge of a new and strong personality it doesn't read like a first novel at all.

It is full of excellent little vignettes—the "extra girl" or whatever she is and her attitude on love, and the diverse yet identical attitude of the two principal women on Sammy. Especially toward the end it gets the feeling of Hollywood with extraordinary vividness. Altogether I congratulate you on publishing this fine book and I hope it has all the success it deserves.

Sincerely,

(Signed) F. Scott Fitzgerald

2. A letter written by John O'Hara, author of *Appointment in Samara*, *Pal Joey*, etc.:

January 28, 1941

RANDOM HOUSE, INC.

Gentlemen:

Here is a fine book by Budd Schulberg, the novelist. It is interesting that it is Schulberg's first book; and because it is his first, I hope he isn't satisfied with it (although I hasten to add that *I'm* satisfied with it). The important thing is, here is this book, first novel or fiftieth, and that with it its author now stands up there with the good writers of our day.

(Signed) John O'Hara

Excerpts from important reviews will be printed on the jacket of future editions.

RANDOM HOUSE · NEW YORK

Dust jacket of *What Makes Sammy Run?* with Fitzgerald's letter

On the evening of December 20, Fitzgerald felt well enough to accompany Graham to the press preview at Hollywood's Pantages Theatre of *This Thing Called Love,* a film comedy starring Rosalind Russell and Melvyn Douglas. After the movie was over, Graham saw Fitzgerald "stagger, as if someone had struck him off balance. He had to lean down and grab the arm rest for support." Thinking he had stumbled, she took his arm, and he said, "I feel awful—everything started to go as it did in Schwab's." Once they got outside, "the air revived him," and he rejected her suggestion that they notify his doctor, reminding her that he was due to visit him the next day.[71]

The next day, after a good night's sleep, Fitzgerald worked on his novel and looked through the mail that Frances Kroll brought from his previous apartment, to which it was still being delivered, as she regularly did. This day it included the most recent issue of the *Princeton Alumni Weekly.* After Graham prepared lunch, he "seemed restless," wandering around the apartment and announcing that he was going to Schwab's to get some ice cream. When she pointed out that if he left he might miss the doctor's visit, adding, "if it's something sweet you want, I've got some Hershey bars," he agreed not to leave. He picked up the *Princeton Alumni Weekly* and, munching on the chocolate, began "making notes on the margin of an article about the Princeton football team." Then, in Graham's account, "I saw him suddenly start up out of his chair, clutch the mantelpiece and, without a sound, fall to the floor. He lay flat on his back, his eyes closed, breathing heavily." Then, "there was a choking, gasping sound in his throat." After she tried unsuccessfully to revive him with some brandy—"it spilled over on his face and ran down his chin and neck"—she summoned the building manager, who felt Fitzgerald's pulse, and told her he was dead.[72]

Fitzgerald in Death

Fitzgerald's body was taken to a funeral parlor on Washington Boulevard, which, "as one observer remarked, '—to Beverly Hills—is on the other side of the tracks in downtown Los Angeles,'" where he was placed not "in the chapel but in a back room named the William Wordsworth room," which "no doubt seemed to the undertaker the appropriate place for a literary man." In an ironic echo of the funeral of Jay Gatsby, "almost no one came to see him."[73] One who did, Frank Scully, observed:

He was laid out to look like a cross between a floor-walker and a wax dummy in the window of a two-pants tailor. But in technicolor. Not a line showed on his face. His hair was parted slightly to one side. None of it was gray.

Until you reached his hands, this looked strictly like an *A* production in peace and security. Realism began at his extremities. His hands were horribly wrinkled and thin, the only proof left after death that for all the props of youth, he actually had suffered and died an old man.[74]

Ring later agreed with Scully's description: "The mortician's cosmetics defaced him and he looked like a badly painted portrait, waxed, spiritless, with unlikely pink cheeks. . . . Like a mannequin in a store window."[75] Carrying the echo of *The Great Gatsby* to the ultimate extreme, Dorothy Parker is famously reported "to have stood looking at his body for a long time and then, without taking her eyes off him, to have repeated what 'Owl-eyes' said at Gatsby's funeral: 'The poor son of a bitch.'"[76] Fitzgerald had made it clear that he wished to be buried in Rockville, Maryland, with his father's ancestors. Accordingly, his body was shipped to the Pumphrey Funeral Home in Bethesda, Maryland, where funeral services were held on December 27. In attendance, according to Jeffrey Meyers, were "about twenty people, including Scottie, cousin Cecilia Taylor and her four daughters from Norfolk, Scott's brother-in-law Newman Smith, Gerald and Sara Murphy, Max and Louise Perkins, Harold and Anne Ober, John and Anna Biggs, Ludlow Fowler (the best man at Scott's wedding) and the Turnbulls." Because he had not been a practicing Catholic, church authorities in Maryland did not allow him to be buried in the family's plot at St. Mary's Church in Rockville; he was buried instead at Rockville Union Cemetery.[77]

At his death, Fitzgerald had written forty-four thousand words of his novel, which was published in 1941, incomplete, as *The Last Tycoon*, edited by his Princeton friend Edmund Wilson.[78] His books were not out of print, as many commentators for years after his death declared; in fact, they were in print but not selling: his last royalty statement in August 1940 "reported sales of forty copies (including seven copies of *The Great Gatsby* and nine of *Tender Is the Night*) for a royalty of $13.13."[79] In a May 20, 1940, letter to Perkins, he had offered what can stand as a fitting epitaph: "To die, so completely and unjustly after having given so much. Even now there is little published in American fiction that doesn't slightly bare my stamp—in a *small* way I was an original."[80]

NOTES

1. F. Scott Fitzgerald, *Correspondence of F. Scott Fitzgerald*, ed. Matthew J. Bruccoli and Margaret M. Duggan (New York: Random House, 1980), 561.

2. Fitzgerald, *Correspondence*, 562.

3. Graham provides a detailed account of their breakup in her autobiography *Beloved Infidel*. Sheilah Graham and Gerold Frank, *Beloved Infidel: The Education of a Woman* (New York: Henry Holt, 1958), 294–304.

4. Fitzgerald, *Correspondence*, 564–65.

5. Graham and Frank, *Beloved Infidel*, 306.

6. Graham and Frank, *Beloved Infidel*, 308, 309.

7. Sheilah Graham, *The Real F. Scott Fitzgerald: Thirty-Five Years Later* (New York: Grosset and Dunlap, 1976), 200.

8. Frances K. Ring, *Against the Current: As I Remember F. Scott Fitzgerald* (Berkeley, Calif.: Creative Arts, 1985), 90, 91.

9. Graham and Frank, *Beloved Infidel*, 309–10.

10. Graham and Frank, *Beloved Infidel*, 310. There was in fact at least one other photograph taken of Fitzgerald and Graham together (see page 374).

11. Ring, *Against the Current*, 89.

12. Ring, *Against the Current*, 90.

13. F. Scott Fitzgerald, *The Letters of F. Scott Fitzgerald*, ed. Andrew Turnbull (New York: Charles Scribner's Sons, 1963), 428.

14. Fitzgerald, *Correspondence*, 578.

15. Fitzgerald, *Correspondence*, 582–83.

16. The Pat Hobby stories Fitzgerald submitted between January and March 1940 were "A Patriotic Short" (submitted on January 8; published in December 1940); "Pat Hobby and Orson Welles" (submitted on February 6; published in May 1940); "On the Trail of Pat Hobby" (submitted on February 14; published in January 1941); "Pat Hobby's Secret" (submitted on March 9; published in June 1940); "Pat Hobby Does His Best" (submitted on March 18; published in September 1940); and "The Homes of the Stars" (submitted on March 28; published in August 1940). See Mary Jo Tate, *F. Scott Fitzgerald A to Z: The Essential Reference to His Life and Work* (New York: Facts on File, 1998), 190, 183, 123, 188, 189. *Esquire* published a Fitzgerald story in each of its monthly issues between November 1939 and July 1941; a Pat Hobby story appeared in each issue between January 1940 and May 1941. "The Woman from 21" was published (as "The Woman from Twenty-One") in *Esquire* in June 1941. See Matthew J. Bruccoli, *F. Scott Fitzgerald: A Descriptive Bibliography*, rev. ed. (Pittsburgh: University of Pittsburgh Press, 1987), 341–43. Gingrich rejected "Dearly Beloved" and it was not published until 1969, when it appeared in the *Fitzgerald/ Hemingway Annual*; he also rejected "Beloved Infidel," which was first published in Sheilah Graham and Gerold Frank's *Beloved Infidel*. Fitzgerald, *Correspondence*, 581; see also Graham and Frank, *Beloved Infidel*, 194–95.

17. Gingrich never used this pseudonym, but he did posthumously publish Fitz-

gerald's story "On an Ocean Wave" under the pseudonym Paul Elgin in February 1941 (undoubtedly because the Pat Hobby story "Fun in an Artist's Studio" also appeared in that issue). Fitzgerald, *Correspondence*, 581; Bruccoli, *Scott Fitzgerald: Bibliography*, 343.

18. Fitzgerald, *Correspondence*, 581.

19. Fitzgerald, *Correspondence*, 585.

20. Fitzgerald, *Correspondence*, 595.

21. F. Scott Fitzgerald, *Letters to His Daughter*, ed. Andrew Turnbull (New York: Charles Scribner's Sons, 1963), 103.

22. Matthew J. Bruccoli cites these figures and says that Fitzgerald and Cowan agreed on these terms "in March 1940." Bruccoli, *Some Sort of Epic Grandeur: The Life of F. Scott Fitzgerald*, 2nd rev. ed. (Columbia: University of South Carolina Press, 2002), 481. Aaron Latham contends the deal was made "in late January" and sets the terms at one thousand dollars for the rights and three hundred dollars per week for the adaptation. Latham, *Crazy Sundays: F. Scott Fitzgerald in Hollywood* (New York: Viking, 1971), 239. Jeffrey Meyers says that "in April 1940," Fitzgerald "sold the screen rights of his best story, 'Babylon Revisited,' to . . . Lester Cowan for one thousand dollars [and] . . . received another five thousand dollars for completing a screenplay." Jeffrey Meyers, *F. Scott Fitzgerald: A Biography* (New York: Harper/Collins, 1994), 316. Graham mentions the same terms but does not give a date. Graham and Frank, *Beloved Infidel*, 309. While the letter to Scottie seems to confirm Latham's earlier date, as late as March 19, Fitzgerald wrote his wife, "Nothing has developed here. I write these 'Pat Hobby' stories—and wait." Jackson R. Bryer and Cathy W. Barks, eds., *Dear Scott, Dearest Zelda: The Love Letters of F. Scott and Zelda Fitzgerald*, with an introduction by Eleanor Lanahan (New York: St. Martin's Press, 2002, 331). This letter implies that he may not have started writing the screenplay until later in March, an inference that seems verified by his remark, in an April 11 letter to Scottie, "I go to cinema work tomorrow on a sort of half-pay, half-'spec' (speculation) business on my own story 'Babylon Revisited.'" Fitzgerald, *Letters to His Daughter*, 110. As to the terms, in a July 29 letter, Fitzgerald told his wife that Cowan "bought my *Babylon Revisited* . . . for $900" and "then, in a beautifully avaricious way, knowing I'd been sick and was probably hard up, . . . hired me to do the script on a percentage basis . . . what worked out to a few hundred a week." Bryer and Barks, *Dear Scott, Dearest Zelda*, 355–56. For a detailed account of how Cowan approached Fitzgerald for the project, see Latham, *Crazy Sundays*, 238–40.

23. Meyers contends that, "in March 1940 when he was . . . flying across the country," Fitzgerald was "overcome by [an] . . . imaginary illness": "He suddenly felt terribly sick, panicked and rather grandly asked the airline stewardess to wire for a doctor, nurse and ambulance to meet him at Tucson airport. By the time they landed, Fitzgerald had miraculously recovered and decided to remain on the plane." Meyers, *Fitzgerald*, 332. No other biographer mentions this incident or that Fitzgerald left California at this time, but the account is bolstered by a letter Fitzgerald wrote Perkins on April 19 about a bill for fifty dollars from "of all things an undertaker" who claimed he owed him for "an ambulance which he claims that I ordered." Denying that he had ordered the ambulance, Fitzgerald instructed Perkins to ignore the claim. Fitzgerald, *Correspondence*, 594. The editors of Fitzgerald's correspondence

offer no explanation for this letter. There is no other mention of this incident in Fitzgerald's correspondence.

24. Fitzgerald, *Letters to His Daughter,* 110, 117; Bryer and Barks, *Dear Scott, Dearest Zelda,* 341.

25. Quoted in in Latham, *Crazy Sundays,* 240.

26. Latham says that "adapting 'Babylon Revisited' for the movies brought [Graham and Fitzgerald] back together. They even began to act out some of the scenes in the new script. . . . Sheilah played the little girl in the story, Scott the father whom she looked up to." Latham, *Crazy Sundays,* 245.

27. Ring, *Against the Current,* 92, 94.

28. Bryer and Barks, *Dear Scott, Dearest Zelda,* 328.

29. Bryer and Barks, *Dear Scott, Dearest Zelda,* 329. Between the time she was released from Highland in early April and her death in a fire there on March 10, 1948, Zelda Fitzgerald spent most of her time in Montgomery. She returned to the hospital from August 1943 until February 1944, from early 1946 until the end of the summer of 1946, and for the last time from November 2, 1947, until her death. Nancy Milford, *Zelda: A Biography* (New York: Harper and Row, 1970), 374–75, 382–83.

30. Bryer and Barks, *Dear Scott, Dearest Zelda,* 343.

31. At some point, Fitzgerald renamed the little girl in the screenplay Victoria in honor of Budd Schulberg's newborn baby, who was born on May 26. F. Scott Fitzgerald, *Babylon Revisited: The Screenplay* (New York: Carroll and Graf, 1993), 11. He also sent Schulberg a copy of *Tender Is the Night* inscribed "For Victoria Schulberg in memory of a three-day mountain-climbing trip with her illustrious father—who pulled me out of crevices into which I sank and away from avalanches—with affection to you both." Latham, *Crazy Sundays,* 245–46; see also Fitzgerald, *Correspondence,* 598.

32. Fitzgerald, *Correspondence,* 599–600.

33. Fitzgerald, *Letters to His Daughter,* 125; Fitzgerald, *Correspondence,* 600–601.

34. Bryer and Barks, *Dear Scott, Dearest Zelda,* 334; Fitzgerald, *Letters to His Daughter,* 112.

35. Graham says that she found the apartment for Fitzgerald and that, "to economize, we shared the same maid, each paying half of her salary. We dined at each other's apartment on alternate nights: one night she cooked his dinner and I was his guest, the next she cooked mine and he was my guest. Again, like a married couple, we went shopping at night in the supermarkets on Sunset Boulevard, or spent an hour in Schwab's drugstore, five minutes away, browsing among the magazines and ending our visit sipping chocolate malted milks at the ice-cream counter. On the way home we chanted poetry to each other, swinging hands as we walked in the darkness." Graham and Frank, *Beloved Infidel,* 310–11.

36. Graham, *Real Fitzgerald,* 206.

37. Tate, *Fitzgerald A to Z,* 68.

38. Fitzgerald, *Letters to His Daughter,* 132.

39. Bryer and Barks, *Dear Scott, Dearest Zelda,* 355.

40. Bryer and Barks, *Dear Scott, Dearest Zelda,* 352.

41. Quoted in Latham, *Crazy Sundays,* 255–56.

42. Quoted in Latham, *Crazy Sundays,* 256.

43. Fitzgerald, *Correspondence*, 604.

44. Bryer and Barks, *Dear Scott, Dearest Zelda*, 356, 357.

45. Bryer and Barks, *Dear Scott, Dearest Zelda*, 364.

46. Latham, *Crazy Sundays*, 256. Several years later, Cowan sold the rights to "Babylon Revisited" to RKO for either one hundred thousand dollars (Latham, *Crazy Sundays*, 257; Fitzgerald, *Babylon Revisited*, 11–12) or forty thousand dollars (Tate, *Fitzgerald A to Z*, 42). At about the same time, RKO bought the rights to Elliot Paul's 1942 memoir *The Last Time I Saw Paris*; they hired twin brothers Julius J. and Philip G. Epstein (who had cowritten *Casablanca*) and Richard Brooks to write a screenplay based on both Paul's memoir and Fitzgerald's "Babylon Revisited." The film, directed by Brooks and titled *The Last Time I Saw Paris*, was released in 1954 and starred Elizabeth Taylor (as Helen Ellswirth), Van Johnson (as Charles Wills), Donna Reed (as Marion Ellswirth), Eva Gabor (as Lorraine Quarl), and Sandy Descher (playing the much-reduced role of the character renamed Vicki). In the early 1990s, Budd Schulberg found a copy of Fitzgerald's screenplay in a carton marked "other people's manuscripts," and, with the assistance of Matthew J. Bruccoli, arranged to have it published by Carroll and Graf in 1993 as *Babylon Revisited: The Screenplay*, with an introduction by Schulberg and an afterword by Bruccoli.

47. Bryer and Barks, *Dear Scott, Dearest Zelda*, 360.

48. Latham, *Crazy Sundays*, 260.

49. Bryer and Barks, *Dear Scott, Dearest Zelda*, 360.

50. Bryer and Barks, *Dear Scott, Dearest Zelda*, 366.

51. Latham, *Crazy Sundays*, 267–68; quoted in Latham, *Crazy Sundays*, 173.

52. For an extensive description of Fitzgerald's screenplay of *The Light of Heart*, including numerous quotations from the script (included because "20th Century-Fox proved to be the most generous studio with permissions"), see Latham, *Crazy Sundays*, 263, 261–66. Bruccoli says that at about this time, Fitzgerald "was also involved in a story conference for *Everything Happens at Night*, a Sonja Henie vehicle, and he may have worked briefly on 'Brooklyn Bridge,' a proposed movie about the building of the bridge." Bruccoli, *Epic Grandeur*, 484.

53. Bryer and Barks, *Dear Scott, Dearest Zelda*, 367, 370.

54. Bryer and Barks, *Dear Scott, Dearest Zelda*, 370, 371, 373.

55. Bryer and Barks, *Dear Scott, Dearest Zelda*, 374, 375–76, 376, 379.

56. Ring, *Against the Current*, 95.

57. Graham and Frank, *Beloved Infidel*, 322; see also 318–21.

58. Fitzgerald, *Correspondence*, 611.

59. F. Scott Fitzgerald, *A Life in Letters*, ed. Matthew J. Bruccoli (New York: Charles Scribner's Sons, 1994), 469.

60. Bryer and Barks, *Dear Scott, Dearest Zelda*, 374.

61. F. Scott Fitzgerald, *The Notebooks of F. Scott Fitzgerald*, ed. Matthew J. Bruccoli (New York: Harcourt Brace Jovanovich / Bruccoli Clark, 1978), 335.

62. Scott Donaldson, *Hemingway vs. Fitzgerald: The Rise and Fall of a Literary Friendship* (Woodstock, N.Y.: Overlook, 1999), 220.

63. Bryer and Barks, *Dear Scott, Dearest Zelda*, 382.

64. Ring, *Against the Current*, 103–4.

65. Ring, *Against the Current*, 104.

66. Graham and Frank, *Beloved Infidel,* 322–23.

67. Bryer and Barks, *Dear Scott, Dearest Zelda,* 381, 382.

68. Bryer and Barks, *Dear Scott, Dearest Zelda,* 382.

69. John Kuehl and Jackson R. Bryer, eds., *Dear Scott / Dear Max: The Fitzgerald-Perkins Correspondence* (New York: Charles Scribner's Sons, 1971), 268.

70. Fitzgerald, *Correspondence,* 604–5.

71. Graham and Frank, *Beloved Infidel,* 326–27.

72. Graham and Frank, *Beloved Infidel,* 329–31; see also Graham, *Real Fitzgerald,* 215–16.

73. Arthur Mizener, *The Far Side of Paradise: A Biography of F. Scott Fitzgerald* (Boston: Houghton Mifflin, 1951), 298.

74. Frank Scully, *Rogue's Gallery* (Hollywood, Calif.: Murray and Gee, 1943), 268–69.

75. Ring, *Against the Current,* 109.

76. Mizener, *Far Side of Paradise,* 298.

77. Meyers, *Fitzgerald,* 335; see also Mizener, *Far Side of Paradise,* 299. Zelda's remains were interred with Scott's in Rockville Cemetery when she died in a fire at Highland Hospital in 1948. In 1975, the Fitzgeralds' remains were reinterred in the St. Mary's Church cemetery.

78. In 1993, Matthew J. Bruccoli published *The Love of the Last Tycoon: A Western* in the Cambridge Edition of the Works of F. Scott Fitzgerald, which presented not only all the text that Fitzgerald left at his death but also his working notes, an inventory of his drafts, textual notes, Wilson's alterations to the 1941 edition, and explanatory notes by Bruccoli. See also Matthew J. Bruccoli, *"The Last of the Novelists": F. Scott Fitzgerald and "The Last Tycoon"* (Carbondale: Southern Illinois University Press, 1977).

79. Bruccoli, *Epic Grandeur,* 486.

80. Kuehl and Bryer, *Dear Scott / Dear Max,* 261.

Acknowledgments

"Are you and your friends ever going to leave that poor man in peace?"

The editors wish to thank Erik Anderson and the University of Minnesota Press for matching our enthusiasm for this project and making the journey into print highly personable and professional. To Fitzgerald Society president Jackson R. Bryer, we offer our gratitude for his initial support; Jackson was the first contributor we secured, which made for an encouraging start. We would like to acknowledge the work of the F. Scott Fitzgerald Society and Fitzgerald Society Executive Board in fostering the scholarly appreciation of Fitzgerald, while maintaining a companionable forum for Fitzgerald enthusiasts and researchers. When Helen Turner told her mother about this project, the response was, "Are you and your friends ever going to leave that poor man in peace?" Fitzgerald enthusiasts have their own reasons for failing to do so, and that makes, we think, a particularly strong case for combining those varied perspectives here.

Jackson R. Bryer, James L. W. West III, and Kirk Curnutt offered all kinds of assistance as our idea for a composite Fitzgerald biography coalesced into a physical book. Stu Wilson and Mel Barker were supportive of our project and provided the initial contact with the University of Minnesota Press. Our volume has been enriched enormously by illustrations from the F. Scott Fitzgerald Papers, 1897–1944 (Princeton University Library) and the Matthew J. and Arlyn Bruccoli Collection of F. Scott Fitzgerald (University of South Carolina Libraries). The editors are highly appreciative of the permission granted by these institutions to reprint these images in this book.

We are equally grateful for the permissions and assistance offered by the following individuals: Dr. Anna Greek, head of the Department of Languages and Faculty of Arts and Humanities at Linnaeus University; Robert Westbrook and Wendy Fairey, coexecutors of the Sheilah Graham Westbrook Estate; Elizabeth Sudduth, associate dean for Special Collections and director of the Irvin Department of Rare Books and Special Collections at the University of South Carolina; Fred Nace, user-services librarian, at the University of South Carolina; AnnaLee Pauls and Brianna Cregle, special collections assistants at Princeton University's Firestone Library; Amelia H. Chase, digital assets archivist, Alabama Department of Archives and History; Greg Schmidt, head of Auburn University Libraries Special Collections and Archives; and Shawn Sudia-Skehan, board member of the Fitzgerald Museum in Montgomery, Alabama.

To Sarah Carpenter and Randall Stevenson, thank you for the cups of tea, excellent dinner, and even better company during our editorial rendezvous in Edinburgh. An island of trust in the perilous waters of publishing, Emma Saks, editorial assistant at the University of Minnesota Press, helped with everything, especially securing images and permissions. We are also very grateful for the generous support from the Friends of the St. Paul Public Library. Finally, we recognize our indebtedness to Anna Ishchenko, editing research assistant at Linnaeus University, who provided invaluable assistance in obtaining images and assembling the final manuscript.

CONTRIBUTORS

Jade Broughton Adams is an independent scholar. She is the author of *F. Scott Fitzgerald's Short Fiction: From Ragtime to Swing Time*.

Ronald Berman (1930–2022) was professor emeritus of English literature at the University of California San Diego. His works of Fitzgerald scholarship include *The Great Gatsby and Modern Times*; *Fitzgerald, Hemingway, and the Twenties*; and *Fitzgerald–Wilson–Hemingway*.

William Blazek is professor of American literature and modern culture at Liverpool Hope University. He is vice president of the F. Scott Fitzgerald Society and a founding coeditor of *The F. Scott Fitzgerald Review*. He edited the Oxford World's Classics second edition of *The Beautiful and Damned* and coedited the collections *F. Scott Fitzgerald's "The Beautiful and Damned": New Critical Essays* (with Kirk Curnutt and David W. Ullrich) and *Twenty-First-Century Readings of "Tender Is the Night"* (with Laura Rattray).

Elisabeth Bouzonviller is professor of American literature at Jean Monnet University, Saint-Etienne, France. She is author of *Francis Scott Fitzgerald, ou La Plénitude du silence*; *Francis Scott Fitzgerald, écrivain du déséquilibre*; *Louise Erdrich: Métissage et écriture*; *Histoires d'Amérique*; coeditor of *Mémoires, traces, empreintes*; and editor of *"Home, Sweet Home": Places of Belonging in Anglophone Narratives*.

Jackson R. Bryer is professor emeritus of English at the University of Maryland. He is cofounder and president of the F. Scott Fitzgerald Society. Among his books on Fitzgerald are *F. Scott Fitzgerald in the Twenty-First Century*; *Dear Scott, Dearest Zelda: The Love Letters of F. Scott and Zelda Fitzgerald*; *F. Scott Fitzgerald: New Perspectives*; *French Connections: Hemingway and Fitzgerald Abroad*; *New Essays on F. Scott Fitzgerald's Neglected Stories*; *The Short Stories of F. Scott Fitzgerald: New Approaches in Criticism*; *Dear Scott / Dear Max: The Fitzgerald–Perkins Correspondence*; and *F. Scott Fitzgerald in His Own Time: A Miscellany*.

Kirk Curnutt is professor of English at Troy University. He coedited, with William Blazek and David W. Ullrich, a collection of centennial essays on *The Beautiful and Damned* and, with Sara Kosiba, a volume on the Fitzgeralds' relationship to the South, *The Romance of Regionalism in the Work of F. Scott and Zelda Fitzgerald: The South Side of Paradise.* He is executive director of the F. Scott Fitzgerald Society and managing editor of its annual, the *F. Scott Fitzgerald Review.*

Catherine Delesalle-Nancey is professor of English literature at the University of Lyon 3 in France. She is author of *La Divine comédie ivre: Repetition, ressassement et reprise dans l'oeuvre an prose de Malcom Lowry* and coeditor of *Expériences de l'histoire, poétiques de la mémoire: J. Conrad "Au cœur des ténèbres," C. Simon "L'Acacia," A. L. Antunes "Le Cul de Judas."*

Scott Donaldson (1928–2020) was Louise G. T. Cooley Professor of English Emeritus, College of William and Mary. Among his many books are *Fool for Love: F. Scott Fitzgerald* (Minnesota, 2012), *Hemingway vs. Fitzgerald: The Rise and Fall of a Literary Friendship,* and *The Impossible Craft: Literary Biography.*

Kayla Forrest is a PhD candidate at the University of North Carolina Greensboro and an English instructor at Surry Community College in Dobson, North Carolina.

Marie-Agnès Gay is professor of American literature at University Jean Moulin Lyon 3 in France. She is author of *Epiphanie et fracture: L'Évolution du point de vue narratif dans les romans de F. Scott Fitzgerald* and *Richard Ford: "A Multitude of Sins."* She coedited, with Elisabeth Bouzonviller, the essay collection *F. Scott Fitzgerald: "Tender Is the Night."*

Joel Kabot is a speechwriter at the U.S. Senate.

Sara Kosiba, an independent scholar, is editor of *A Scattering Time: How Modernism Met Midwestern Culture* and coeditor (with Kirk Curnutt) of *The Romance of Regionalism in the Work of F. Scott and Zelda Fitzgerald: The South Side of Paradise.*

Arne Lunde is associate professor of European languages and transcultural studies at UCLA. He is author of *Nordic Exposures: Scandinavian Identities in Classical Hollywood Cinema* and coeditor of *Nordic Film Cultures and Cinemas of Elsewhere.*

Bryant Mangum, professor of English at Virginia Commonwealth University, is author of *A Fortune Yet: Money in the Art of F. Scott Fitzgerald's Short Stories* and *Understanding Alice Adams* and editor of *F. Scott Fitzgerald in Context* and *The Best Early Stories of F. Scott Fitzgerald*. His essays have been published in the *F. Scott Fitzgerald Review* and *Cambridge Companion to F. Scott Fitzgerald*.

Martina Mastandrea teaches English at Liceo Ugo Morin, Venice. She is author of *F. Scott Fitzgerald on Silent Film* and coauthor of *Hemingway and the Harvard Poets*.

Philip McGowan is professor of American literature at Queen's University Belfast. He is author of *American Carnival* and *Anne Sexton and Middle Generation Poetry* and coeditor of *After Thirty Falls: New Essays on John Berryman*. He has edited editions of *This Side of Paradise* and *The Great Gatsby*.

David Page, a retired writing instructor at Inver Hills Community College, has worked on five books on Fitzgerald, including *F. Scott Fitzgerald in Minnesota: The Writer and His Friends at Home* (Minnesota, 2017) and *The Thoughtbook of F. Scott Fitzgerald: A Secret Boyhood Diary* (Minnesota, 2013). He served on committees that organized two International F. Scott Fitzgerald Conferences in St. Paul, and with his wife, Mecca, created a series of videos on Fitzgerald for the Friends of the St. Paul Public Library.

Walter Raubicheck is professor of English at Pace University, New York. His essays on Fitzgerald's work have been published in the *F. Scott Fitzgerald Review* and *Twenty-First Century Interpretations of F. Scott Fitzgerald*. He edited several books on Alfred Hitchcock's films, including *Hitchcock and the Cold War* and (with Walter Srebnick) *Scripting Hitchcock*.

David Rennie teaches English at St. Machar Academy, Scotland. He is author of *American Writers and World War I* and *Sir Alexander Ogston, 1844–1929: A Life at Medical and Military Frontlines* and editor of *Scottish Literature and World War I*.

Niklas Salmose is professor of English at Linnaeus University in Sweden, where he studies F. Scott Fitzgerald, modernism, nostalgia, intermediality, and environmental humanities. He is coauthor of *Intermedial Ecocriticism: The Climate Crisis through Art and Media* and coeditor of *Once upon a Time: Nostalgic Narratives in Transition; Transmediations:*

Communication across Media Borders; and *Cultural Comets and Other Celestials*.

Ross K. Tangedal is associate professor of English and director of the Cornerstone Press at the University of Wisconsin Stevens Point. He is author of *The Preface: American Authorship in the Twentieth Century* and coeditor of *Editing the Harlem Renaissance* and *Michigan Salvage: The Fiction of Bonnie Jo Campbell*.

Helen Turner is an affiliated lecturer at Linnaeus University in Sweden and a classroom teacher in the United Kingdom. She is author of *Breaking Down Fitzgerald* and the forthcoming *Ready to Teach: "The Great Gatsby."* She is coeditor of *The Routledge Companion to F. Scott Fitzgerald* due for publication in 2025.

James L. W. West III is Edwin Erle Sparks Professor of English Emeritus at Pennsylvania State University. He is author of *William Styron: A Life* and general editor of the Cambridge Edition of the Works of F. Scott Fitzgerald.

‖ ILLUSTRATION CREDITS ‖

The University of Minnesota Press gratefully acknowledges the following institutions and individuals who provided permission to reproduce the illustrations in this book.

Pages 8, 13, 20, 29, 43, 49, 54, 59, 93, 120, 121, 124, 135, 140, 143, 153, 171, 174, 185, 188, 204, 228, 236, 261, 268, 275, 275, 280, 298, 308, 321, 332, 333, 374: F. Scott Fitzgerald Papers, Manuscripts Division, Department of Special Collections, Princeton University Library. Copyright 2023 William Morris Endeavor Entertainment, LLC.

Page 28: *Buffalo Courier,* May 10, 1896.

Page 32: *Evening Star,* Washington, D.C., May 25, 1899. Chronicling America: Historic American Newspapers. Library of Congress. https://chroniclingamerica.loc.gov/lccn/sn83045462/1899-05-25/ed-1/seq-13/.

Page 33: Historic American Buildings Survey, creator. Cairo Hotel, Q Street Northwest, Washington, D.C. Library of Congress. www.loc.gov/item/dc0042/.

Page 74: Frank Lloyd Wright, Larkin Administration Building, circa 1940. Frank A. Waugh Papers (FS 088). Special Collections and University Archives, University of Massachusetts Amherst Libraries.

Page 76: Mary Evans / Grenville Collins Postcard Collection.

Page 77: "St. Paul's Church, Buffalo, N.Y." The New York Public Library Digital Collections, 1903–1904. The Miriam and Ira D. Wallach Division of Art, Prints, and Photographs: Photography Collection, The New York Public Library. https://digitalcollections.nypl.org/items/510d47d9-a58b-a3d9-e040-e00a18064a99.

Page 97: Bain News Service, publisher. Ted Coy, captain of Yale Varsity football team [graphic], 1909 (date created or published later by Bain). One negative, glass, 5 × 7 inches or smaller. LC-B2-913–1. https://lccn.loc.gov/2014684334.

Page 100: National Automotive History Collection, Detroit Public Library.

Page 108: *St. Paul Pioneer Press,* October 3, 1915.

Page 111: George Latimer Central Library, St. Paul Public Library, *St. Paul*

Pioneer Press, April 18, 1915, section 3. https://sppl.bibliocommons.com/v2 /record/S138C1016228.

Page 113: *Los Angeles Times,* February 7, 1906.

Page 114: Photograph by Dave Page.

Page 133: Newman School postcard, 1910. Courtesy of Niklas Salmose.

Page 139: Photograph by Jeff Krueger.

Page 156: W. (Truman Ward) Ingersoll, Minnesota Historical Society.

Page 161: Minnesota Historical Society.

Page 183: *This Side of Paradise.* F. Scott Fitzgerald Papers, C0187, Manuscripts Division, Department of Special Collections, Princeton University Library. NIK, page 2.

Page 190: Alabama Department of Archives and History.

Page 193: Courtesy of Auburn University Libraries Special Collections and Archives.

Page 193: Alabama Department of Archives and History Postcard Collection.

Page 205: Photograph by Walther Raubicheck.

Pages 221, 237, 249, 320, 366, 372, 375, 386, 388: Matthew J. Bruccoli Papers, Irvin Department of Rare Books and Special Collections, University of South Carolina Libraries. Copyright 2023 William Morris Endeavor Entertainment, LLC.

Page 225: F. Scott Fitzgerald, *Tales of the Jazz Age,* 1922. The Rare Book and Manuscript Collections, Cornell University Library.

Page 238: Estate of Honoria Murphy Donnelly. Licensed by VAGA at Artists Rights Society (ARS), N.Y.

Page 257: From an advertisement by Charles Scribner's Sons for *All the Sad Young Men,* in the *Chicago Tribune,* February 27, 1926, as submitted. Copyright 1926 Charles Scribner's Sons; reprinted with the permission of Scribner, a division of Simon and Schuster, Inc.; all rights reserved.

Page 281: Delaware Public Archives, Board of Agriculture Glass Negative Collection.

Page 301: *Washington, D.C., Evening Star,* August 30, 1931. Chronicling America: Historic American Newspapers. Library of Congress. https://chroniclingamerica.loc.gov/lccn/sn83045462/1931-08-30/ed-1/seq-77/.

Page 314: The Chesney Archives of Johns Hopkins Medicine, Nursing, and Public Health.

Page 343: "Skyland Hotel, Hendersonville, N.C." In North Carolina Postcard Collection (P052), North Carolina Collection Photographic Archives, Wilson Library, UNC–Chapel Hill.

Page 361: Library of Congress, Prints and Photographs Division, Carl Van Vechten Collection.

Page 364: Courtesy of the Sheilah Graham Westbrook Estate. Matthew J. Bruccoli Papers, Irvin Department of Rare Books and Special Collections, University of South Carolina Libraries.

Page 376: *Three Comrades,* directed by Frank Borzage, 1938. MGM. Photograph by Arne Lunde.

Page 395: Photograph by Mary C. Hartig.

INDEX